THE LEGEND OF ZELDA
THE MINISH CAP

D0126365

THE MINISH CAP—THE GAME

The Legend of Zelda™: The Minish Cap was released in North America in 2005 for the Game Boy Advance and went on to win several awards. The game took advantage of the Game Boy Advance platform to introduce several new game-play elements and enhance the experience for the player.

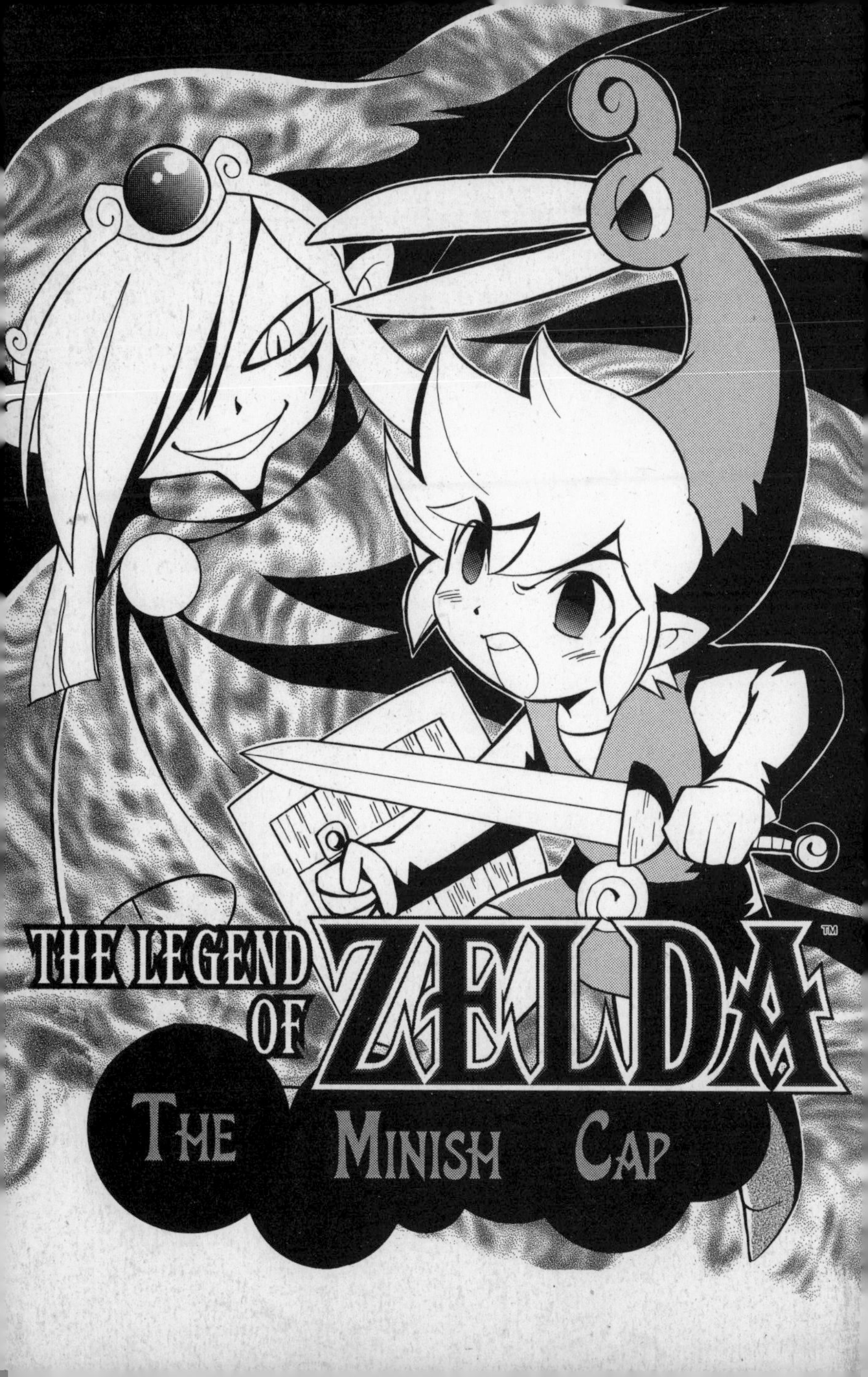
THE LEGEND OF ZELDA™
THE MINISH CAP

THE LEGEND OF ZELDA™

THE MINISH CAP

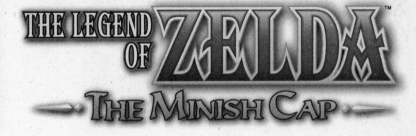

CONTENTS

THE MINISH CAP

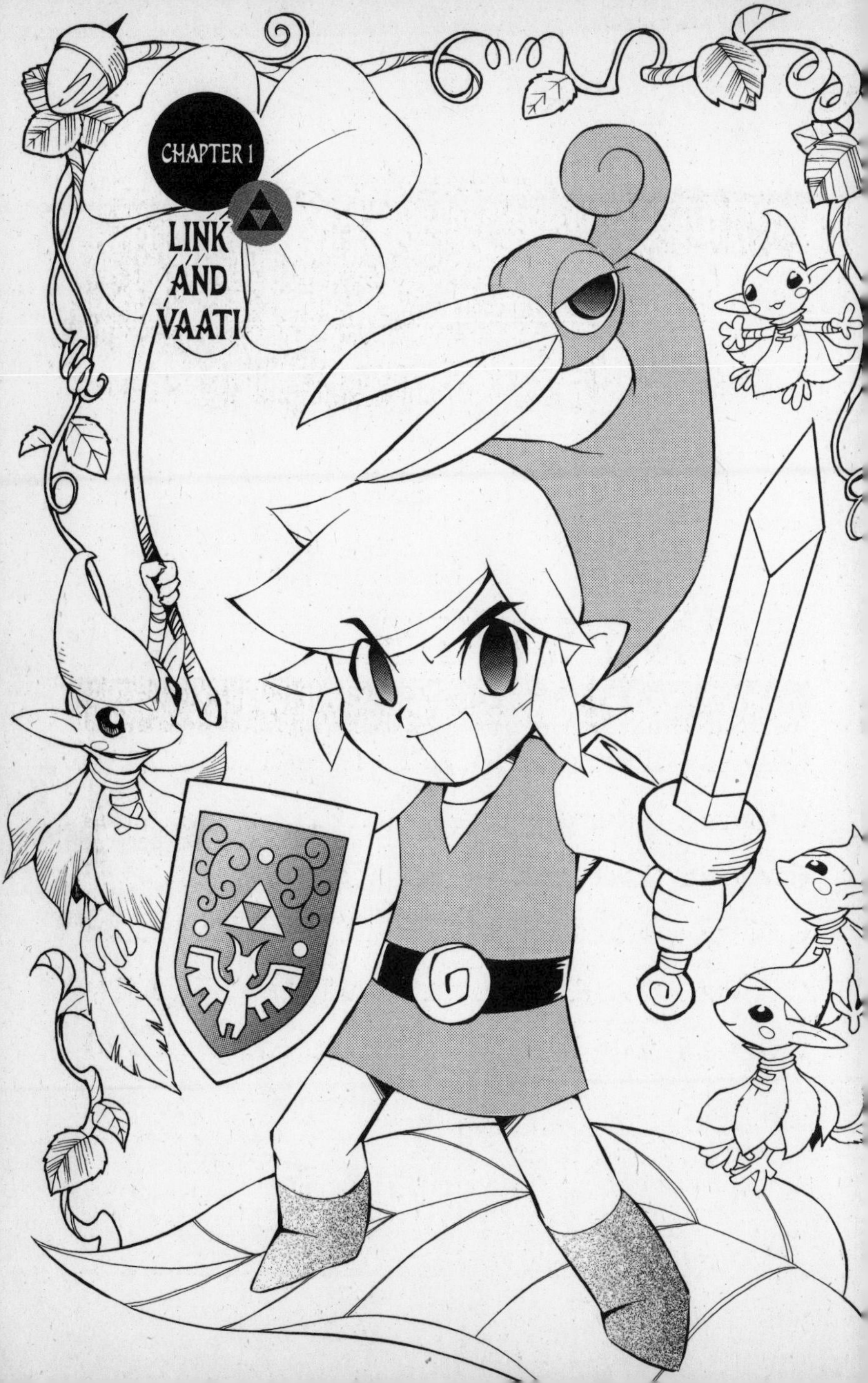
CHAPTER 1
LINK AND VAATI

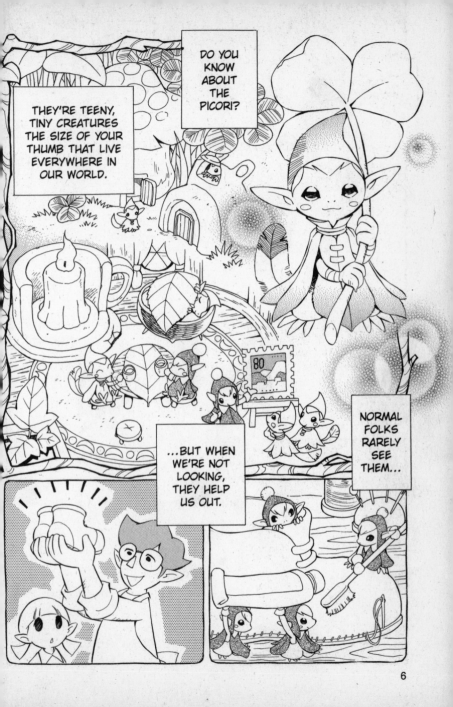

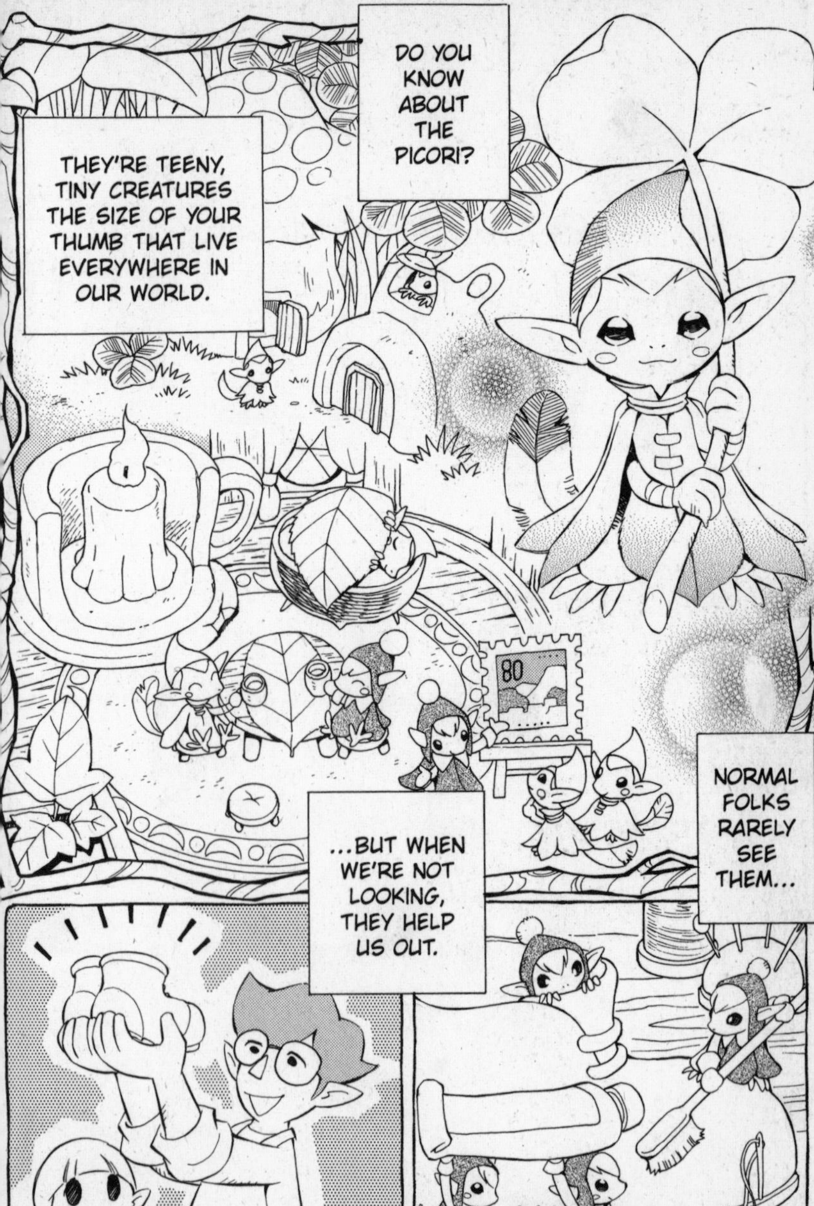
DO YOU KNOW ABOUT THE PICORI?
THEY'RE TEENY, TINY CREATURES THE SIZE OF YOUR THUMB THAT LIVE EVERYWHERE IN OUR WORLD.
80
NORMAL FOLKS RARELY SEE THEM...
...BUT WHEN WE'RE NOT LOOKING, THEY HELP US OUT.

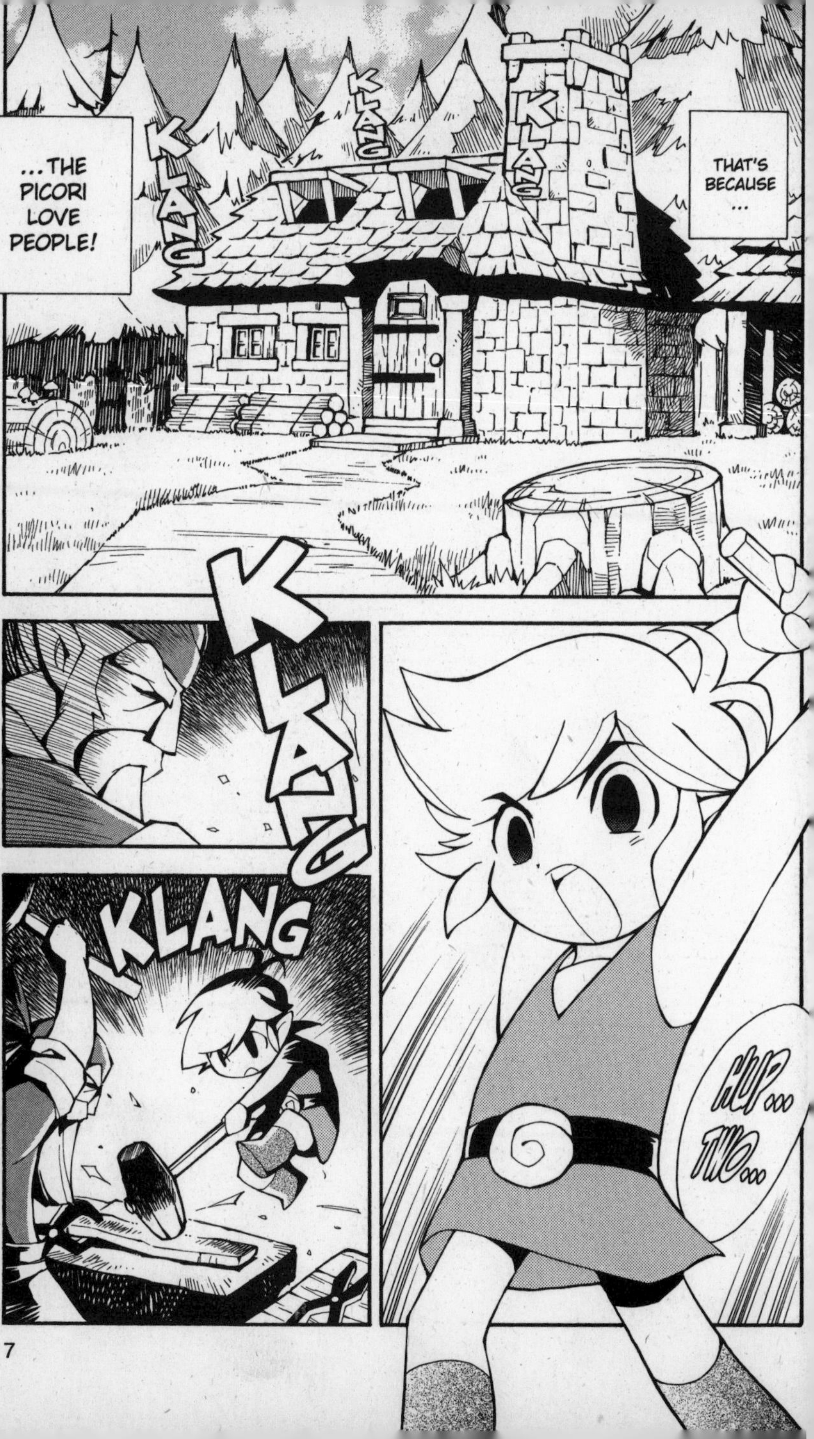
THAT'S BECAUSE ...
KLANG
KLANG
KLANG
...THE PICORI LOVE PEOPLE!
HUP...
TWO...
KLANG
KLANG

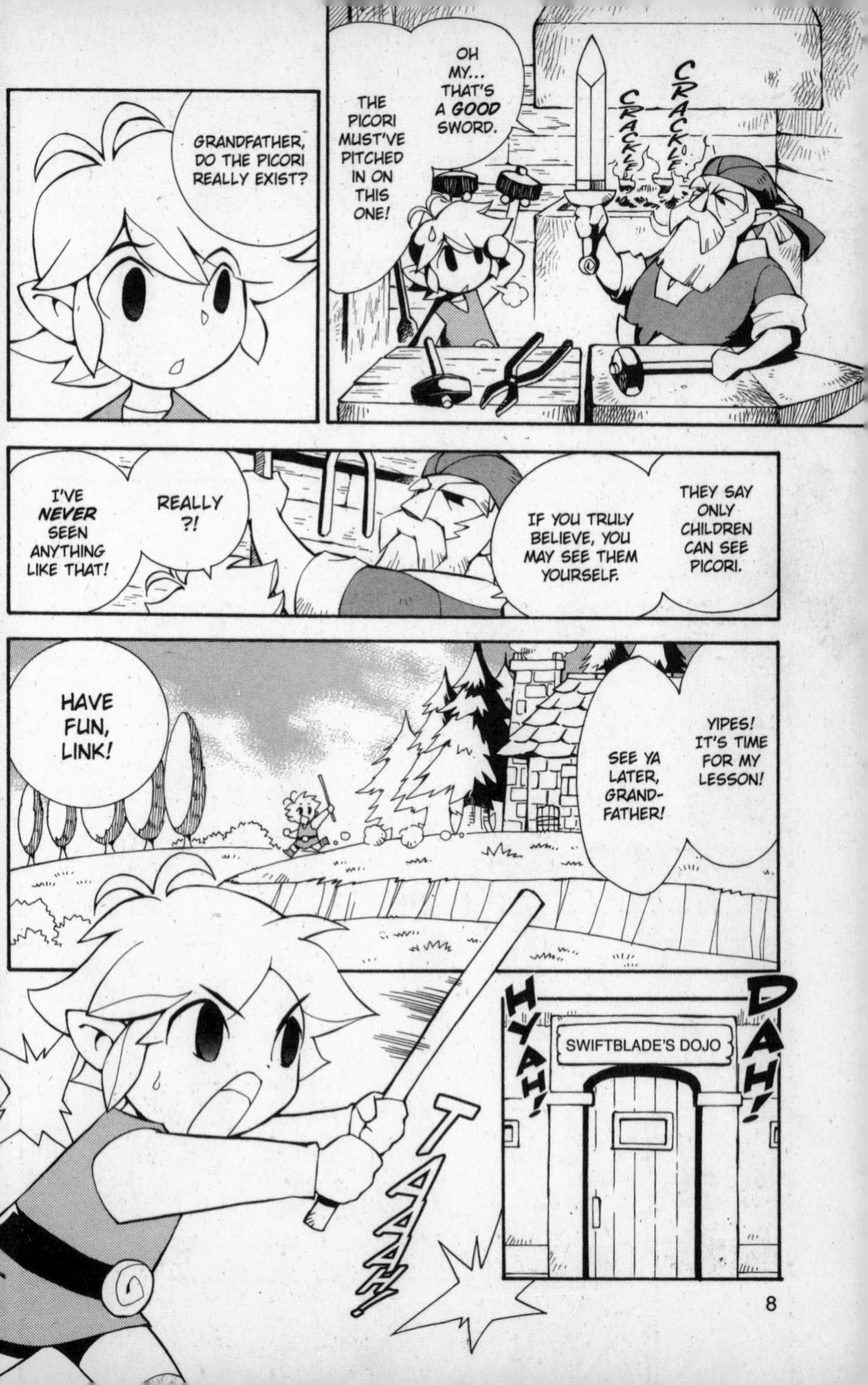
OH MY... THAT'S A GOOD SWORD.
THE PICORI MUST'VE PITCHED IN ON THIS ONE!
CRACKLE
CRACKLE
GRANDFATHER, DO THE PICORI REALLY EXIST?
THEY SAY ONLY CHILDREN CAN SEE PICORI.
IF YOU TRULY BELIEVE, YOU MAY SEE THEM YOURSELF.
REALLY ?!
I'VE NEVER SEEN ANYTHING LIKE THAT!
YIPES! IT'S TIME FOR MY LESSON!
SEE YA LATER, GRAND-FATHER!
HAVE FUN, LINK!
DAH!
SWIFTBLADE'S DOJO
HYAH!
TAAAAAH!

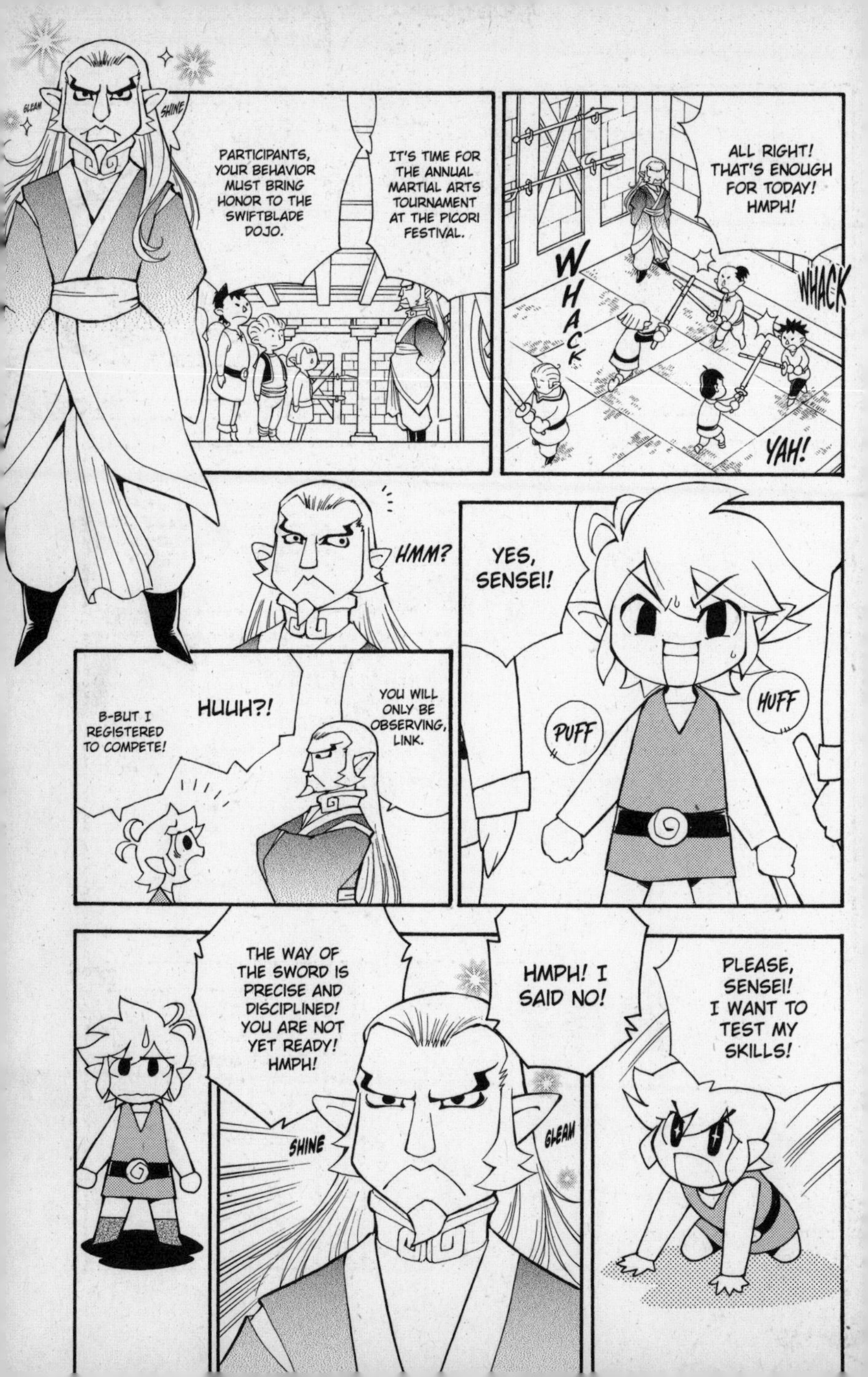
ALL RIGHT! THAT'S ENOUGH FOR TODAY! HMPH!
WHACK
WHACK
YAH!
IT'S TIME FOR THE ANNUAL MARTIAL ARTS TOURNAMENT AT THE PICORI FESTIVAL.
PARTICIPANTS, YOUR BEHAVIOR MUST BRING HONOR TO THE SWIFTBLADE DOJO.
SHINE
GLEAM
YES, SENSEI!
HUFF
PUFF
HMM?
YOU WILL ONLY BE OBSERVING, LINK.
HUUH?!
B-BUT I REGISTERED TO COMPETE!
PLEASE, SENSEI! I WANT TO TEST MY SKILLS!
HMPH! I SAID NO!
THE WAY OF THE SWORD IS PRECISE AND DISCIPLINED! YOU ARE NOT YET READY! HMPH!
GLEAM
SHINE

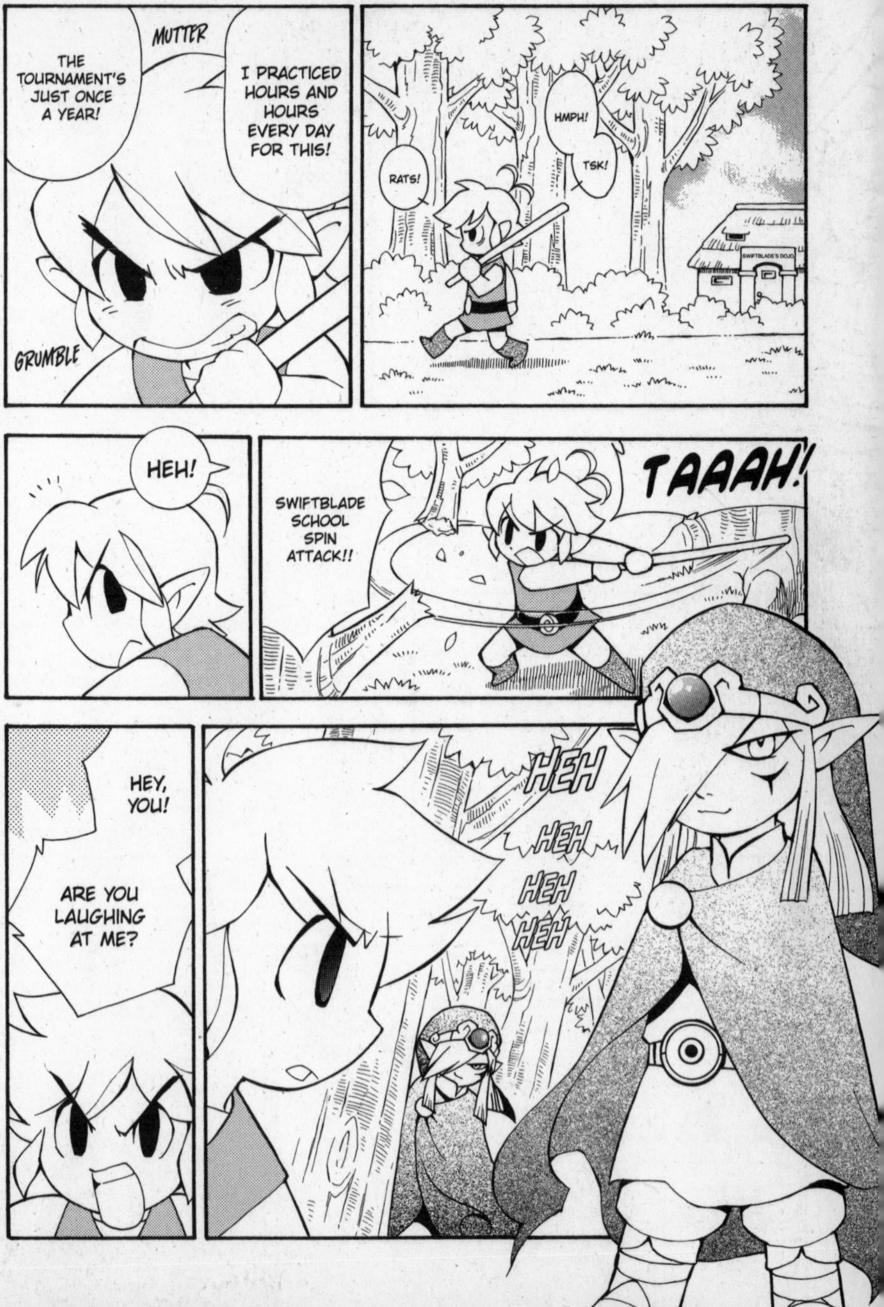
HMPH!
TSK!
RATS!
SWIFTBLADE'S DOJO
I PRACTICED HOURS AND HOURS EVERY DAY FOR THIS!
MUTTER
THE TOURNAMENT'S JUST ONCE A YEAR!
GRUMBLE
TAAAH!
SWIFTBLADE SCHOOL SPIN ATTACK!!
HEH!
HEH
HEH
HEH
HEH
HEY, YOU!
ARE YOU LAUGHING AT ME?

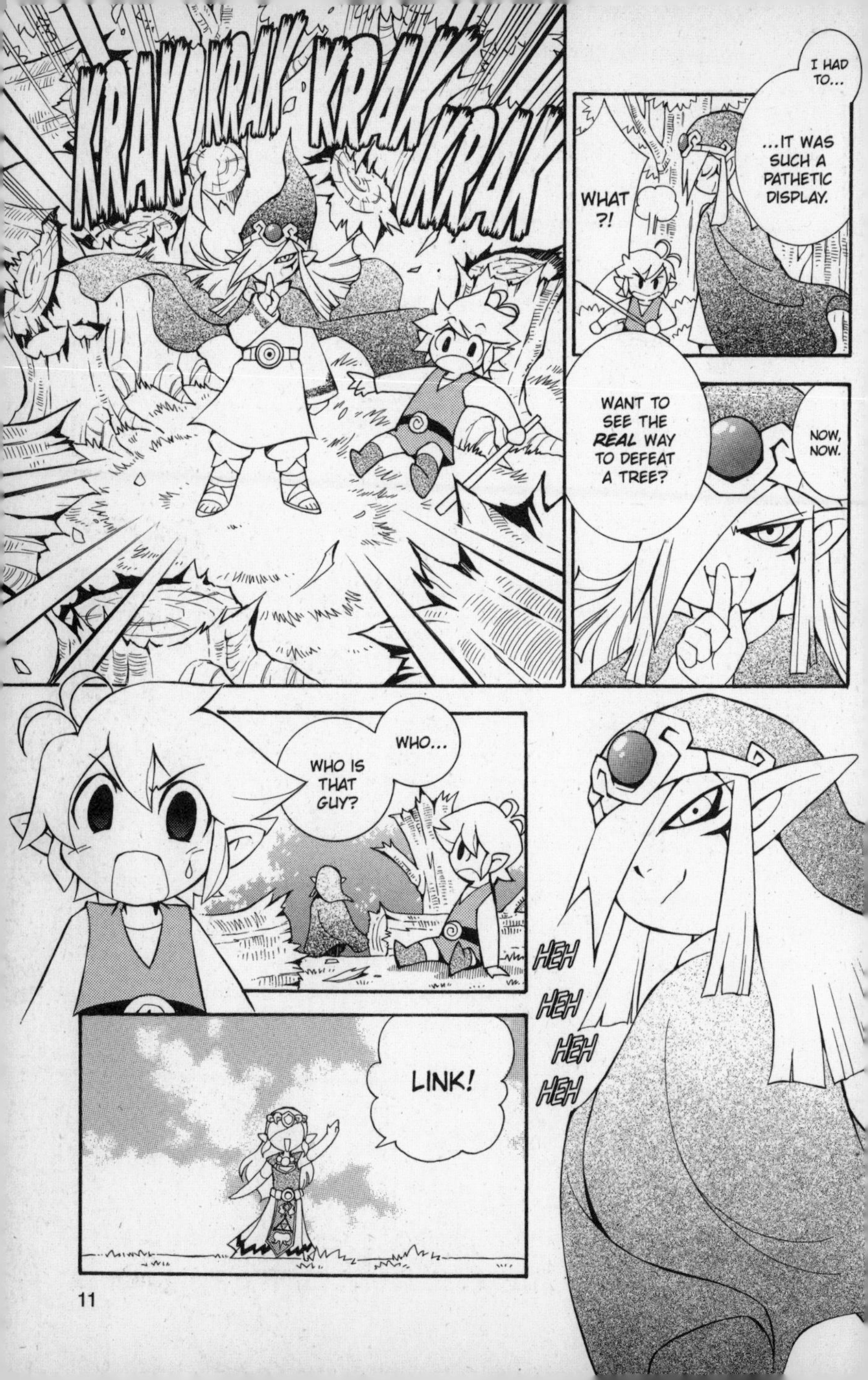
I HAD TO...
...IT WAS SUCH A PATHETIC DISPLAY.
WHAT?!
NOW, NOW.
WANT TO SEE THE REAL WAY TO DEFEAT A TREE?
KRAK KRAK KRAK KRAK
HEH HEH HEH HEH
WHO...
WHO IS THAT GUY?
LINK!

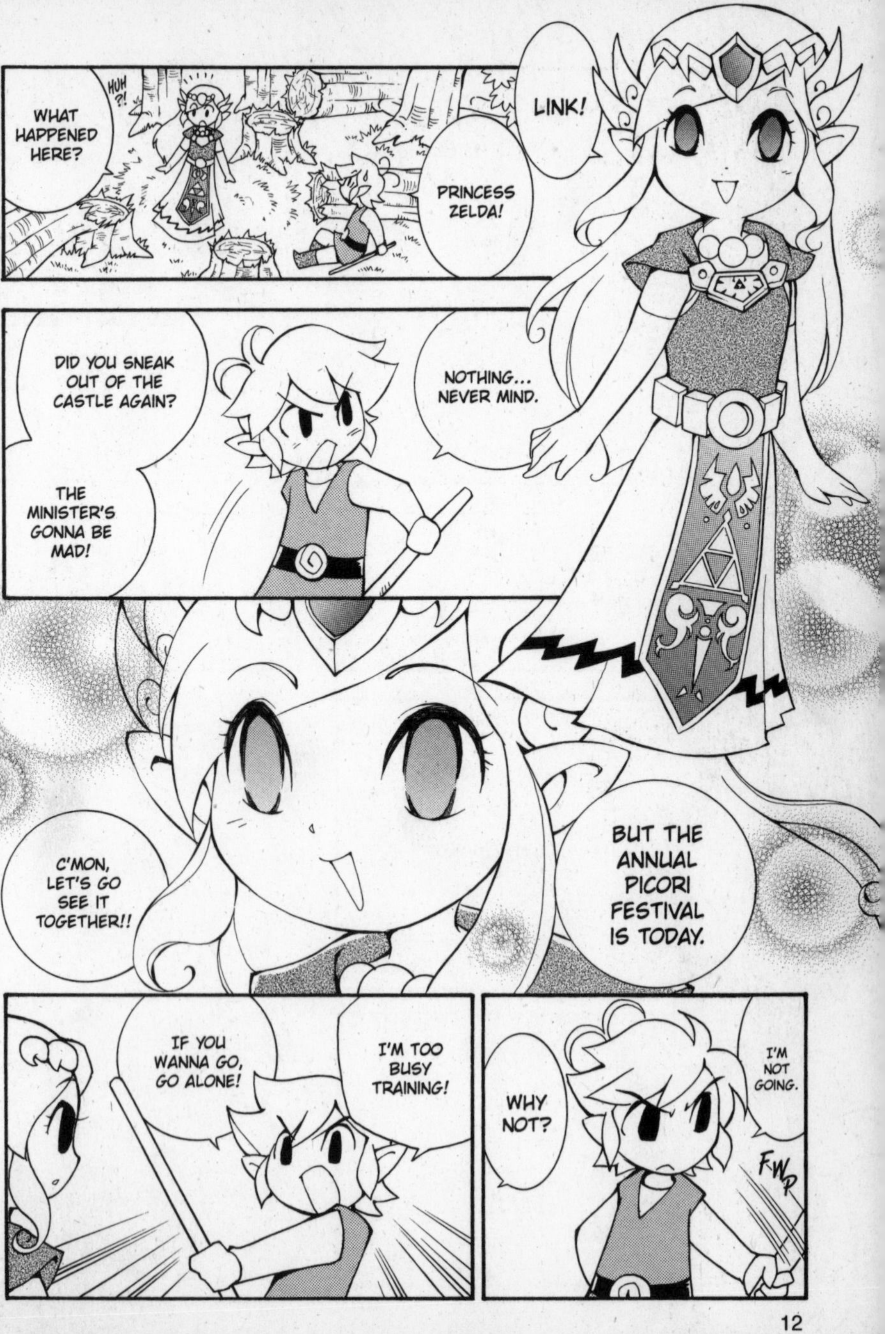

LINK!
PRINCESS ZELDA!
HUH ?!
WHAT HAPPENED HERE?
NOTHING... NEVER MIND.
DID YOU SNEAK OUT OF THE CASTLE AGAIN?
THE MINISTER'S GONNA BE MAD!
BUT THE ANNUAL PICORI FESTIVAL IS TODAY.
C'MON, LET'S GO SEE IT TOGETHER!!
I'M NOT GOING.
F-WP
WHY NOT?
I'M TOO BUSY TRAINING!
IF YOU WANNA GO, GO ALONE!

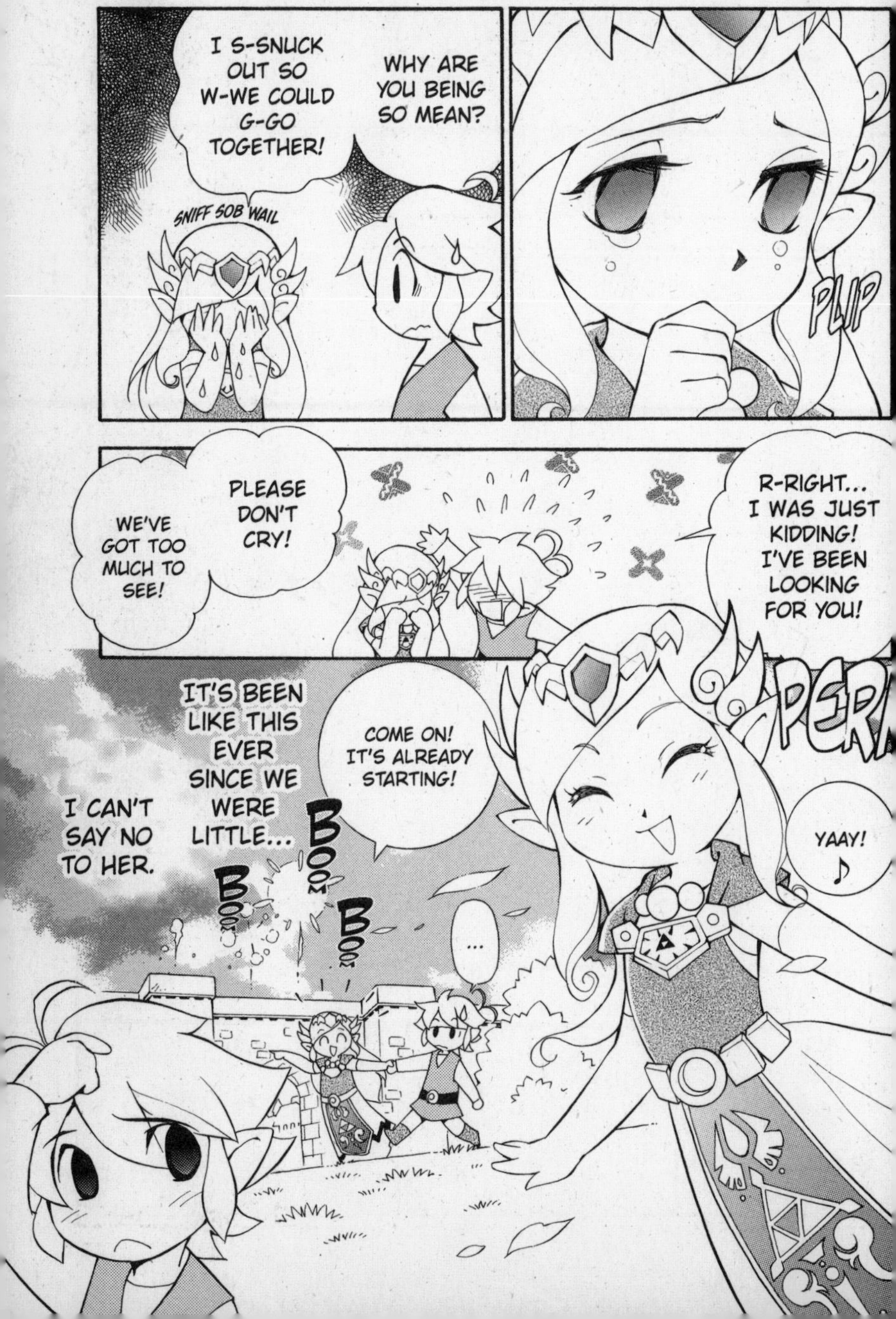
PLIP
WHY ARE YOU BEING SO MEAN?
I S-SNUCK OUT SO W-WE COULD G-GO TOGETHER!
SNIFF SOB WAIL
R-RIGHT... I WAS JUST KIDDING! I'VE BEEN LOOKING FOR YOU!
PLEASE DON'T CRY!
WE'VE GOT TOO MUCH TO SEE!
PER
YAAY! ♪
COME ON! IT'S ALREADY STARTING!
BOOM
BOOM
BOOM
...
IT'S BEEN LIKE THIS EVER SINCE WE WERE LITTLE...
I CAN'T SAY NO TO HER.

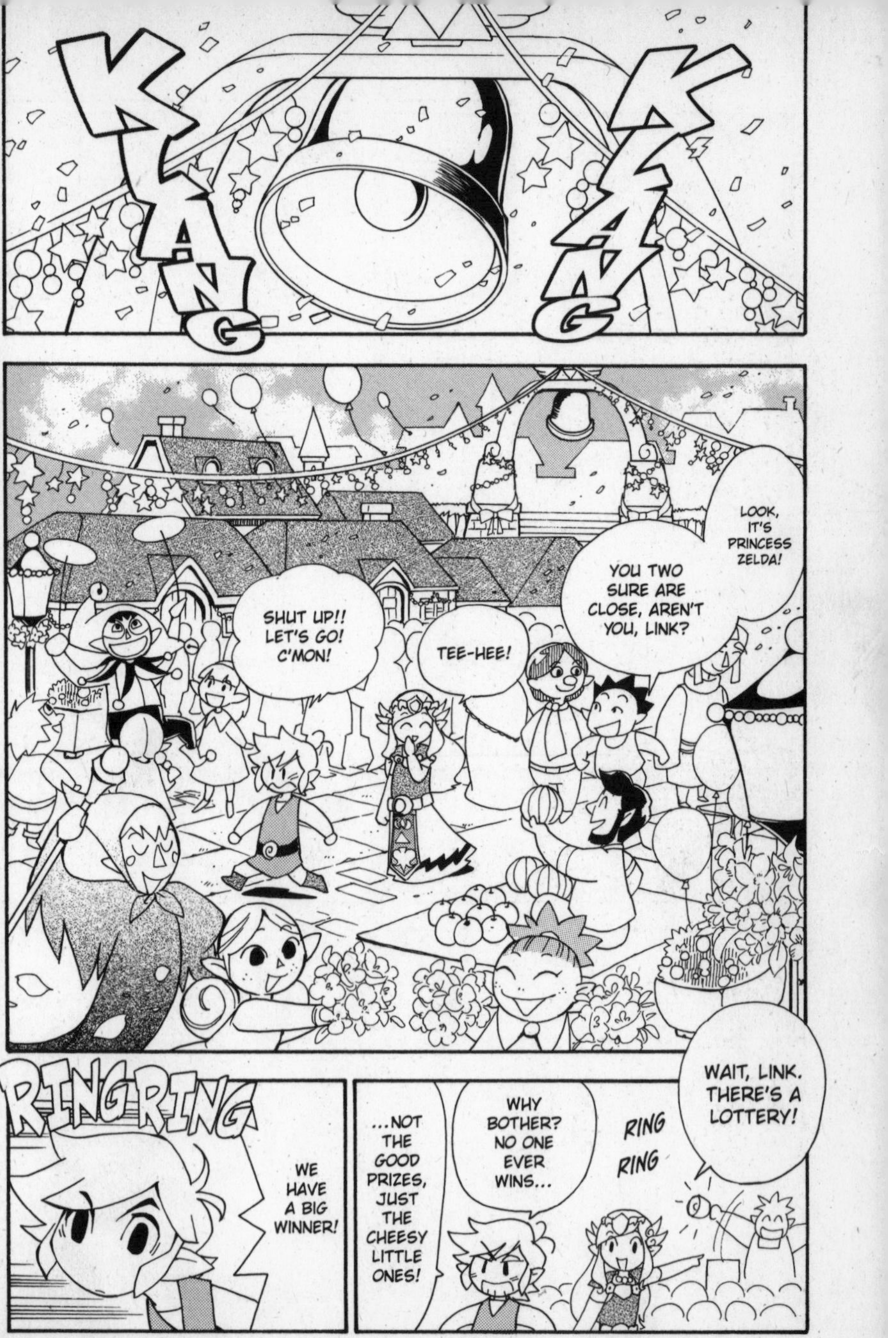
KANG
KANG
LOOK, IT'S PRINCESS ZELDA!
YOU TWO SURE ARE CLOSE, AREN'T YOU, LINK?
TEE-HEE!
SHUT UP!! LET'S GO! C'MON!
WAIT, LINK. THERE'S A LOTTERY!
RING RING
WHY BOTHER? NO ONE EVER WINS...
...NOT THE GOOD PRIZES, JUST THE CHEESY LITTLE ONES!
RING RING
WE HAVE A BIG WINNER!

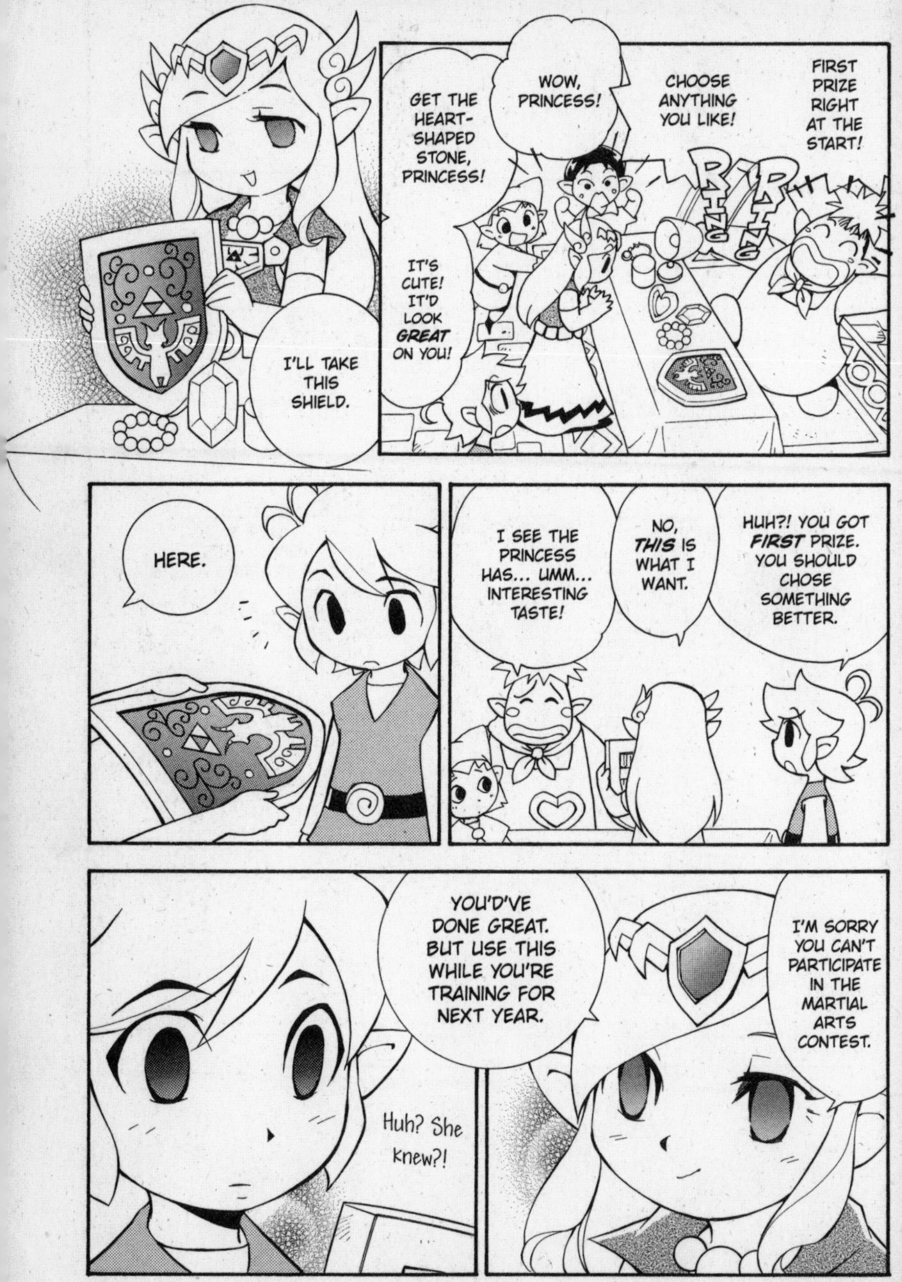
FIRST PRIZE RIGHT AT THE START!
RING RING
CHOOSE ANYTHING YOU LIKE!
WOW, PRINCESS!
GET THE HEART-SHAPED STONE, PRINCESS!
IT'S CUTE! IT'D LOOK *GREAT* ON YOU!
I'LL TAKE THIS SHIELD.
HUH?! YOU GOT *FIRST* PRIZE. YOU SHOULD CHOSE SOMETHING BETTER.
NO, *THIS* IS WHAT I WANT.
I SEE THE PRINCESS HAS... UMM... INTERESTING TASTE!
HERE.
I'M SORRY YOU CAN'T PARTICIPATE IN THE MARTIAL ARTS CONTEST.
YOU'D'VE DONE GREAT. BUT USE THIS WHILE YOU'RE TRAINING FOR NEXT YEAR.
Huh? She knew?!

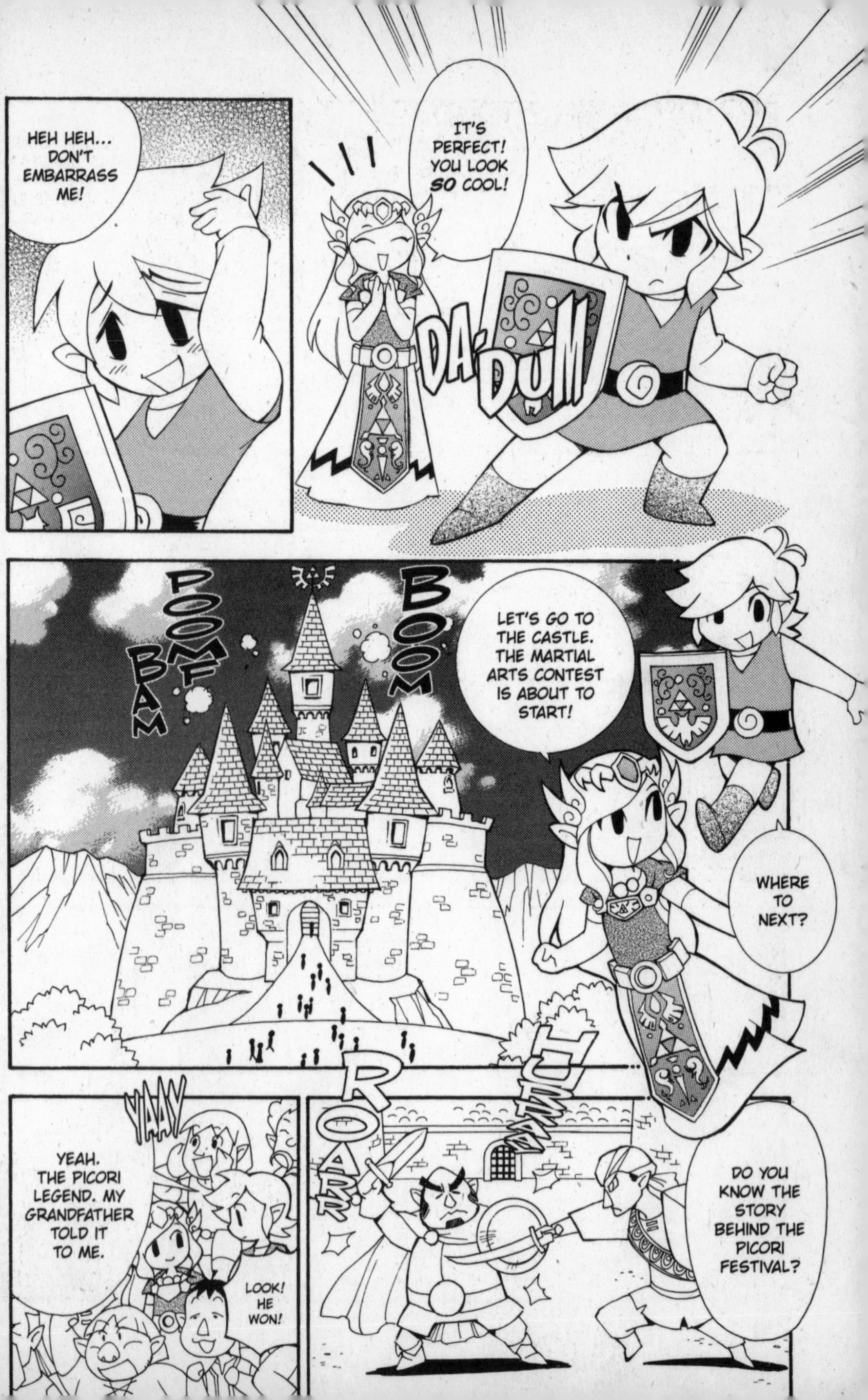
IT'S PERFECT! YOU LOOK SO COOL!
DA-DUM
HEH HEH... DON'T EMBARRASS ME!
BOOOOM
POOOMF
BAM
LET'S GO TO THE CASTLE. THE MARTIAL ARTS CONTEST IS ABOUT TO START!
WHERE TO NEXT?
ROARR
DO YOU KNOW THE STORY BEHIND THE PICORI FESTIVAL?
YAAY
YEAH. THE PICORI LEGEND. MY GRANDFATHER TOLD IT TO ME.
LOOK! HE WON!

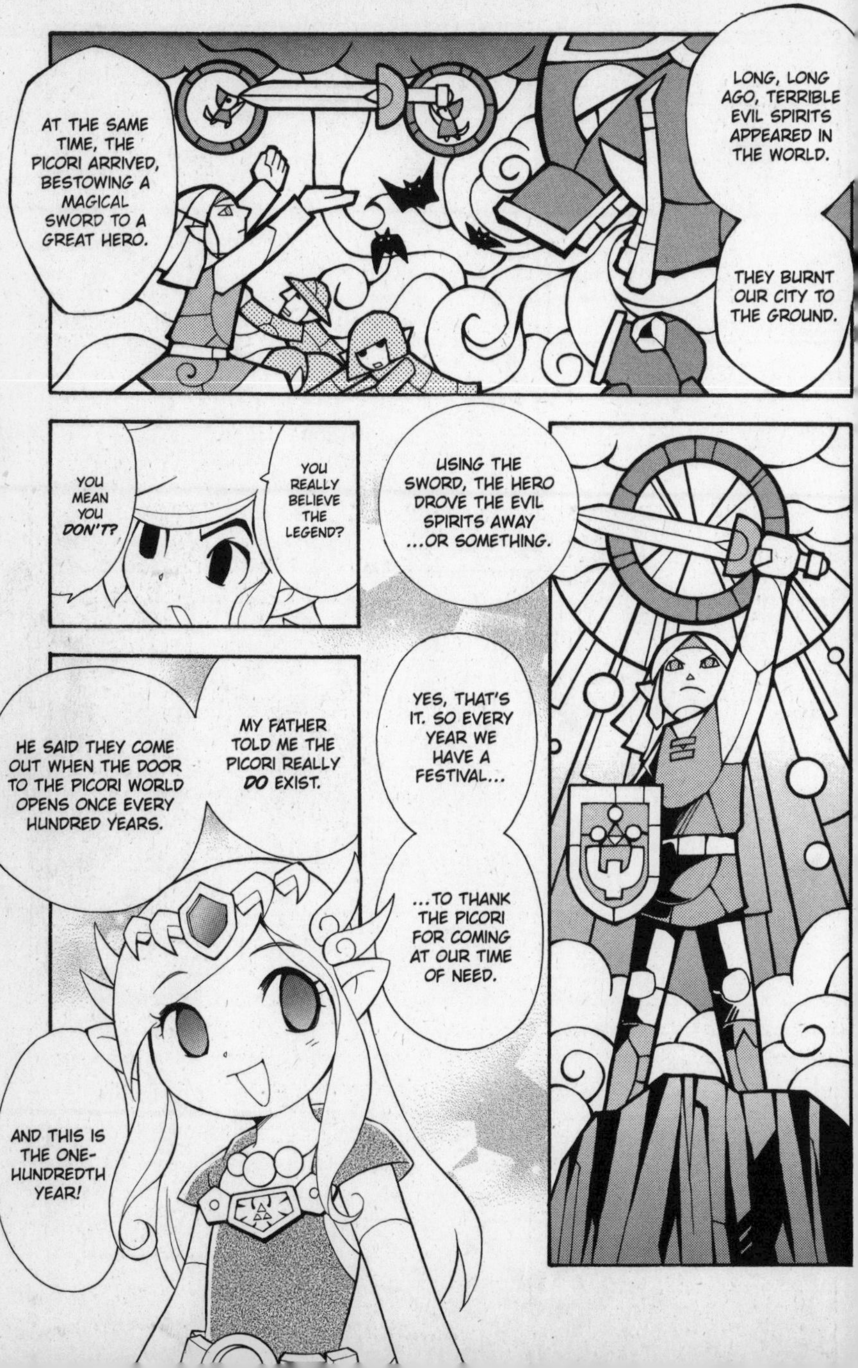
LONG, LONG AGO, TERRIBLE EVIL SPIRITS APPEARED IN THE WORLD.
THEY BURNT OUR CITY TO THE GROUND.
AT THE SAME TIME, THE PICORI ARRIVED, BESTOWING A MAGICAL SWORD TO A GREAT HERO.
USING THE SWORD, THE HERO DROVE THE EVIL SPIRITS AWAY ...OR SOMETHING.
YOU REALLY BELIEVE THE LEGEND?
YOU MEAN YOU *DON'T*?
YES, THAT'S IT. SO EVERY YEAR WE HAVE A FESTIVAL...
...TO THANK THE PICORI FOR COMING AT OUR TIME OF NEED.
MY FATHER TOLD ME THE PICORI REALLY *DO* EXIST.
HE SAID THEY COME OUT WHEN THE DOOR TO THE PICORI WORLD OPENS ONCE EVERY HUNDRED YEARS.
AND THIS IS THE ONE-HUNDREDTH YEAR!

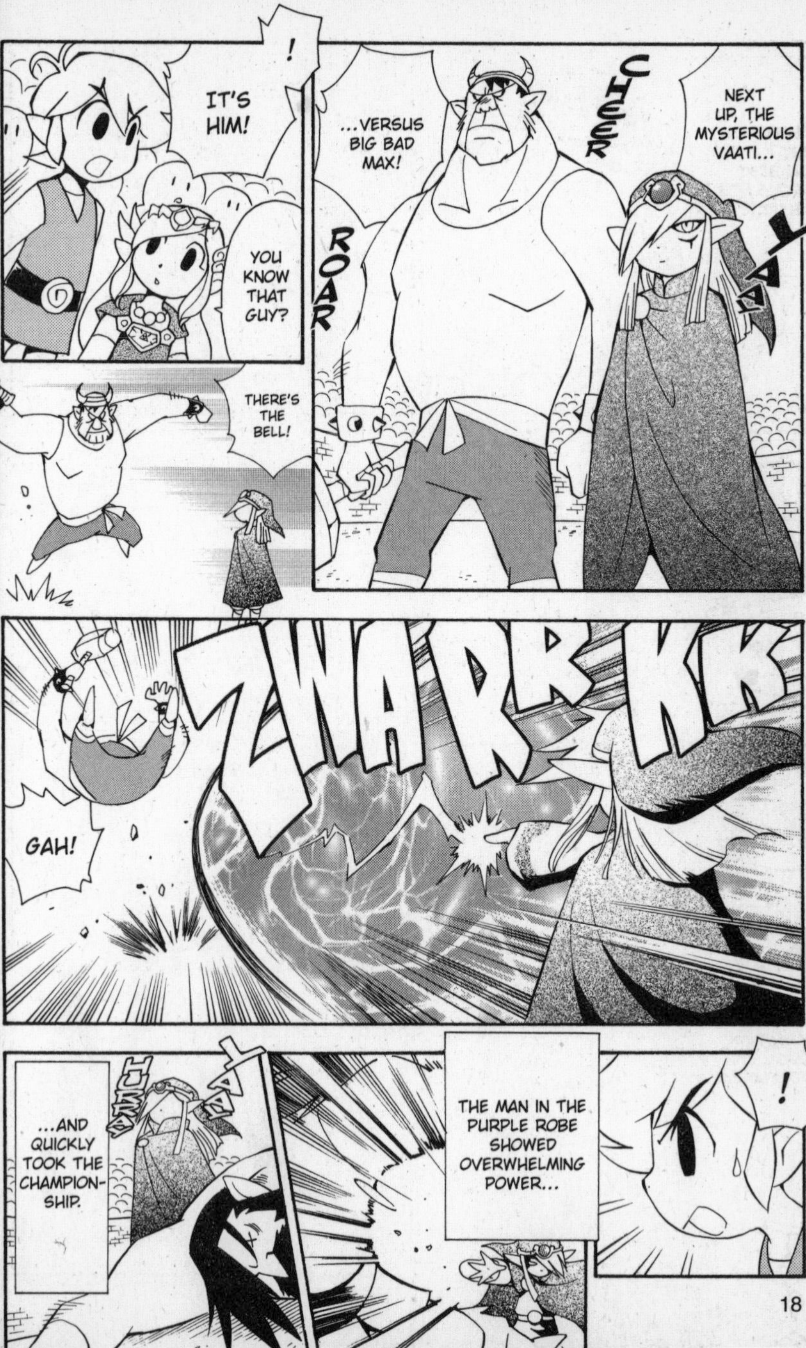

NEXT UP, THE MYSTERIOUS VAATI...
YAAY
CHEER
...VERSUS BIG BAD MAX!
ROAR
!
IT'S HIM!
YOU KNOW THAT GUY?
THERE'S THE BELL!
ZWARRKK
GAH!
!
THE MAN IN THE PURPLE ROBE SHOWED OVERWHELMING POWER...
YAAY
HURRAY
...AND QUICKLY TOOK THE CHAMPION-SHIP.

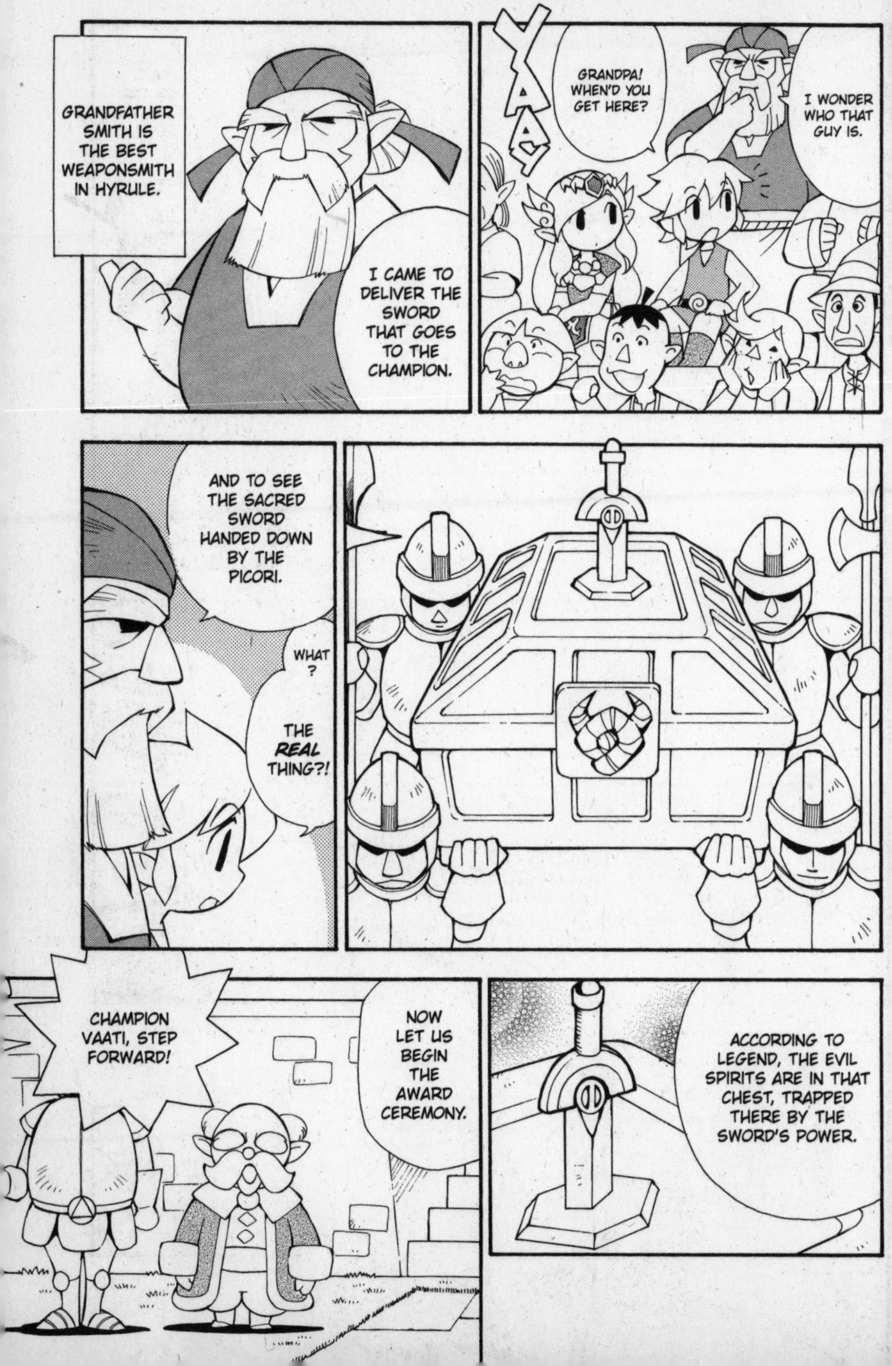
YAAY
I WONDER WHO THAT GUY IS.
GRANDPA! WHEN'D YOU GET HERE?
GRANDFATHER SMITH IS THE BEST WEAPONSMITH IN HYRULE.
I CAME TO DELIVER THE SWORD THAT GOES TO THE CHAMPION.
AND TO SEE THE SACRED SWORD HANDED DOWN BY THE PICORI.
WHAT?
THE *REAL* THING?!
ACCORDING TO LEGEND, THE EVIL SPIRITS ARE IN THAT CHEST, TRAPPED THERE BY THE SWORD'S POWER.
NOW LET US BEGIN THE AWARD CEREMONY.
CHAMPION VAATI, STEP FORWARD!

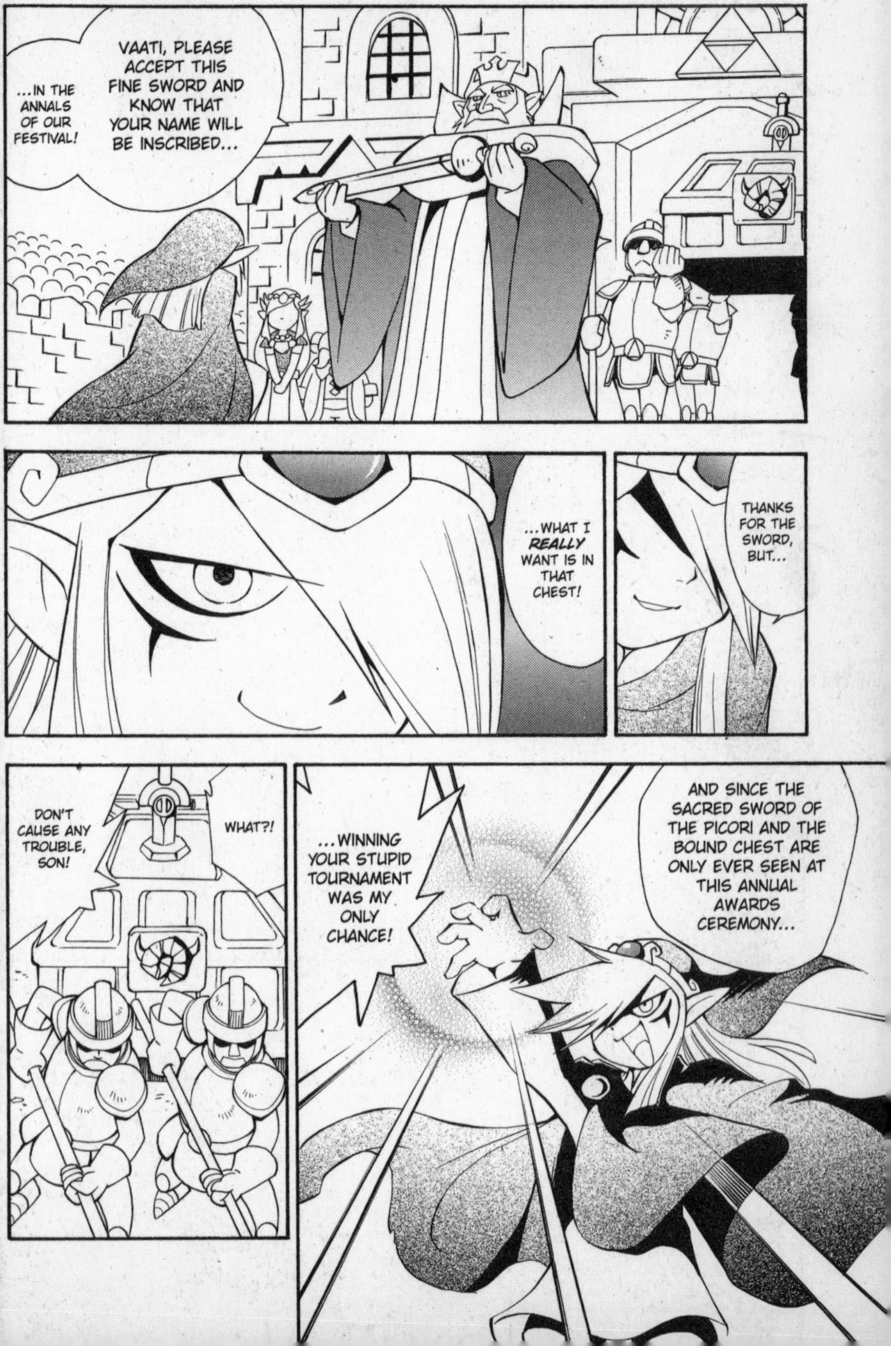
VAATI, PLEASE ACCEPT THIS FINE SWORD AND KNOW THAT YOUR NAME WILL BE INSCRIBED...
...IN THE ANNALS OF OUR FESTIVAL!
THANKS FOR THE SWORD, BUT...
...WHAT I REALLY WANT IS IN THAT CHEST!
AND SINCE THE SACRED SWORD OF THE PICORI AND THE BOUND CHEST ARE ONLY EVER SEEN AT THIS ANNUAL AWARDS CEREMONY...
...WINNING YOUR STUPID TOURNAMENT WAS MY ONLY CHANCE!
WHAT?!
DON'T CAUSE ANY TROUBLE, SON!

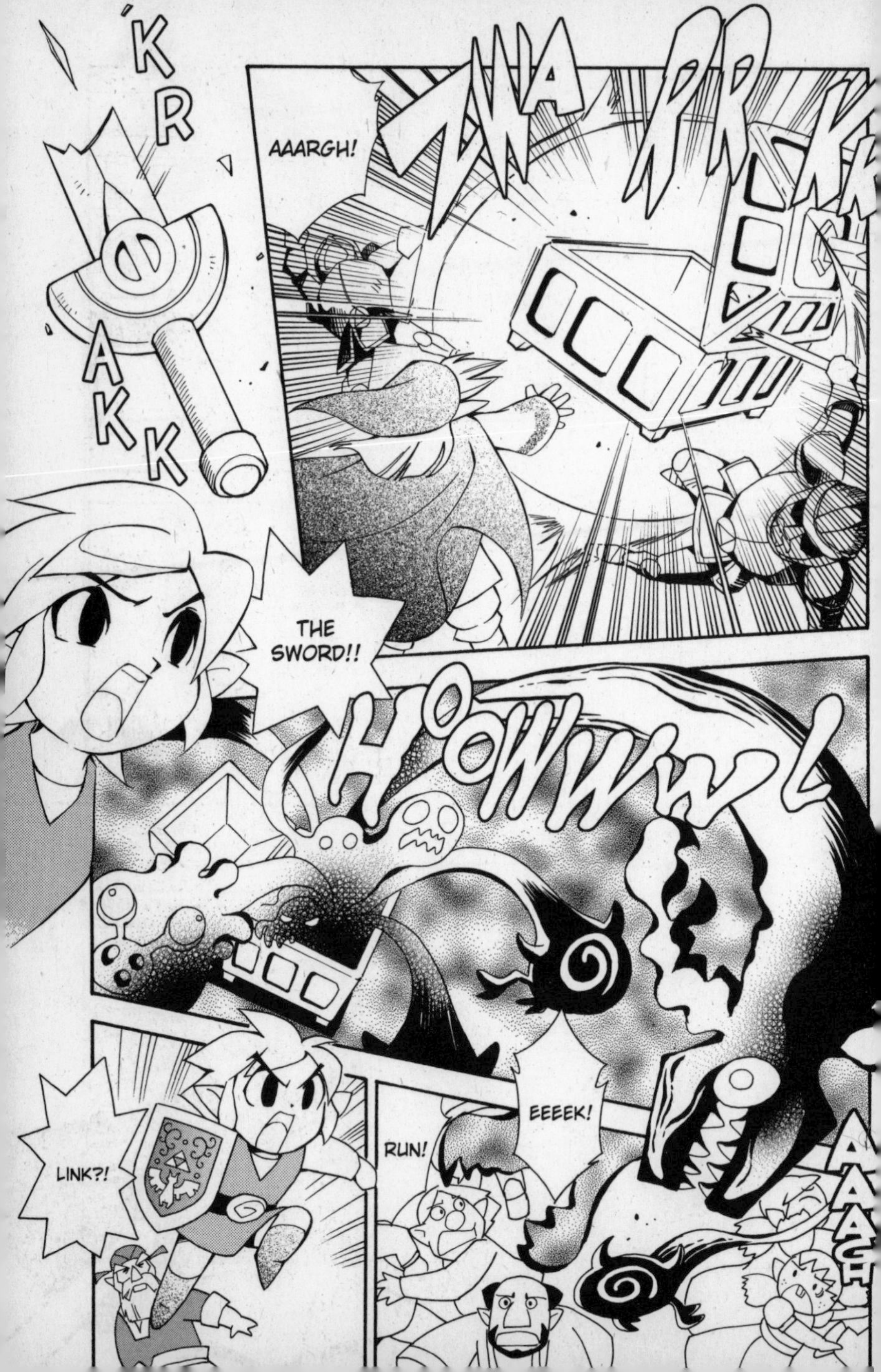
AAARGH!
KRAKK
THE SWORD!!
HOOWWL
EEEEK!
RUN!
AAAGH
LINK?!

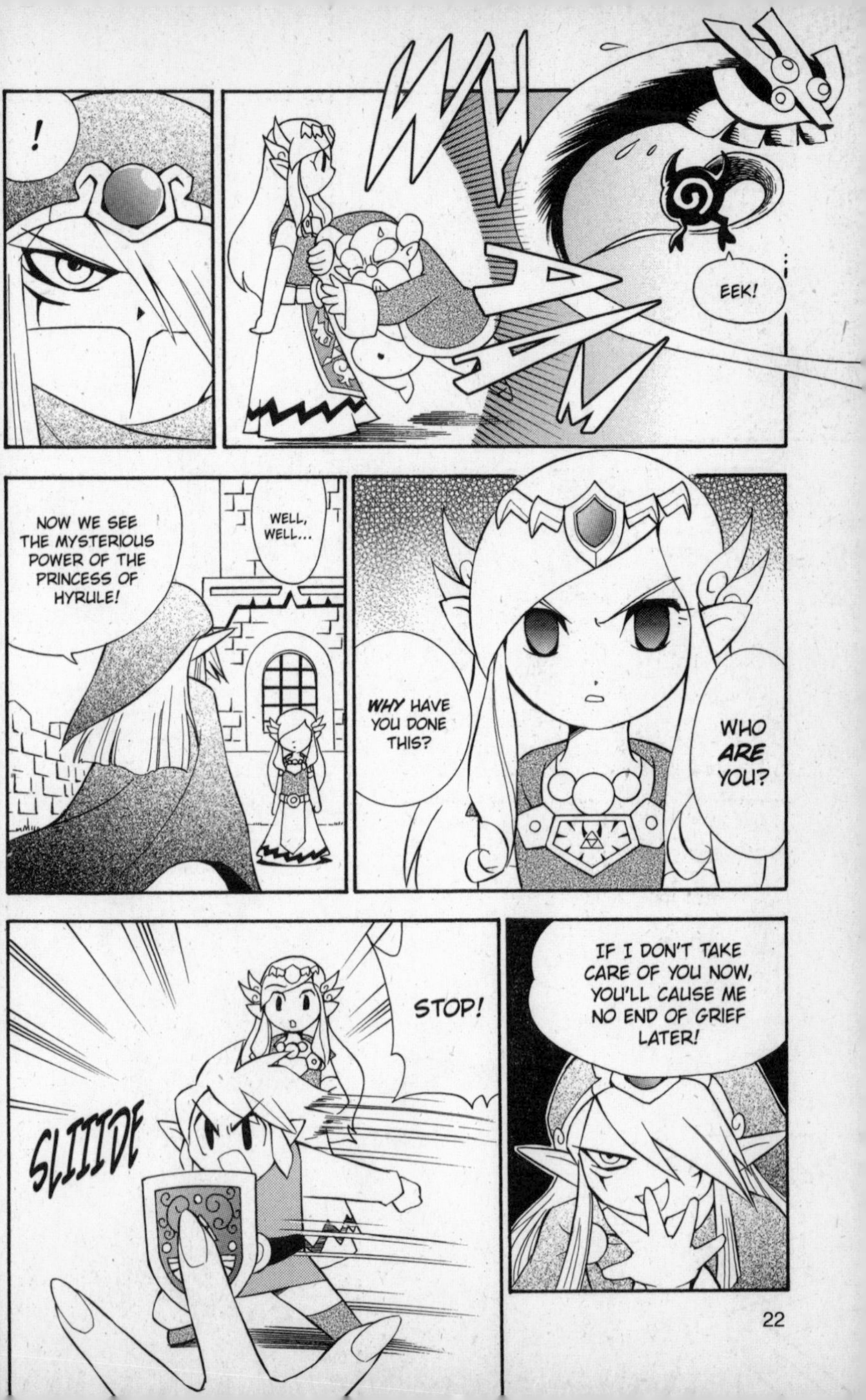
EEK!
!
WHO ARE YOU?
WHY HAVE YOU DONE THIS?
WELL, WELL...
NOW WE SEE THE MYSTERIOUS POWER OF THE PRINCESS OF HYRULE!
IF I DON'T TAKE CARE OF YOU NOW, YOU'LL CAUSE ME NO END OF GRIEF LATER!
STOP!
SLIIIDE

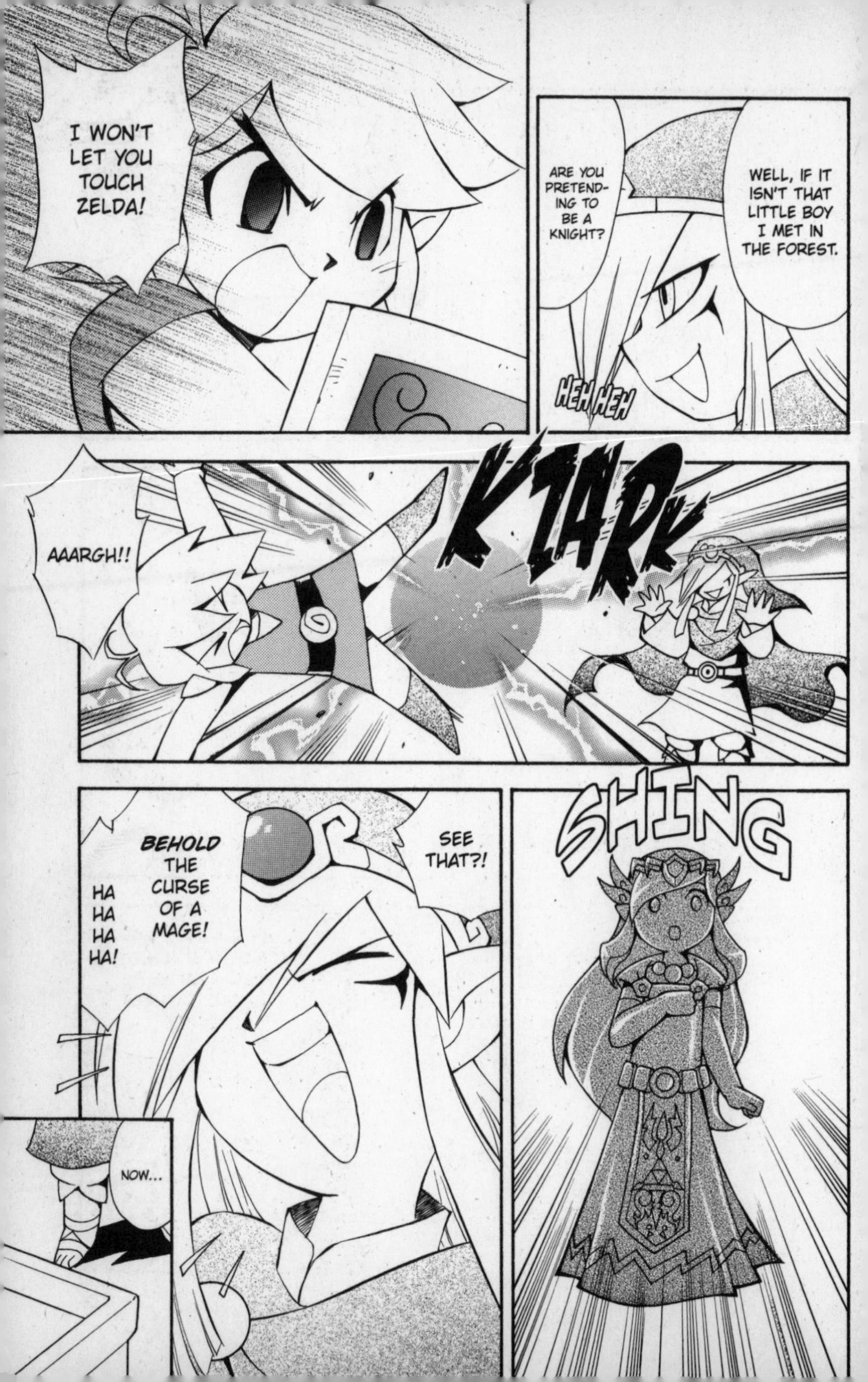
WELL, IF IT ISN'T THAT LITTLE BOY I MET IN THE FOREST.
ARE YOU PRETENDING TO BE A KNIGHT?
HEH HEH
I WON'T LET YOU TOUCH ZELDA!
KZARK
AAARGH!!
SHING
SEE THAT?!
BEHOLD THE CURSE OF A MAGE!
HA HA HA HA!
NOW...

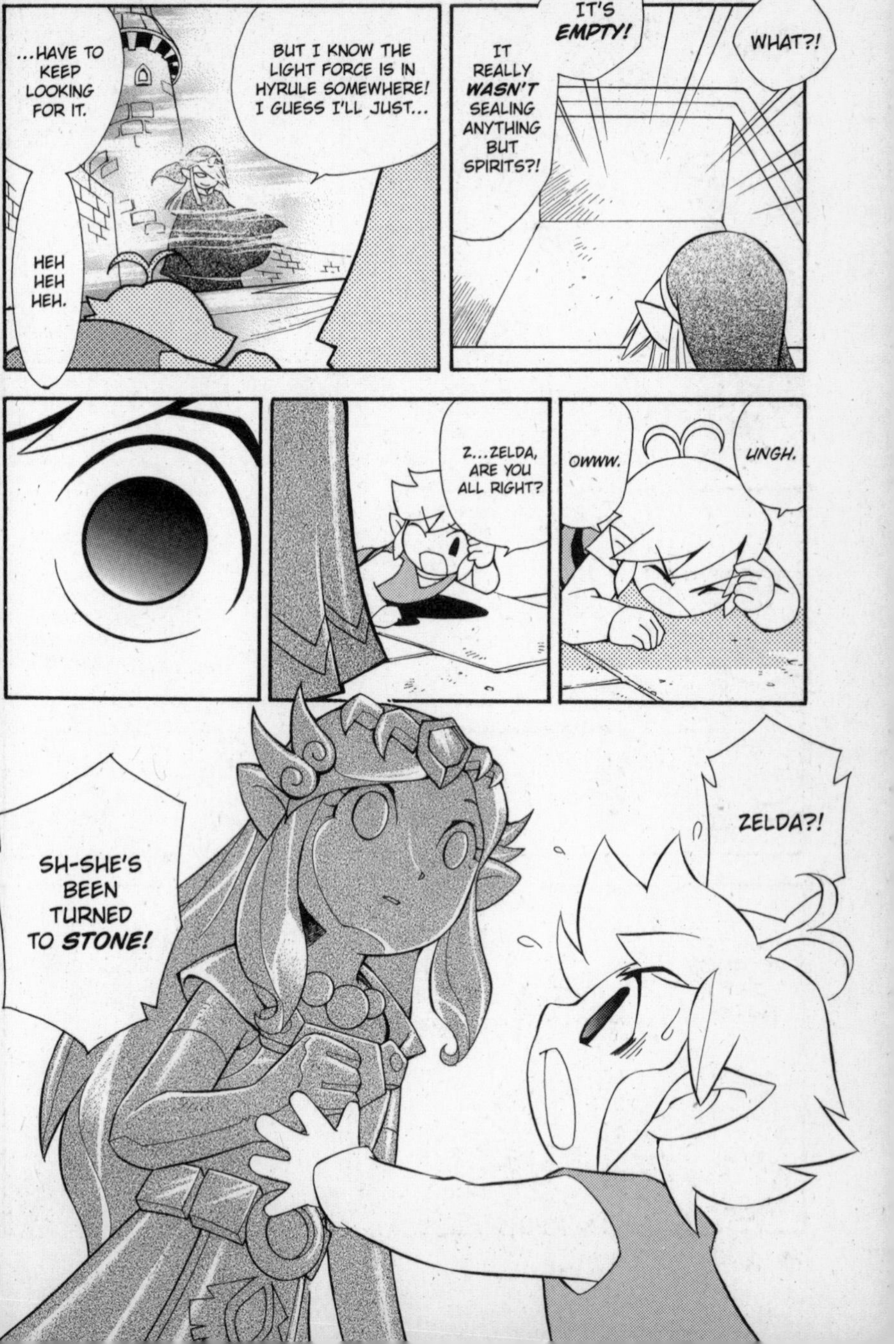
WHAT?!
IT'S EMPTY!
IT REALLY WASN'T SEALING ANYTHING BUT SPIRITS?!
BUT I KNOW THE LIGHT FORCE IS IN HYRULE SOMEWHERE! I GUESS I'LL JUST...
...HAVE TO KEEP LOOKING FOR IT.
HEH HEH HEH.
UNGH.
OWWW.
Z...ZELDA, ARE YOU ALL RIGHT?
ZELDA?!
SH-SHE'S BEEN TURNED TO STONE!

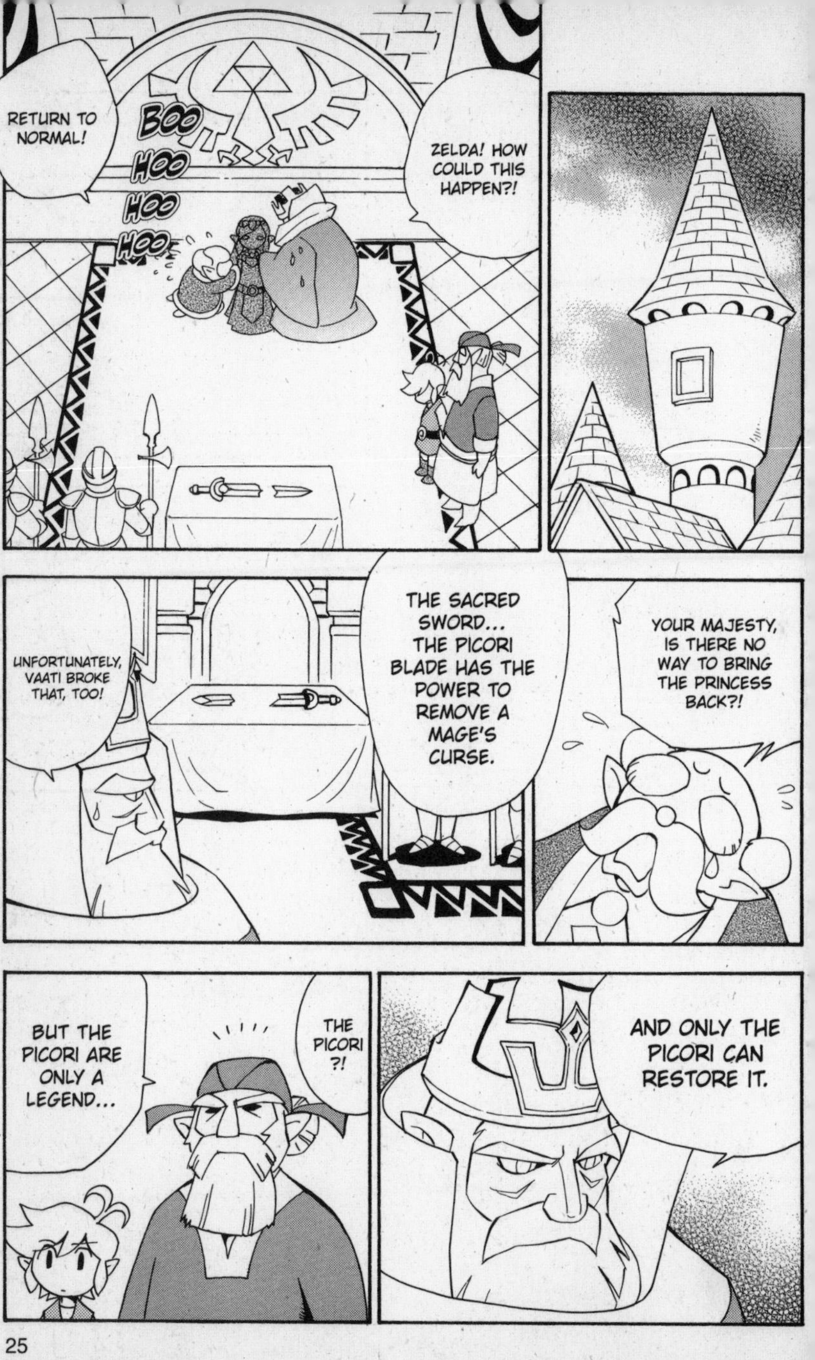
ZELDA! HOW COULD THIS HAPPEN?!
BOO HOO HOO HOO
RETURN TO NORMAL!
YOUR MAJESTY, IS THERE NO WAY TO BRING THE PRINCESS BACK?!
THE SACRED SWORD... THE PICORI BLADE HAS THE POWER TO REMOVE A MAGE'S CURSE.
UNFORTUNATELY, VAATI BROKE THAT, TOO!
AND ONLY THE PICORI CAN RESTORE IT.
THE PICORI ?!
BUT THE PICORI ARE ONLY A LEGEND...

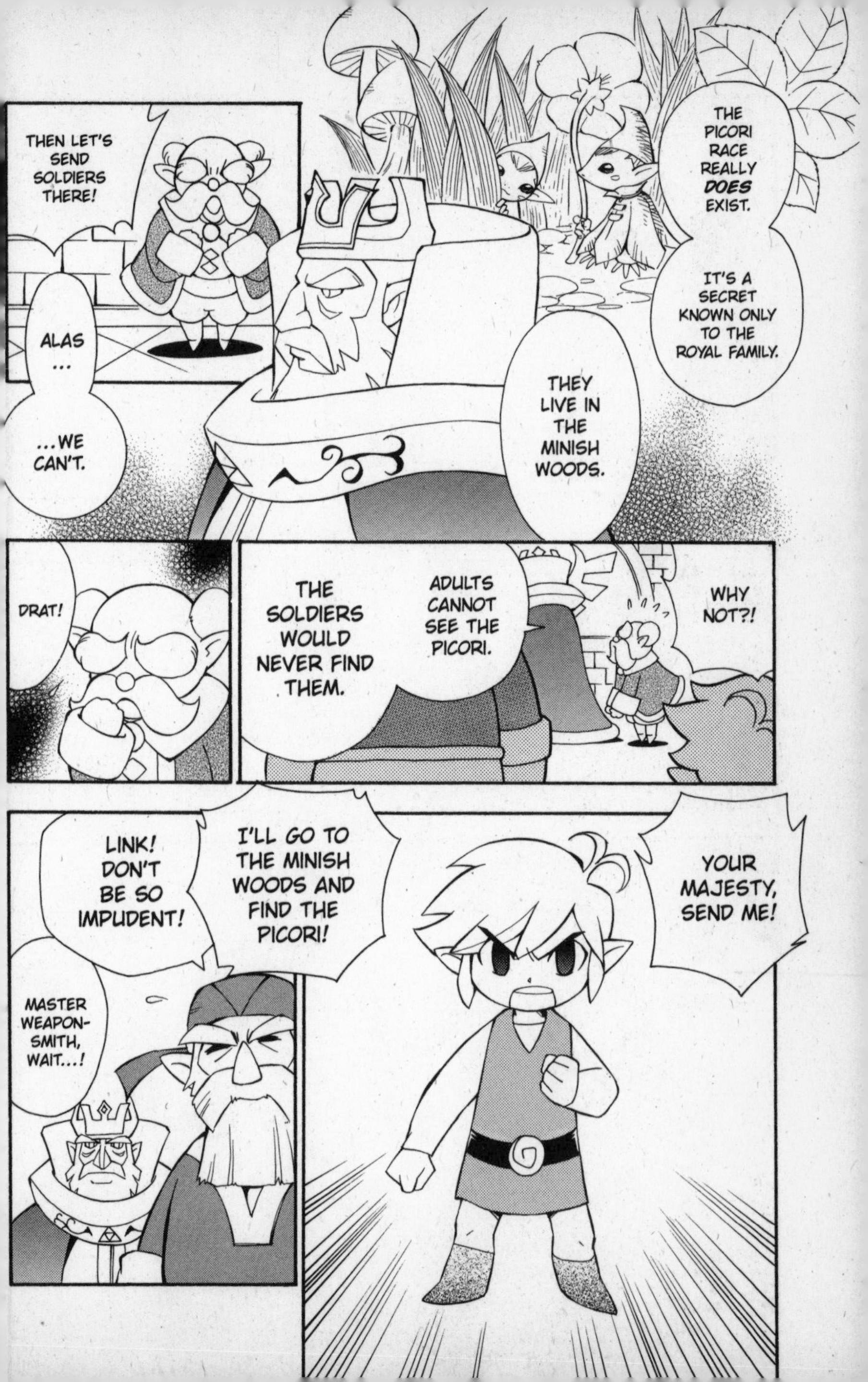
THE PICORI RACE REALLY **DOES** EXIST.
IT'S A SECRET KNOWN ONLY TO THE ROYAL FAMILY.
THEY LIVE IN THE MINISH WOODS.
THEN LET'S SEND SOLDIERS THERE!
ALAS ...
...WE CAN'T.
WHY NOT?!
ADULTS CANNOT SEE THE PICORI.
THE SOLDIERS WOULD NEVER FIND THEM.
DRAT!
YOUR MAJESTY, SEND ME!
I'LL GO TO THE MINISH WOODS AND FIND THE PICORI!
LINK! DON'T BE SO IMPUDENT!
MASTER WEAPON-SMITH, WAIT...!

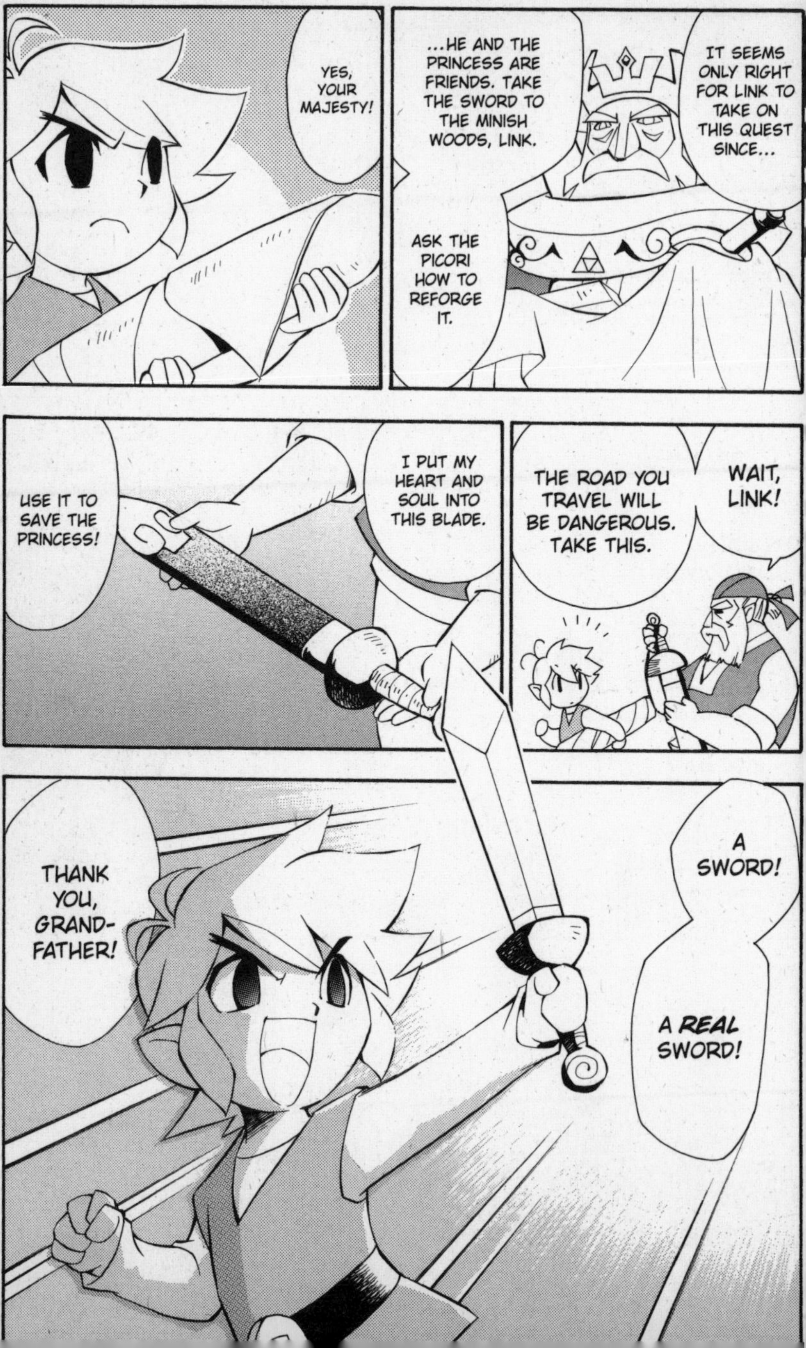
IT SEEMS ONLY RIGHT FOR LINK TO TAKE ON THIS QUEST SINCE...
...HE AND THE PRINCESS ARE FRIENDS. TAKE THE SWORD TO THE MINISH WOODS, LINK.
ASK THE PICORI HOW TO REFORGE IT.
YES, YOUR MAJESTY!
WAIT, LINK!
THE ROAD YOU TRAVEL WILL BE DANGEROUS. TAKE THIS.
I PUT MY HEART AND SOUL INTO THIS BLADE.
USE IT TO SAVE THE PRINCESS!
A SWORD!
A *REAL* SWORD!
THANK YOU, GRAND-FATHER!

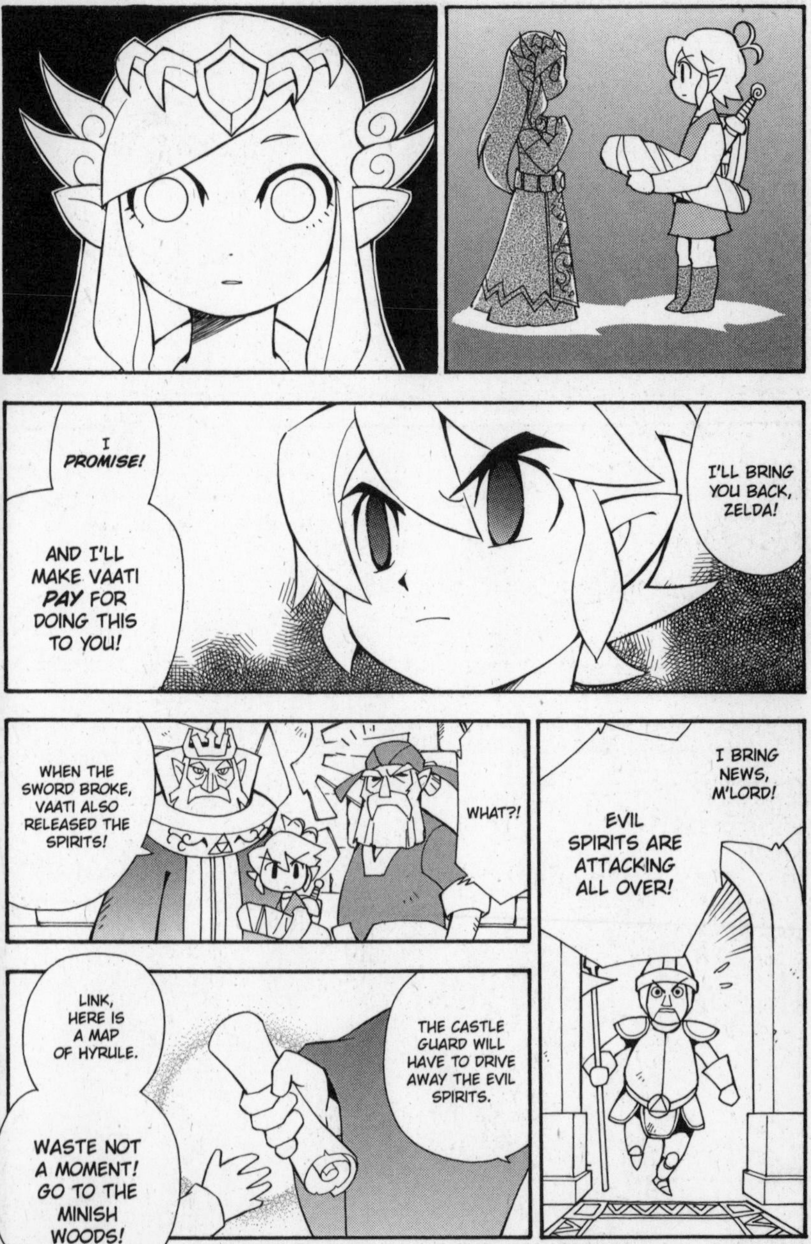
I'LL BRING YOU BACK, ZELDA!
I *PROMISE!*
AND I'LL MAKE VAATI *PAY* FOR DOING THIS TO YOU!
I BRING NEWS, M'LORD!
EVIL SPIRITS ARE ATTACKING ALL OVER!
WHAT?!
WHEN THE SWORD BROKE, VAATI ALSO RELEASED THE SPIRITS!
THE CASTLE GUARD WILL HAVE TO DRIVE AWAY THE EVIL SPIRITS.
LINK, HERE IS A MAP OF HYRULE.
WASTE NOT A MOMENT! GO TO THE MINISH WOODS!

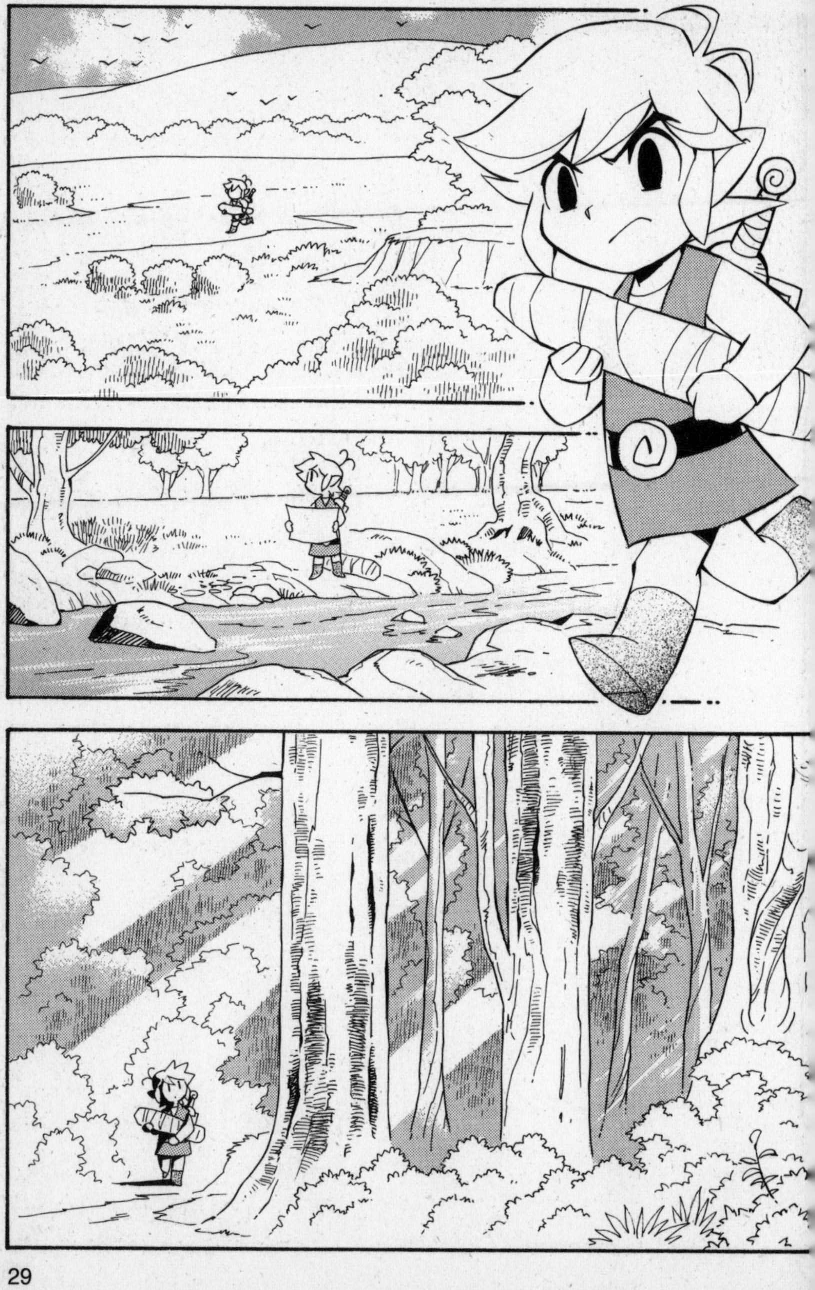

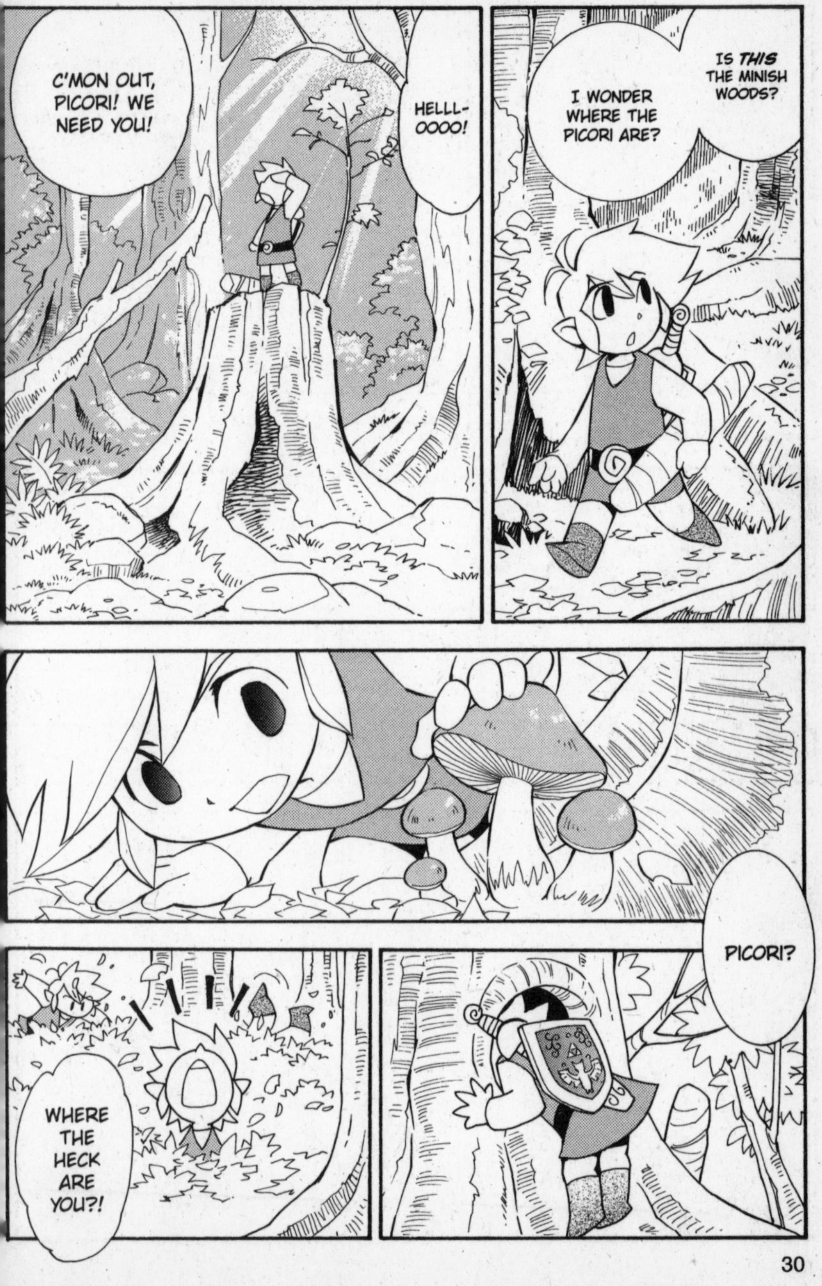
IS THIS THE MINISH WOODS?
I WONDER WHERE THE PICORI ARE?
HELLL-OOOO!
C'MON OUT, PICORI! WE NEED YOU!
PICORI?
WHERE THE HECK ARE YOU?!

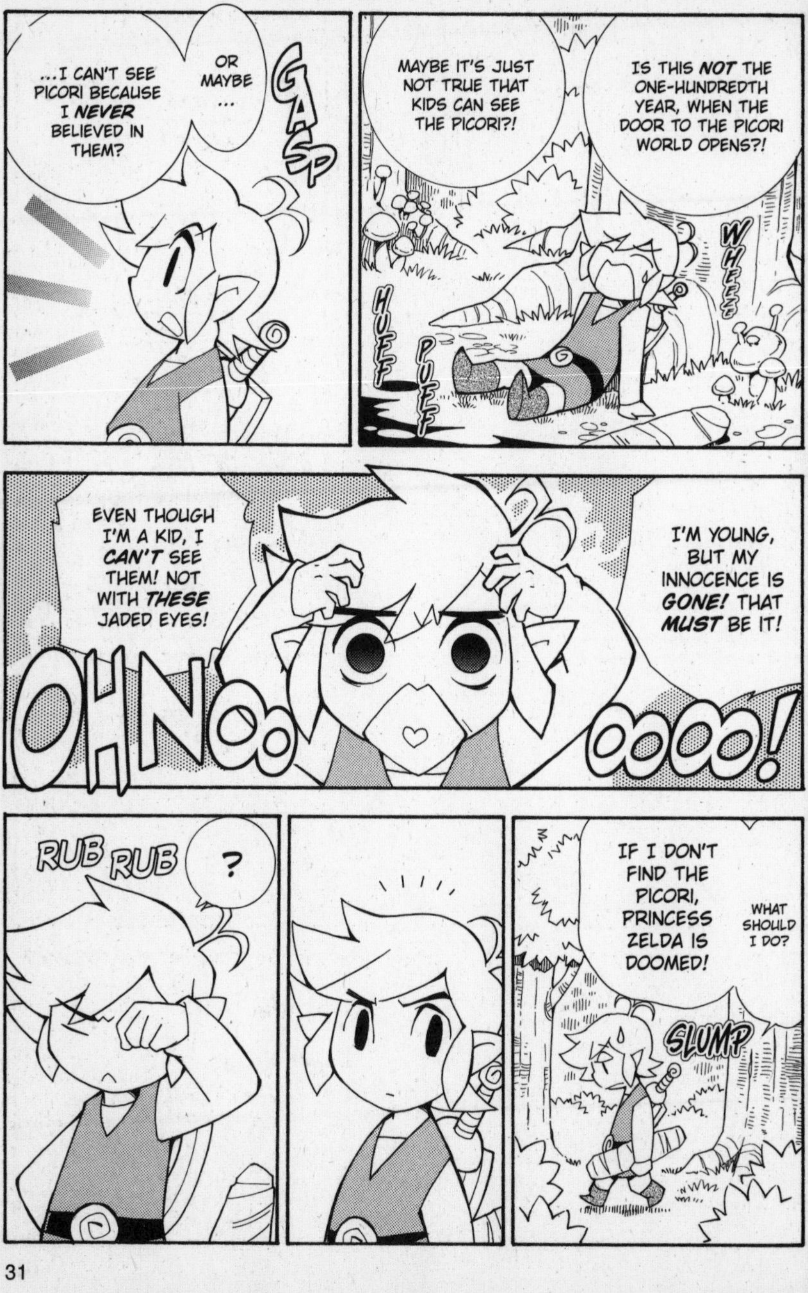
IS THIS *NOT* THE ONE-HUNDREDTH YEAR, WHEN THE DOOR TO THE PICORI WORLD OPENS?!
MAYBE IT'S JUST NOT TRUE THAT KIDS CAN SEE THE PICORI?!
WHEEZE
HUFF PUFF
GASP
OR MAYBE...
...I CAN'T SEE PICORI BECAUSE I *NEVER* BELIEVED IN THEM?
I'M YOUNG, BUT MY INNOCENCE IS *GONE!* THAT *MUST* BE IT!
EVEN THOUGH I'M A KID, I *CAN'T* SEE THEM! NOT WITH *THESE* JADED EYES!
OHNOOOOOOO!
IF I DON'T FIND THE PICORI, PRINCESS ZELDA IS DOOMED!
WHAT SHOULD I DO?
SLUMP
?
RUB RUB

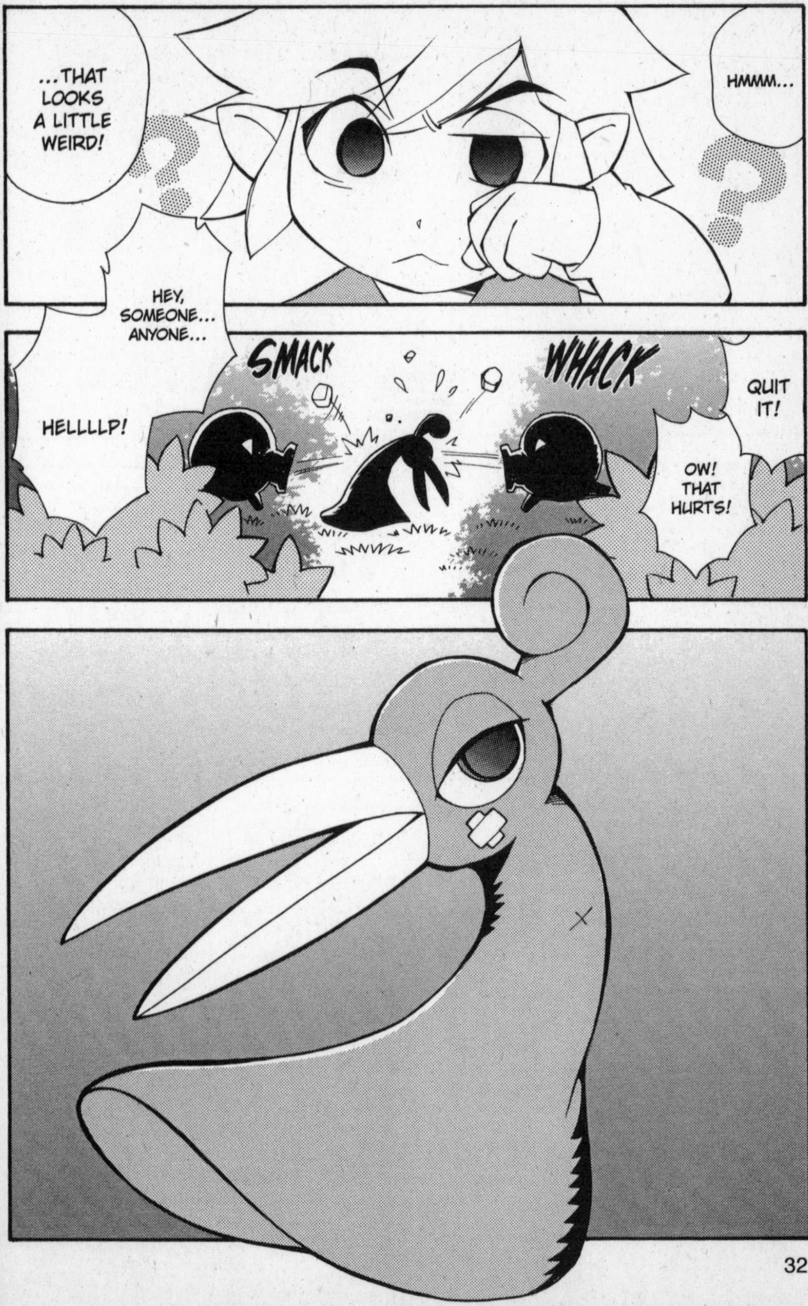
HMMM...
...THAT LOOKS A LITTLE WEIRD!
QUIT IT!
WHACK
OW! THAT HURTS!
SMACK
HEY, SOMEONE... ANYONE...
HELLLLP!

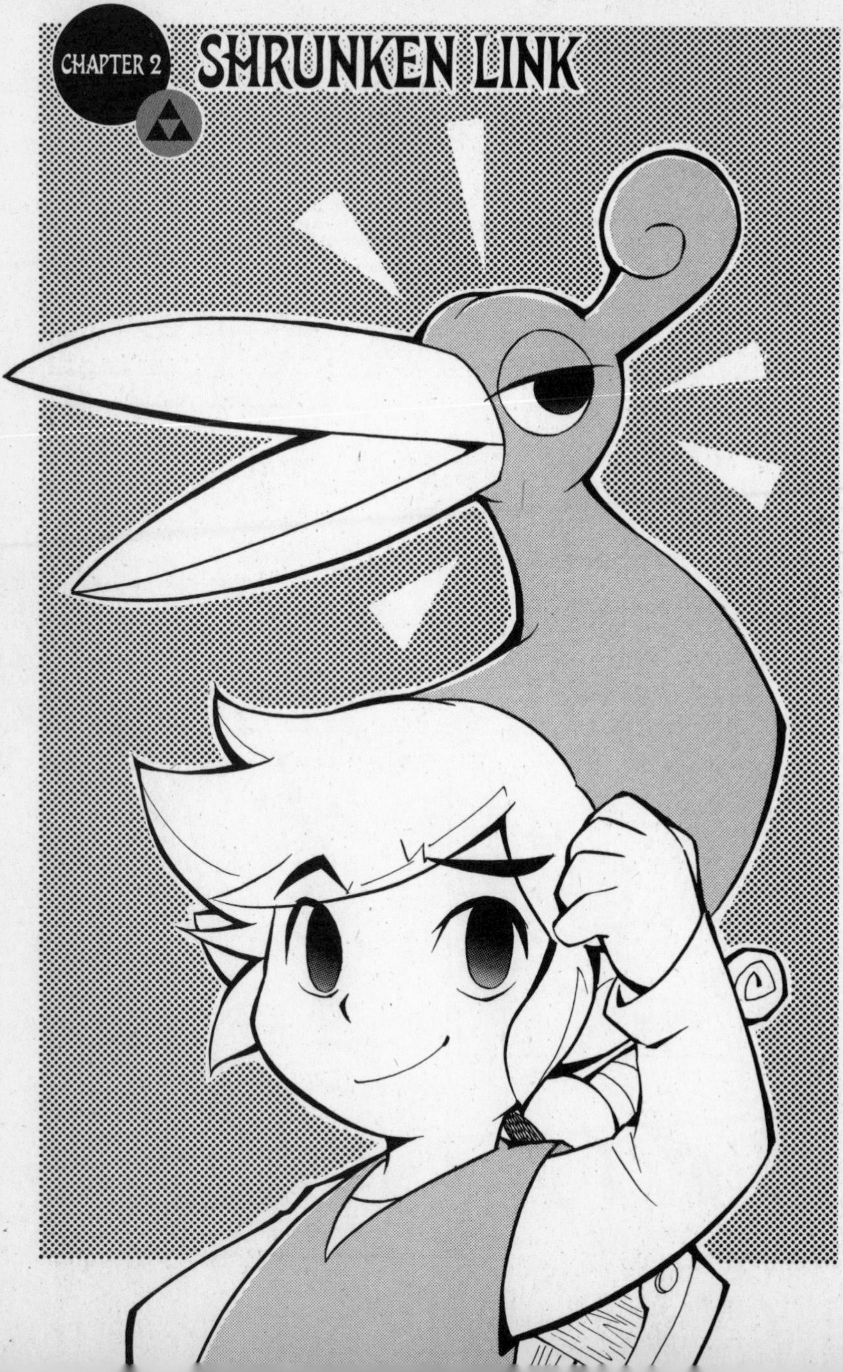
CHAPTER 2
SHRUNKEN LINK

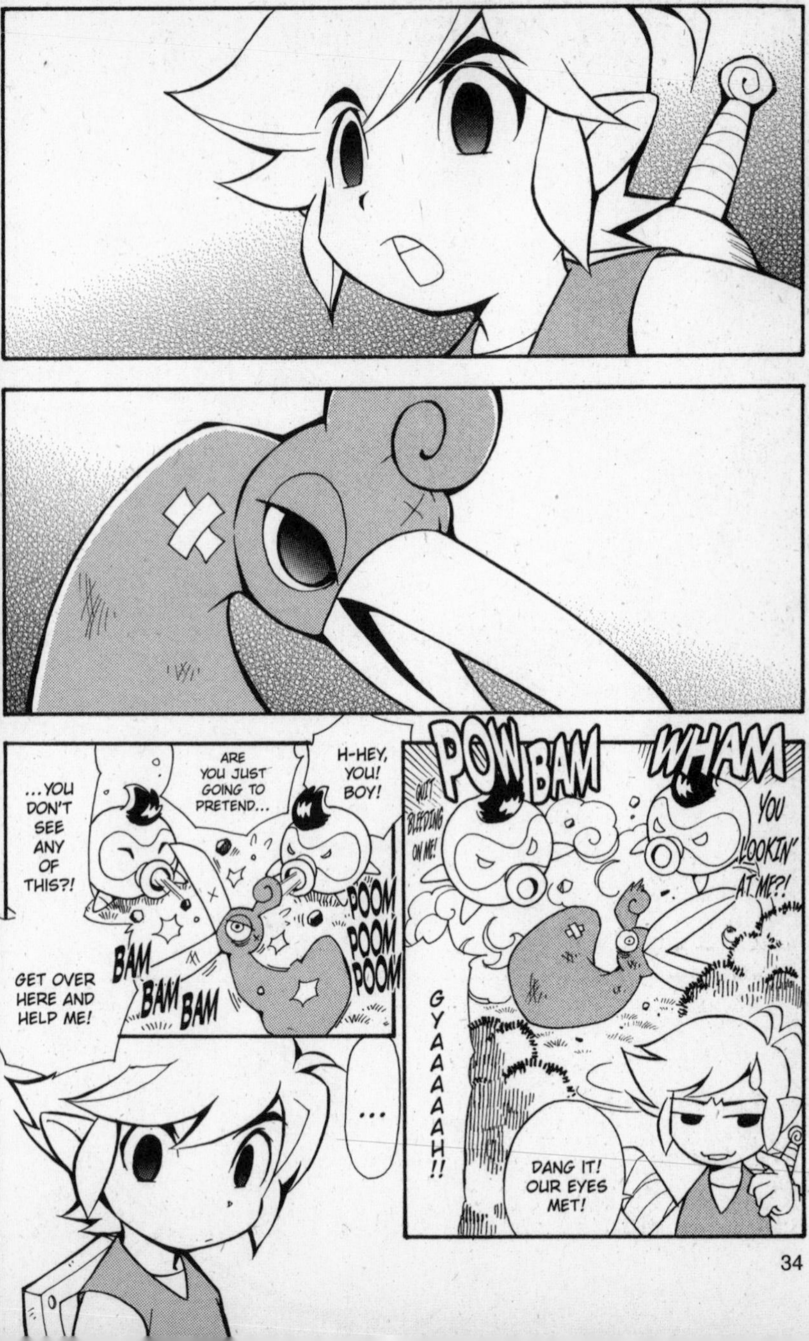

WHAM
BAM
POW
YOU LOOKIN' AT ME?!
QUIT BLEEDING ON ME!
GYAAAAAAH!!
DANG IT! OUR EYES MET!
H-HEY, YOU! BOY!
ARE YOU JUST GOING TO PRETEND...
...YOU DON'T SEE ANY OF THIS?!
POOM POOM POOM
BAM BAM BAM
GET OVER HERE AND HELP ME!
...

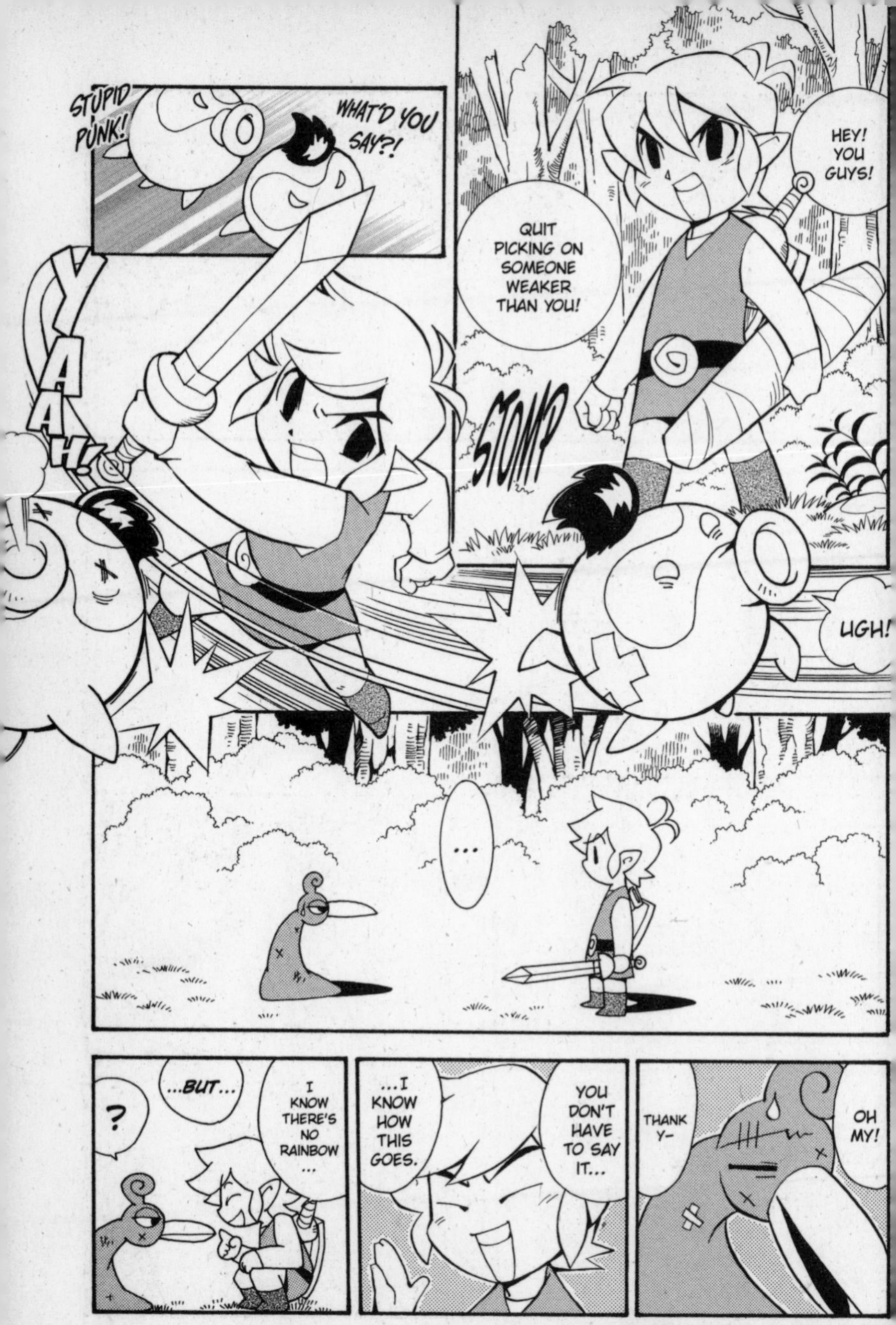
HEY! YOU GUYS!
QUIT PICKING ON SOMEONE WEAKER THAN YOU!
STUPID PUNK!
WHAT'D YOU SAY?!
STOMP
UGH!
YAAAH!
...
OH MY!
THANK Y-
YOU DON'T HAVE TO SAY IT...
...I KNOW HOW THIS GOES.
I KNOW THERE'S NO RAINBOW...
...BUT...
?

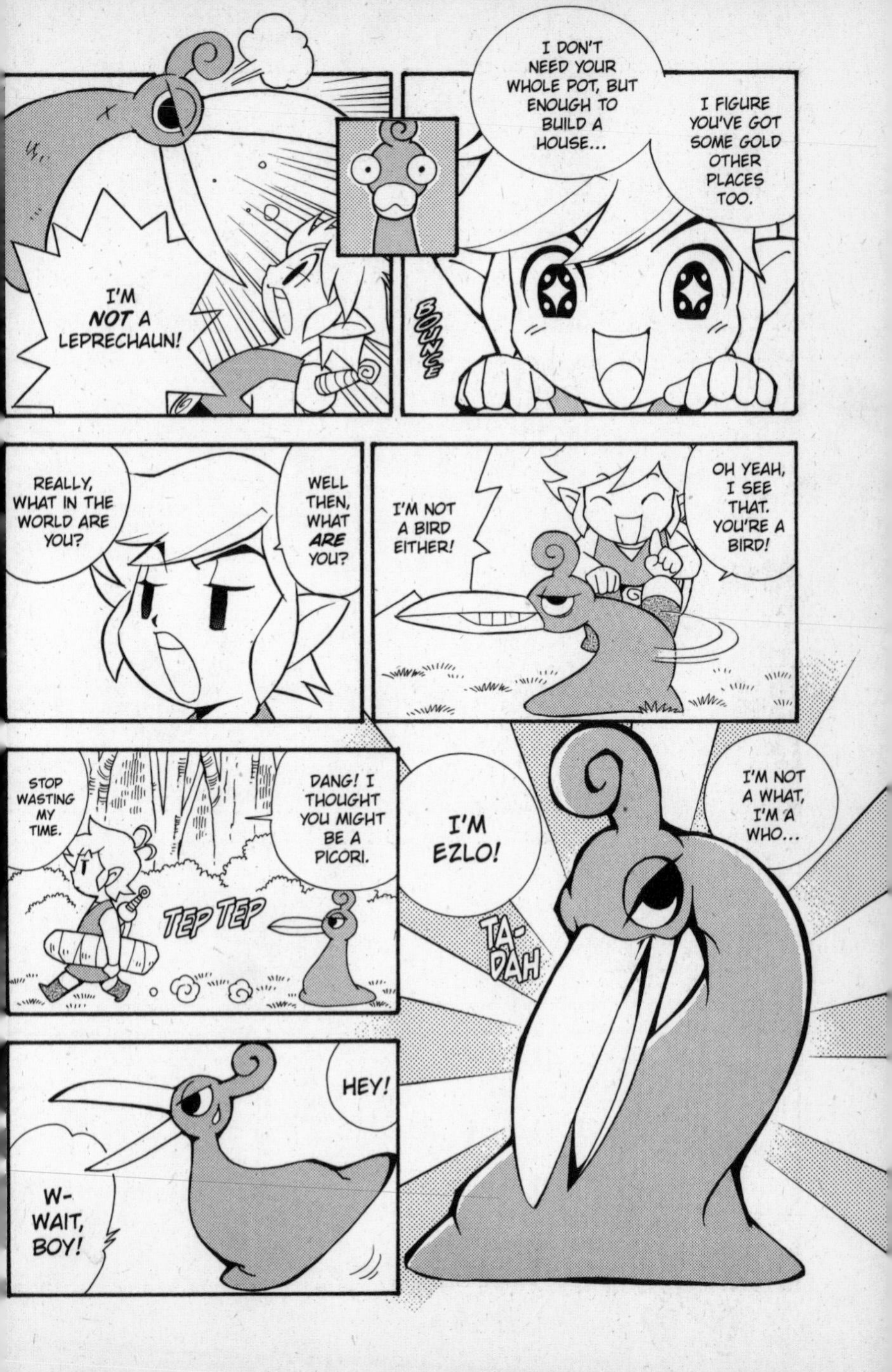
I DON'T NEED YOUR WHOLE POT, BUT ENOUGH TO BUILD A HOUSE...
I FIGURE YOU'VE GOT SOME GOLD OTHER PLACES TOO.
BOUNCE
I'M NOT A LEPRECHAUN!
OH YEAH, I SEE THAT. YOU'RE A BIRD!
I'M NOT A BIRD EITHER!
WELL THEN, WHAT ARE YOU?
REALLY, WHAT IN THE WORLD ARE YOU?
I'M NOT A WHAT, I'M A WHO...
I'M EZLO!
TA-DAH
DANG! I THOUGHT YOU MIGHT BE A PICORI.
STOP WASTING MY TIME.
TEP TEP
HEY!
W-WAIT, BOY!

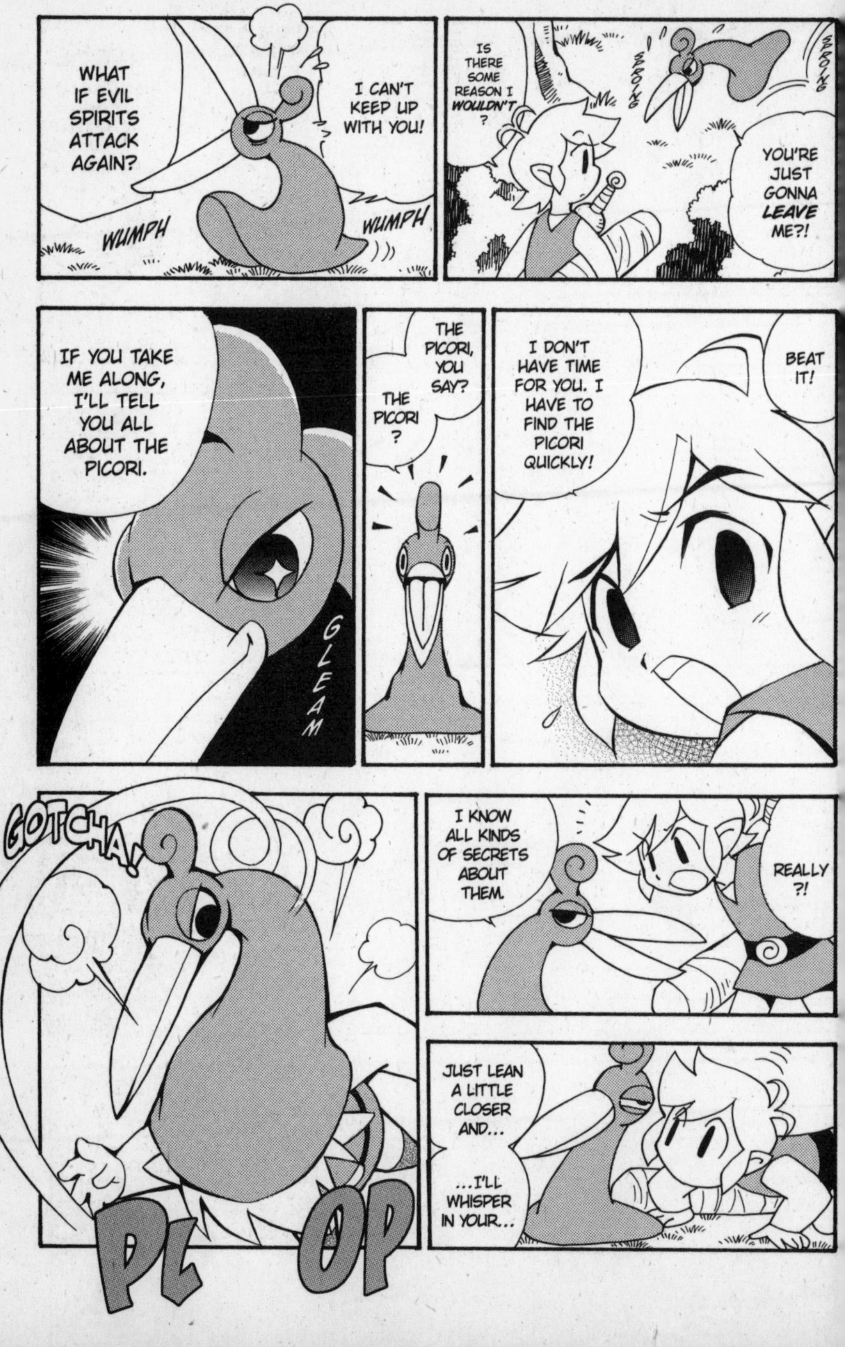
SPROING
YOU'RE JUST GONNA LEAVE ME?!
SPROING
IS THERE SOME REASON I WOULDN'T?
I CAN'T KEEP UP WITH YOU!
WHAT IF EVIL SPIRITS ATTACK AGAIN?
WUMPH
WUMPH
BEAT IT!
I DON'T HAVE TIME FOR YOU. I HAVE TO FIND THE PICORI QUICKLY!
THE PICORI, YOU SAY?
THE PICORI?
IF YOU TAKE ME ALONG, I'LL TELL YOU ALL ABOUT THE PICORI.
GLEAM
REALLY?!
I KNOW ALL KINDS OF SECRETS ABOUT THEM.
JUST LEAN A LITTLE CLOSER AND...
...I'LL WHISPER IN YOUR...
GOTCHA!
PLOP

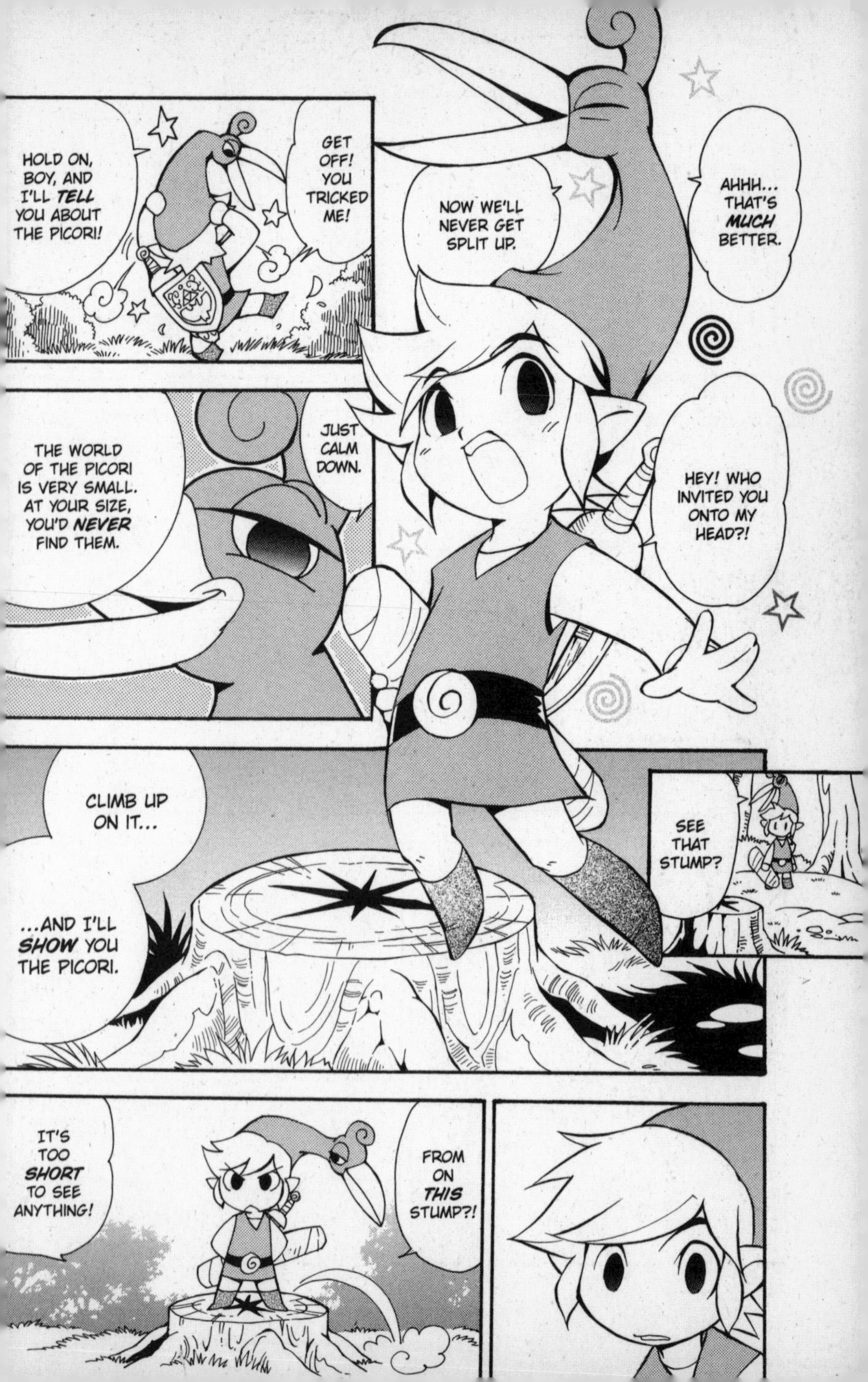
AHHH... THAT'S ***MUCH*** BETTER.
NOW WE'LL NEVER GET SPLIT UP.
HEY! WHO INVITED YOU ONTO MY HEAD?!
GET OFF! YOU TRICKED ME!
HOLD ON, BOY, AND I'LL ***TELL*** YOU ABOUT THE PICORI!
JUST CALM DOWN.
THE WORLD OF THE PICORI IS VERY SMALL. AT YOUR SIZE, YOU'D ***NEVER*** FIND THEM.
SEE THAT STUMP?
CLIMB UP ON IT...
...AND I'LL ***SHOW*** YOU THE PICORI.
FROM ON ***THIS*** STUMP?!
IT'S TOO ***SHORT*** TO SEE ANYTHING!

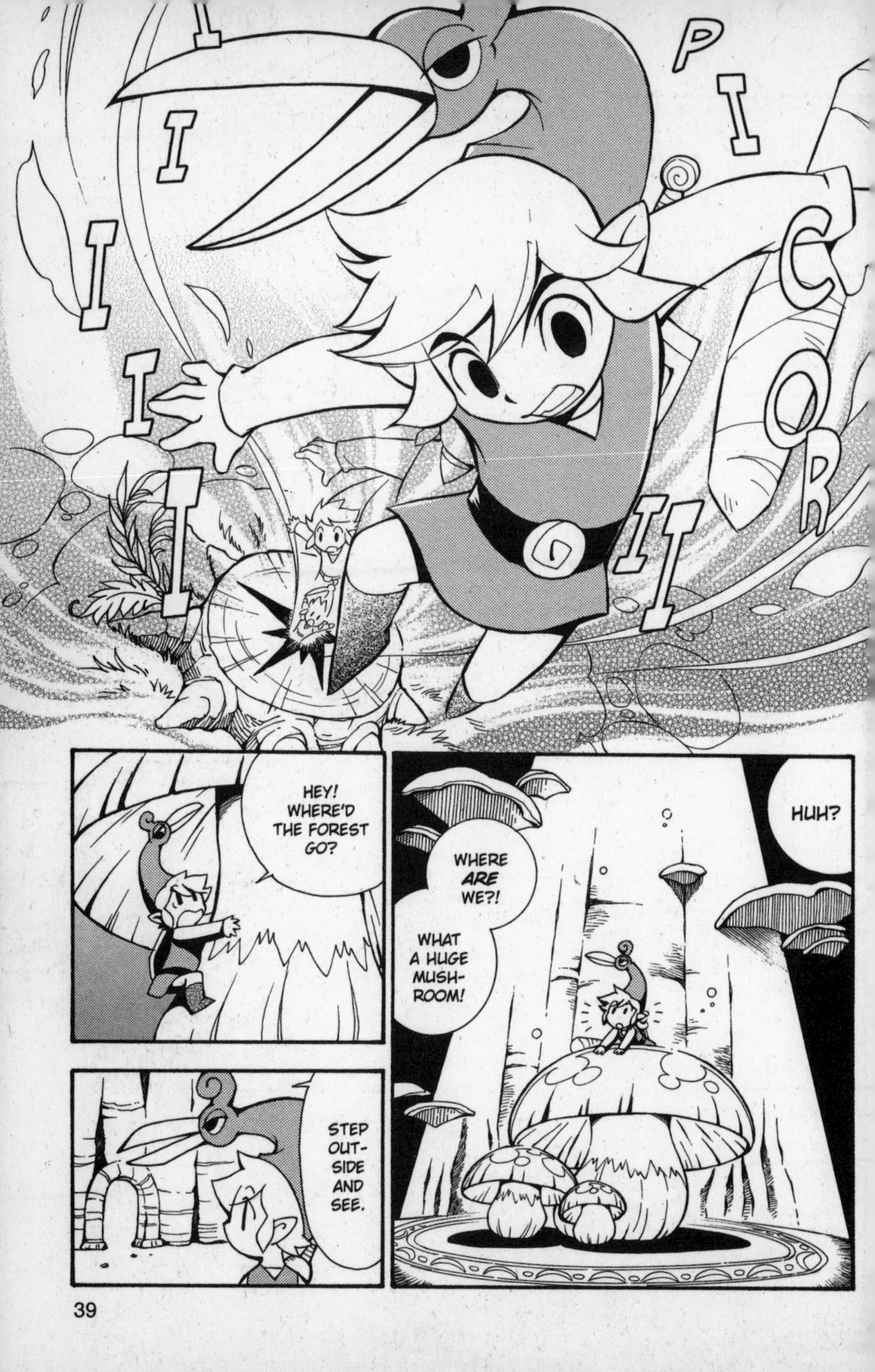
PICORIIIII
HUH?
WHERE *ARE* WE?!
WHAT A HUGE MUSH-ROOM!
HEY! WHERE'D THE FOREST GO?
STEP OUT-SIDE AND SEE.

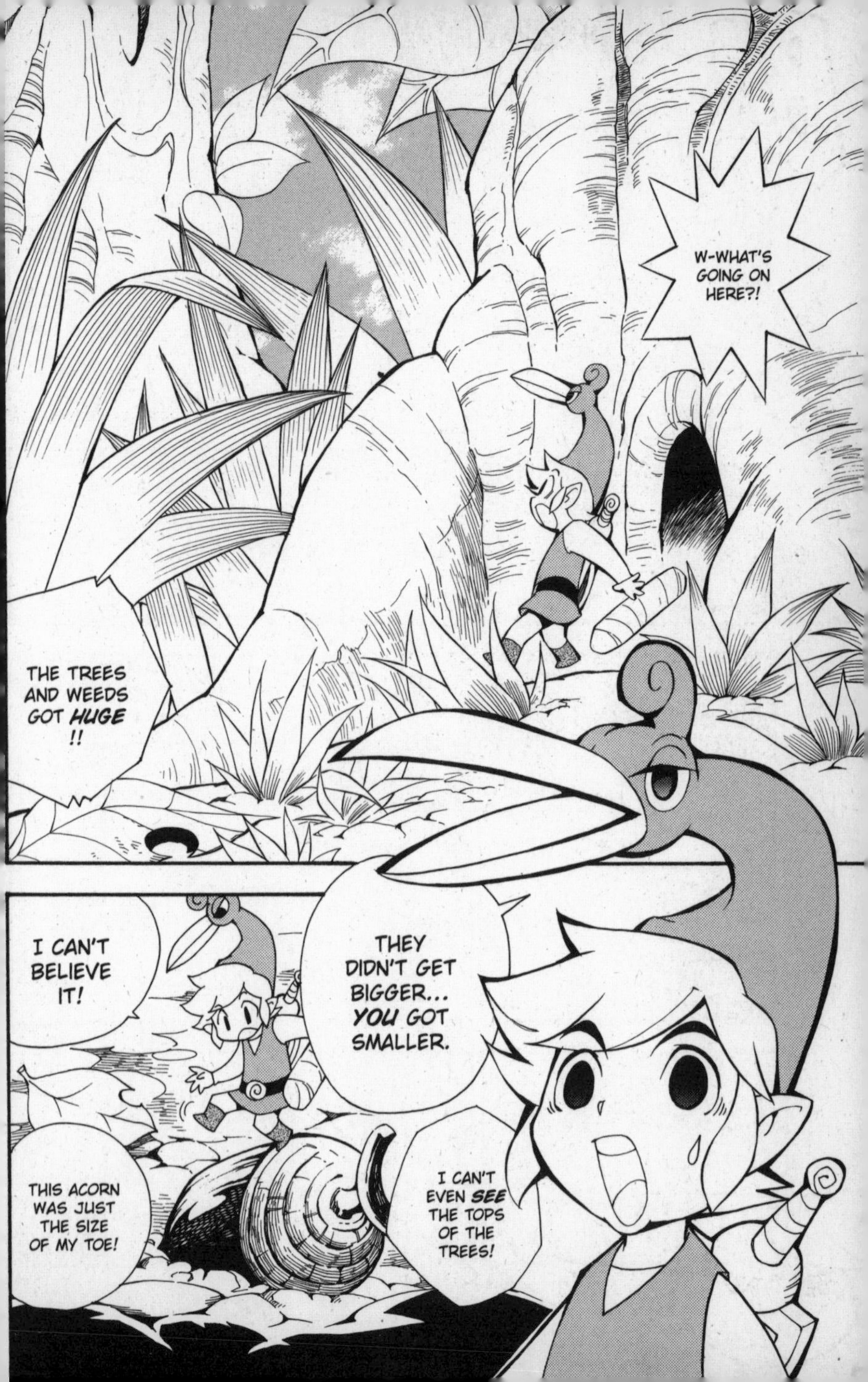
W-WHAT'S GOING ON HERE?!
THE TREES AND WEEDS GOT HUGE!!
THEY DIDN'T GET BIGGER... YOU GOT SMALLER.
I CAN'T EVEN SEE THE TOPS OF THE TREES!
I CAN'T BELIEVE IT!
THIS ACORN WAS JUST THE SIZE OF MY TOE!

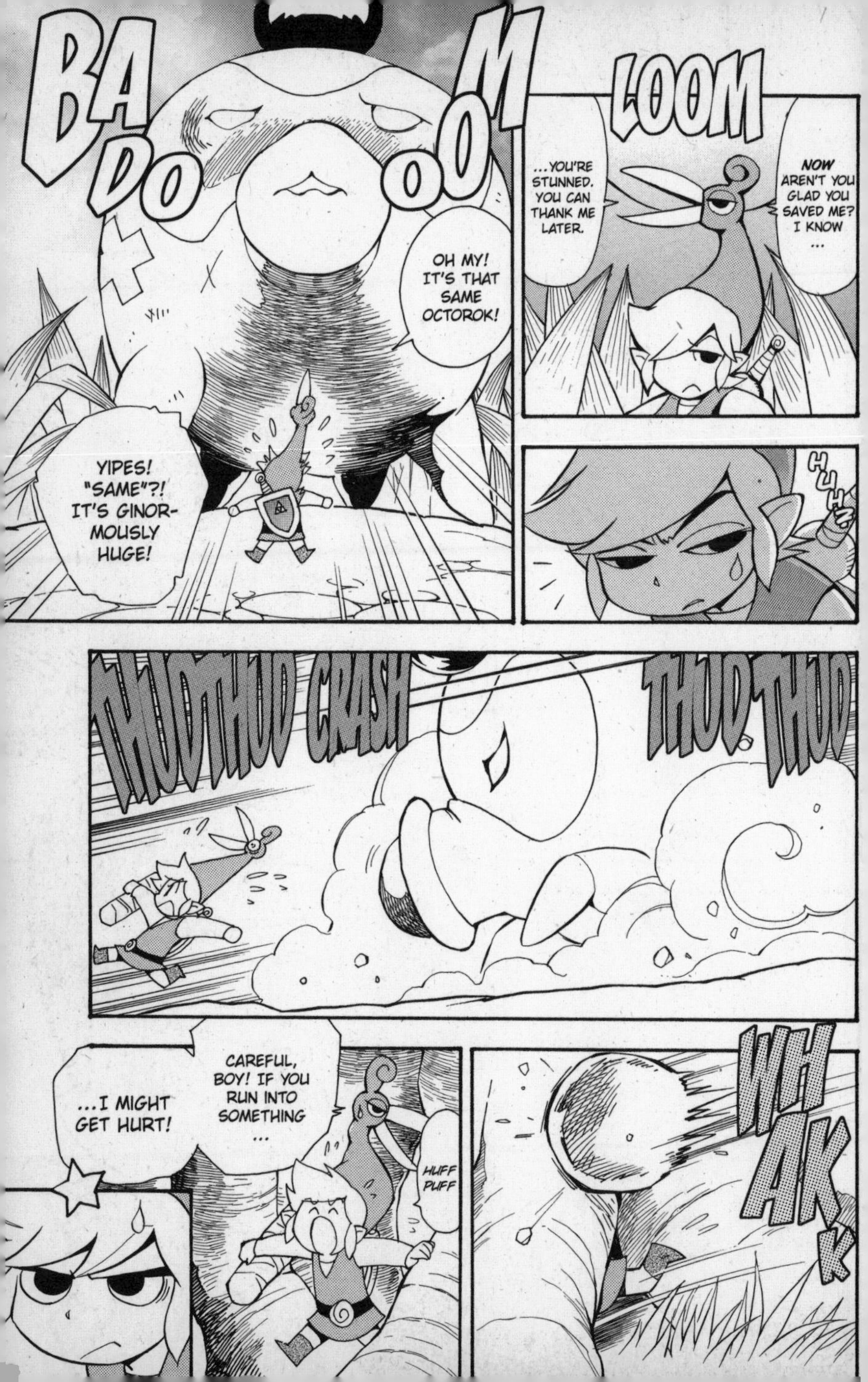
LOOM
NOW AREN'T YOU GLAD YOU SAVED ME? I KNOW ...
...YOU'RE STUNNED. YOU CAN THANK ME LATER.
HUH
BADOoOM
OH MY! IT'S THAT SAME OCTOROK!
YIPES! "SAME"?! IT'S GINOR-MOUSLY HUGE!
THUD THUD
THUDTHUD CRASH
WHAKK
HUFF PUFF
CAREFUL, BOY! IF YOU RUN INTO SOMETHING ...
...I MIGHT GET HURT!

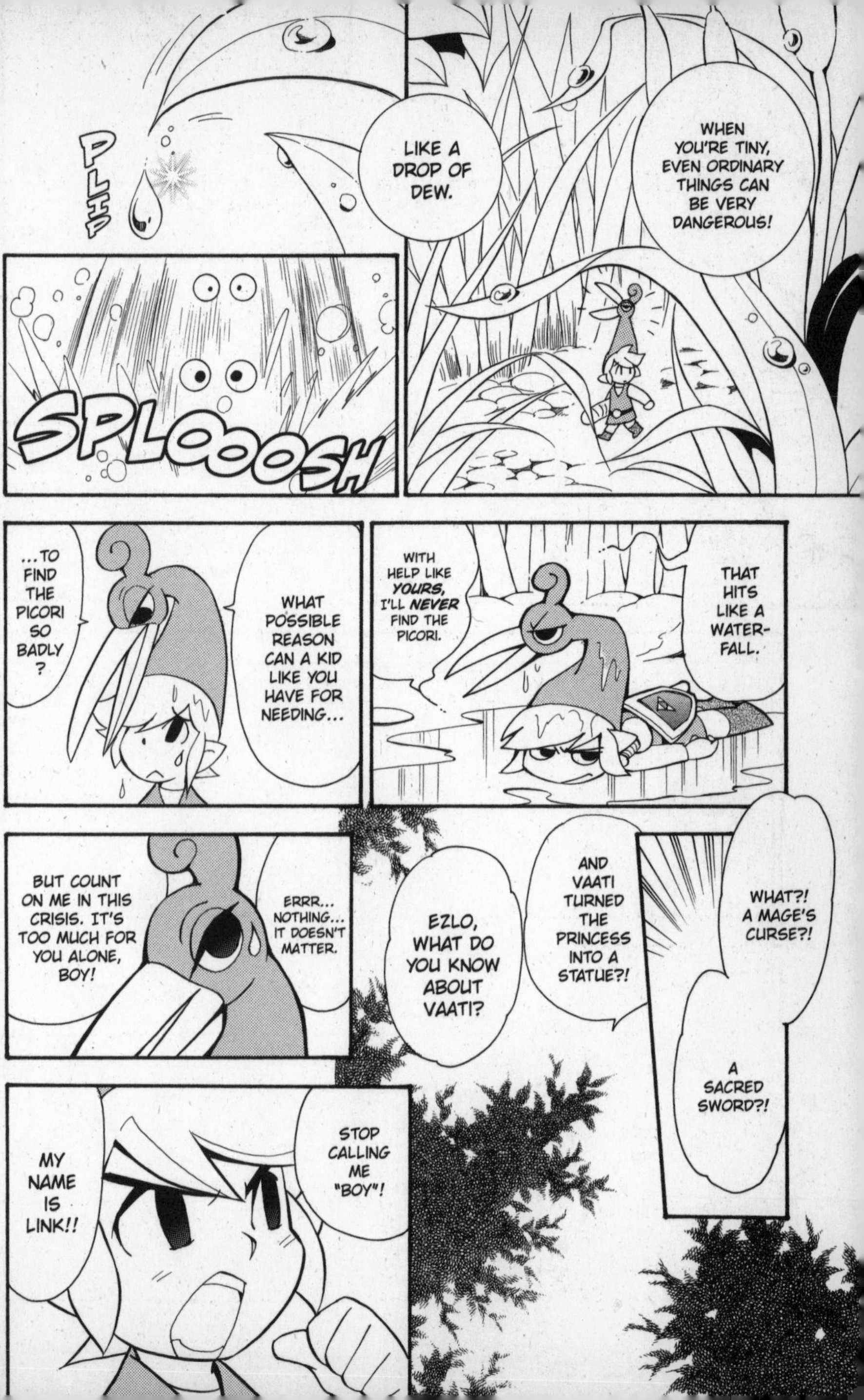
WHEN YOU'RE TINY, EVEN ORDINARY THINGS CAN BE VERY DANGEROUS!
LIKE A DROP OF DEW.
PLIP
SPLOOOSH
THAT HITS LIKE A WATER-FALL.
WITH HELP LIKE *YOURS*, I'LL *NEVER* FIND THE PICORI.
WHAT POSSIBLE REASON CAN A KID LIKE YOU HAVE FOR NEEDING...
...TO FIND THE PICORI SO BADLY?
WHAT?! A MAGE'S CURSE?!
A SACRED SWORD?!
AND VAATI TURNED THE PRINCESS INTO A STATUE?!
EZLO, WHAT DO YOU KNOW ABOUT VAATI?
ERRR... NOTHING... IT DOESN'T MATTER.
BUT COUNT ON ME IN THIS CRISIS. IT'S TOO MUCH FOR YOU ALONE, BOY!
STOP CALLING ME "BOY"!
MY NAME IS LINK!!

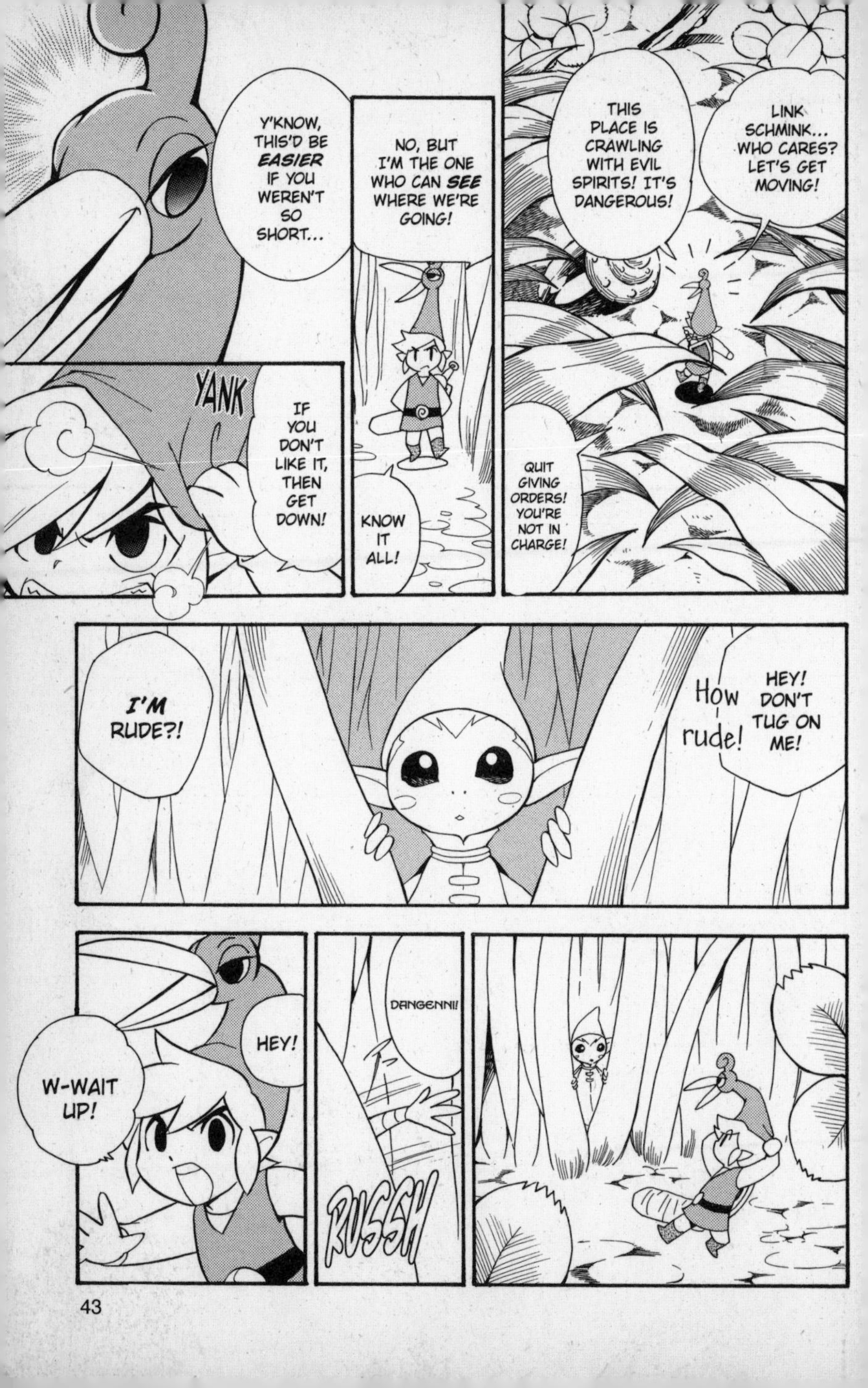
LINK SCHMINK... WHO CARES? LET'S GET MOVING!
THIS PLACE IS CRAWLING WITH EVIL SPIRITS! IT'S DANGEROUS!
QUIT GIVING ORDERS! YOU'RE NOT IN CHARGE!
NO, BUT I'M THE ONE WHO CAN *SEE* WHERE WE'RE GOING!
KNOW IT ALL!
Y'KNOW, THIS'D BE *EASIER* IF YOU WEREN'T SO SHORT...
YANK
IF YOU DON'T LIKE IT, THEN GET DOWN!
HEY! DON'T TUG ON ME!
How rude!
I'M RUDE?!
DANGENNI!
RUSSH
HEY!
W-WAIT UP!

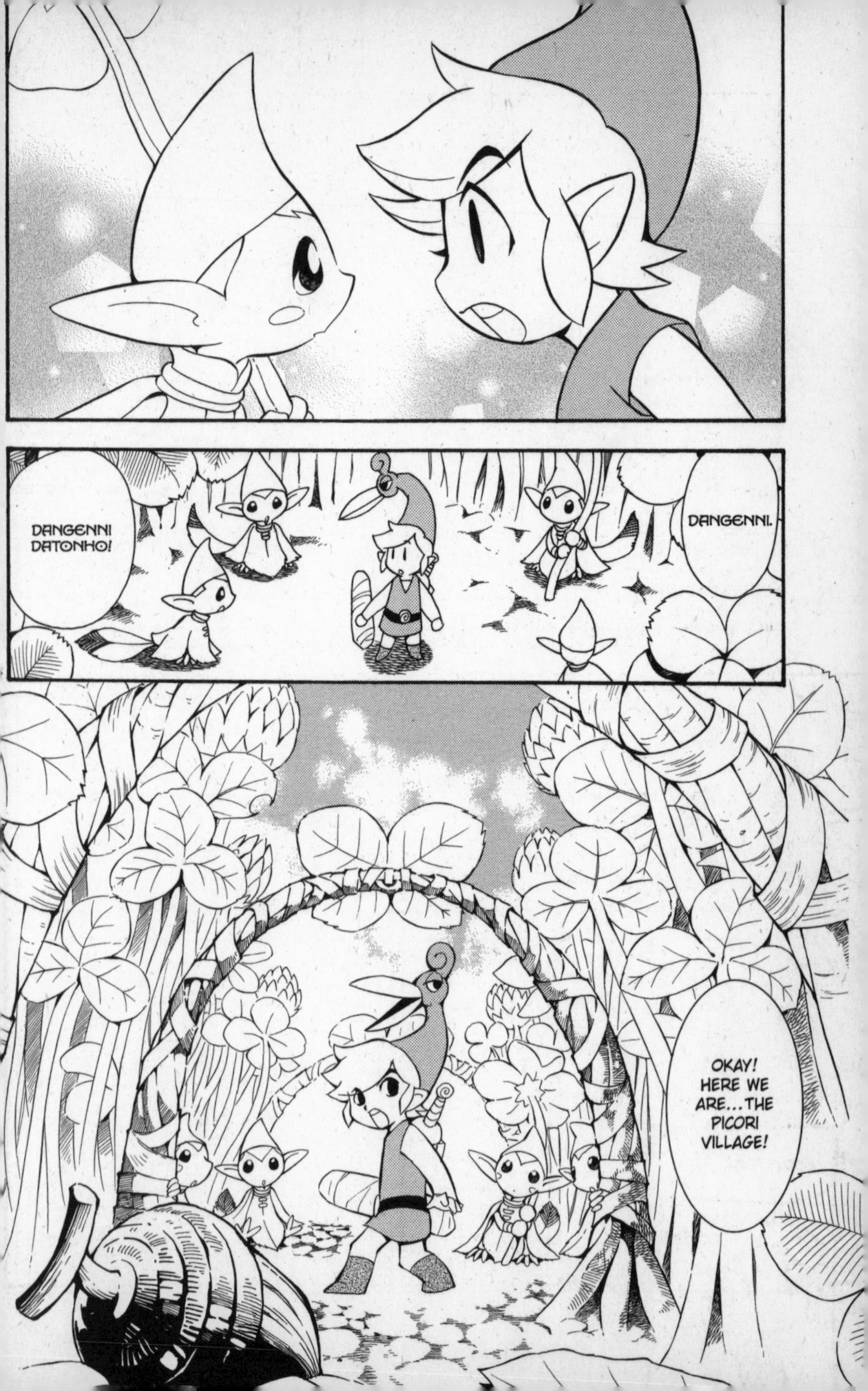
DANGENNI.
DANGENNI DATONHO!
OKAY! HERE WE ARE...THE PICORI VILLAGE!

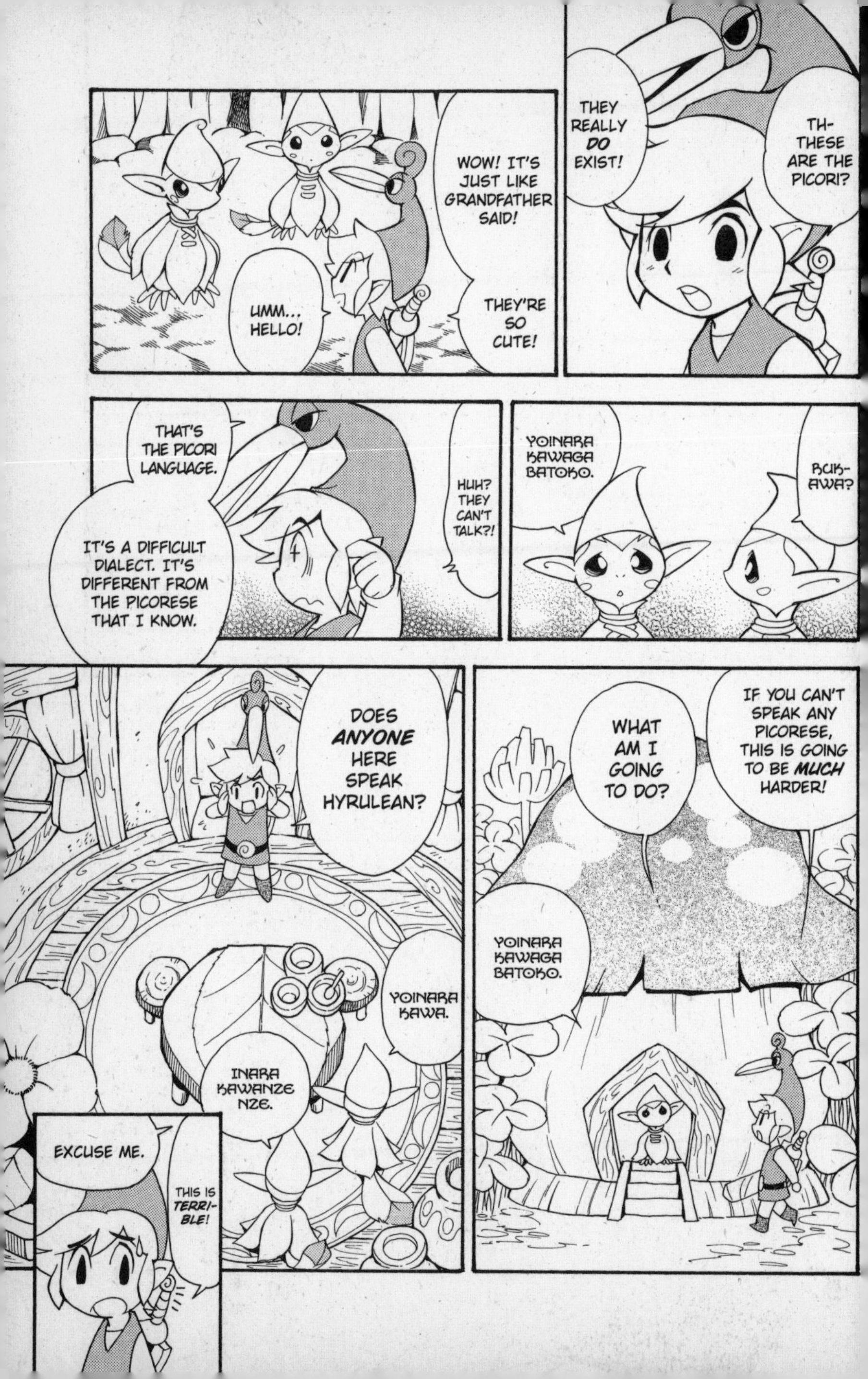
TH-THESE ARE THE PICORI?
THEY REALLY DO EXIST!
WOW! IT'S JUST LIKE GRANDFATHER SAID!
THEY'RE SO CUTE!
UMM... HELLO!
BUK-AWA?
YOINARA KAWAGA BATOKO.
HUH? THEY CAN'T TALK?!
THAT'S THE PICORI LANGUAGE.
IT'S A DIFFICULT DIALECT. IT'S DIFFERENT FROM THE PICORESE THAT I KNOW.
IF YOU CAN'T SPEAK ANY PICORESE, THIS IS GOING TO BE MUCH HARDER!
WHAT AM I GOING TO DO?
YOINARA KAWAGA BATOKO.
DOES ANYONE HERE SPEAK HYRULEAN?
YOINARA KAWA.
INARA KAWANZE NZE.
EXCUSE ME.
THIS IS TERRIBLE!

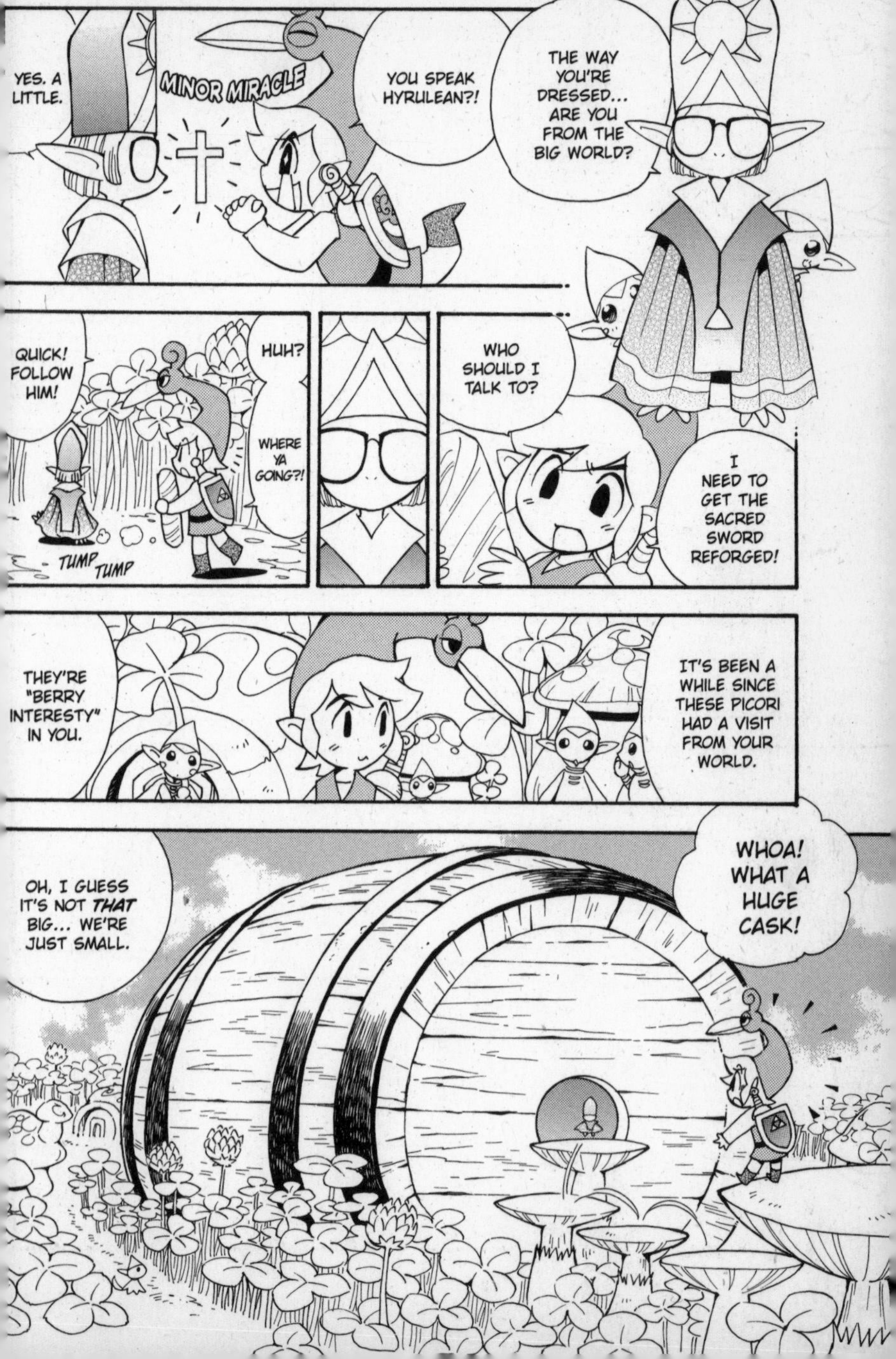
THE WAY YOU'RE DRESSED... ARE YOU FROM THE BIG WORLD?
YOU SPEAK HYRULEAN?!
MINOR MIRACLE
YES. A LITTLE.
WHO SHOULD I TALK TO?
I NEED TO GET THE SACRED SWORD REFORGED!
HUH?
WHERE YA GOING?!
QUICK! FOLLOW HIM!
TUMP TUMP
IT'S BEEN A WHILE SINCE THESE PICORI HAD A VISIT FROM YOUR WORLD.
THEY'RE "BERRY INTERESTY" IN YOU.
WHOA! WHAT A HUGE CASK!
OH, I GUESS IT'S NOT *THAT* BIG... WE'RE JUST SMALL.

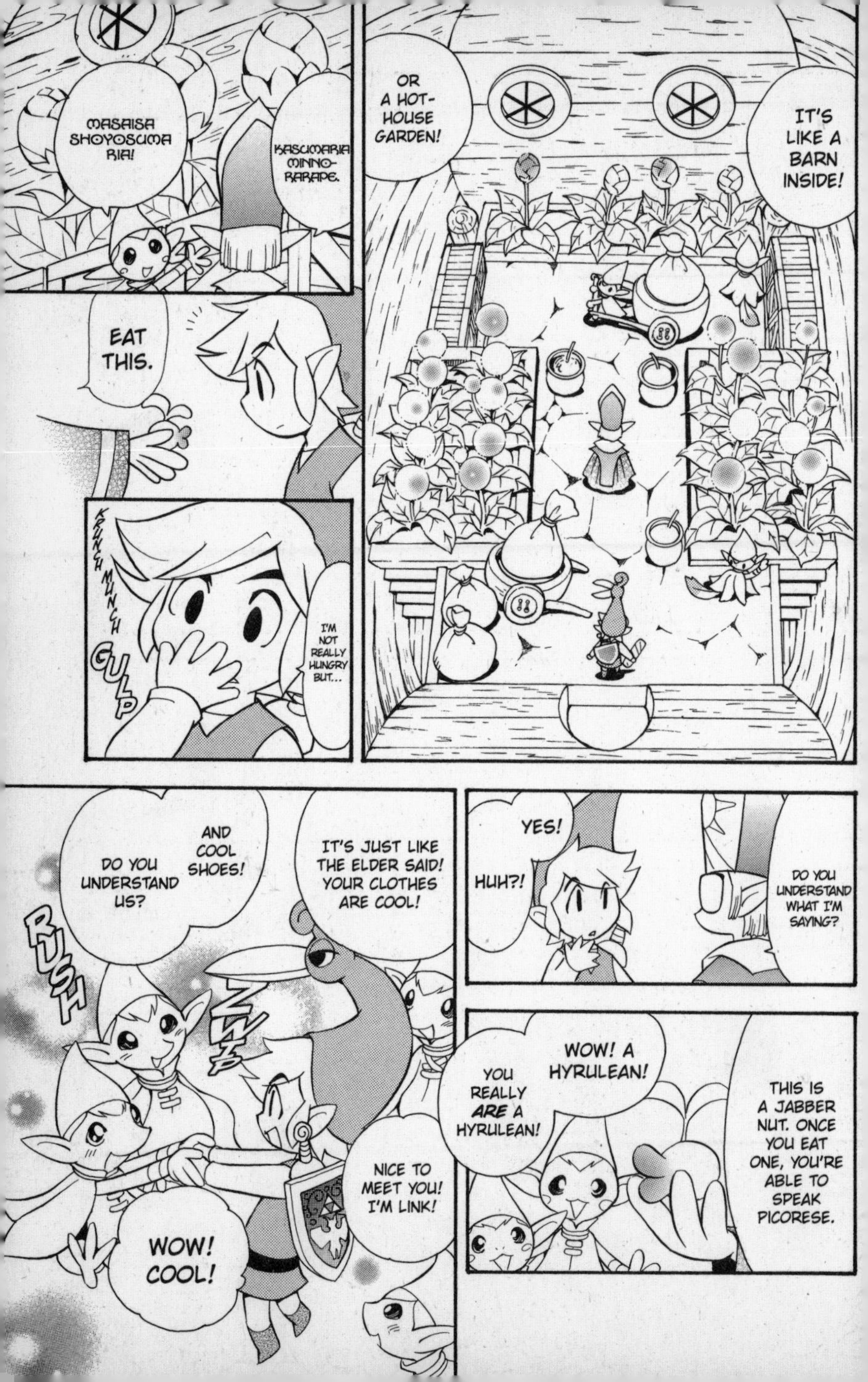
IT'S LIKE A BARN INSIDE!
OR A HOT-HOUSE GARDEN!
KASUMARIA MINNO-RARAPE.
MASAISA SHOYOSUMA RIA!
EAT THIS.
I'M NOT REALLY HUNGRY BUT...
KRUNCH MUNCH GULP
DO YOU UNDERSTAND WHAT I'M SAYING?
YES!
HUH?!
THIS IS A JABBER NUT. ONCE YOU EAT ONE, YOU'RE ABLE TO SPEAK PICORESE.
WOW! A HYRULEAN!
YOU REALLY *ARE* A HYRULEAN!
IT'S JUST LIKE THE ELDER SAID! YOUR CLOTHES ARE COOL!
AND COOL SHOES!
DO YOU UNDERSTAND US?
ZWIP
RUSH
NICE TO MEET YOU! I'M LINK!
WOW! COOL!

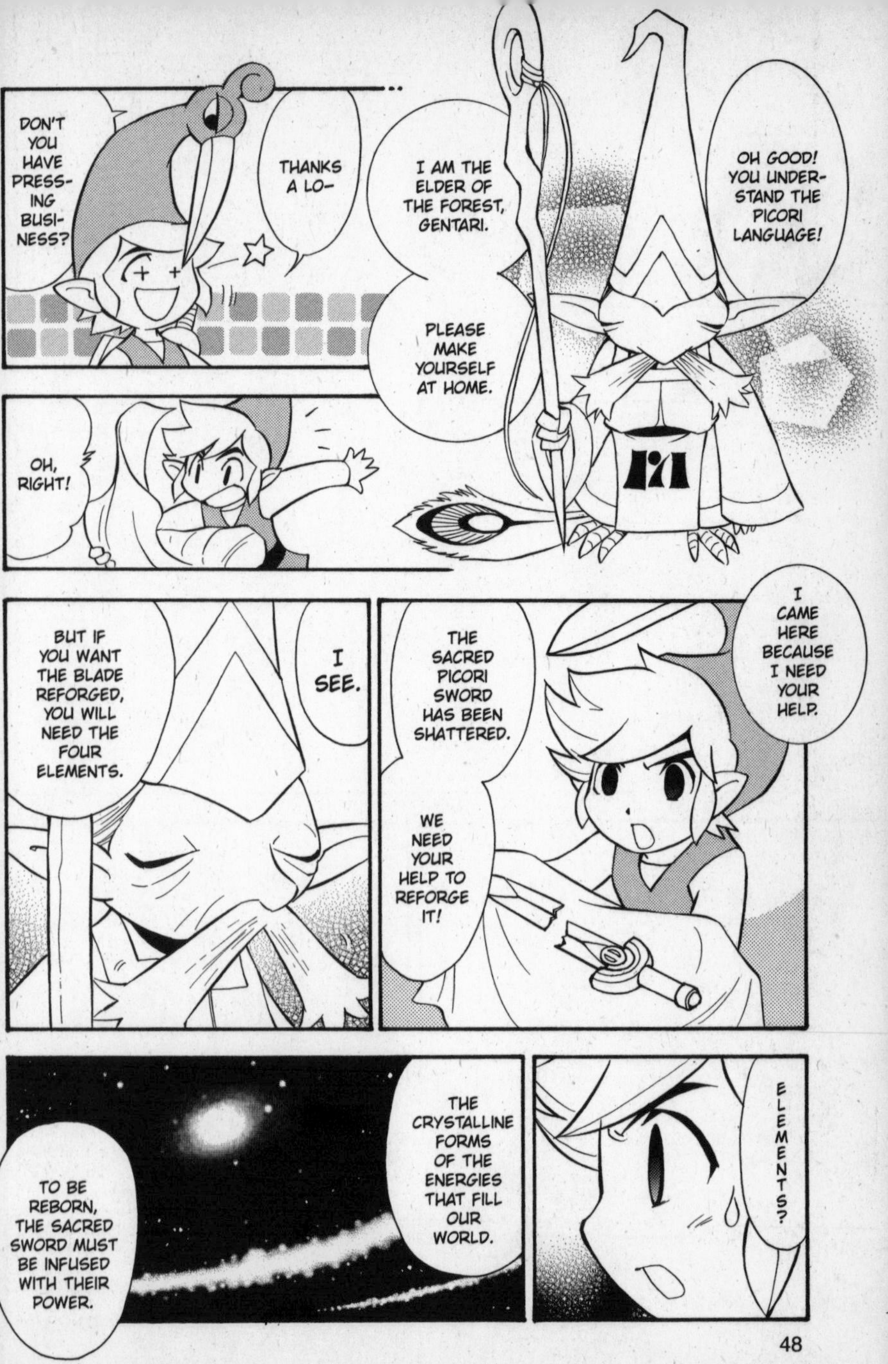
DON'T YOU HAVE PRESS-ING BUSI-NESS?
THANKS A LO-
I AM THE ELDER OF THE FOREST, GENTARI.
OH GOOD! YOU UNDER-STAND THE PICORI LANGUAGE!
PLEASE MAKE YOURSELF AT HOME.
OH, RIGHT!
I CAME HERE BECAUSE I NEED YOUR HELP.
THE SACRED PICORI SWORD HAS BEEN SHATTERED.
WE NEED YOUR HELP TO REFORGE IT!
I SEE.
BUT IF YOU WANT THE BLADE REFORGED, YOU WILL NEED THE FOUR ELEMENTS.
ELEMENTS?
THE CRYSTALLINE FORMS OF THE ENERGIES THAT FILL OUR WORLD.
TO BE REBORN, THE SACRED SWORD MUST BE INFUSED WITH THEIR POWER.

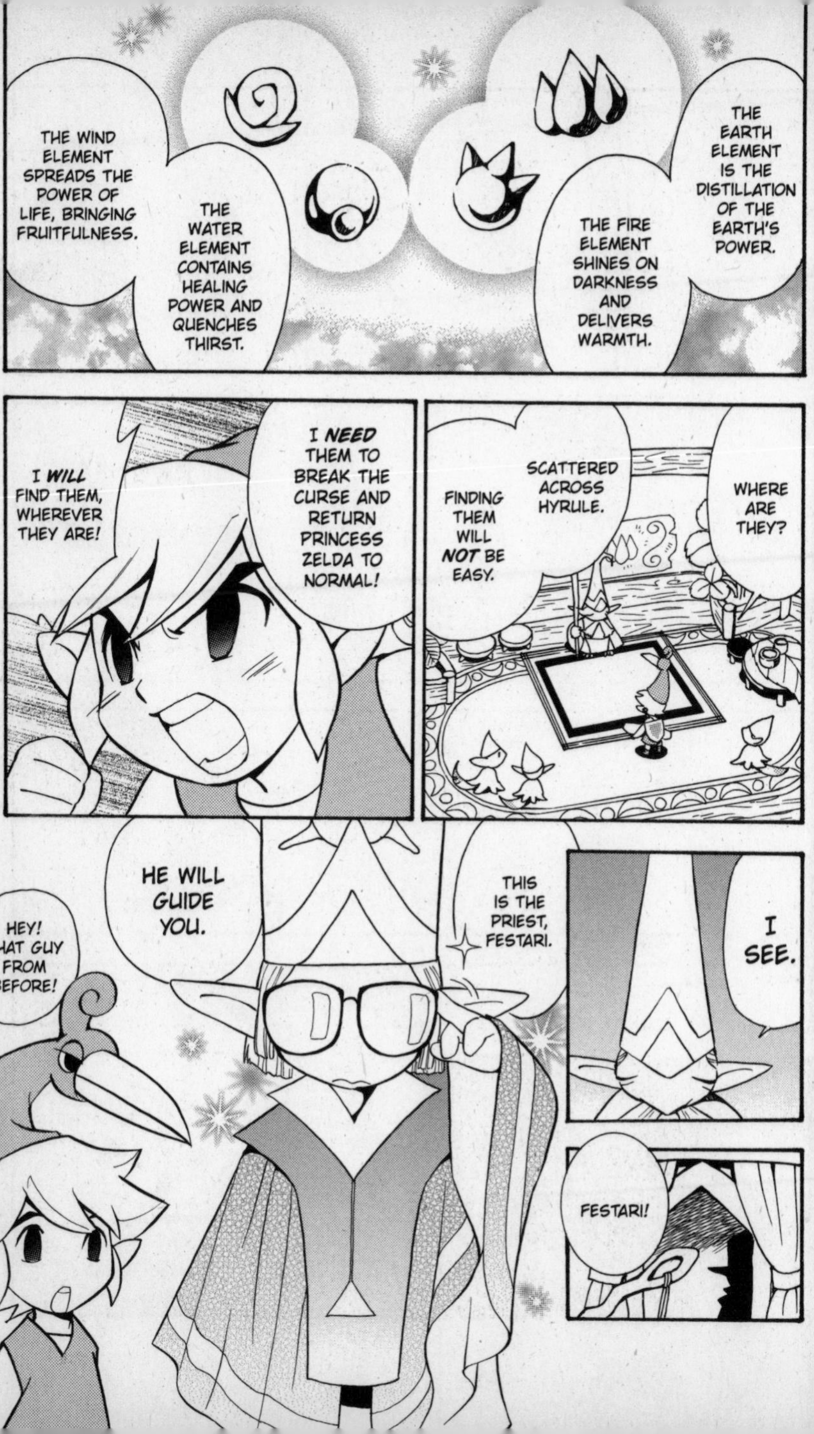
THE EARTH ELEMENT IS THE DISTILLATION OF THE EARTH'S POWER.
THE FIRE ELEMENT SHINES ON DARKNESS AND DELIVERS WARMTH.
THE WATER ELEMENT CONTAINS HEALING POWER AND QUENCHES THIRST.
THE WIND ELEMENT SPREADS THE POWER OF LIFE, BRINGING FRUITFULNESS.
WHERE ARE THEY?
SCATTERED ACROSS HYRULE.
FINDING THEM WILL *NOT* BE EASY.
I *NEED* THEM TO BREAK THE CURSE AND RETURN PRINCESS ZELDA TO NORMAL!
I *WILL* FIND THEM, WHEREVER THEY ARE!
I SEE.
FESTARI!
THIS IS THE PRIEST, FESTARI.
HE WILL GUIDE YOU.
HEY! THAT GUY FROM BEFORE!

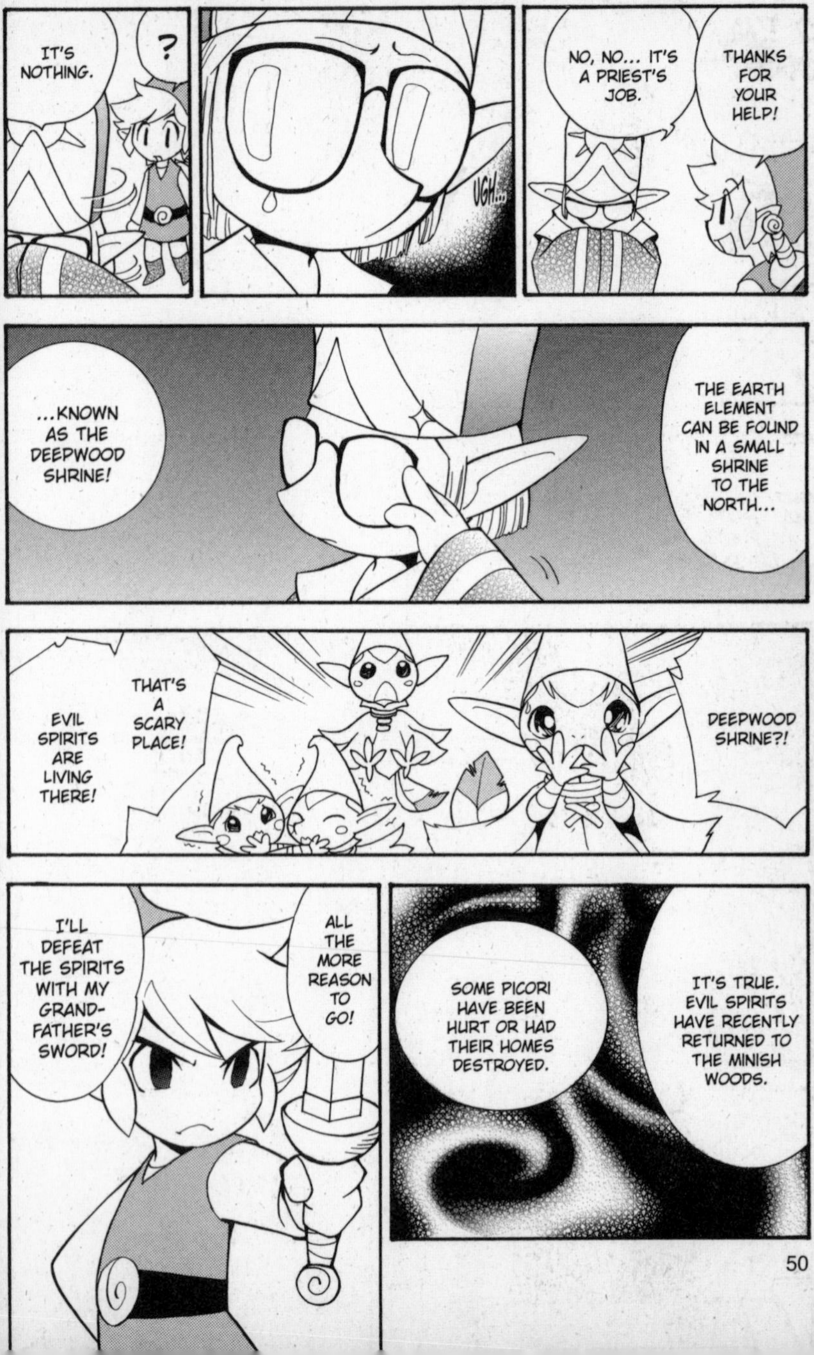
THANKS FOR YOUR HELP!
NO, NO... IT'S A PRIEST'S JOB.
UGH...
?
IT'S NOTHING.
THE EARTH ELEMENT CAN BE FOUND IN A SMALL SHRINE TO THE NORTH...
...KNOWN AS THE DEEPWOOD SHRINE!
DEEPWOOD SHRINE?!
THAT'S A SCARY PLACE!
EVIL SPIRITS ARE LIVING THERE!
IT'S TRUE. EVIL SPIRITS HAVE RECENTLY RETURNED TO THE MINISH WOODS.
SOME PICORI HAVE BEEN HURT OR HAD THEIR HOMES DESTROYED.
ALL THE MORE REASON TO GO!
I'LL DEFEAT THE SPIRITS WITH MY GRAND-FATHER'S SWORD!

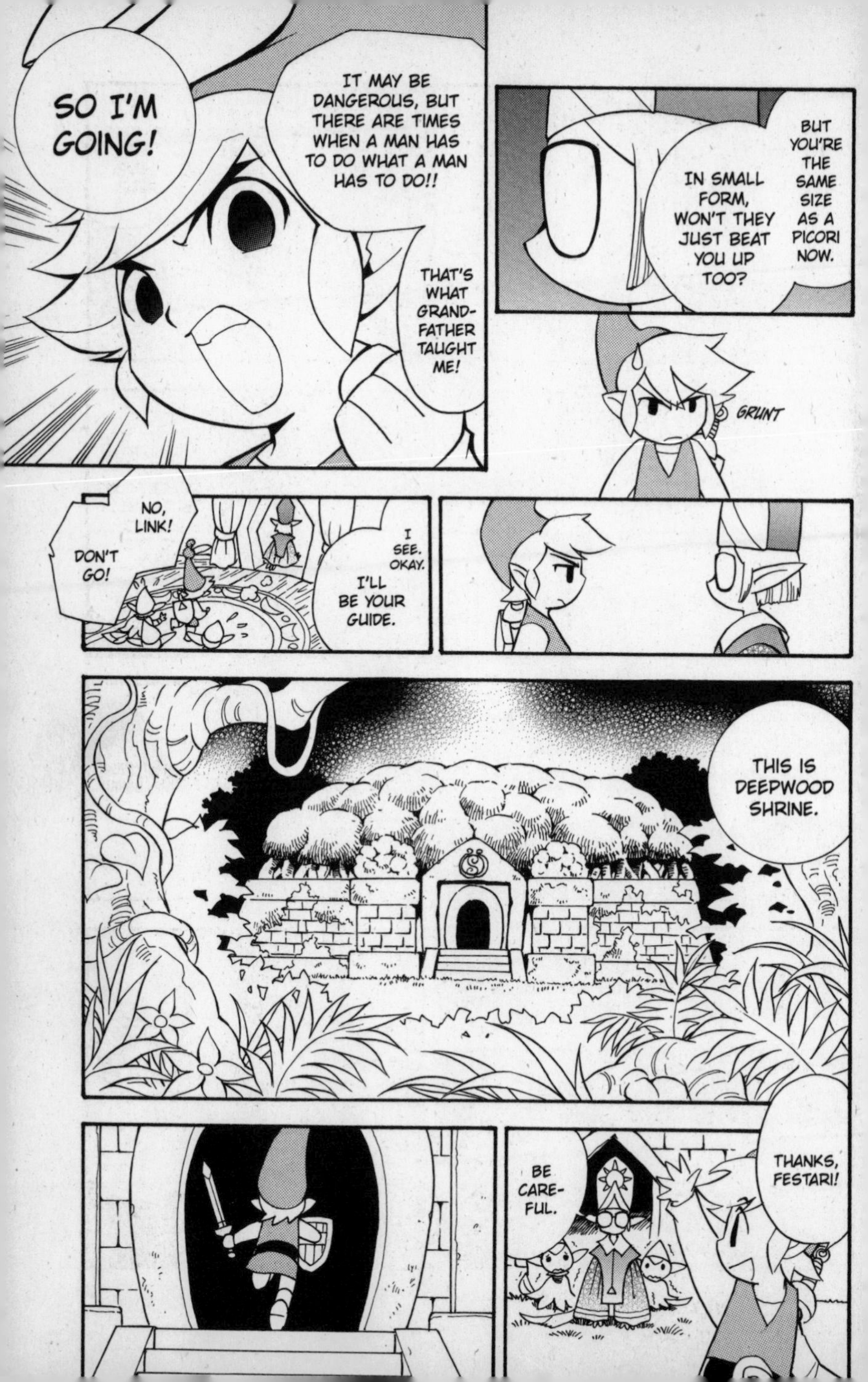
BUT YOU'RE THE SAME SIZE AS A PICORI NOW.
IN SMALL FORM, WON'T THEY JUST BEAT YOU UP TOO?
GRUNT
IT MAY BE DANGEROUS, BUT THERE ARE TIMES WHEN A MAN HAS TO DO WHAT A MAN HAS TO DO!!
THAT'S WHAT GRANDFATHER TAUGHT ME!
SO I'M GOING!
I SEE. OKAY.
I'LL BE YOUR GUIDE.
NO, LINK!
DON'T GO!
THIS IS DEEPWOOD SHRINE.
THANKS, FESTARI!
BE CAREFUL.

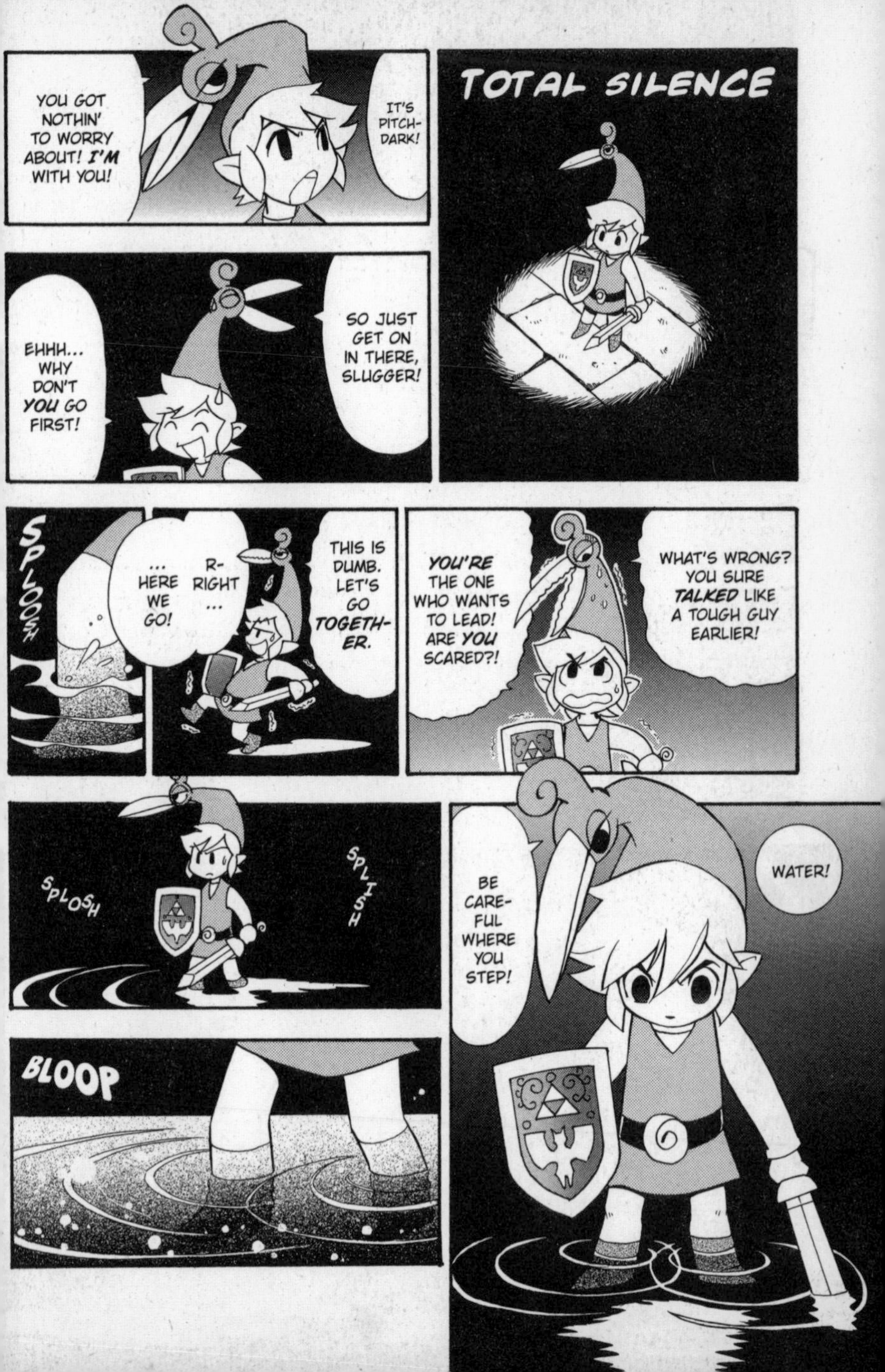
TOTAL SILENCE
IT'S PITCH-DARK!
YOU GOT NOTHIN' TO WORRY ABOUT! I'M WITH YOU!
SO JUST GET ON IN THERE, SLUGGER!
EHHH... WHY DON'T YOU GO FIRST!
WHAT'S WRONG? YOU SURE TALKED LIKE A TOUGH GUY EARLIER!
YOU'RE THE ONE WHO WANTS TO LEAD! ARE YOU SCARED?!
THIS IS DUMB. LET'S GO TOGETHER.
R-RIGHT...
... HERE WE GO!
SPLOOSH
WATER!
BE CARE-FUL WHERE YOU STEP!
SPLISH
SPLOSH
BLOOP

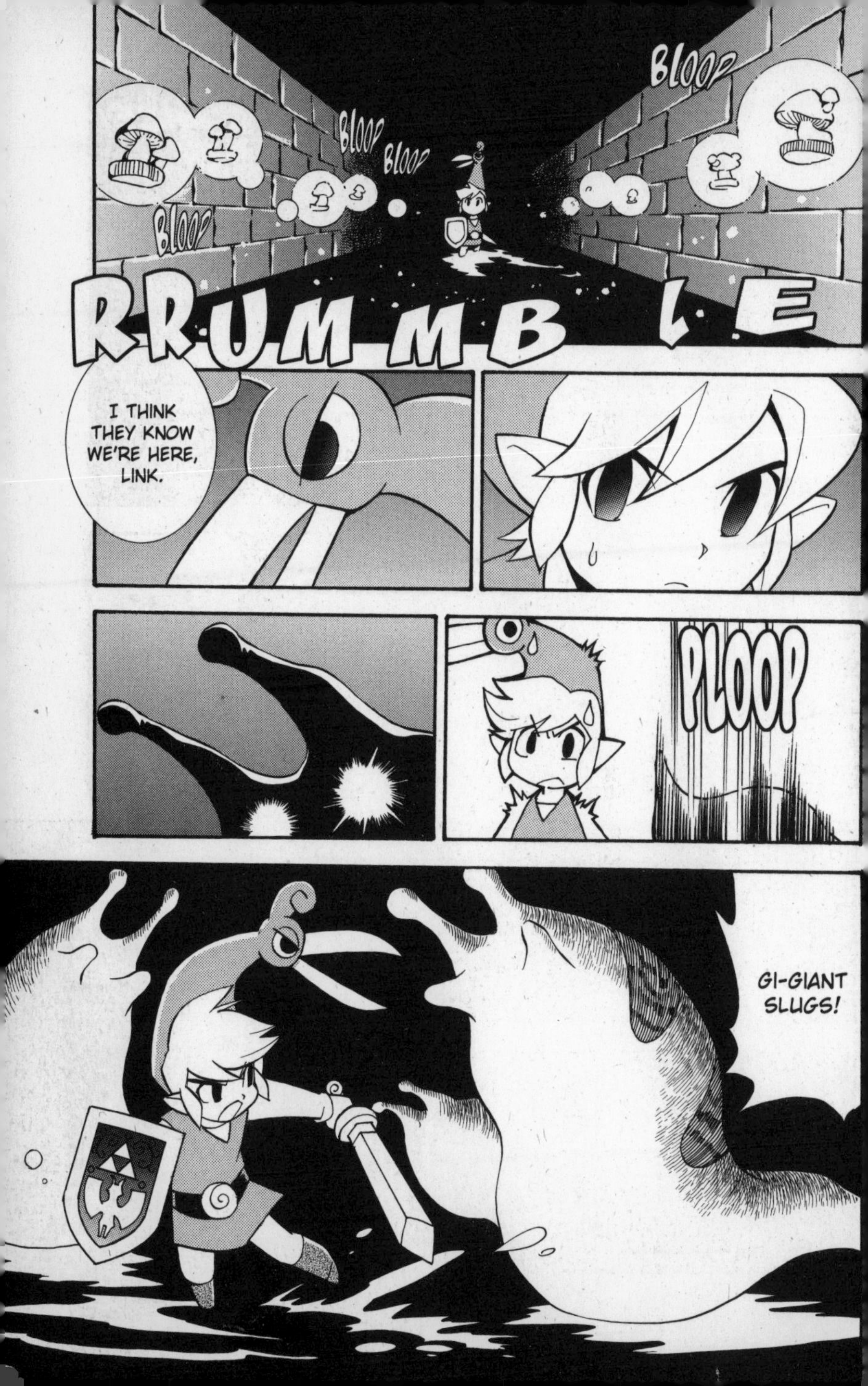
BLOOP
BLOOP
BLOOP
BLOOP
RRUMMBLE
I THINK THEY KNOW WE'RE HERE, LINK.
PLOOP
GI-GIANT SLUGS!

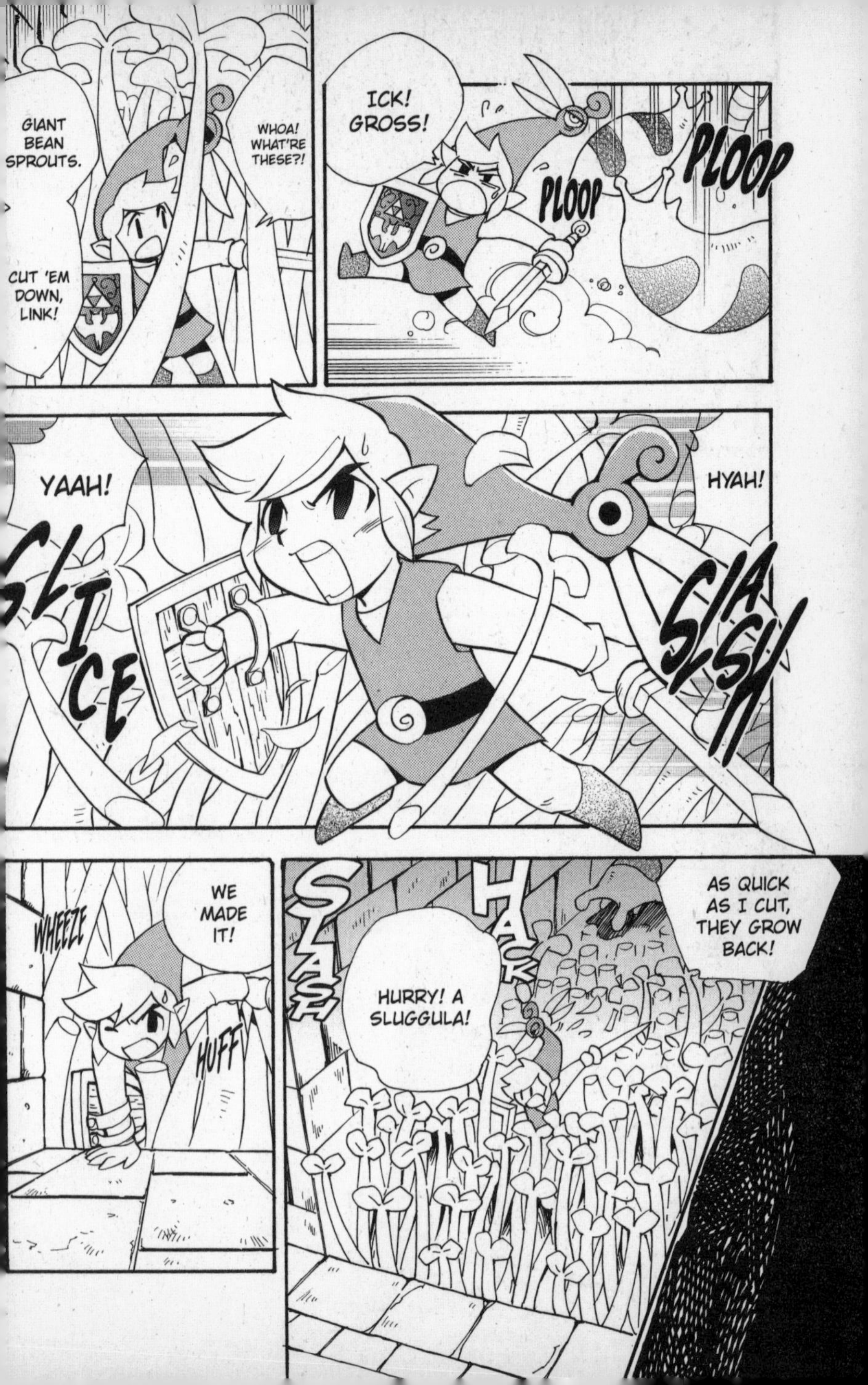
ICK! GROSS!
PLOOP
PLOOP
WHOA! WHAT'RE THESE?!
GIANT BEAN SPROUTS.
CUT 'EM DOWN, LINK!
HYAH!
SLASH
YAAH!
SLICE
AS QUICK AS I CUT, THEY GROW BACK!
HACK
SLASH
HURRY! A SLUGGULA!
WE MADE IT!
WHEEZE
HUFF

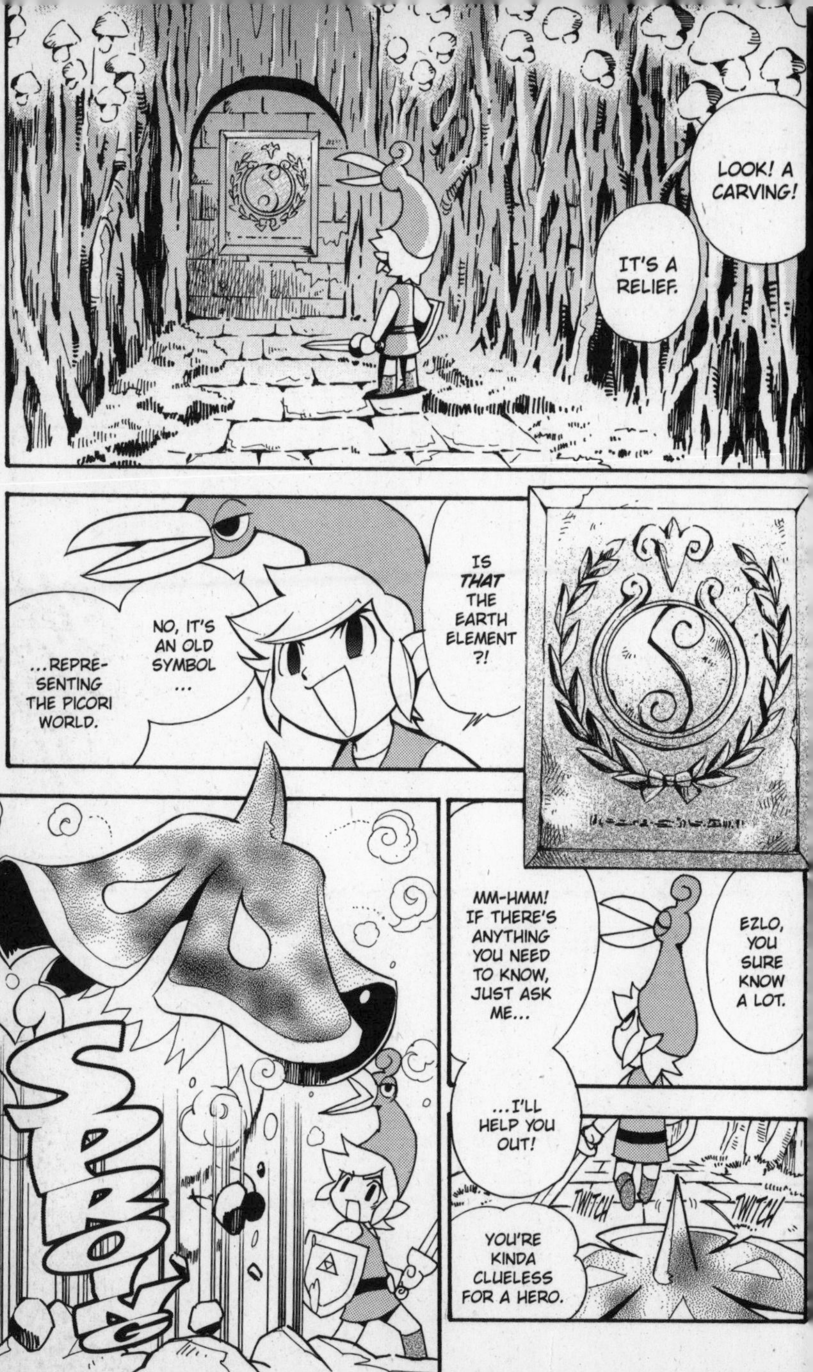
LOOK! A CARVING!
IT'S A RELIEF.
IS *THAT* THE EARTH ELEMENT ?!
NO, IT'S AN OLD SYMBOL ...
...REPRESENTING THE PICORI WORLD.
EZLO, YOU SURE KNOW A LOT.
MM-HMM! IF THERE'S ANYTHING YOU NEED TO KNOW, JUST ASK ME...
...I'LL HELP YOU OUT!
TWITCH
TWITCH
YOU'RE KINDA CLUELESS FOR A HERO.

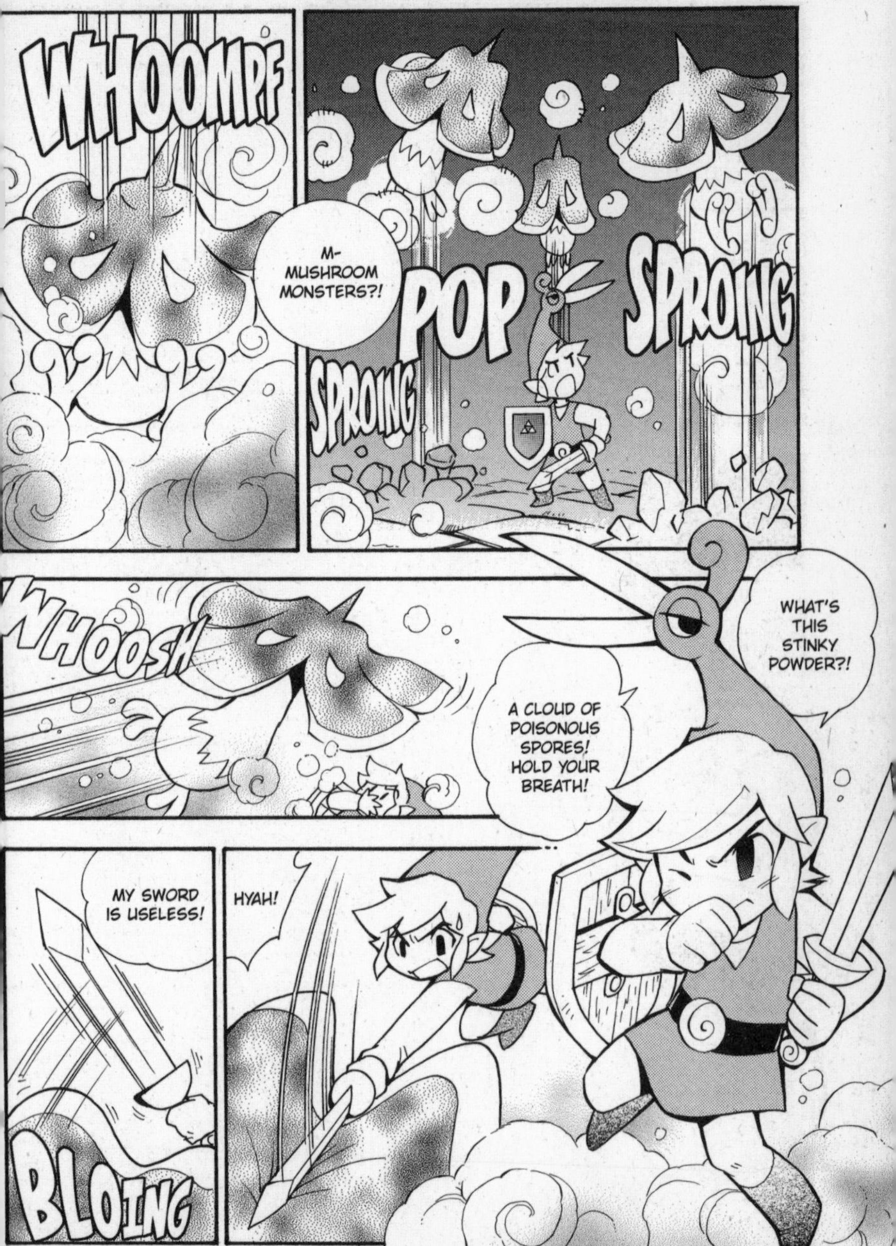
M-MUSHROOM MONSTERS?!
POP
SPROING
SPROING
WHOOMPF
WHAT'S THIS STINKY POWDER?!
A CLOUD OF POISONOUS SPORES! HOLD YOUR BREATH!
WHOOSH
HYAH!
MY SWORD IS USELESS!
BLOING

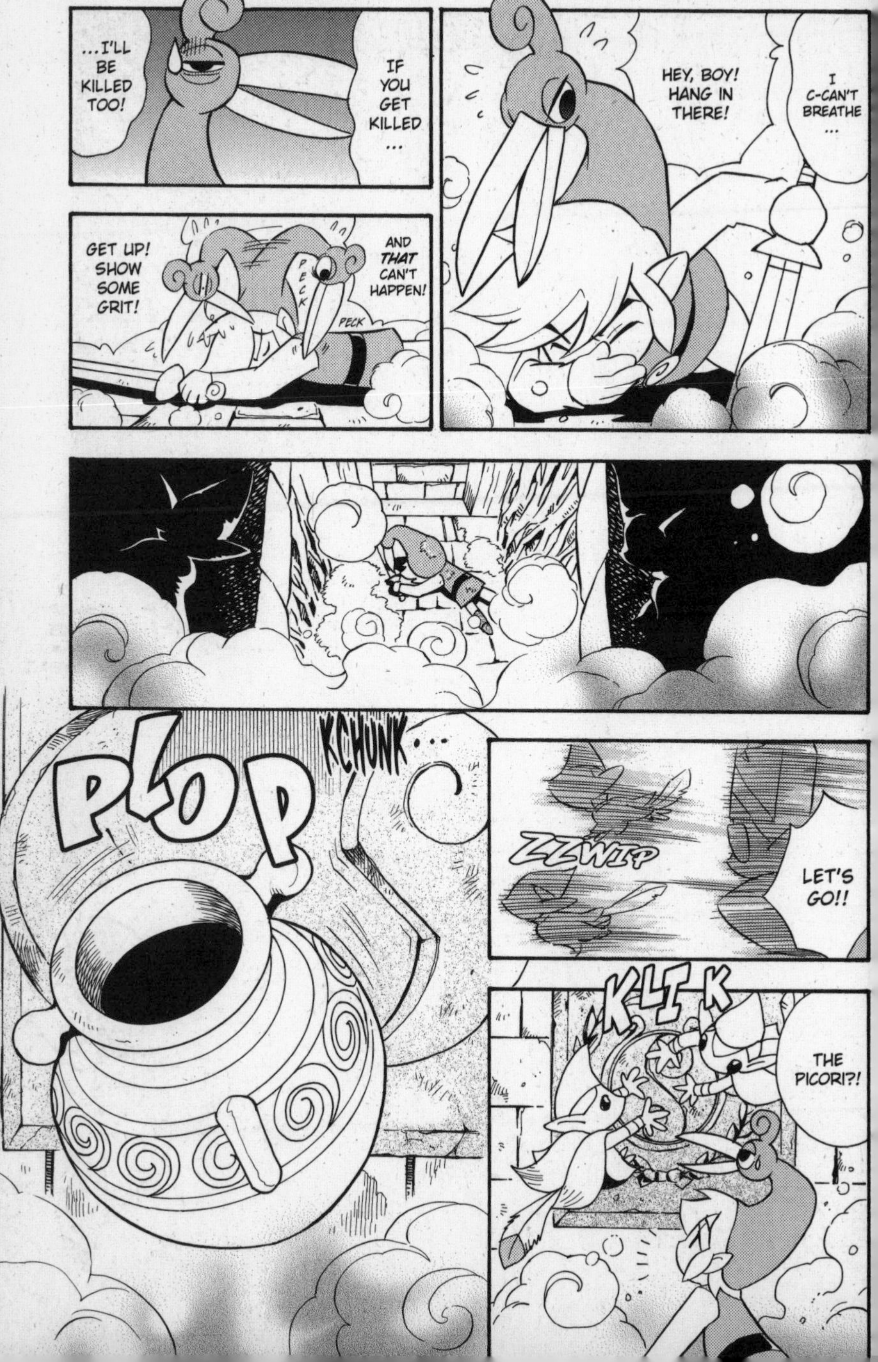
I C-CAN'T BREATHE ...
HEY, BOY! HANG IN THERE!
IF YOU GET KILLED ...
...I'LL BE KILLED TOO!
AND *THAT* CAN'T HAPPEN!
PECK
PECK
GET UP! SHOW SOME GRIT!
LET'S GO!!
ZZWIP
THE PICORI?!
KLIK
KCHUNK...
PLOP

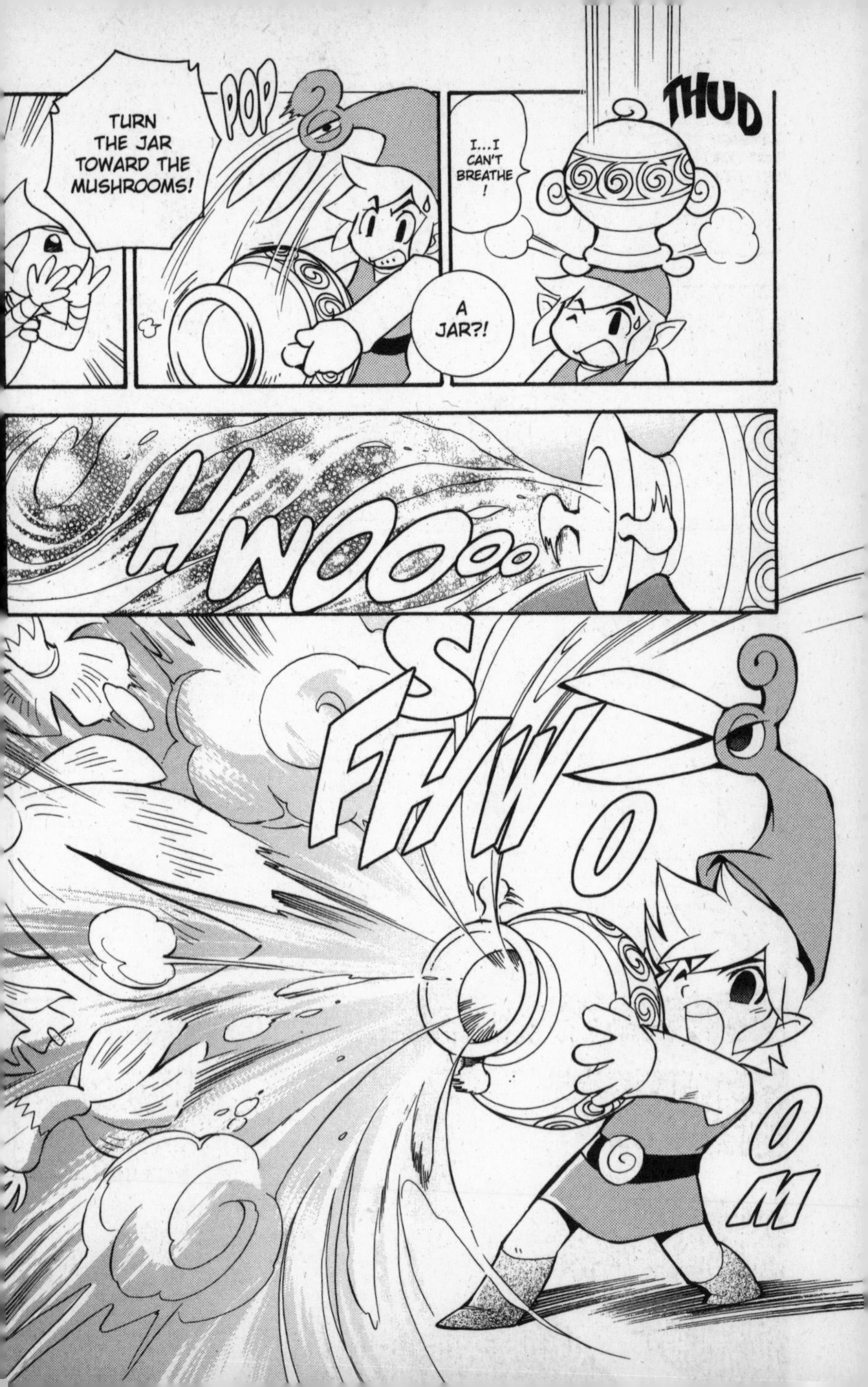
THUD
I...I CAN'T BREATHE!
A JAR?!
POP
TURN THE JAR TOWARD THE MUSHROOMS!
HWOOooo
SFHWOOOM

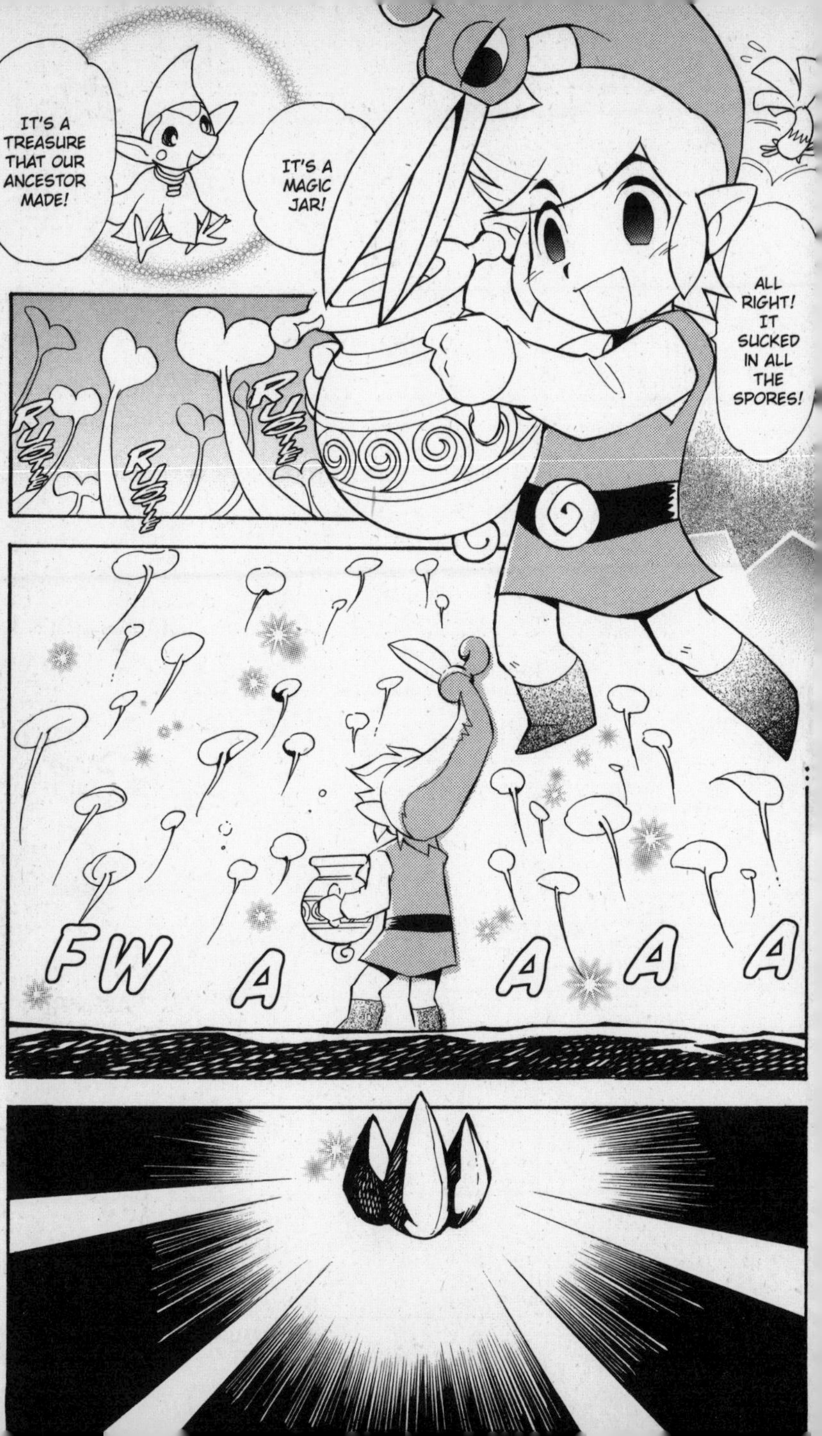
ALL RIGHT! IT SUCKED IN ALL THE SPORES!
IT'S A MAGIC JAR!
IT'S A TREASURE THAT OUR ANCESTOR MADE!
RUSTLE
RUSTLE
RUSTLE
FW A A A A

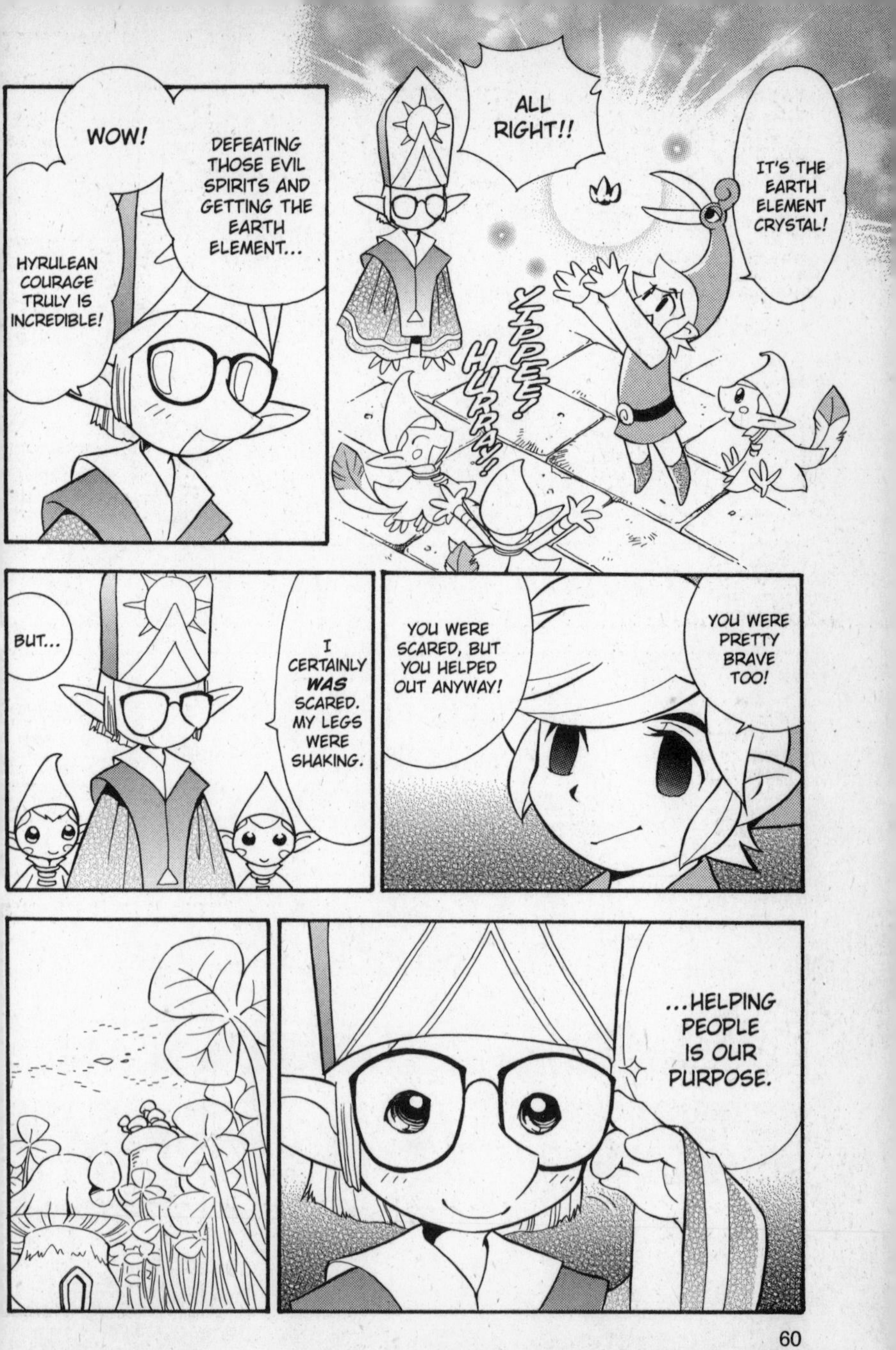
IT'S THE EARTH ELEMENT CRYSTAL!
ALL RIGHT!!
YIPPEE!
HURRA!
WOW!
DEFEATING THOSE EVIL SPIRITS AND GETTING THE EARTH ELEMENT...
HYRULEAN COURAGE TRULY IS INCREDIBLE!
YOU WERE PRETTY BRAVE TOO!
YOU WERE SCARED, BUT YOU HELPED OUT ANYWAY!
I CERTAINLY *WAS* SCARED. MY LEGS WERE SHAKING.
BUT...
...HELPING PEOPLE IS OUR PURPOSE.

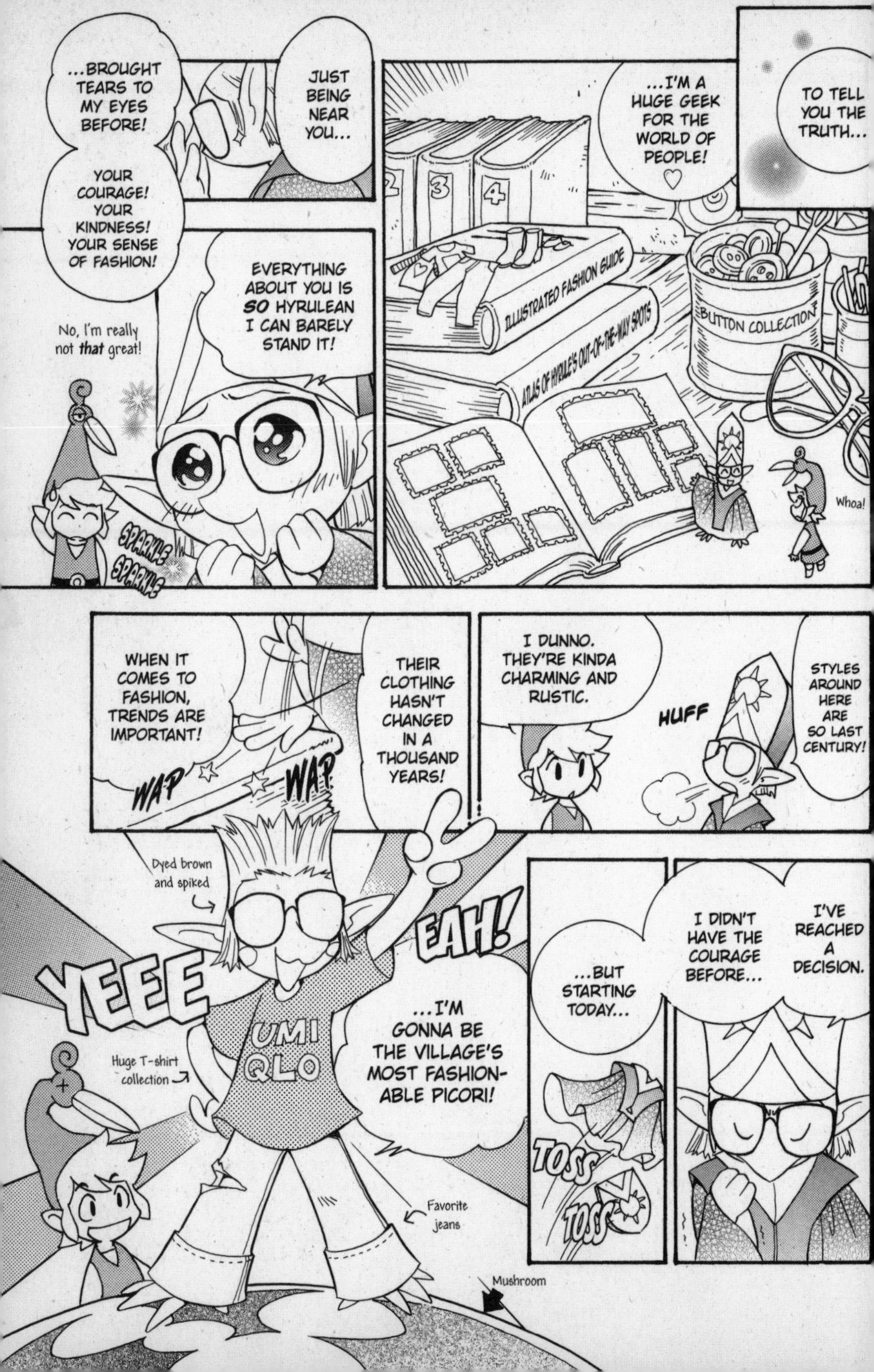
TO TELL YOU THE TRUTH...
...I'M A HUGE GEEK FOR THE WORLD OF PEOPLE! ♡
2
3
4
ILLUSTRATED FASHION GUIDE
ATLAS OF HYRULE'S OUT-OF-THE-WAY SPOTS
BUTTON COLLECTION
Whoa!
JUST BEING NEAR YOU...
...BROUGHT TEARS TO MY EYES BEFORE!
YOUR COURAGE! YOUR KINDNESS! YOUR SENSE OF FASHION!
EVERYTHING ABOUT YOU IS SO HYRULEAN I CAN BARELY STAND IT!
No, I'm really not that great!
SPARKLE SPARKLE
STYLES AROUND HERE ARE SO LAST CENTURY!
HUFF
I DUNNO. THEY'RE KINDA CHARMING AND RUSTIC.
THEIR CLOTHING HASN'T CHANGED IN A THOUSAND YEARS!
WHEN IT COMES TO FASHION, TRENDS ARE IMPORTANT!
WAP
WAP
I'VE REACHED A DECISION.
I DIDN'T HAVE THE COURAGE BEFORE...
...BUT STARTING TODAY...
TOSS
TOSS
...I'M GONNA BE THE VILLAGE'S MOST FASHION-ABLE PICORI!
YEEE
EAH!
Dyed brown and spiked
UMI QLO
Huge T-shirt collection
Favorite jeans
Mushroom

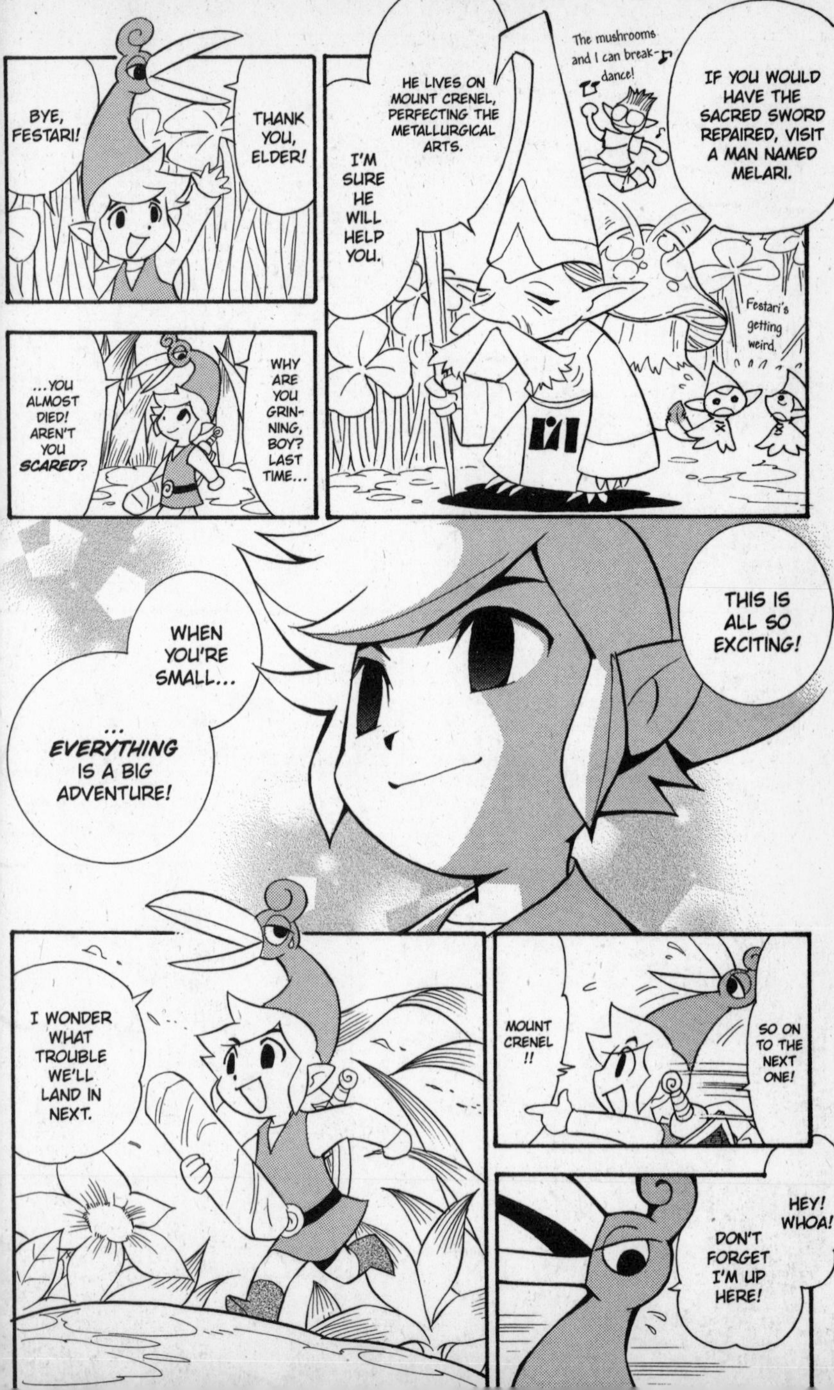
IF YOU WOULD HAVE THE SACRED SWORD REPAIRED, VISIT A MAN NAMED MELARI.
The mushrooms and I can break-dance!
HE LIVES ON MOUNT CRENEL, PERFECTING THE METALLURGICAL ARTS.
I'M SURE HE WILL HELP YOU.
Festari's getting weird.
THANK YOU, ELDER!
BYE, FESTARI!
WHY ARE YOU GRINNING, BOY? LAST TIME...
...YOU ALMOST DIED! AREN'T YOU SCARED?
THIS IS ALL SO EXCITING!
WHEN YOU'RE SMALL...
...EVERYTHING IS A BIG ADVENTURE!
SO ON TO THE NEXT ONE!
MOUNT CRENEL!!
HEY! WHOA!
DON'T FORGET I'M UP HERE!
I WONDER WHAT TROUBLE WE'LL LAND IN NEXT.

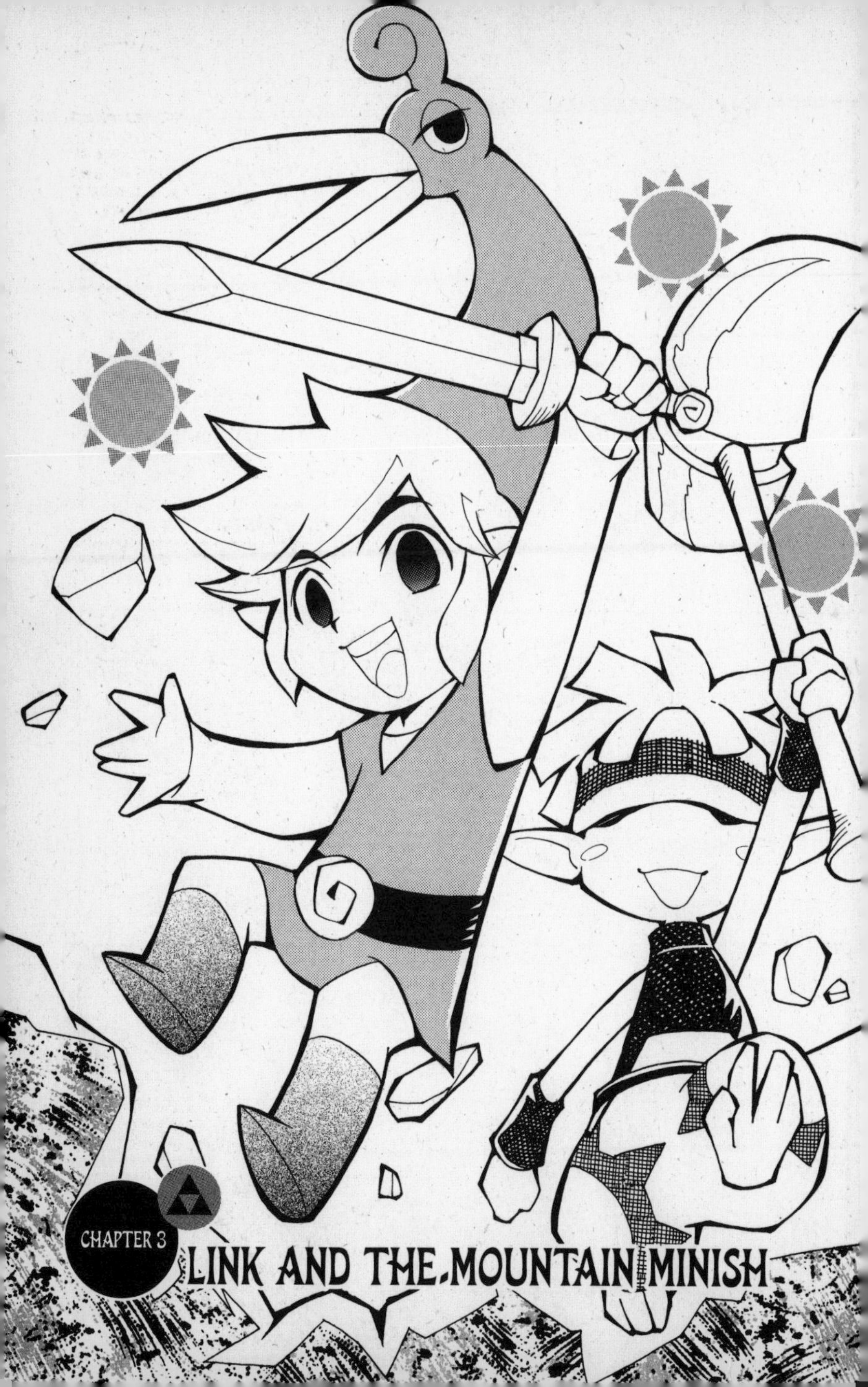
CHAPTER 3
LINK AND THE MOUNTAIN MINISH

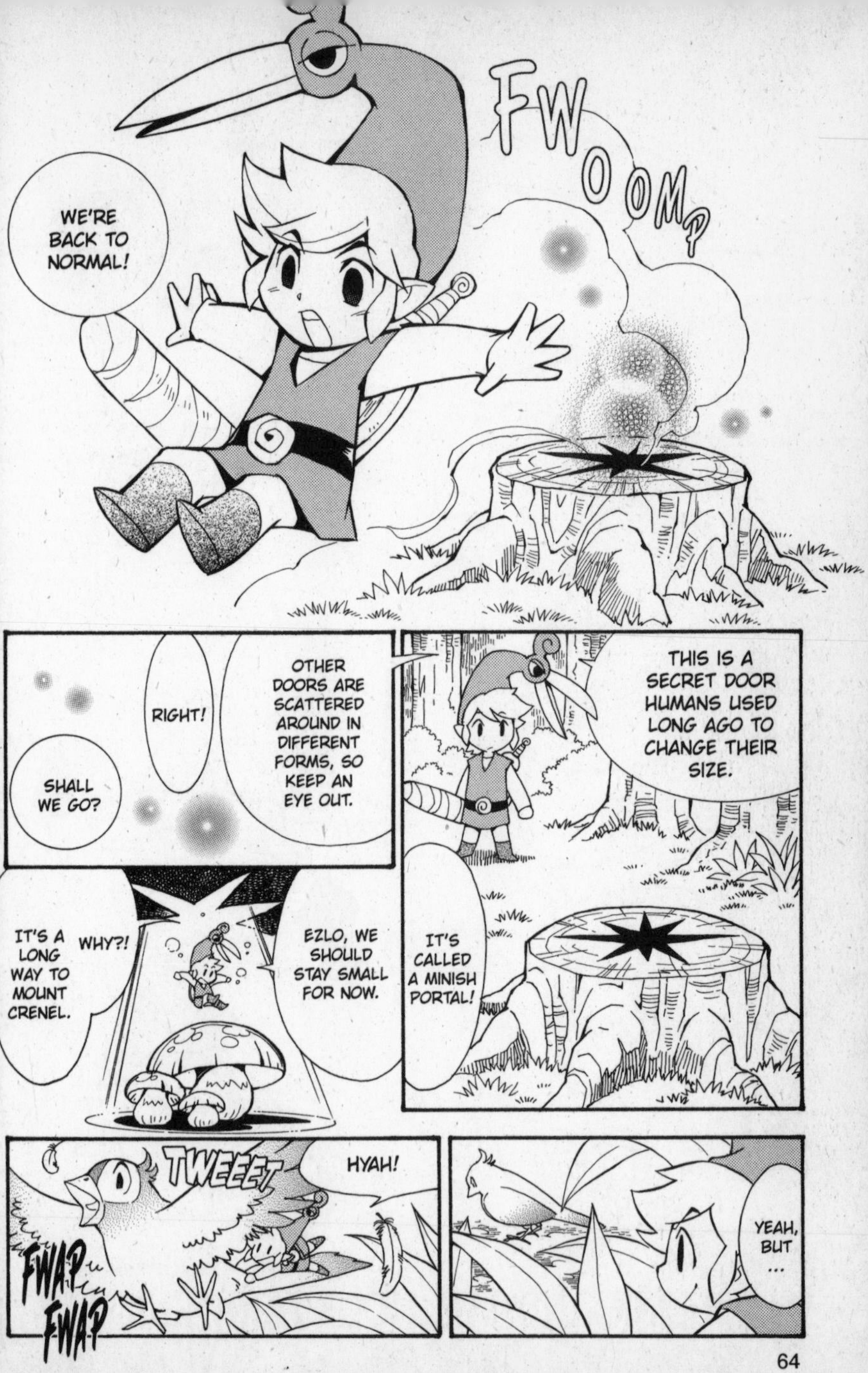

FWOOMP
WE'RE BACK TO NORMAL!
THIS IS A SECRET DOOR HUMANS USED LONG AGO TO CHANGE THEIR SIZE.
IT'S CALLED A MINISH PORTAL!
OTHER DOORS ARE SCATTERED AROUND IN DIFFERENT FORMS, SO KEEP AN EYE OUT.
RIGHT!
SHALL WE GO?
EZLO, WE SHOULD STAY SMALL FOR NOW.
WHY?!
IT'S A LONG WAY TO MOUNT CRENEL.
YEAH, BUT ...
HYAH!
TWEEET
FWAP FWAP

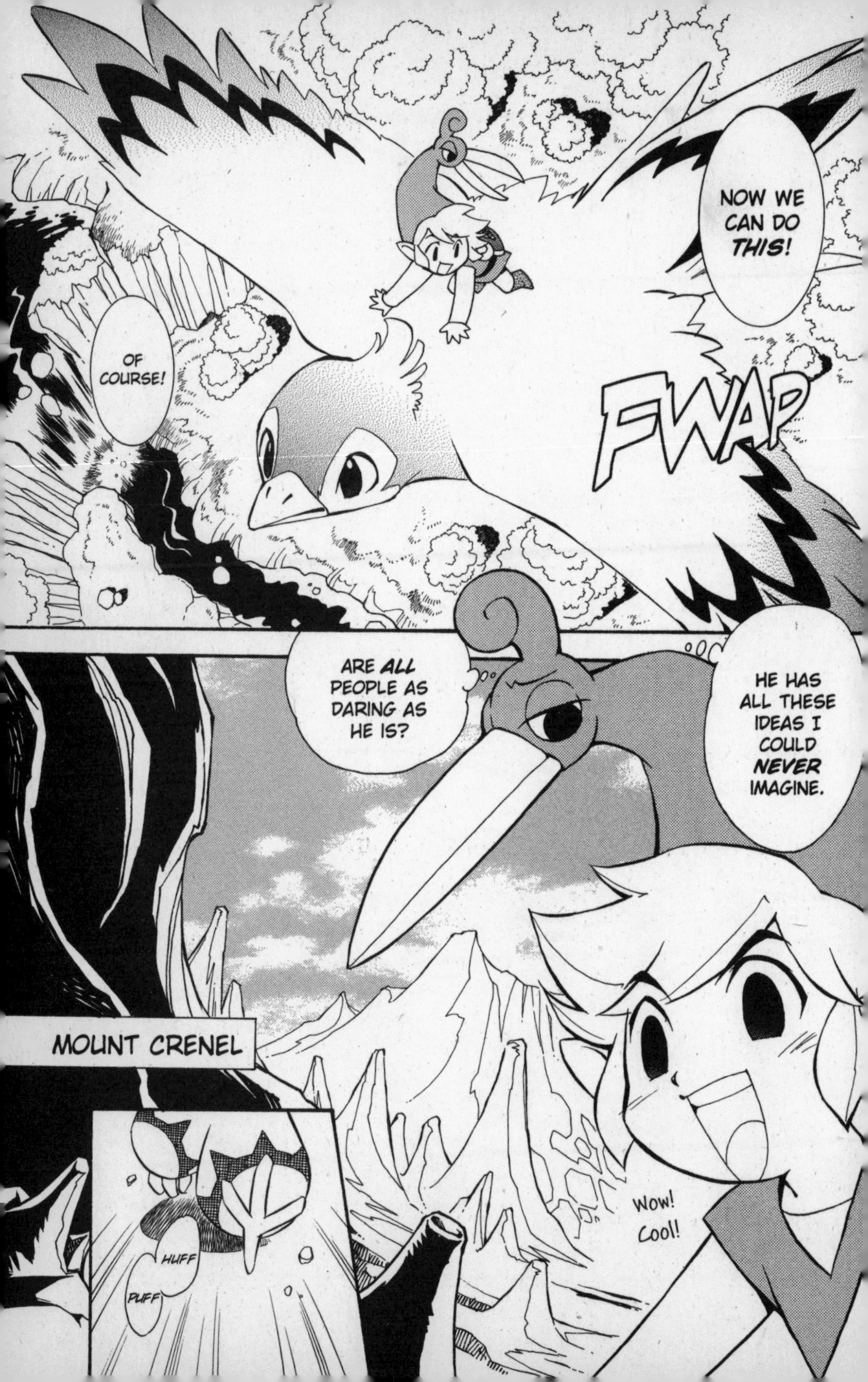
NOW WE CAN DO *THIS*!
OF COURSE!
FWAP
HE HAS ALL THESE IDEAS I COULD *NEVER* IMAGINE.
ARE *ALL* PEOPLE AS DARING AS HE IS?
Wow! Cool!
MOUNT CRENEL
HUFF
PUFF

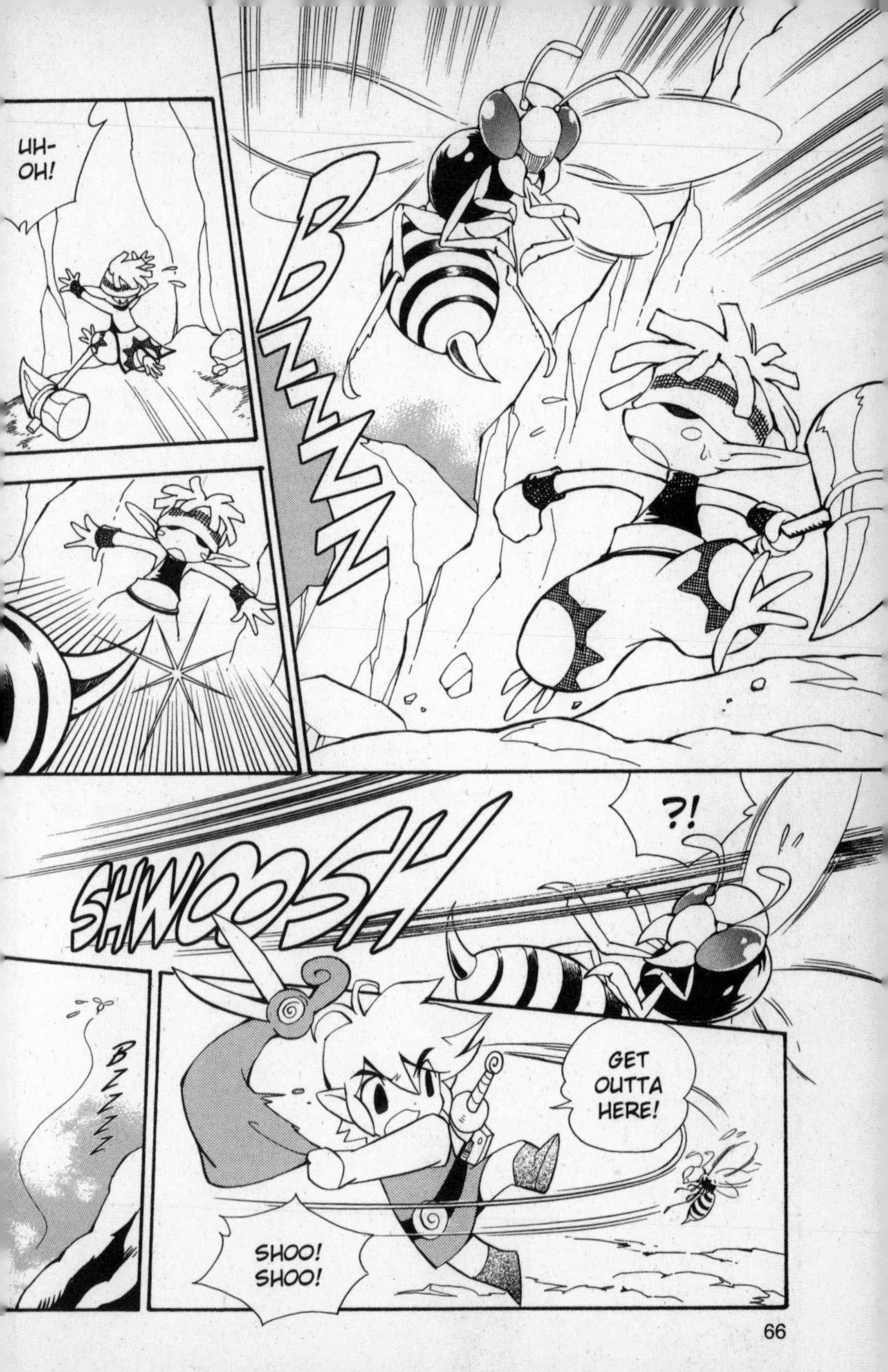
BZZZZ
UH-OH!
SHWOOSH
?!
GET OUTTA HERE!
SHOO! SHOO!
BZZZZZ

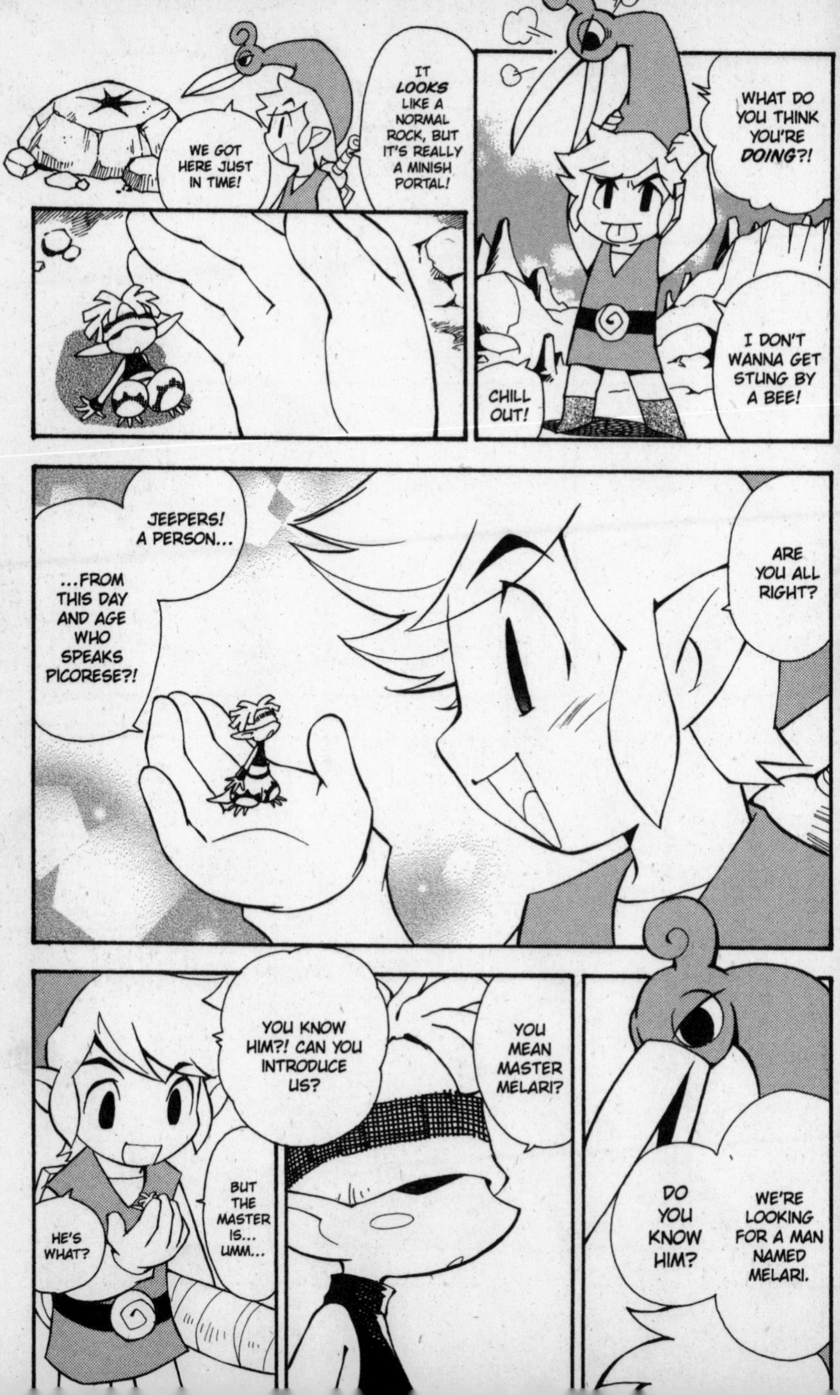
WHAT DO YOU THINK YOU'RE *DOING*?!
I DON'T WANNA GET STUNG BY A BEE!
CHILL OUT!
WE GOT HERE JUST IN TIME!
IT *LOOKS* LIKE A NORMAL ROCK, BUT IT'S REALLY A MINISH PORTAL!
ARE YOU ALL RIGHT?
JEEPERS! A PERSON...
...FROM THIS DAY AND AGE WHO SPEAKS PICORESE?!
WE'RE LOOKING FOR A MAN NAMED MELARI.
DO YOU KNOW HIM?
YOU MEAN MASTER MELARI?
BUT THE MASTER IS... UMM...
YOU KNOW HIM?! CAN YOU INTRODUCE US?
HE'S WHAT?

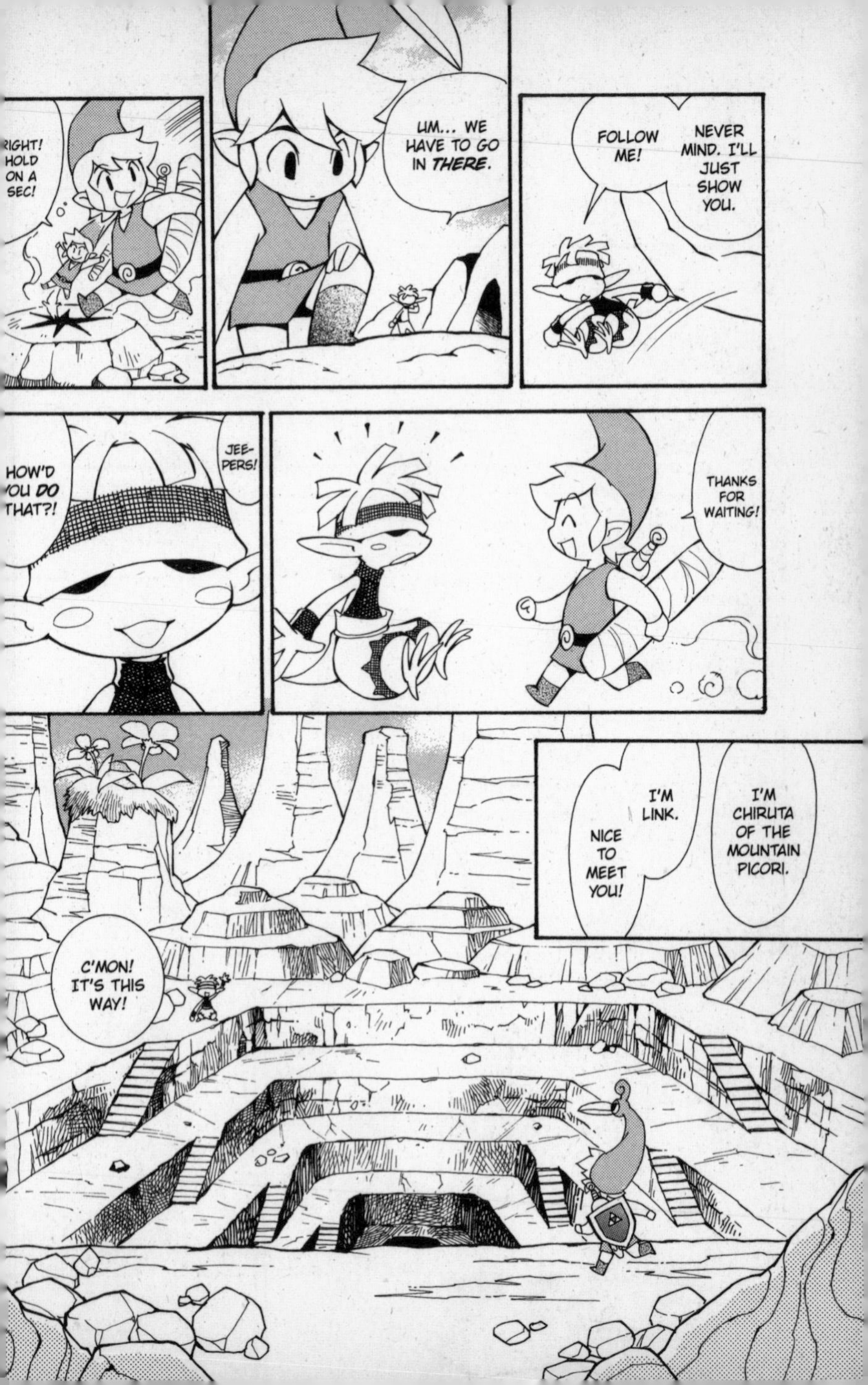
NEVER MIND. I'LL JUST SHOW YOU.
FOLLOW ME!
UM... WE HAVE TO GO IN *THERE*.
RIGHT! HOLD ON A SEC!
THANKS FOR WAITING!
JEE-PERS!
HOW'D YOU *DO* THAT?!
I'M CHIRUTA OF THE MOUNTAIN PICORI.
I'M LINK.
NICE TO MEET YOU!
C'MON! IT'S THIS WAY!

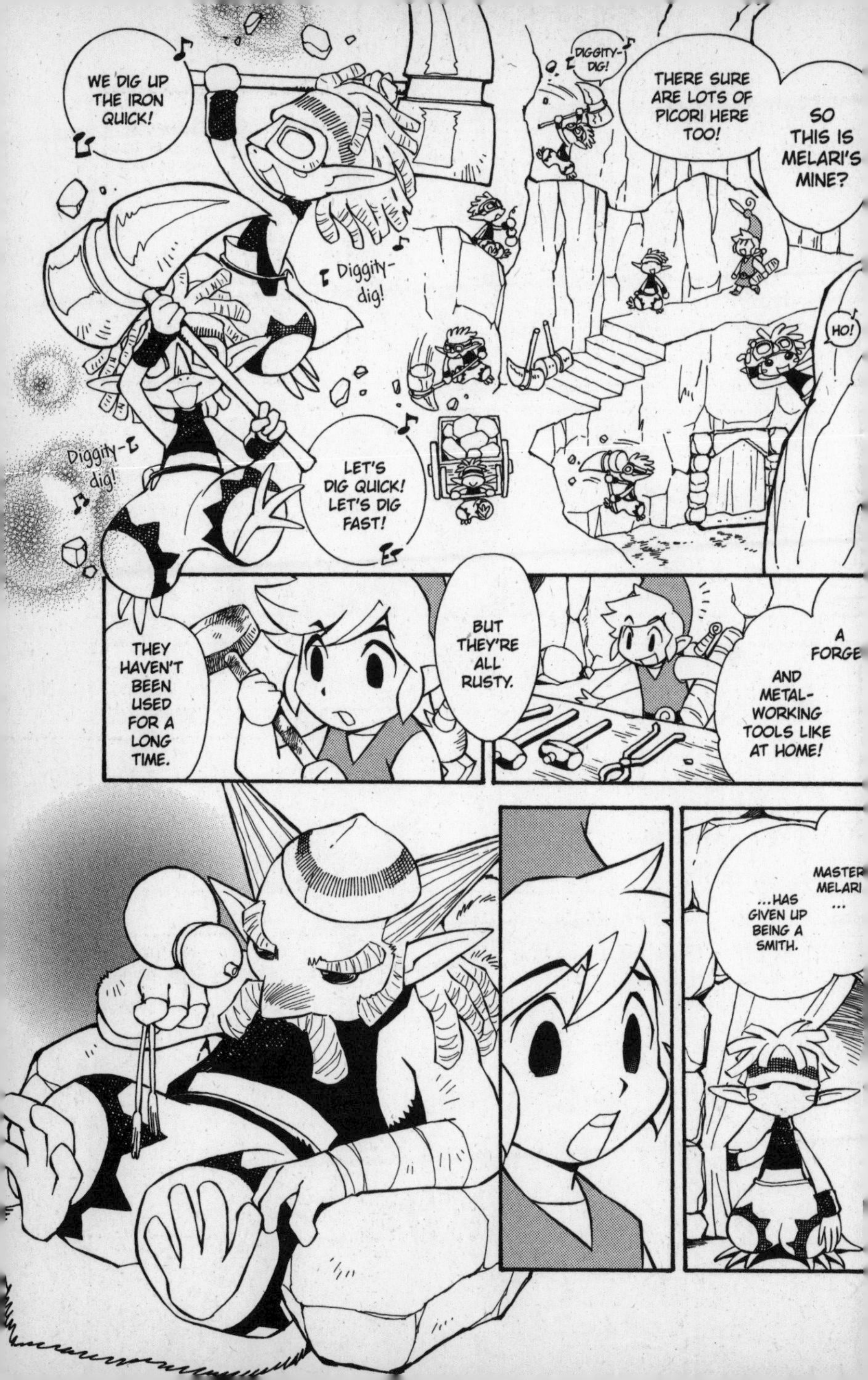
SO THIS IS MELARI'S MINE?
THERE SURE ARE LOTS OF PICORI HERE TOO!
DIGGITY-DIG!
HO!
WE DIG UP THE IRON QUICK!
Diggity-dig!
LET'S DIG QUICK! LET'S DIG FAST!
Diggity-dig!
A FORGE
AND METAL-WORKING TOOLS LIKE AT HOME!
BUT THEY'RE ALL RUSTY.
THEY HAVEN'T BEEN USED FOR A LONG TIME.
MASTER MELARI ...
...HAS GIVEN UP BEING A SMITH.

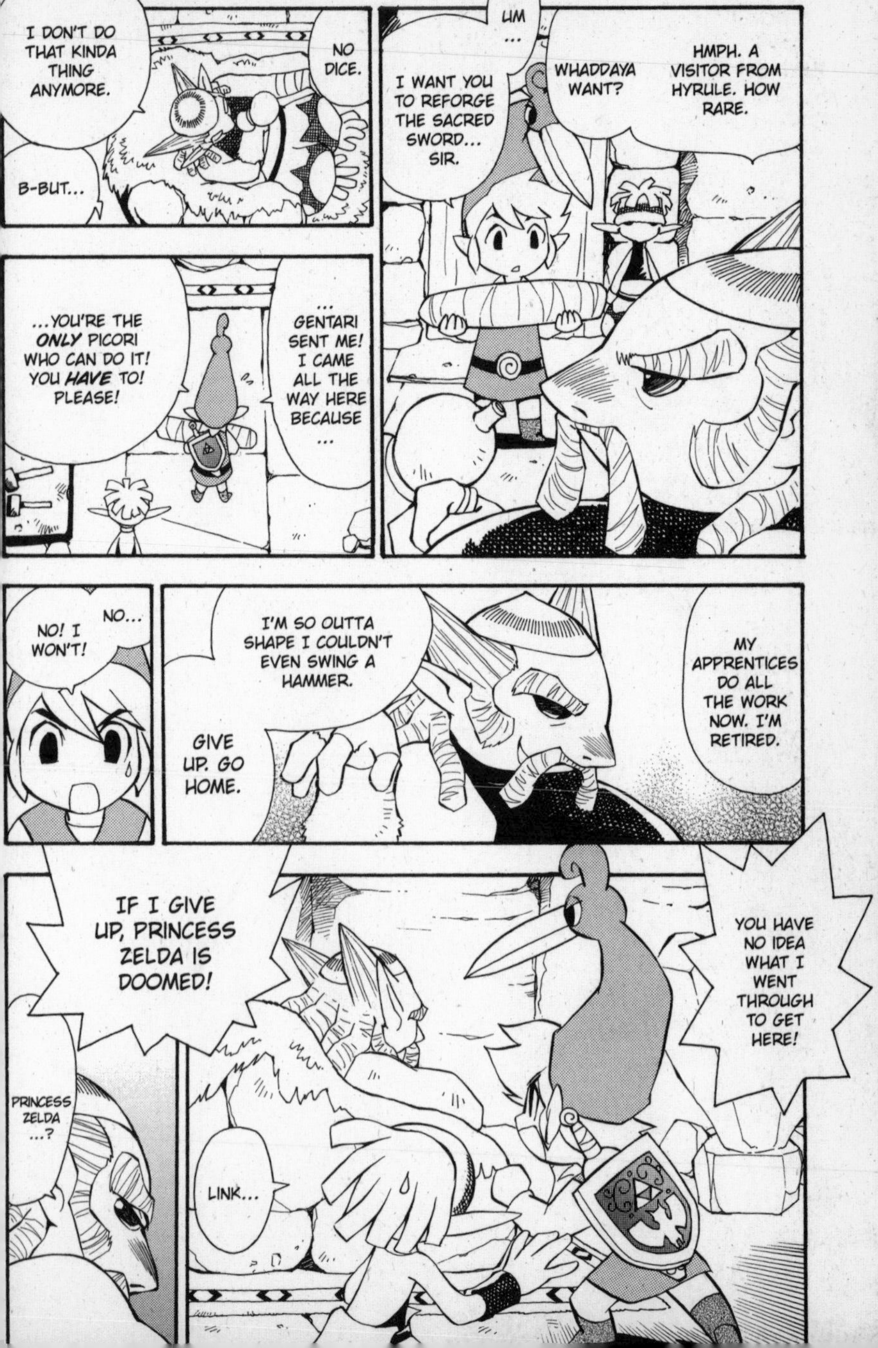
HMPH. A VISITOR FROM HYRULE. HOW RARE.
WHADDAYA WANT?
UM ...
I WANT YOU TO REFORGE THE SACRED SWORD... SIR.
NO DICE.
I DON'T DO THAT KINDA THING ANYMORE.
B-BUT...
... GENTARI SENT ME! I CAME ALL THE WAY HERE BECAUSE ...
...YOU'RE THE *ONLY* PICORI WHO CAN DO IT! YOU *HAVE* TO! PLEASE!
MY APPRENTICES DO ALL THE WORK NOW. I'M RETIRED.
I'M SO OUTTA SHAPE I COULDN'T EVEN SWING A HAMMER.
GIVE UP. GO HOME.
NO...
NO! I WON'T!
YOU HAVE NO IDEA WHAT I WENT THROUGH TO GET HERE!
IF I GIVE UP, PRINCESS ZELDA IS DOOMED!
LINK...
PRINCESS ZELDA ...?

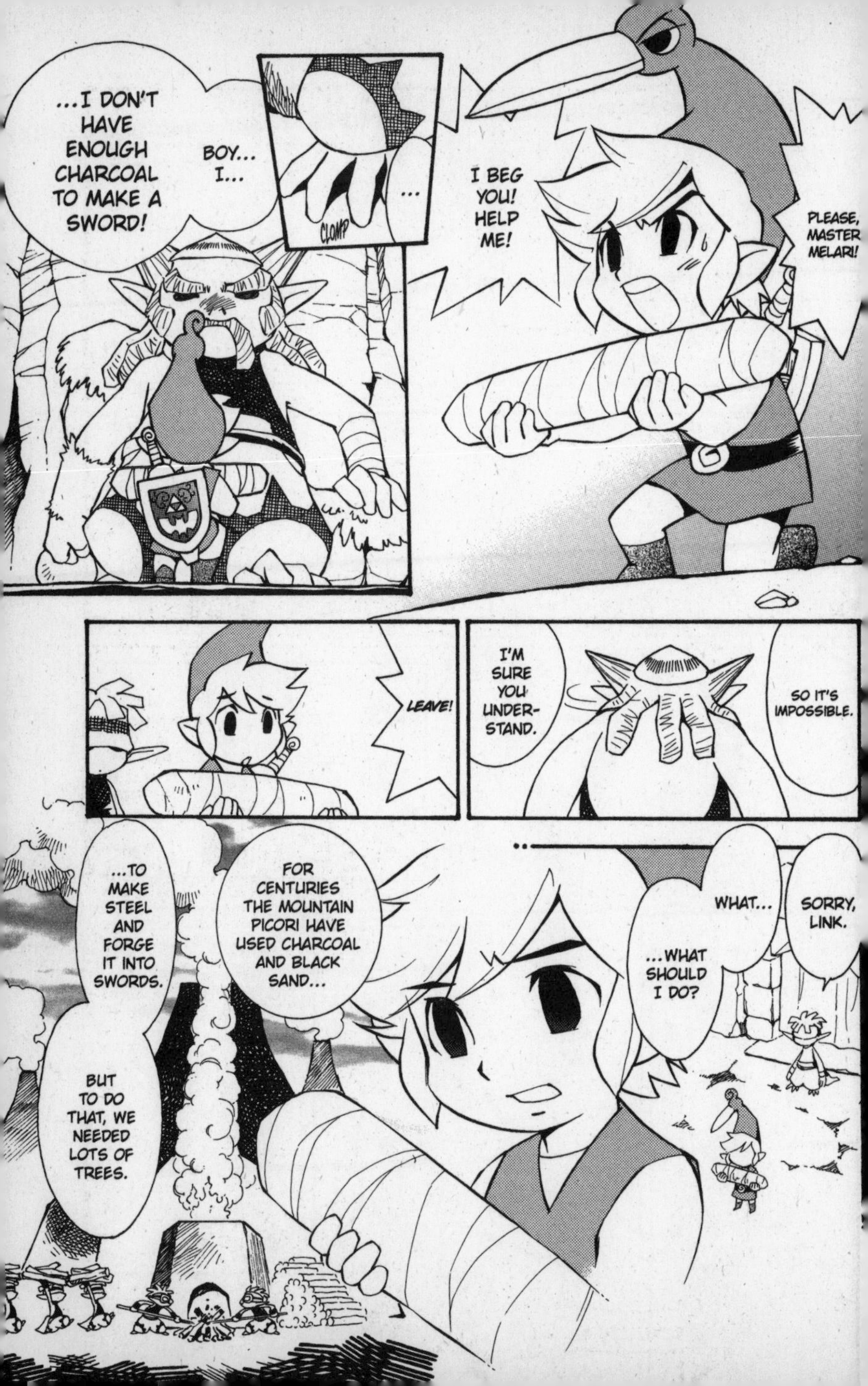
PLEASE, MASTER MELARI!
I BEG YOU! HELP ME!
...
CLOMP
BOY... I...
...I DON'T HAVE ENOUGH CHARCOAL TO MAKE A SWORD!
SO IT'S IMPOSSIBLE.
I'M SURE YOU UNDERSTAND.
LEAVE!
SORRY, LINK.
WHAT...
...WHAT SHOULD I DO?
FOR CENTURIES THE MOUNTAIN PICORI HAVE USED CHARCOAL AND BLACK SAND...
...TO MAKE STEEL AND FORGE IT INTO SWORDS.
BUT TO DO THAT, WE NEEDED LOTS OF TREES.

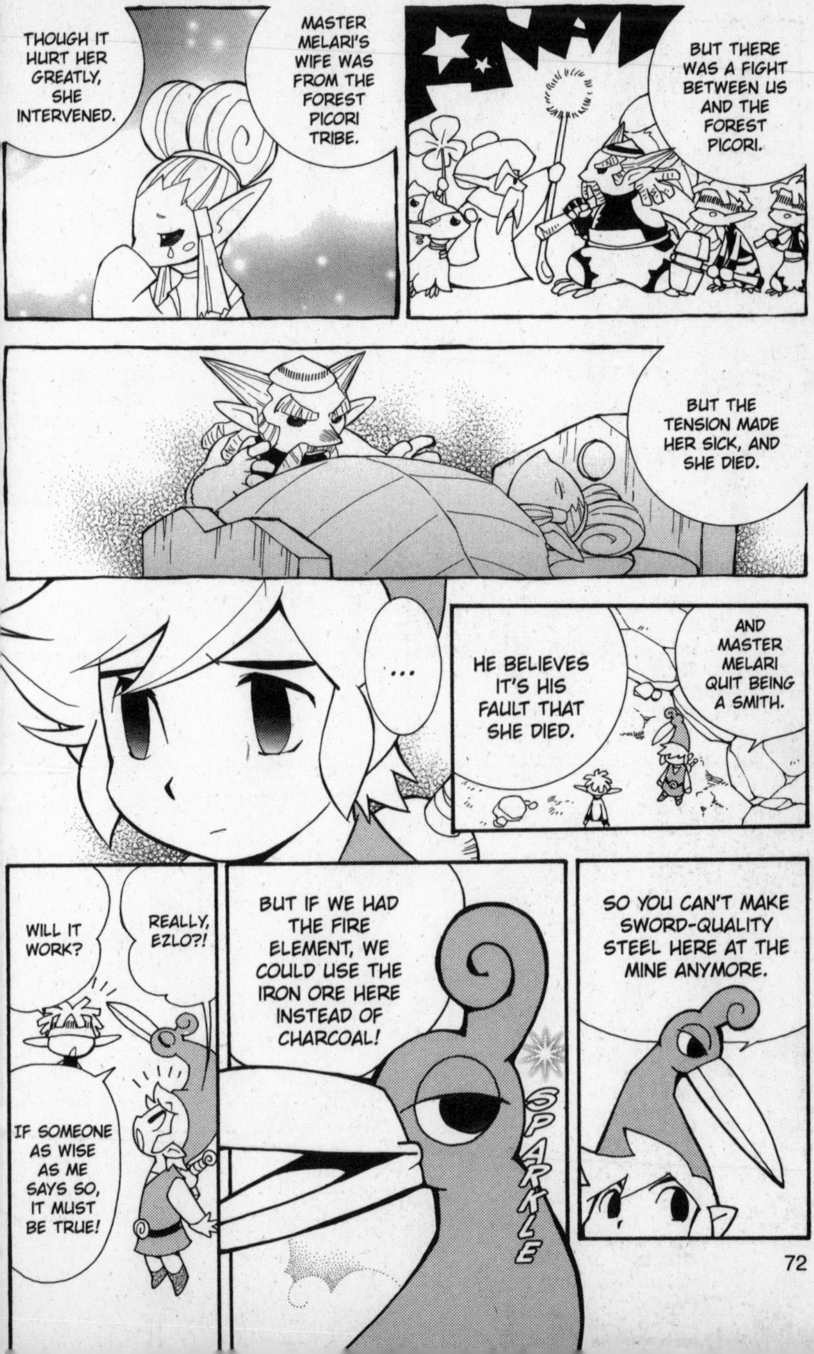
BUT THERE WAS A FIGHT BETWEEN US AND THE FOREST PICORI.
MASTER MELARI'S WIFE WAS FROM THE FOREST PICORI TRIBE.
THOUGH IT HURT HER GREATLY, SHE INTERVENED.
BUT THE TENSION MADE HER SICK, AND SHE DIED.
AND MASTER MELARI QUIT BEING A SMITH.
HE BELIEVES IT'S HIS FAULT THAT SHE DIED.
...
SO YOU CAN'T MAKE SWORD-QUALITY STEEL HERE AT THE MINE ANYMORE.
BUT IF WE HAD THE FIRE ELEMENT, WE COULD USE THE IRON ORE HERE INSTEAD OF CHARCOAL!
SPARKLE
REALLY, EZLO?!
WILL IT WORK?
IF SOMEONE AS WISE AS ME SAYS SO, IT MUST BE TRUE!

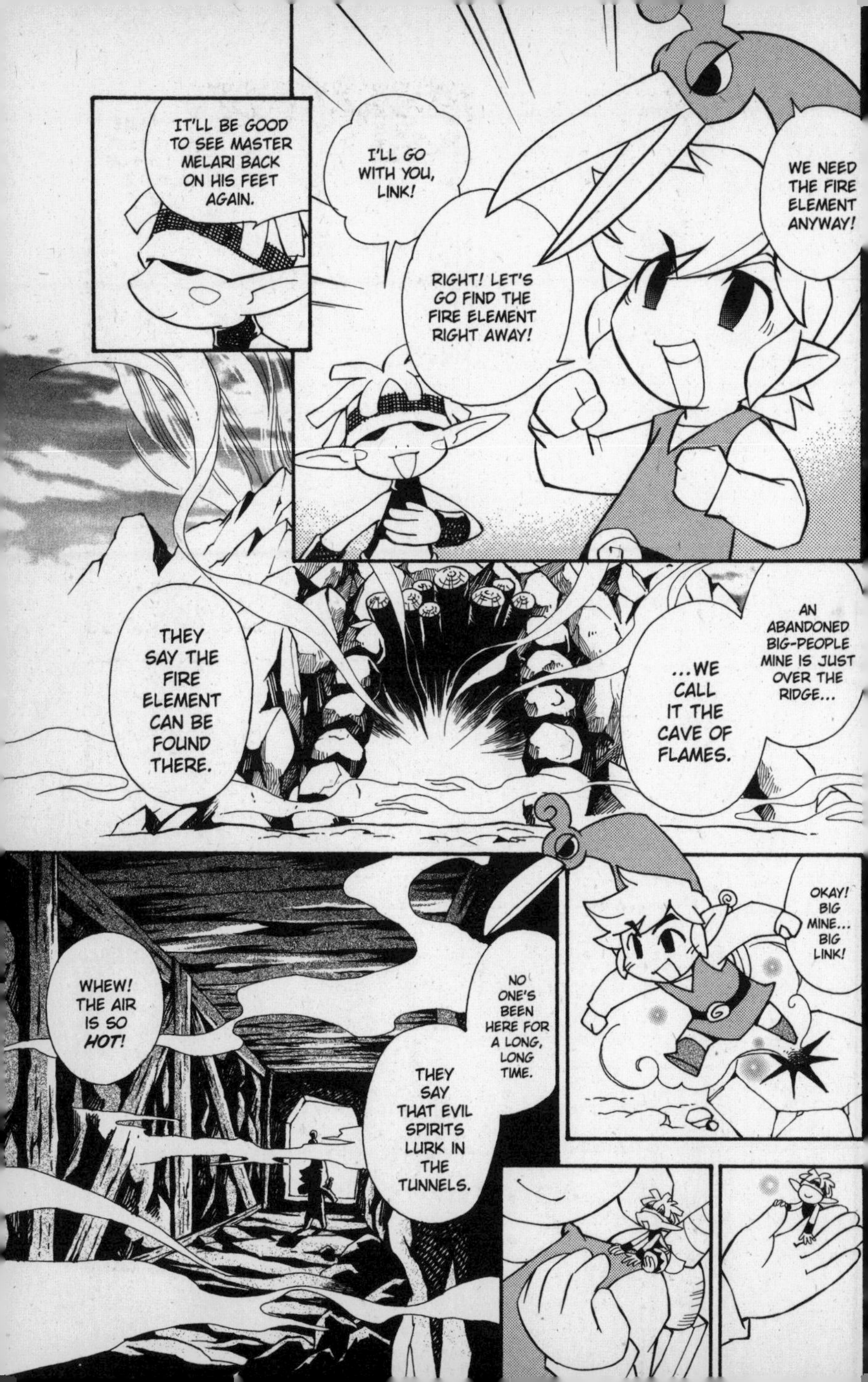
WE NEED THE FIRE ELEMENT ANYWAY!
I'LL GO WITH YOU, LINK!
RIGHT! LET'S GO FIND THE FIRE ELEMENT RIGHT AWAY!
IT'LL BE GOOD TO SEE MASTER MELARI BACK ON HIS FEET AGAIN.
AN ABANDONED BIG-PEOPLE MINE IS JUST OVER THE RIDGE...
...WE CALL IT THE CAVE OF FLAMES.
THEY SAY THE FIRE ELEMENT CAN BE FOUND THERE.
OKAY! BIG MINE... BIG LINK!
NO ONE'S BEEN HERE FOR A LONG, LONG TIME.
THEY SAY THAT EVIL SPIRITS LURK IN THE TUNNELS.
WHEW! THE AIR IS SO *HOT*!

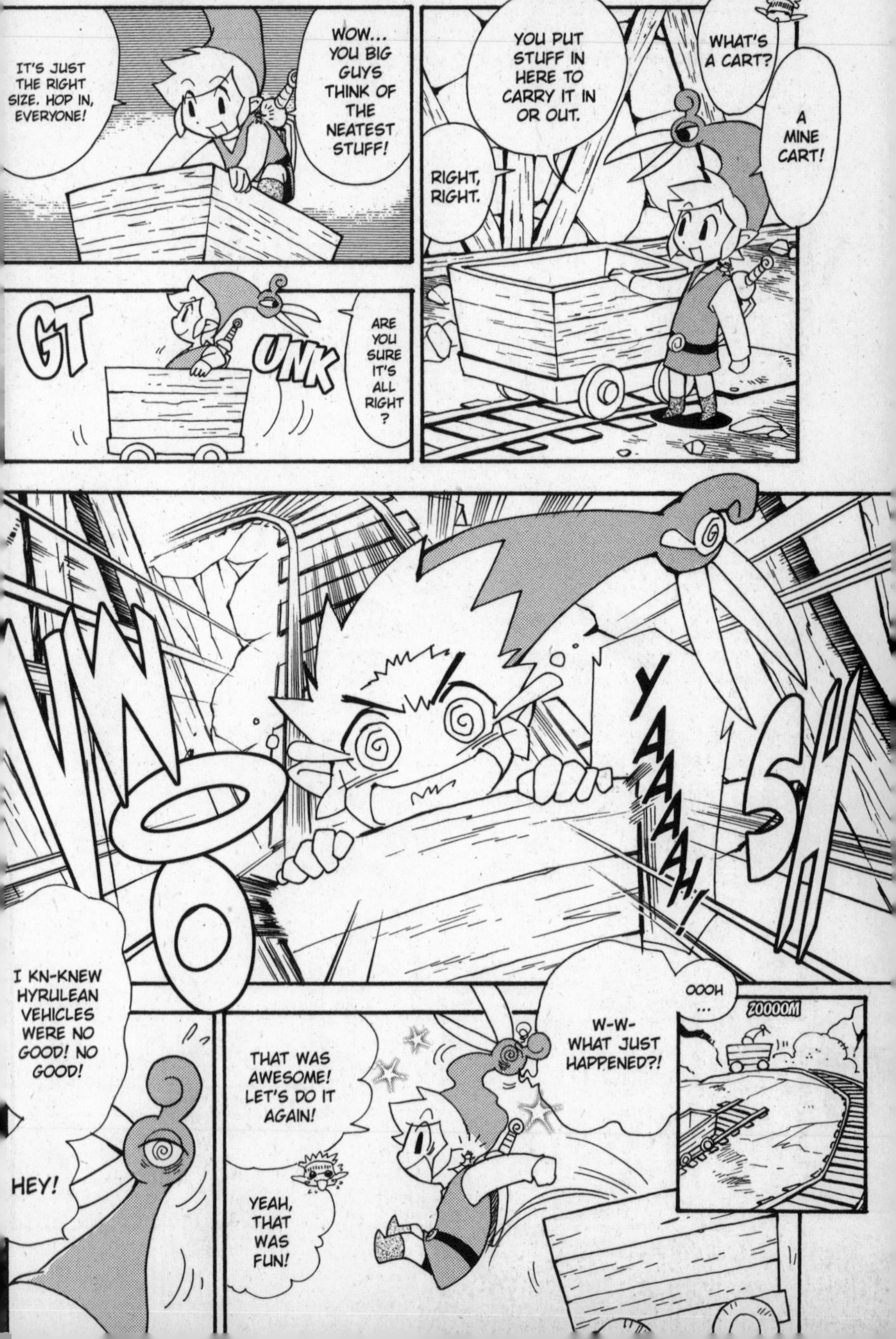
WHAT'S A CART?
A MINE CART!
YOU PUT STUFF IN HERE TO CARRY IT IN OR OUT.
RIGHT, RIGHT.
WOW... YOU BIG GUYS THINK OF THE NEATEST STUFF!
IT'S JUST THE RIGHT SIZE. HOP IN, EVERYONE!
ARE YOU SURE IT'S ALL RIGHT?
GT UNK
YAAAAH!!
WWOOSH
ZOOOOM
OOOH ...
W-W-WHAT JUST HAPPENED?!
THAT WAS AWESOME! LET'S DO IT AGAIN!
YEAH, THAT WAS FUN!
I KN-KNEW HYRULEAN VEHICLES WERE NO GOOD! NO GOOD!
HEY!

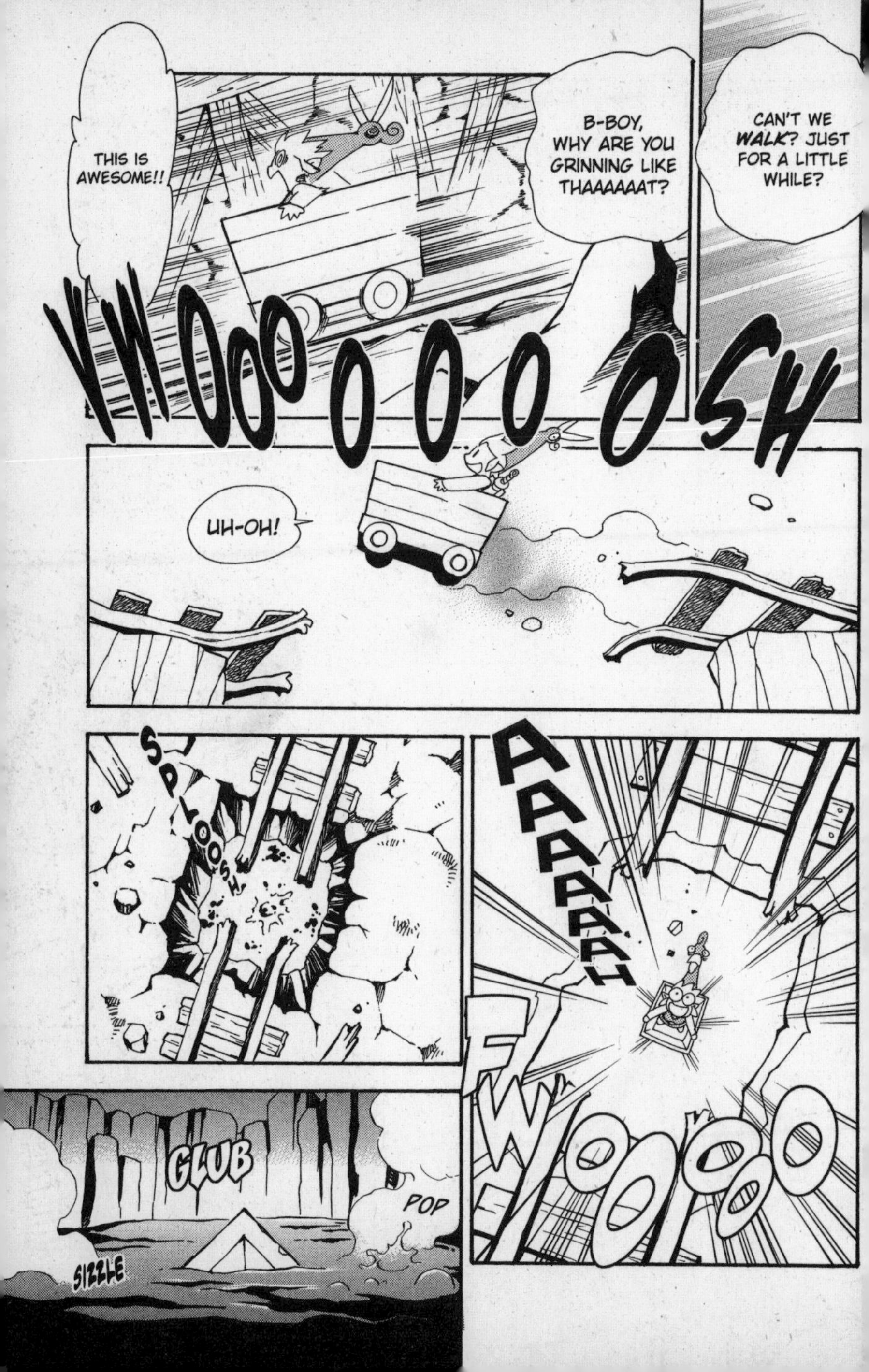
CAN'T WE *WALK*? JUST FOR A LITTLE WHILE?
B-BOY, WHY ARE YOU GRINNING LIKE THAAAAAAT?
THIS IS AWESOME!!
VWOOOOOOOSH
UH-OH!
AAAAAAAH
FWOOOOOO
SPLOOSH
GLUB
POP
SIZZLE

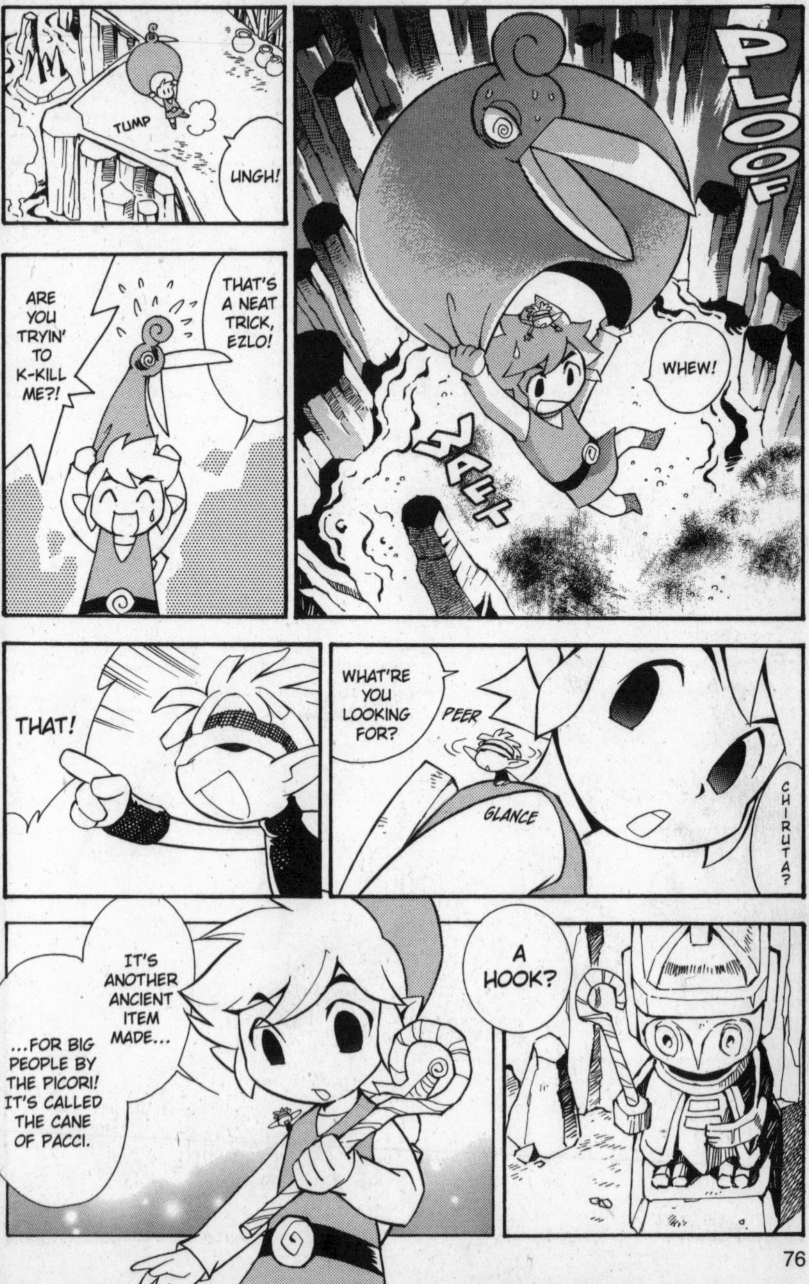
PLOOF
WHEW!
WAFT
TUMP
UNGH!
THAT'S A NEAT TRICK, EZLO!
ARE YOU TRYIN' TO K-KILL ME?!
WHAT'RE YOU LOOKING FOR?
PEER
CHIRUTA?
GLANCE
THAT!
A HOOK?
IT'S ANOTHER ANCIENT ITEM MADE...
...FOR BIG PEOPLE BY THE PICORI! IT'S CALLED THE CANE OF PACCI.

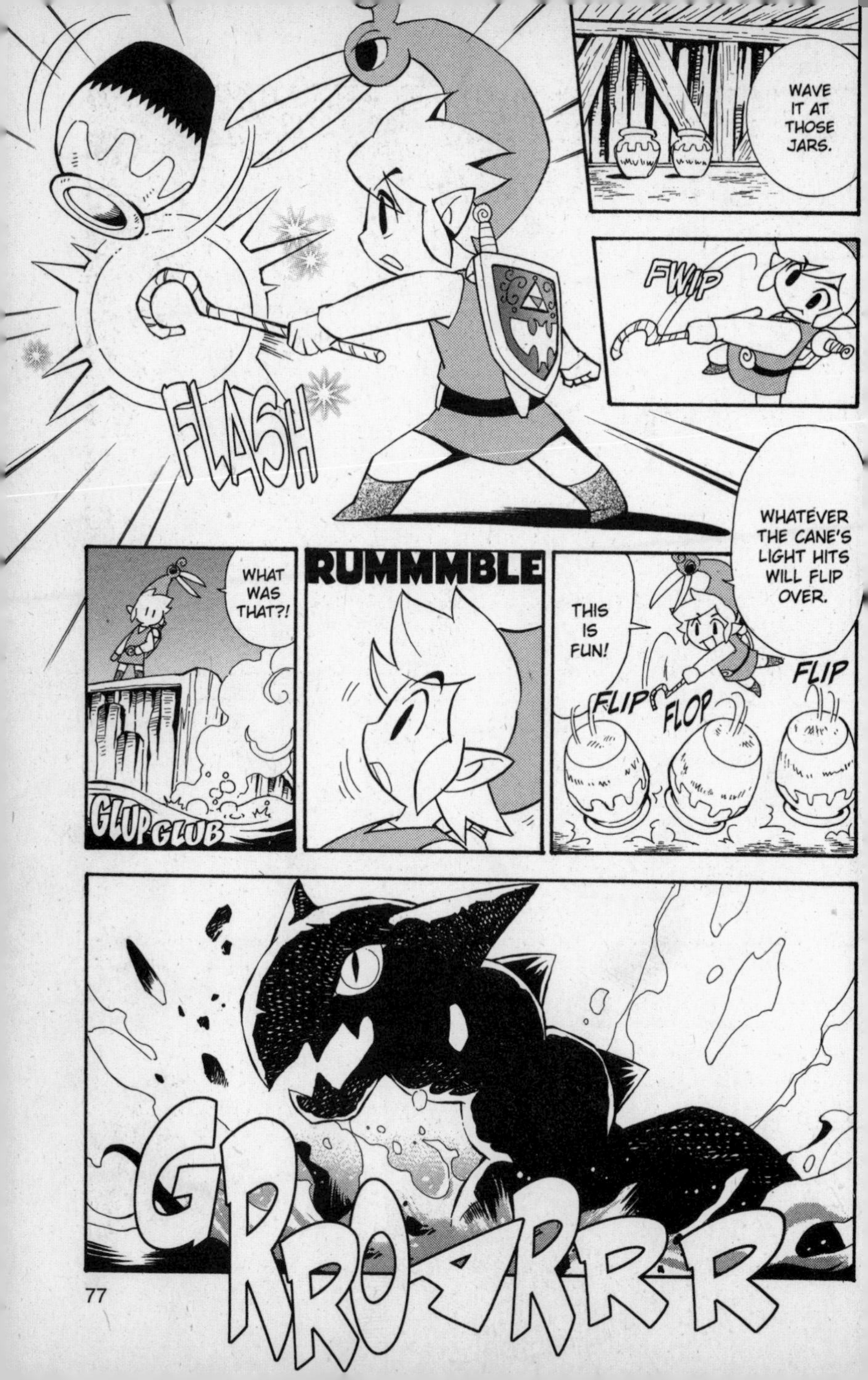
WAVE IT AT THOSE JARS.
FWIP
FLASH
WHATEVER THE CANE'S LIGHT HITS WILL FLIP OVER.
THIS IS FUN!
FLIP
FLOP
FLIP
RUMMMBLE
WHAT WAS THAT?!
GLUP GLUB
GRROARRR

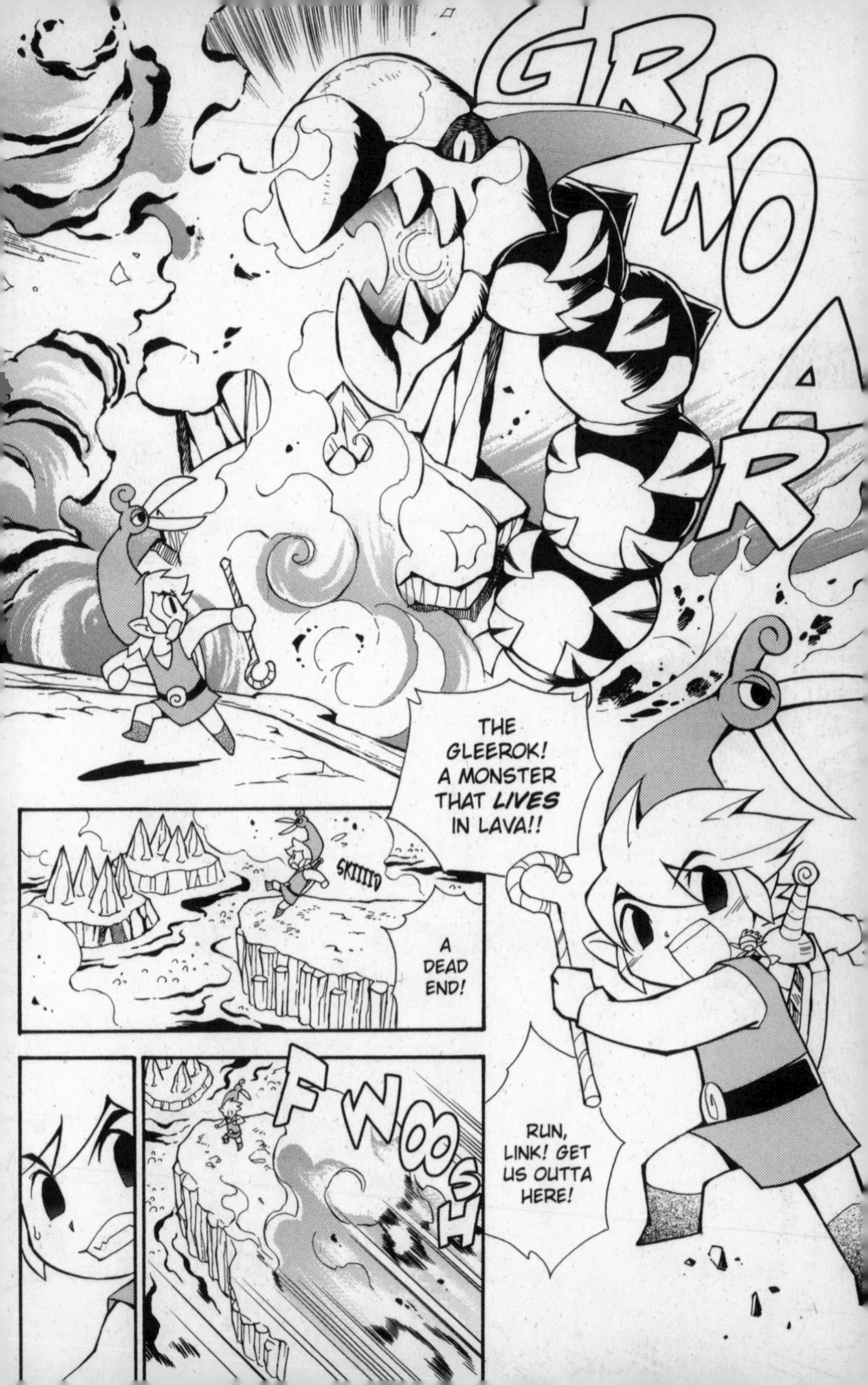
GRROOAAR
THE GLEEROK! A MONSTER THAT *LIVES* IN LAVA!!
RUN, LINK! GET US OUTTA HERE!
SKIIIID
A DEAD END!
FWOOSH

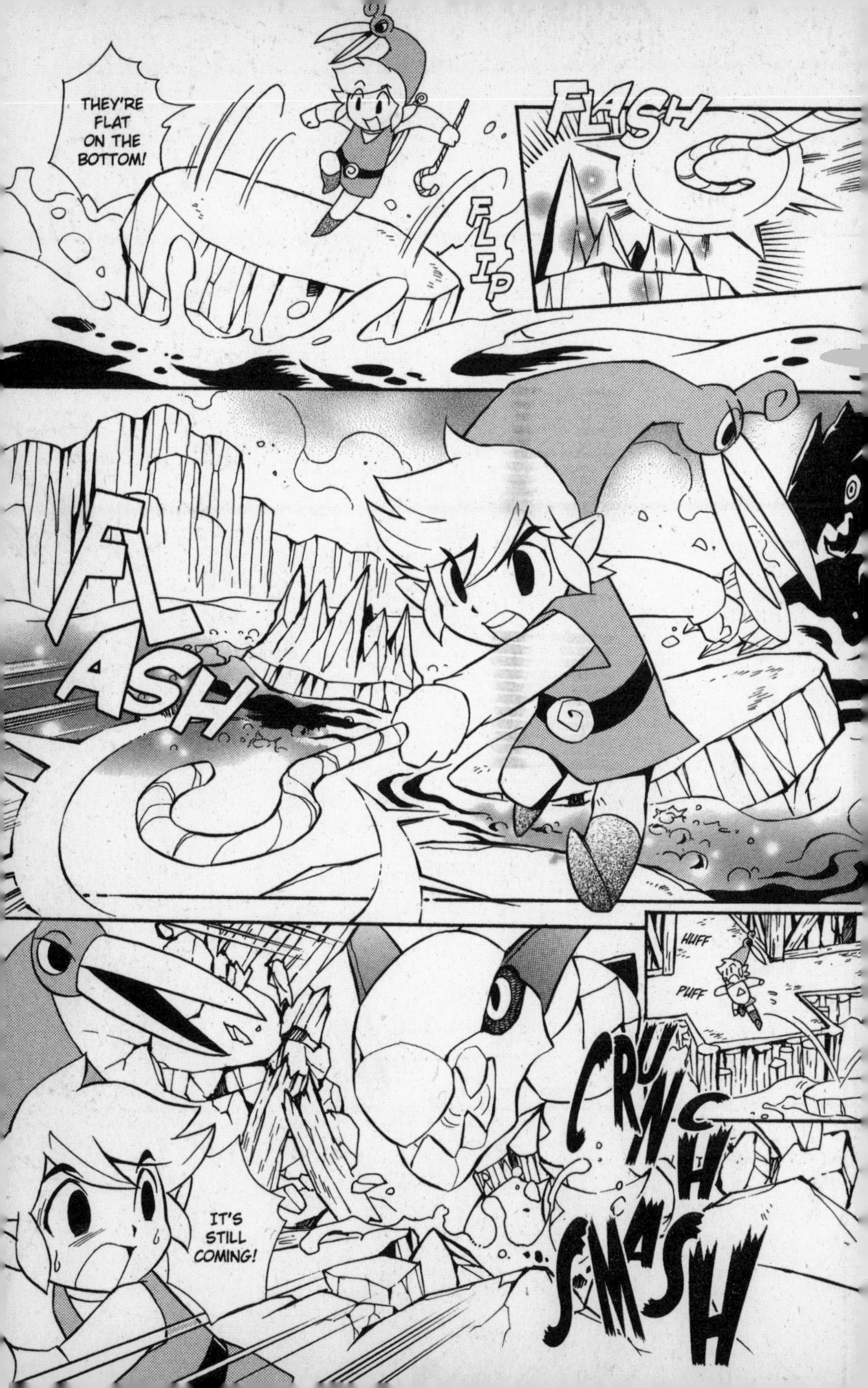
FLASH
FLIP
THEY'RE FLAT ON THE BOTTOM!
FLASH
HUFF
PUFF
CRUNCH
SMASH
IT'S STILL COMING!

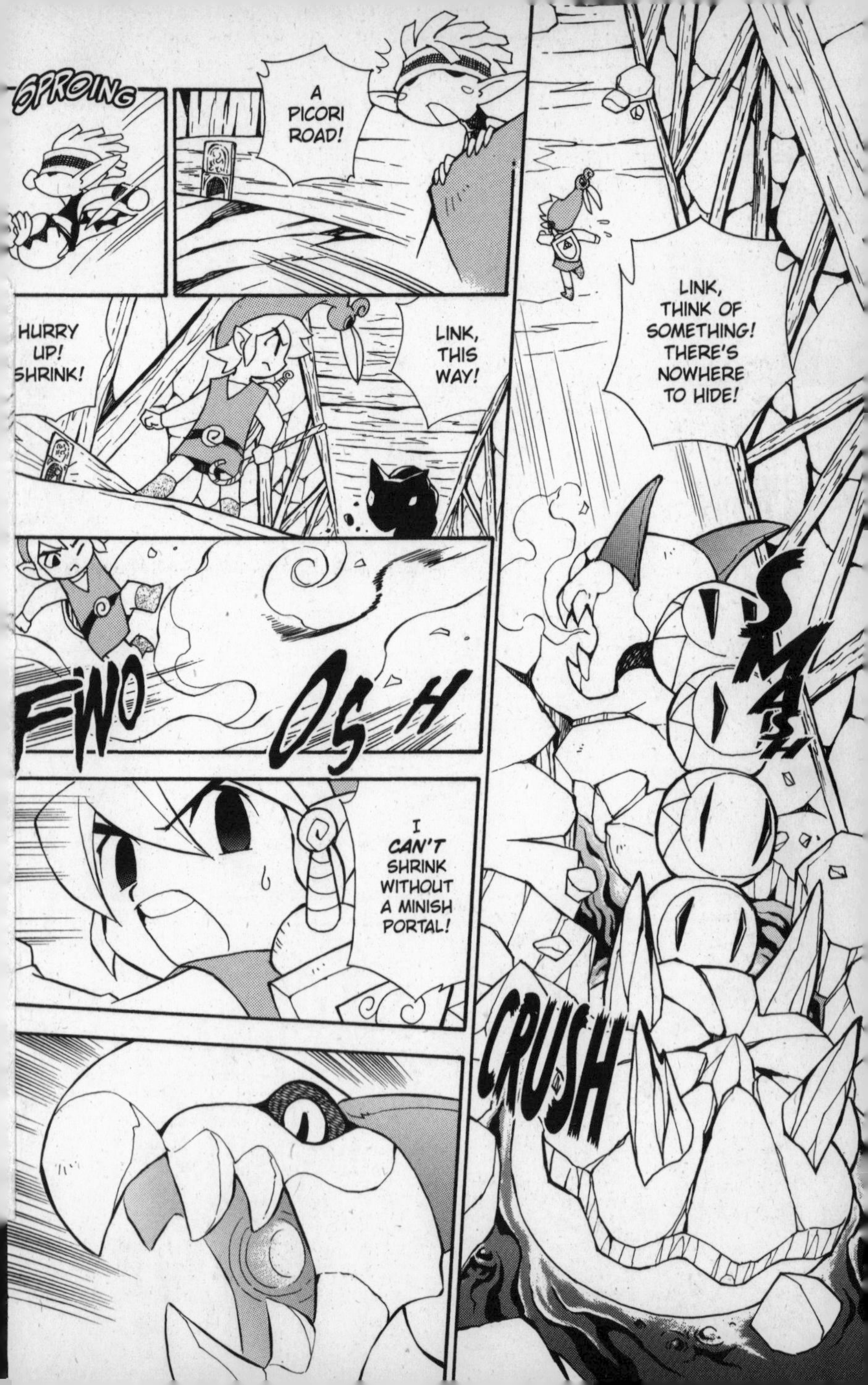
LINK, THINK OF SOMETHING! THERE'S NOWHERE TO HIDE!
SMASH
CRUSH
A PICORI ROAD!
SPROING
LINK, THIS WAY!
HURRY UP! SHRINK!
FWOOSH
I *CAN'T* SHRINK WITHOUT A MINISH PORTAL!

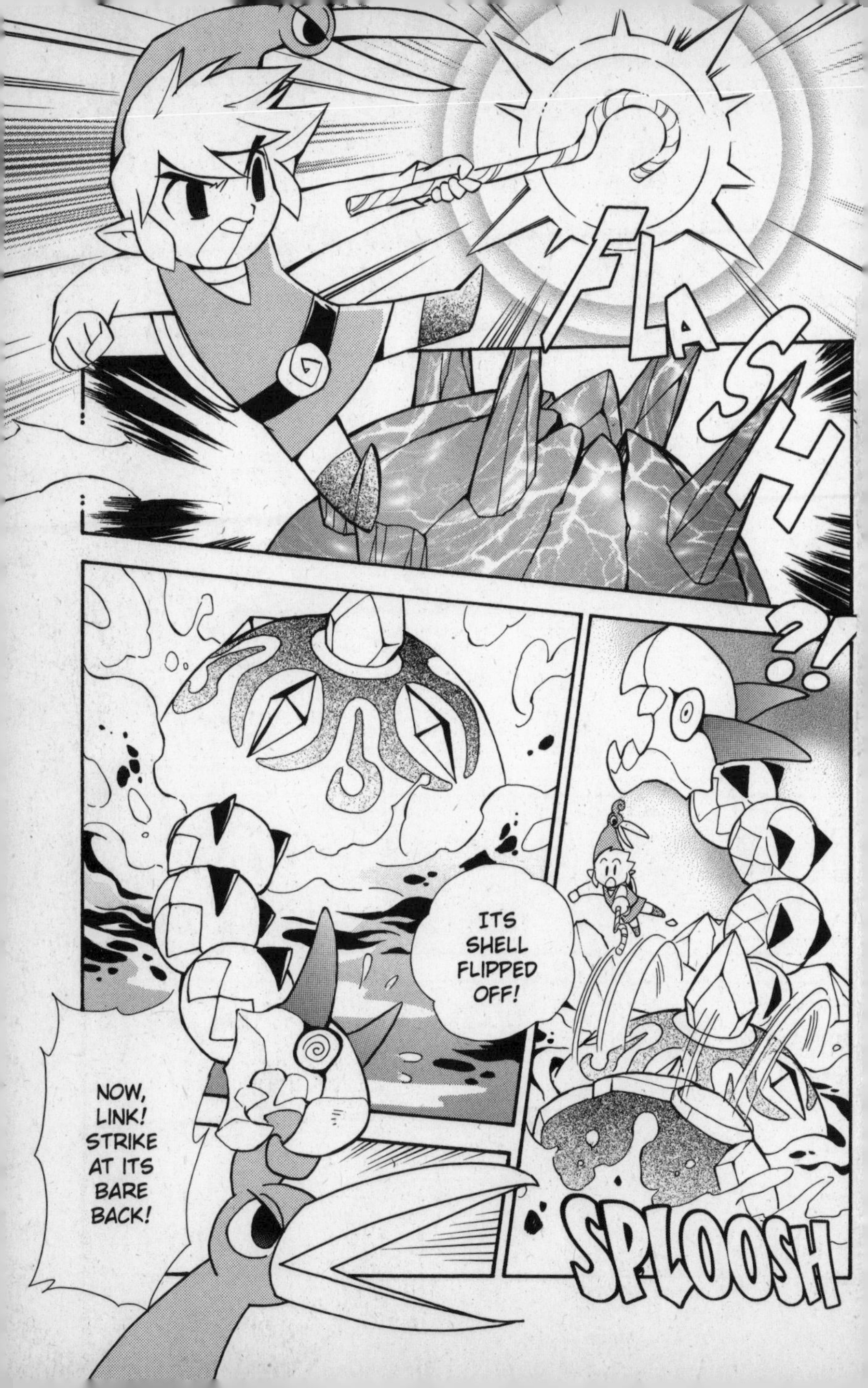
FLASH
?!
ITS SHELL FLIPPED OFF!
SPLOOSH
NOW, LINK! STRIKE AT ITS BARE BACK!

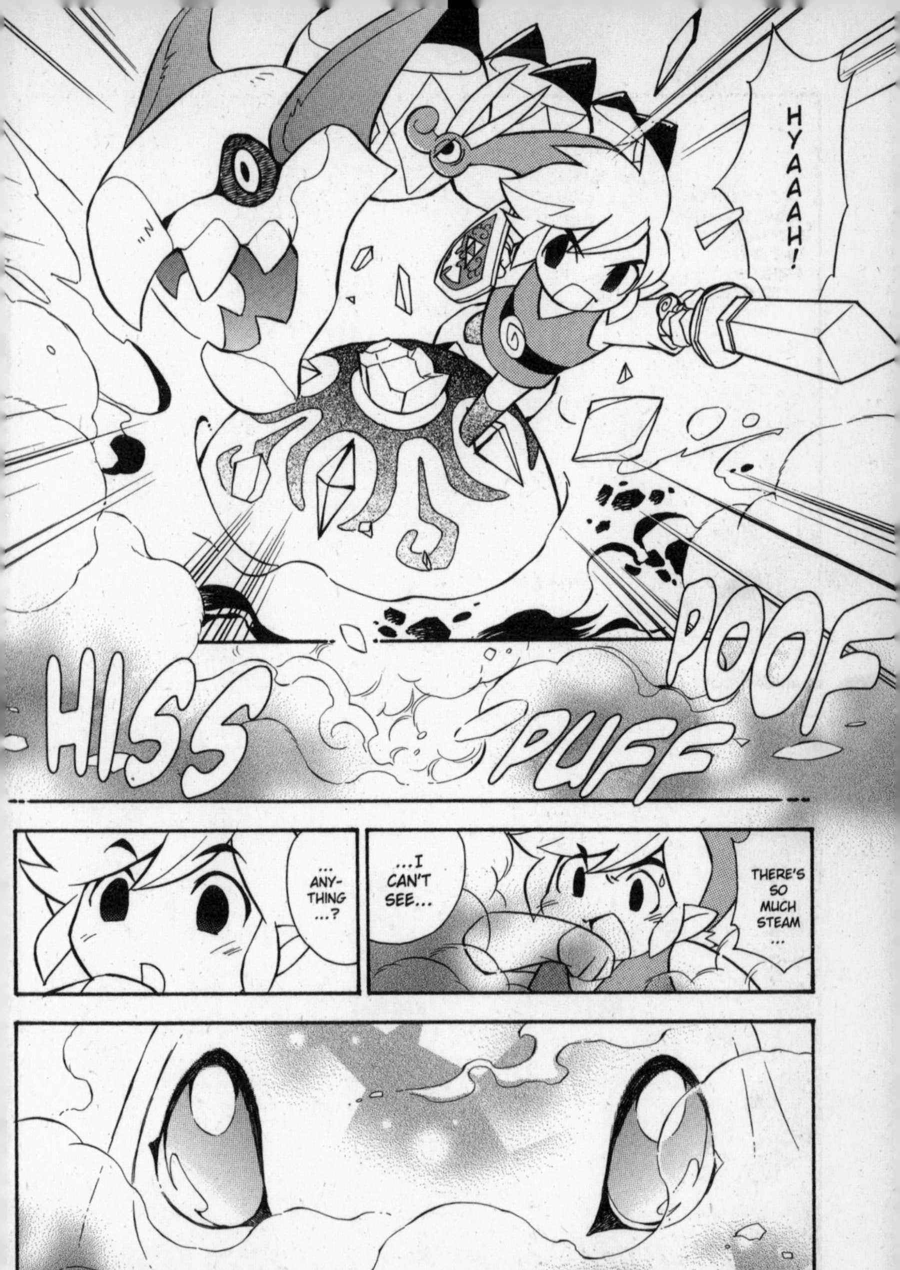
HYAAAH!
POOF
PUFF
HISS
THERE'S SO MUCH STEAM ...
...I CAN'T SEE...
... ANY-THING ...?

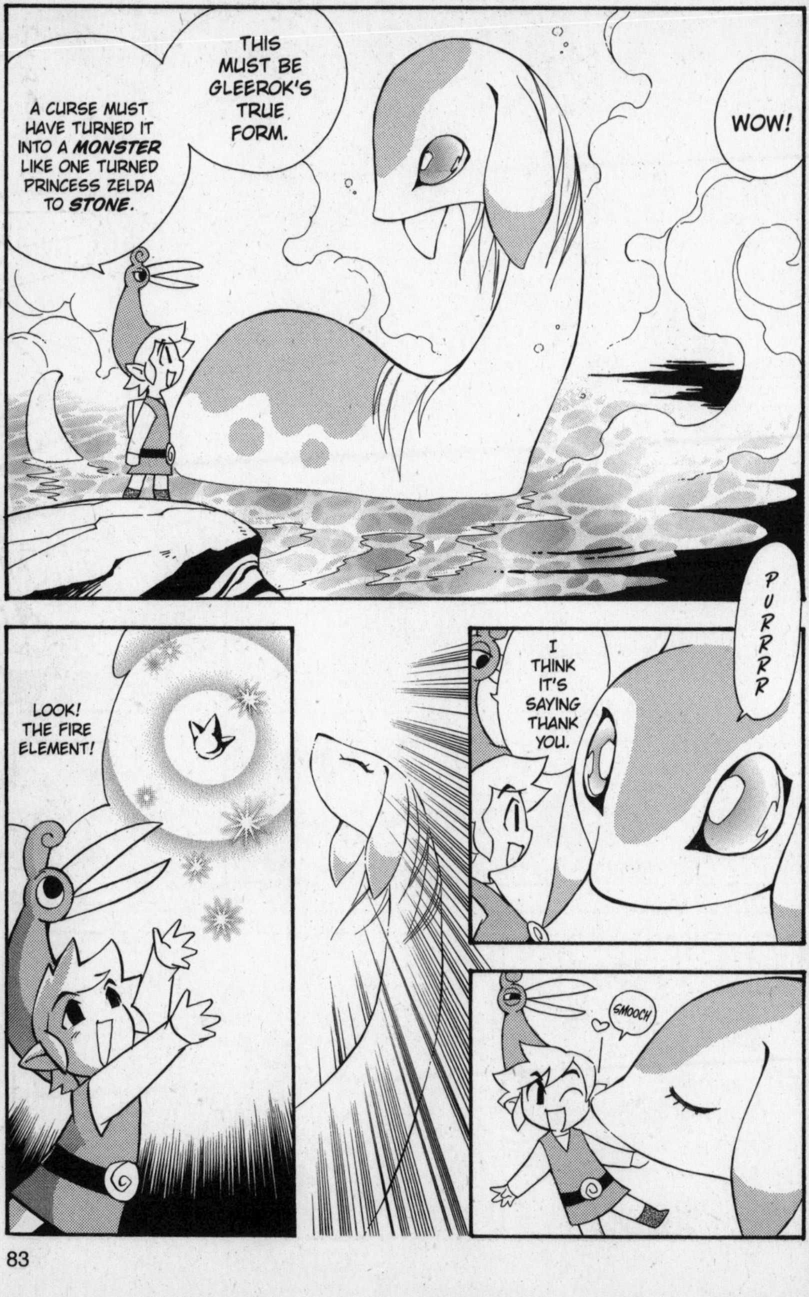
WOW!
THIS MUST BE GLEEROK'S TRUE FORM.
A CURSE MUST HAVE TURNED IT INTO A **MONSTER** LIKE ONE TURNED PRINCESS ZELDA TO **STONE**.
PURRRR
I THINK IT'S SAYING THANK YOU.
SMOOCH
LOOK! THE FIRE ELEMENT!

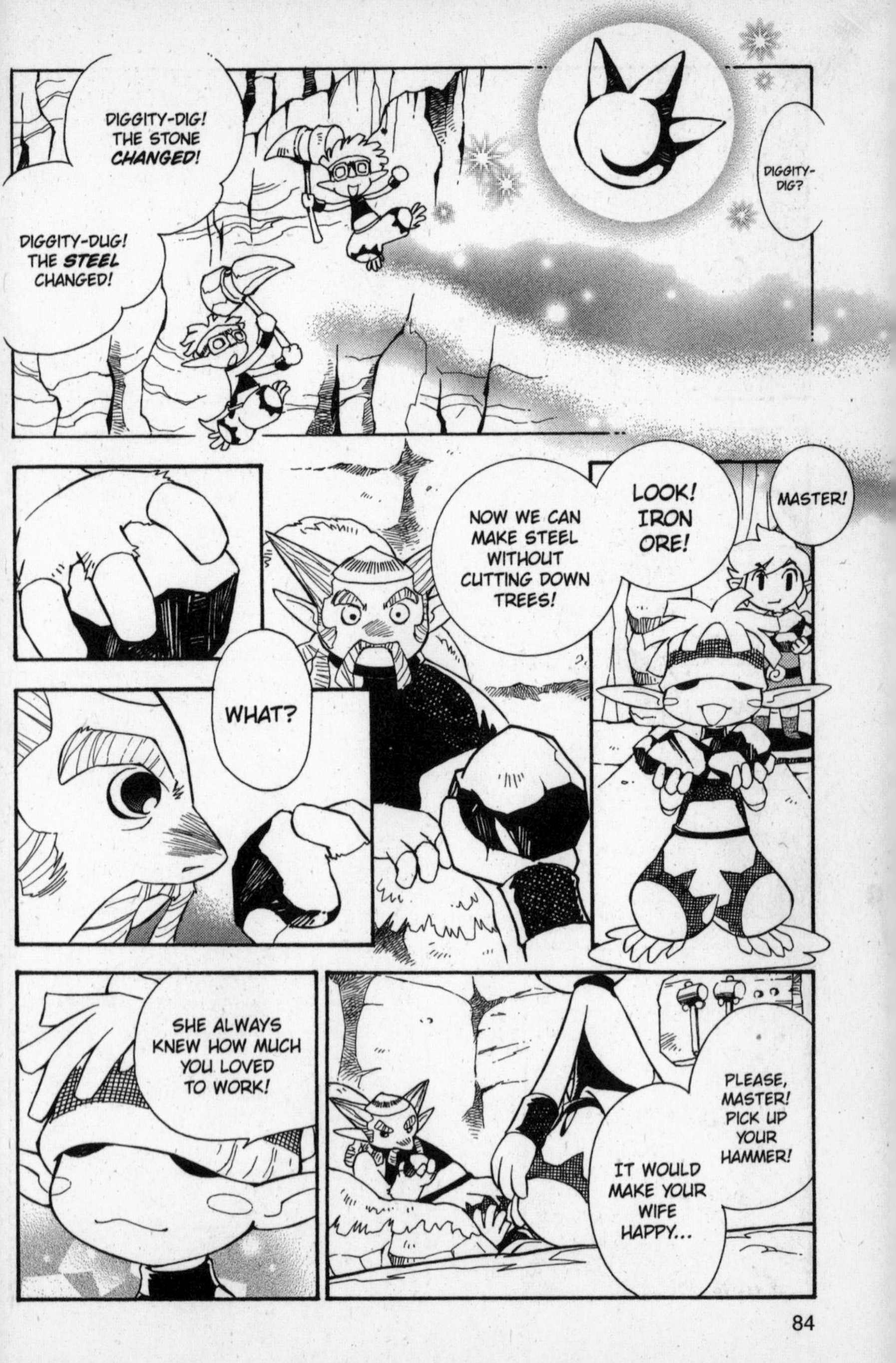
DIGGITY-DIG?
DIGGITY-DIG! THE STONE *CHANGED!*
DIGGITY-DUG! THE *STEEL* CHANGED!
MASTER!
LOOK! IRON ORE!
NOW WE CAN MAKE STEEL WITHOUT CUTTING DOWN TREES!
WHAT?
PLEASE, MASTER! PICK UP YOUR HAMMER!
IT WOULD MAKE YOUR WIFE HAPPY...
SHE ALWAYS KNEW HOW MUCH YOU LOVED TO WORK!

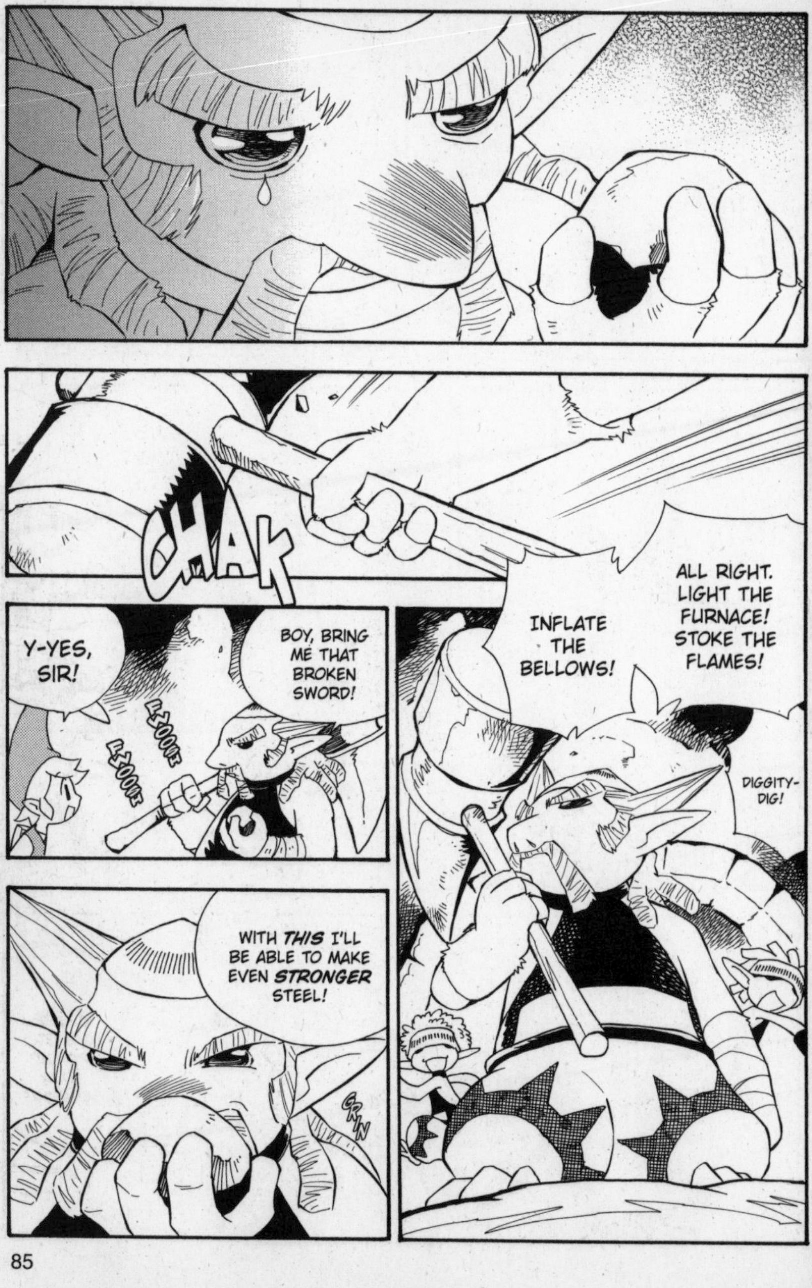
CHAK
ALL RIGHT. LIGHT THE FURNACE! STOKE THE FLAMES!
INFLATE THE BELLOWS!
DIGGITY-DIG!
BOY, BRING ME THAT BROKEN SWORD!
Y-YES, SIR!
WITH *THIS* I'LL BE ABLE TO MAKE EVEN ***STRONGER*** STEEL!
GRIN

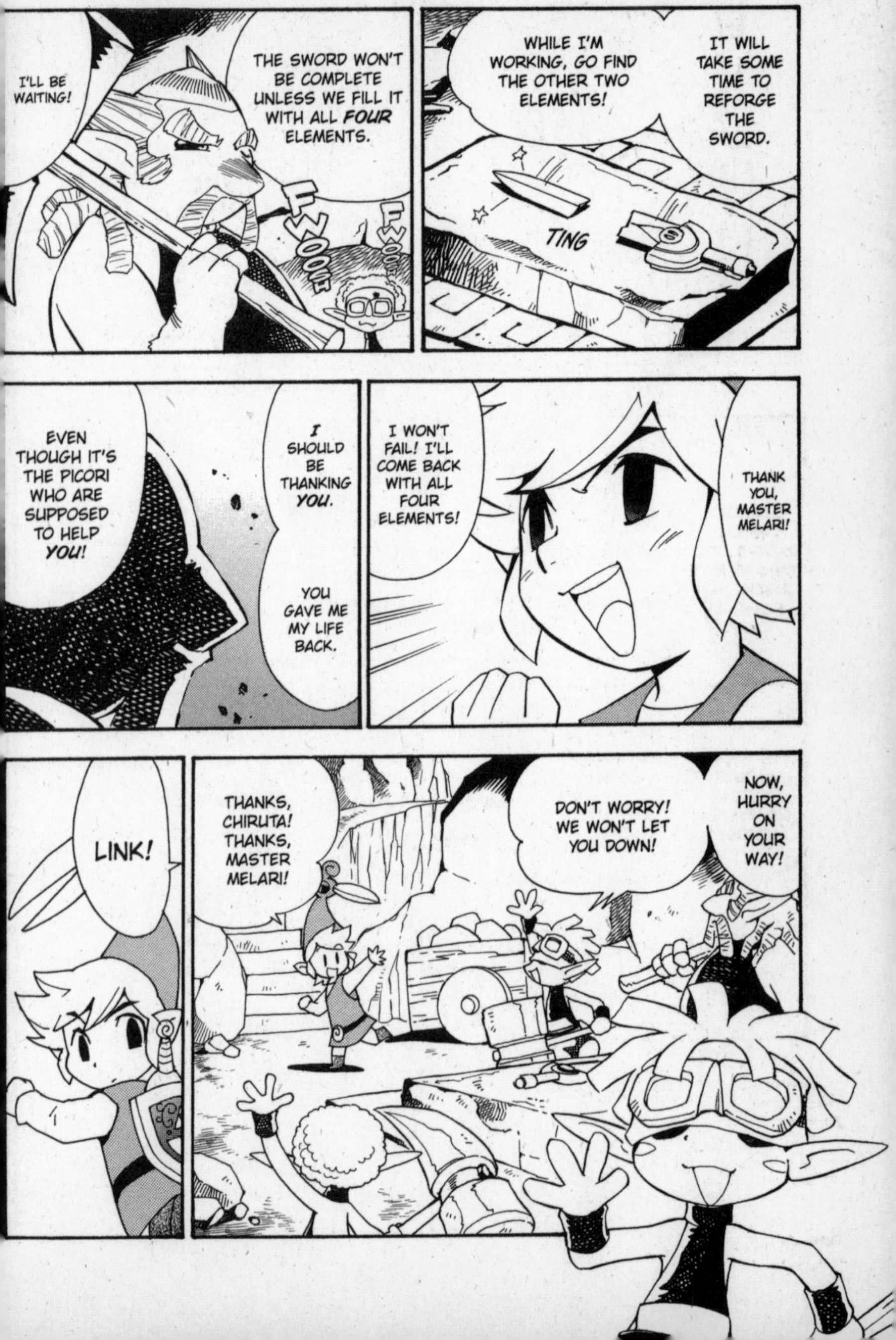
IT WILL TAKE SOME TIME TO REFORGE THE SWORD.
WHILE I'M WORKING, GO FIND THE OTHER TWO ELEMENTS!
TING
THE SWORD WON'T BE COMPLETE UNLESS WE FILL IT WITH ALL *FOUR* ELEMENTS.
I'LL BE WAITING!
THANK YOU, MASTER MELARI!
I WON'T FAIL! I'LL COME BACK WITH ALL FOUR ELEMENTS!
I SHOULD BE THANKING *YOU*.
YOU GAVE ME MY LIFE BACK.
EVEN THOUGH IT'S THE PICORI WHO ARE SUPPOSED TO HELP *YOU*!
NOW, HURRY ON YOUR WAY!
DON'T WORRY! WE WON'T LET YOU DOWN!
THANKS, CHIRUTA! THANKS, MASTER MELARI!
LINK!

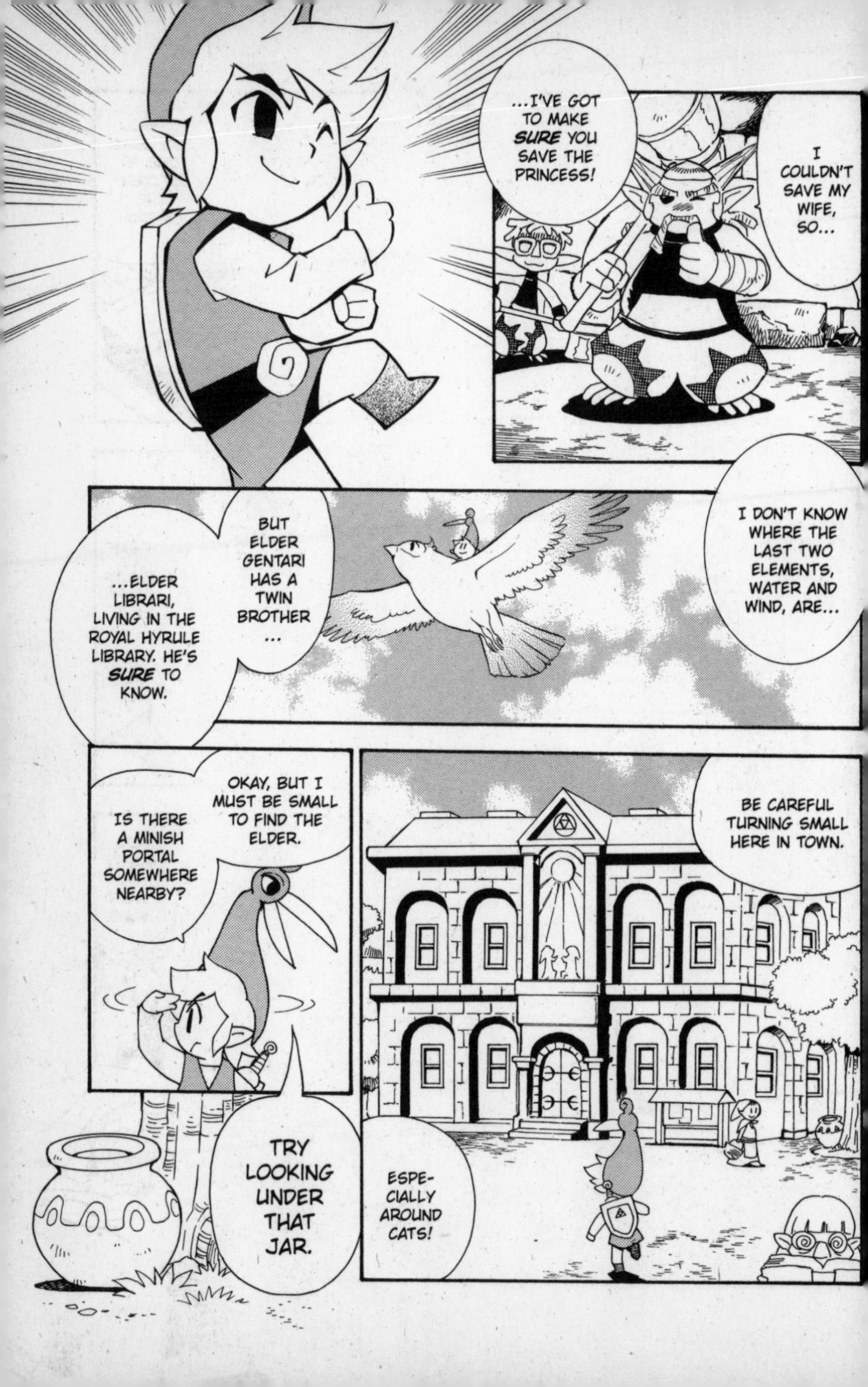
I COULDN'T SAVE MY WIFE, SO...
...I'VE GOT TO MAKE *SURE* YOU SAVE THE PRINCESS!
I DON'T KNOW WHERE THE LAST TWO ELEMENTS, WATER AND WIND, ARE...
BUT ELDER GENTARI HAS A TWIN BROTHER...
...ELDER LIBRARI, LIVING IN THE ROYAL HYRULE LIBRARY. HE'S *SURE* TO KNOW.
BE CAREFUL TURNING SMALL HERE IN TOWN.
ESPE-CIALLY AROUND CATS!
OKAY, BUT I MUST BE SMALL TO FIND THE ELDER.
IS THERE A MINISH PORTAL SOMEWHERE NEARBY?
TRY LOOKING UNDER THAT JAR.

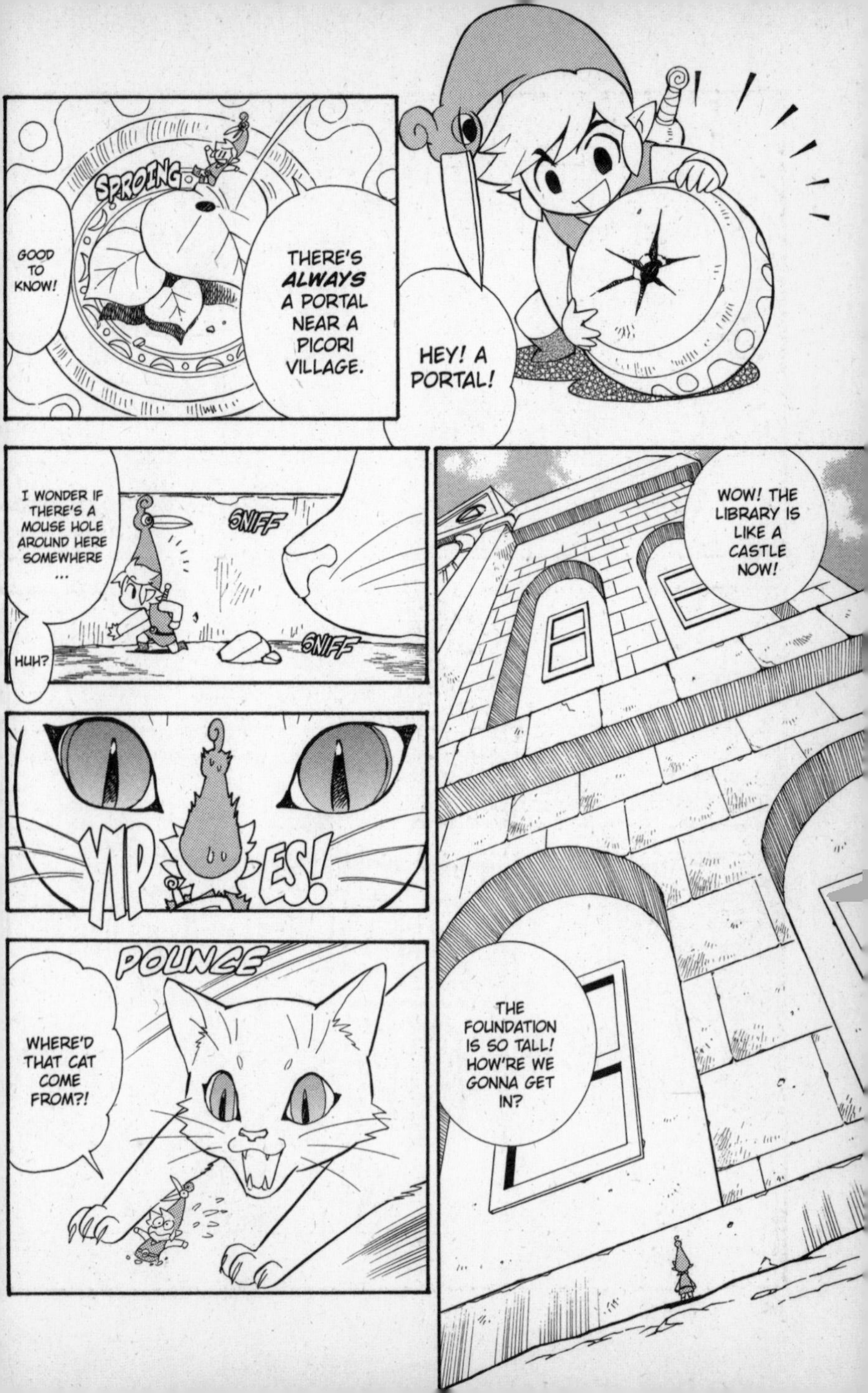
HEY! A PORTAL!
THERE'S **ALWAYS** A PORTAL NEAR A PICORI VILLAGE.
SPROING
GOOD TO KNOW!
WOW! THE LIBRARY IS LIKE A CASTLE NOW!
THE FOUNDATION IS SO TALL! HOW'RE WE GONNA GET IN?
SNIFF
I WONDER IF THERE'S A MOUSE HOLE AROUND HERE SOMEWHERE ...
SNIFF
HUH?
YIPES!
POUNCE
WHERE'D THAT CAT COME FROM?!

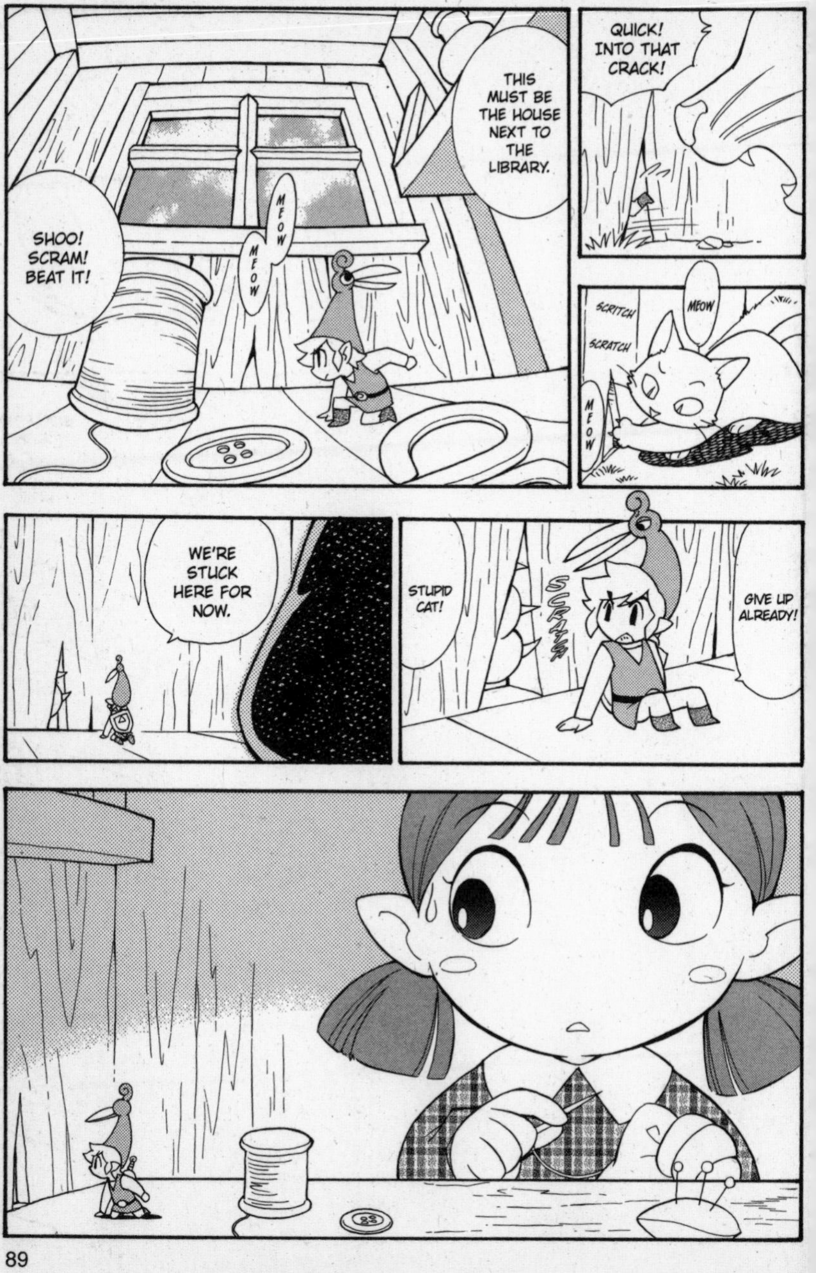
QUICK! INTO THAT CRACK!
MEOW
SCRITCH
SCRATCH
MEOW
THIS MUST BE THE HOUSE NEXT TO THE LIBRARY.
MEOW
MEOW
SHOO! SCRAM! BEAT IT!
GIVE UP ALREADY!
STUPID CAT!
WE'RE STUCK HERE FOR NOW.

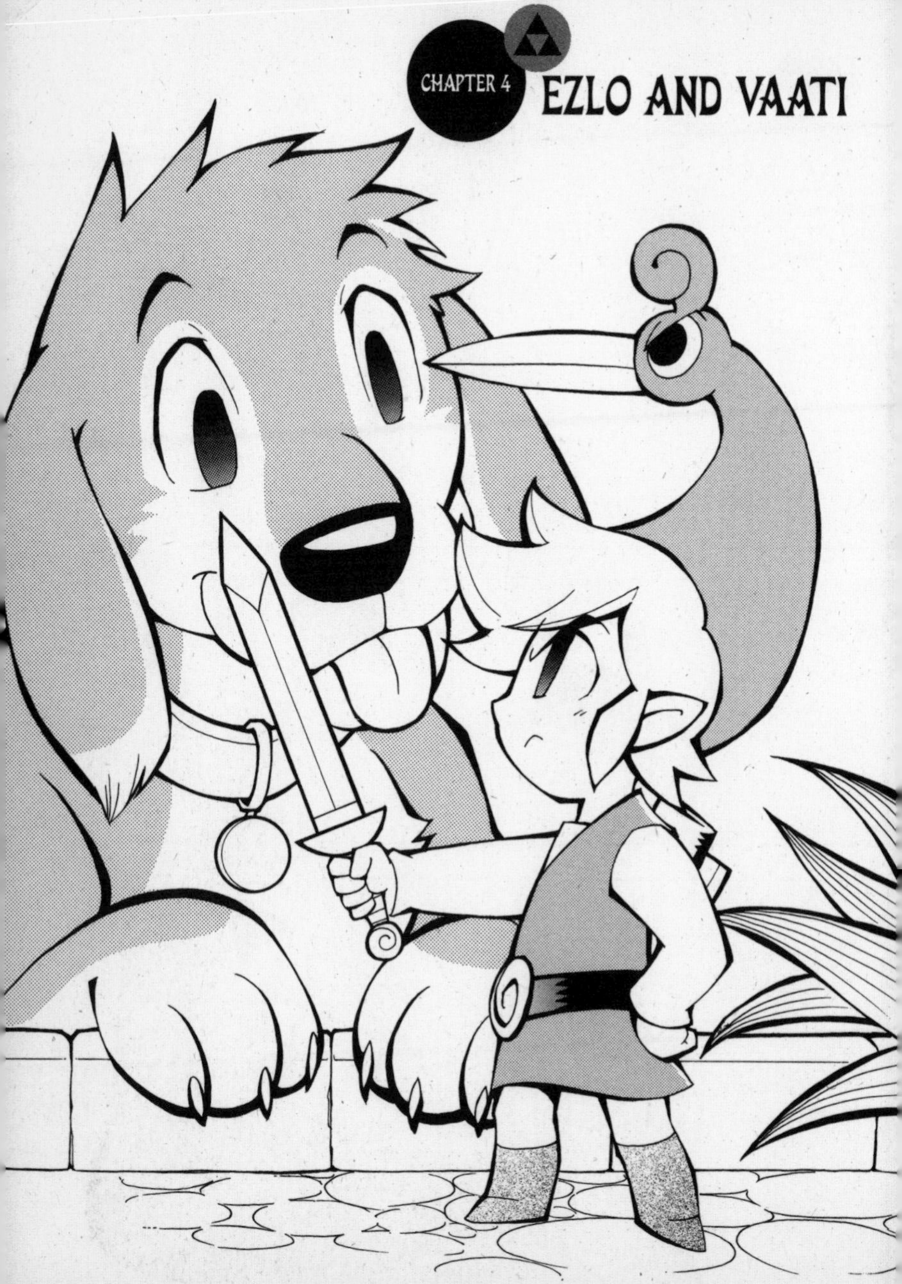
CHAPTER 4
EZLO AND VAATI

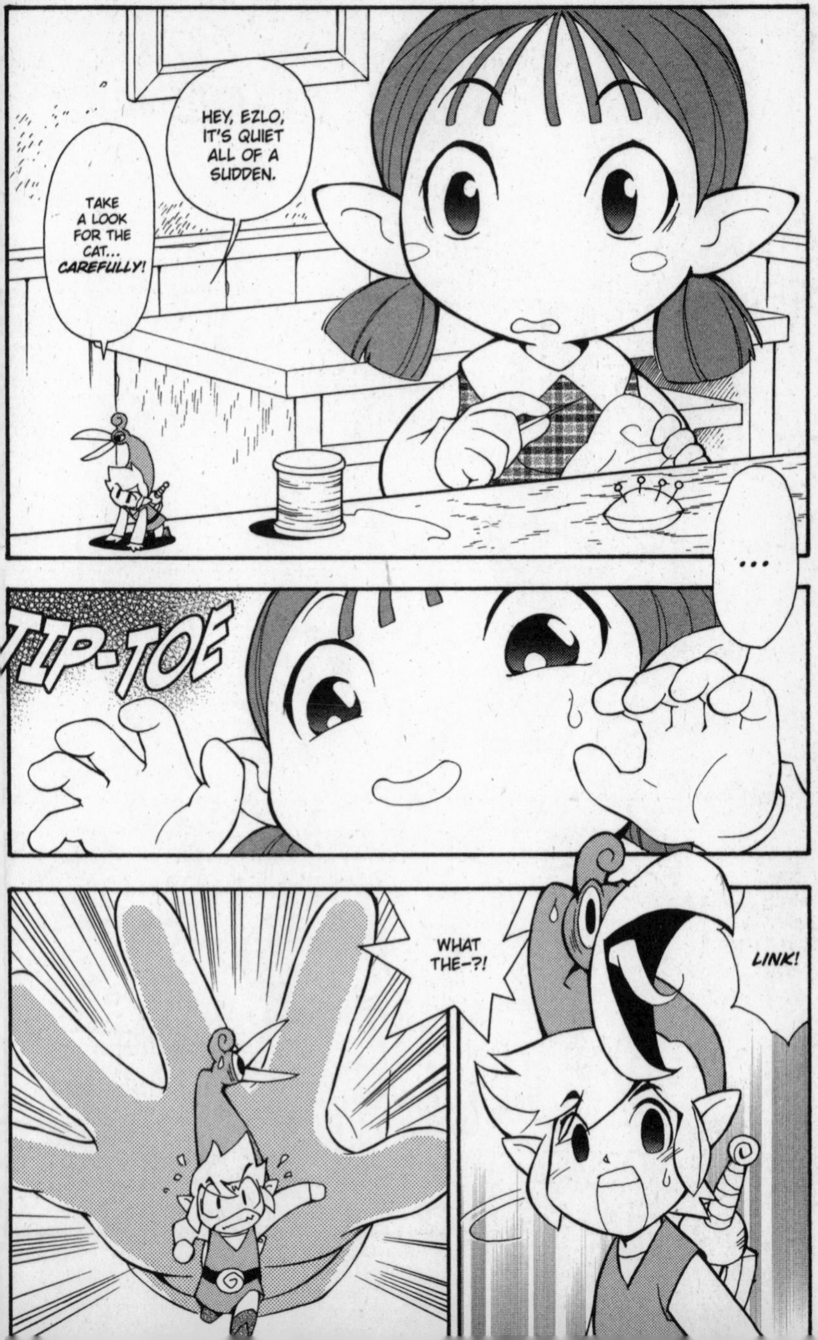
HEY, EZLO, IT'S QUIET ALL OF A SUDDEN.
TAKE A LOOK FOR THE CAT... *CAREFULLY!*
...
TIP-TOE
LINK!
WHAT THE-?!

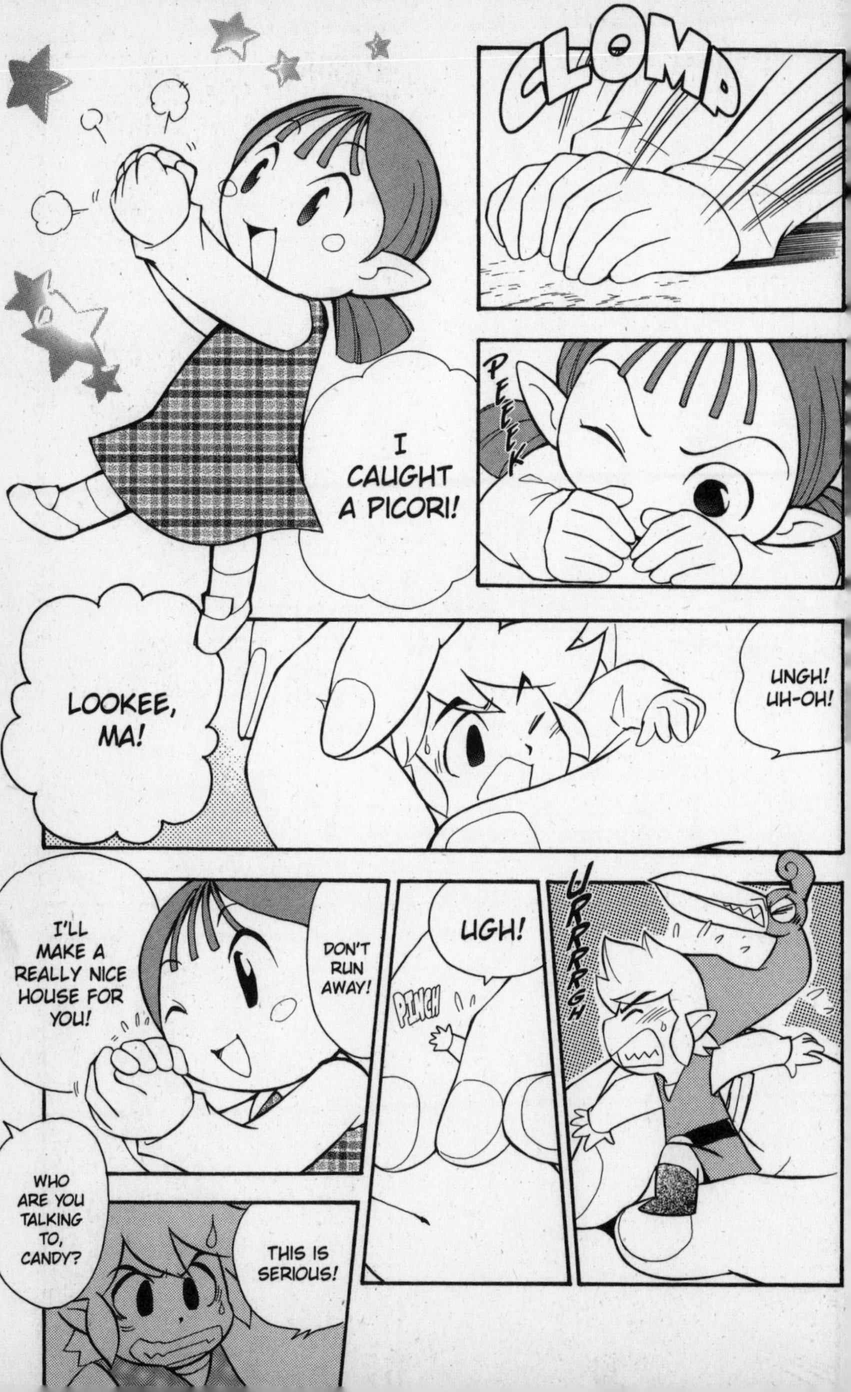
CLOMP
PEEEK
I CAUGHT A PICORI!
LOOKEE, MA!
UNGH! UH-OH!
URRRGH
UGH!
PINCH
DON'T RUN AWAY!
I'LL MAKE A REALLY NICE HOUSE FOR YOU!
WHO ARE YOU TALKING TO, CANDY?
THIS IS SERIOUS!

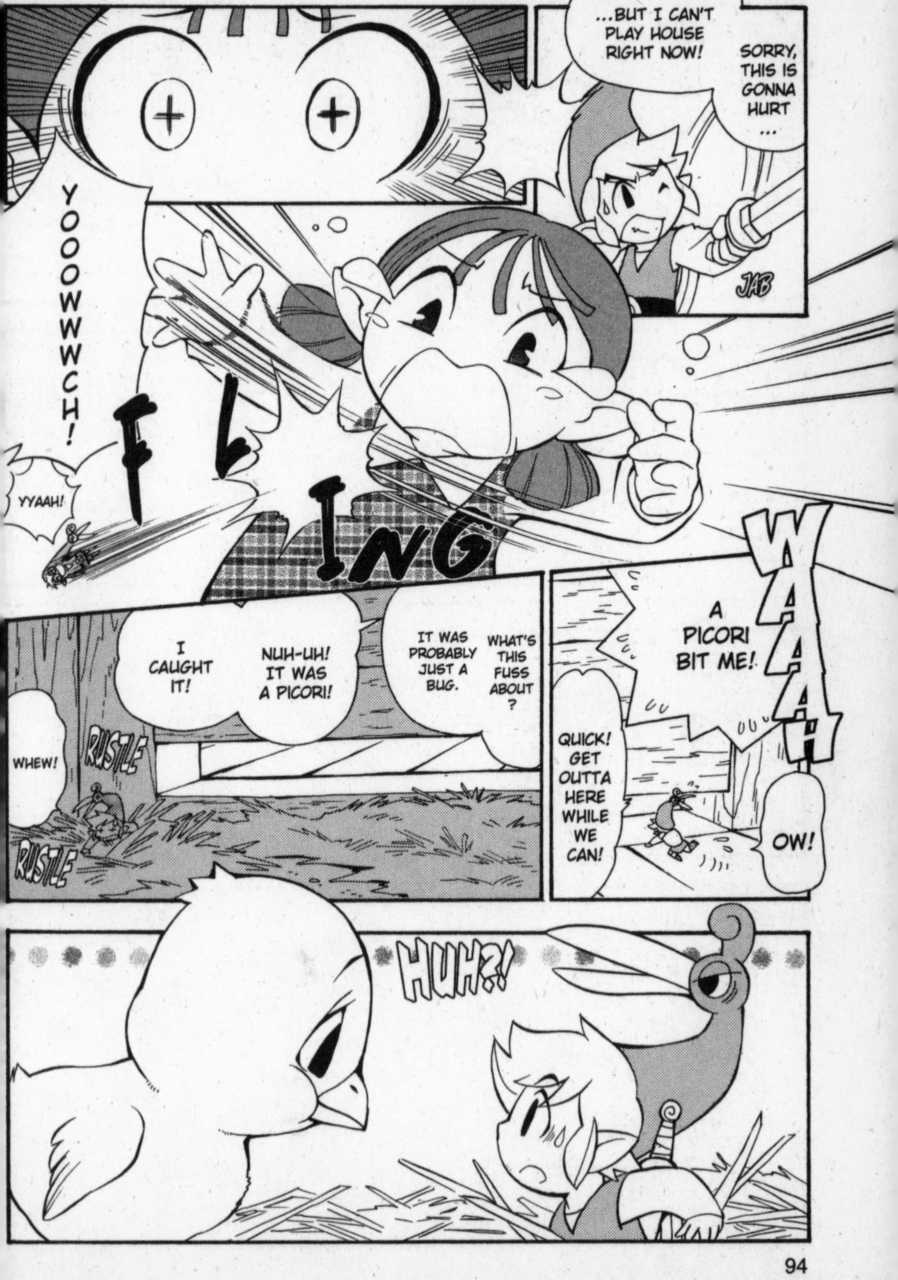
...BUT I CAN'T PLAY HOUSE RIGHT NOW!
SORRY, THIS IS GONNA HURT ...
JAB
YOOOOWWWWCH!
FLING
YYAAH!
WAAAAH
A PICORI BIT ME!
OW!
QUICK! GET OUTTA HERE WHILE WE CAN!
WHAT'S THIS FUSS ABOUT?
IT WAS PROBABLY JUST A BUG.
NUH-UH! IT WAS A PICORI!
I CAUGHT IT!
RUSTLE
WHEW!
RUSTLE
HUH?!

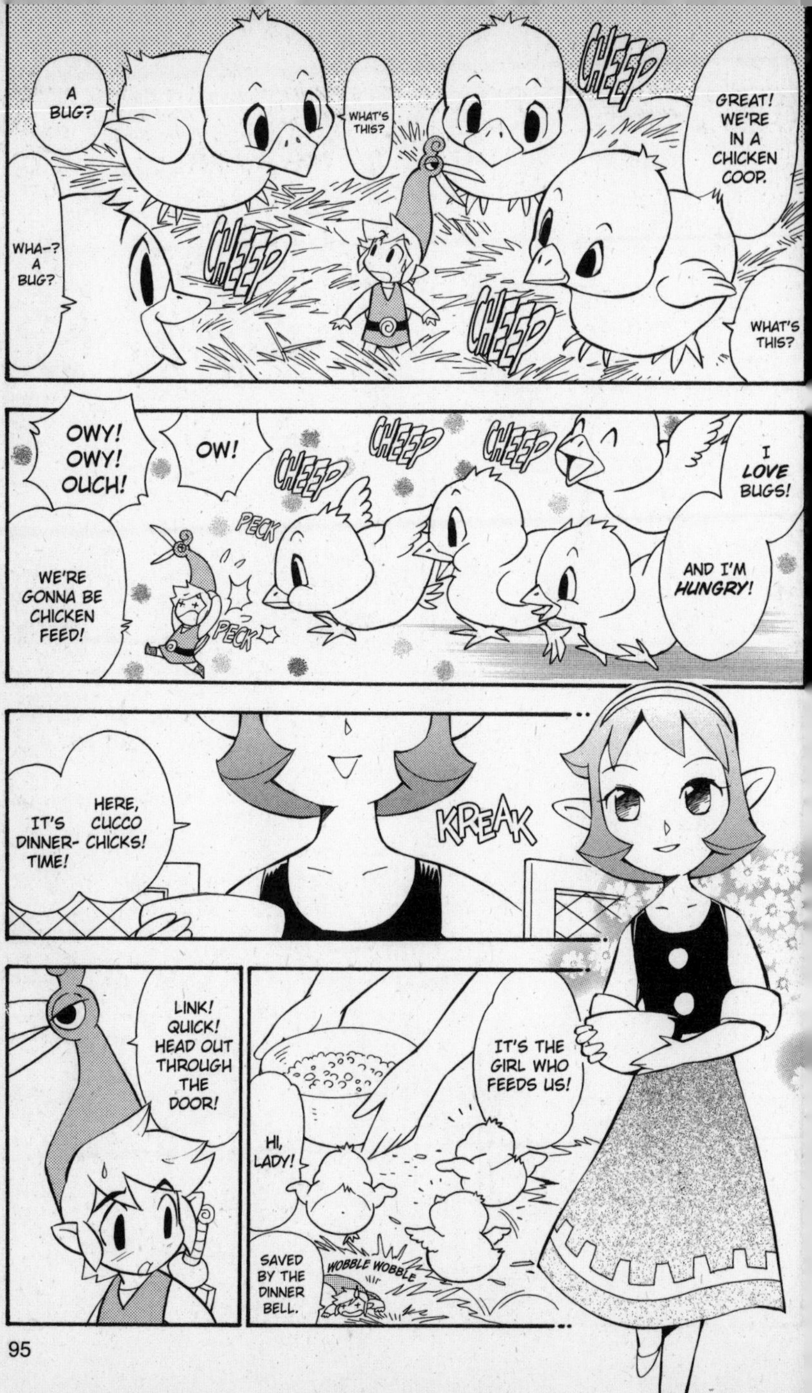
CHEEP
GREAT! WE'RE IN A CHICKEN COOP.
WHAT'S THIS?
WHAT'S THIS?
A BUG?
CHEEP
CHEEP
WHA-? A BUG?
I LOVE BUGS!
AND I'M HUNGRY!
CHEEP
CHEEP
CHEEP
OW!
OWY! OWY! OUCH!
PECK
PECK
WE'RE GONNA BE CHICKEN FEED!
KREAK
HERE, CUCCO CHICKS!
IT'S DINNER-TIME!
IT'S THE GIRL WHO FEEDS US!
HI, LADY!
WOBBLE WOBBLE
SAVED BY THE DINNER BELL.
LINK! QUICK! HEAD OUT THROUGH THE DOOR!

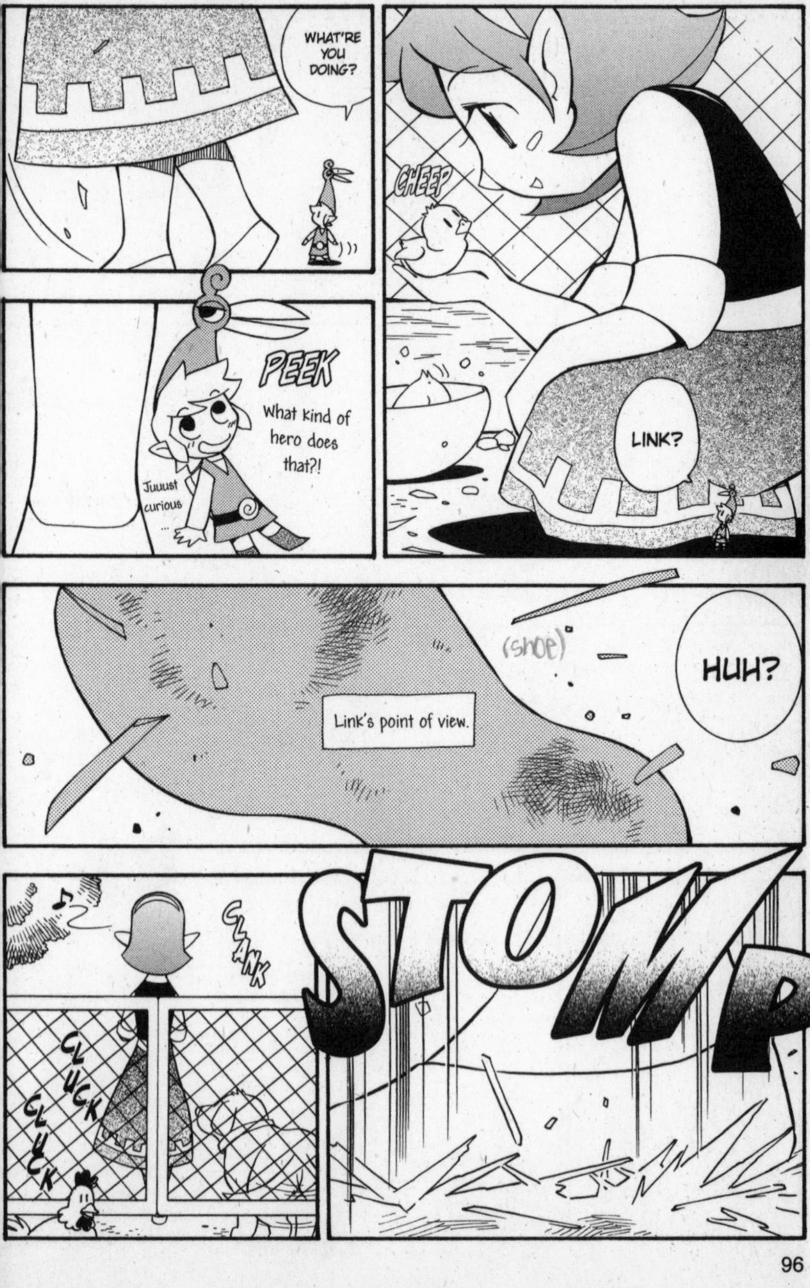
CHEEP
LINK?
WHAT'RE YOU DOING?
PEEK
What kind of hero does that?!
Juuust curious ...
HUH?
(shoe)
Link's point of view.
STOMP
CLANK
CLUCK
CLUCK
CLUCK

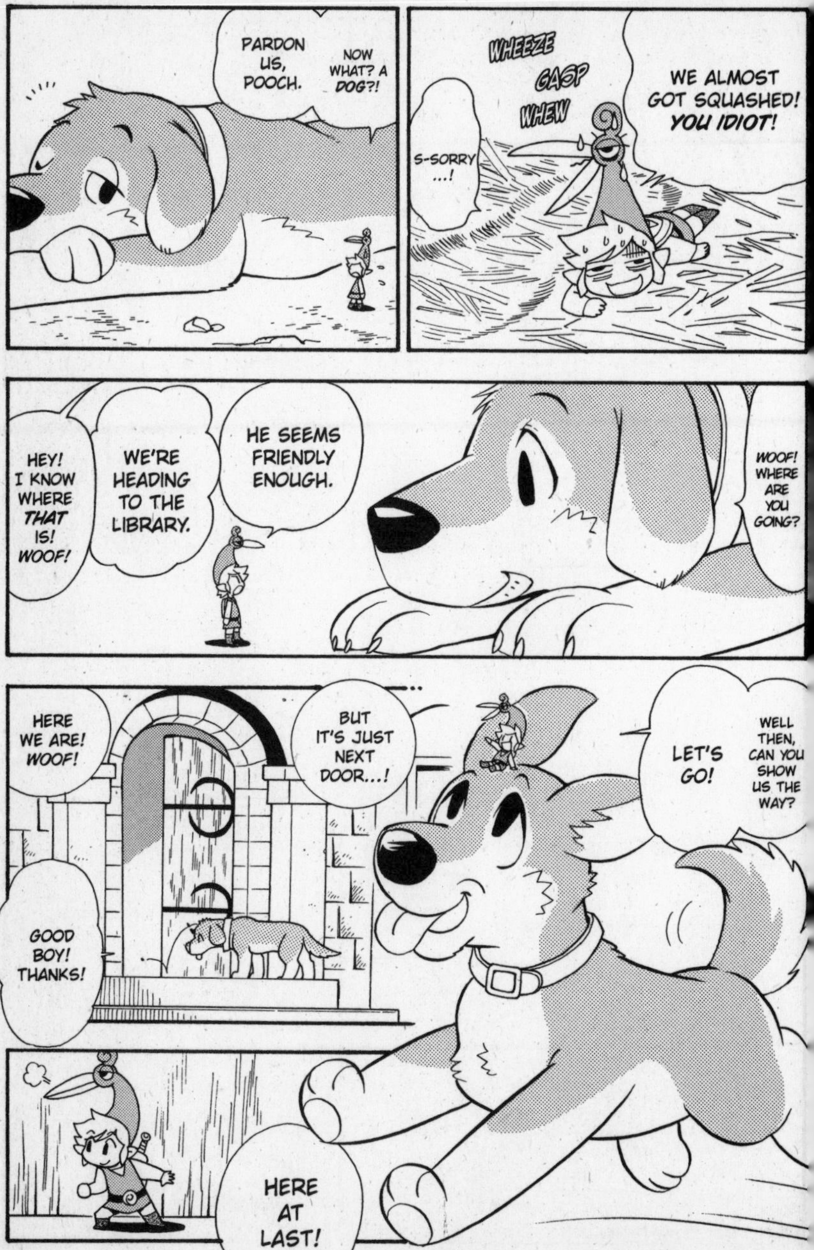
WE ALMOST GOT SQUASHED! *YOU IDIOT!*
WHEEZE
GASP
WHEW
S-SORRY ...!
NOW WHAT? A *DOG?!*
PARDON US, POOCH.
WOOF! WHERE ARE YOU GOING?
HE SEEMS FRIENDLY ENOUGH.
WE'RE HEADING TO THE LIBRARY.
HEY! I KNOW WHERE *THAT* IS! *WOOF!*
WELL THEN, CAN YOU SHOW US THE WAY?
LET'S GO!
BUT IT'S JUST NEXT DOOR...!
HERE WE ARE! *WOOF!*
GOOD BOY! THANKS!
HERE AT LAST!

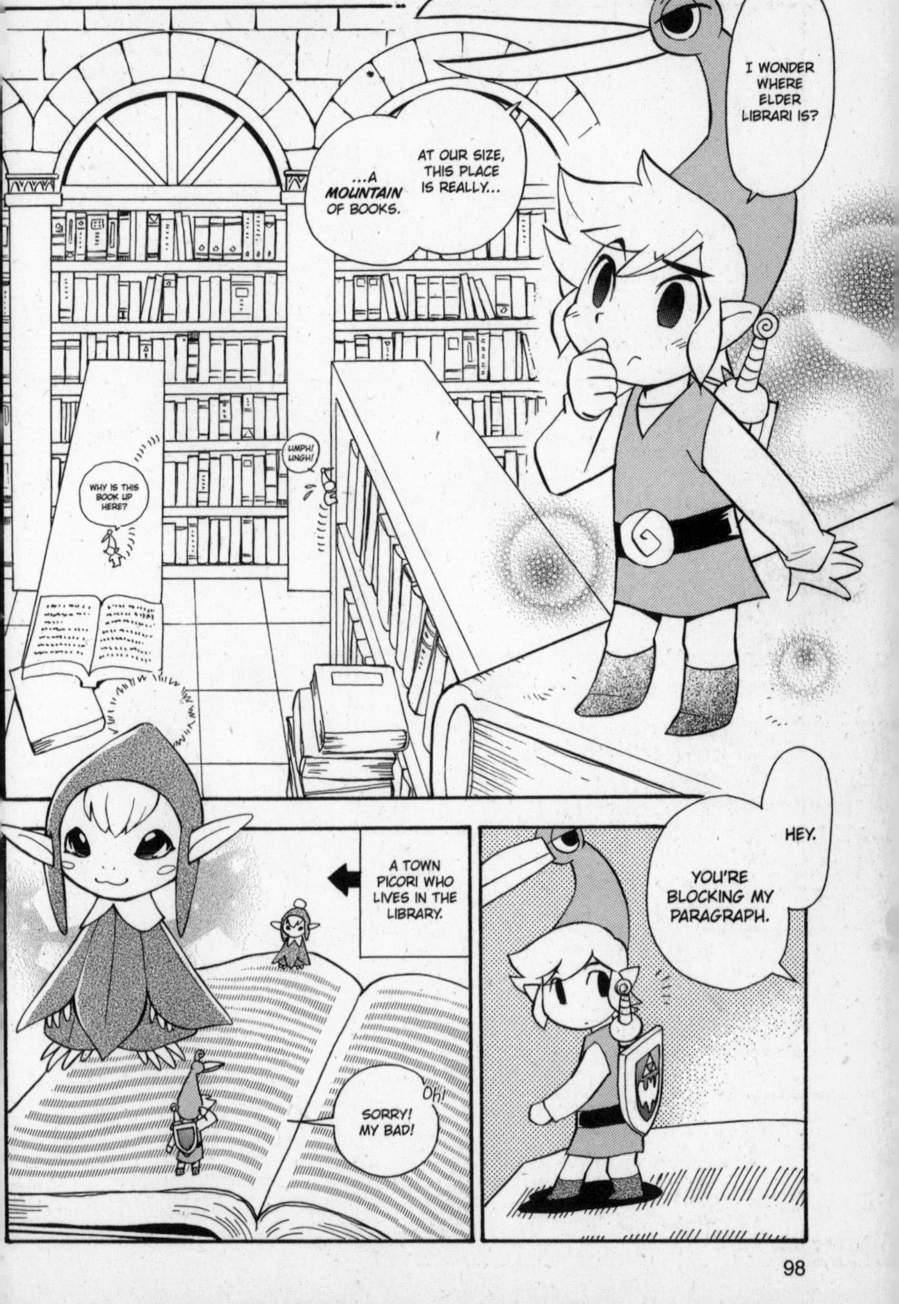
I WONDER WHERE ELDER LIBRARI IS?
AT OUR SIZE, THIS PLACE IS REALLY...
...A *MOUNTAIN* OF BOOKS.
UMPH! UNGH!
WHY IS THIS BOOK UP HERE?
HEY.
YOU'RE BLOCKING MY PARAGRAPH.
A TOWN PICORI WHO LIVES IN THE LIBRARY.
Oh!
SORRY! MY BAD!

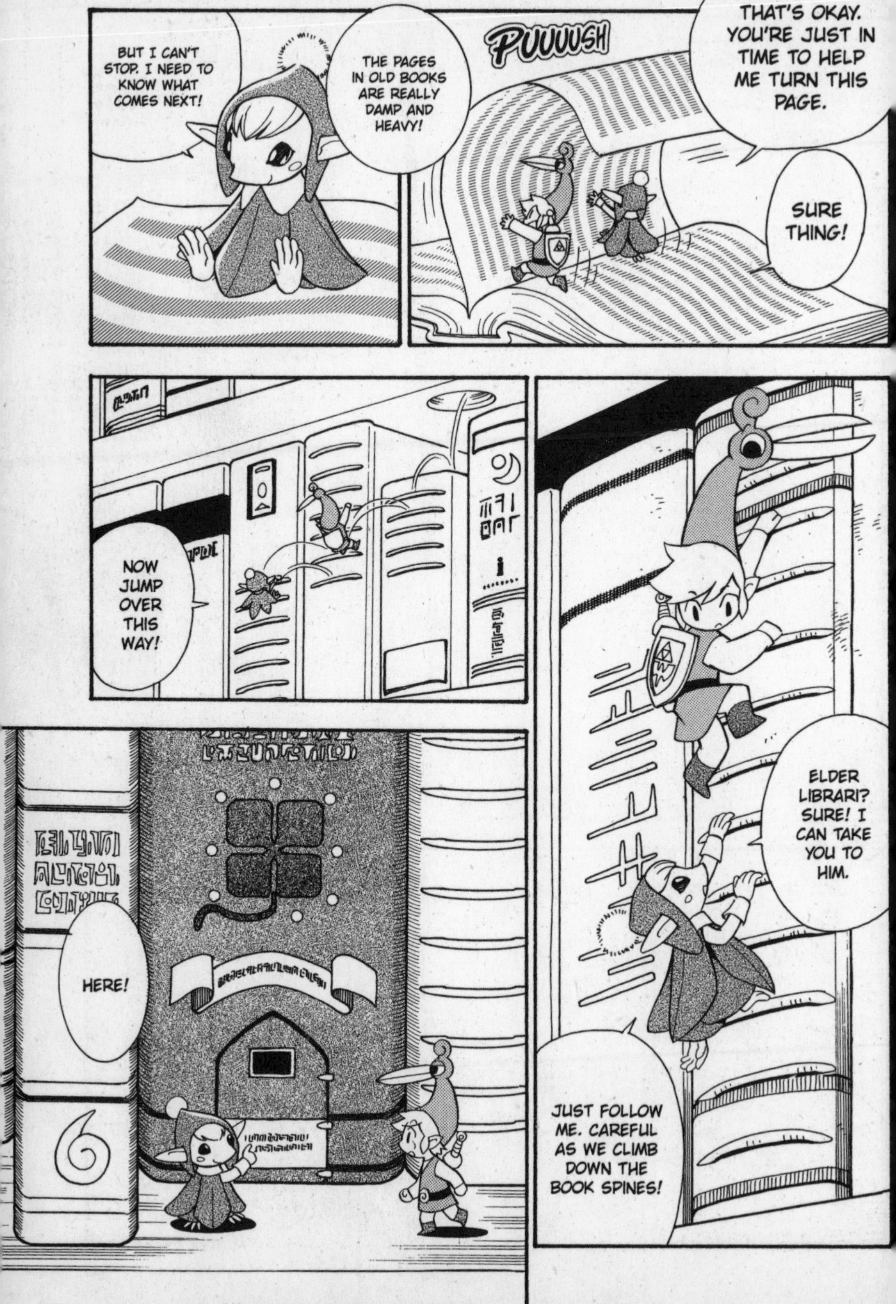
THAT'S OKAY. YOU'RE JUST IN TIME TO HELP ME TURN THIS PAGE.
PUUUUSH
SURE THING!
THE PAGES IN OLD BOOKS ARE REALLY DAMP AND HEAVY!
BUT I CAN'T STOP. I NEED TO KNOW WHAT COMES NEXT!
ELDER LIBRARI? SURE! I CAN TAKE YOU TO HIM.
JUST FOLLOW ME. CAREFUL AS WE CLIMB DOWN THE BOOK SPINES!
NOW JUMP OVER THIS WAY!
HERE!

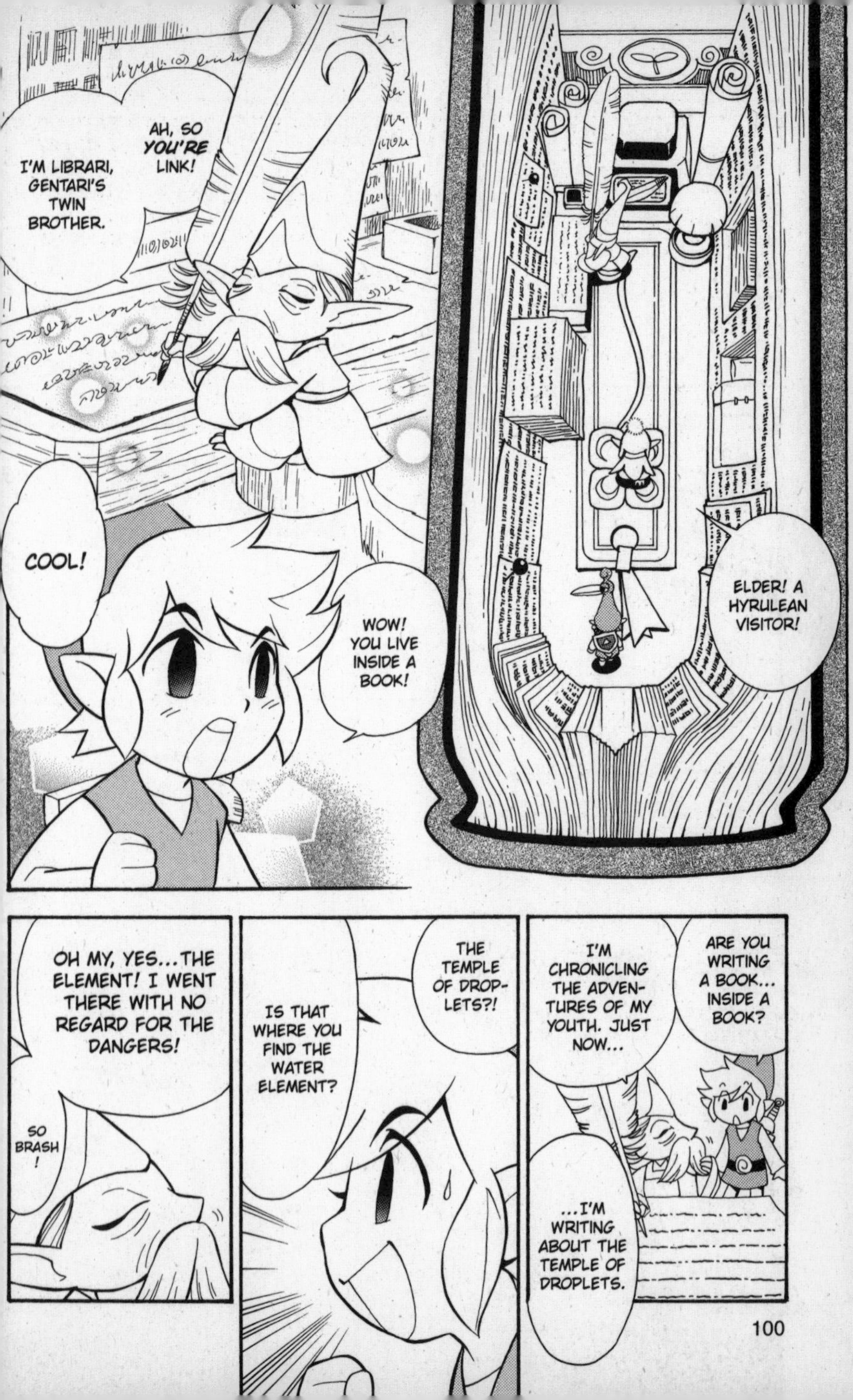
ELDER! A HYRULEAN VISITOR!
AH, SO *YOU'RE* LINK!
I'M LIBRARI, GENTARI'S TWIN BROTHER.
WOW! YOU LIVE INSIDE A BOOK!
COOL!
ARE YOU WRITING A BOOK... INSIDE A BOOK?
I'M CHRONICLING THE ADVENTURES OF MY YOUTH. JUST NOW...
...I'M WRITING ABOUT THE TEMPLE OF DROPLETS.
THE TEMPLE OF DROPLETS?!
IS THAT WHERE YOU FIND THE WATER ELEMENT?
OH MY, YES...THE ELEMENT! I WENT THERE WITH NO REGARD FOR THE DANGERS!
SO BRASH!

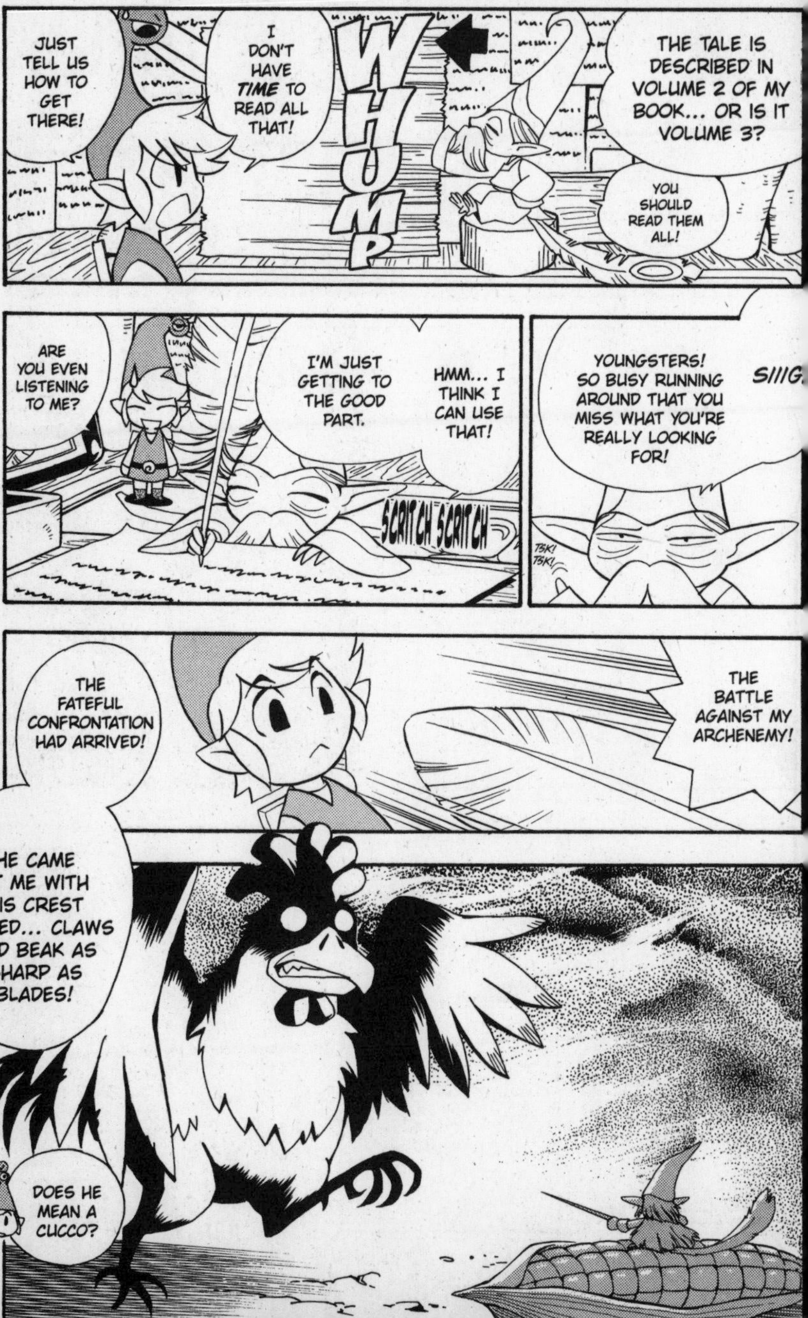
THE TALE IS DESCRIBED IN VOLUME 2 OF MY BOOK... OR IS IT VOLUME 3?
YOU SHOULD READ THEM ALL!
WHUMP
I DON'T HAVE *TIME* TO READ ALL THAT!
JUST TELL US HOW TO GET THERE!
YOUNGSTERS! SO BUSY RUNNING AROUND THAT YOU MISS WHAT YOU'RE REALLY LOOKING FOR!
SIIIG.
TSK! TSK!
HMM... I THINK I CAN USE THAT!
I'M JUST GETTING TO THE GOOD PART.
SCRITCH SCRITCH
ARE YOU EVEN LISTENING TO ME?
THE BATTLE AGAINST MY ARCHENEMY!
THE FATEFUL CONFRONTATION HAD ARRIVED!
HE CAME AT ME WITH HIS CREST RAISED... CLAWS AND BEAK AS SHARP AS BLADES!
DOES HE MEAN A CUCCO?

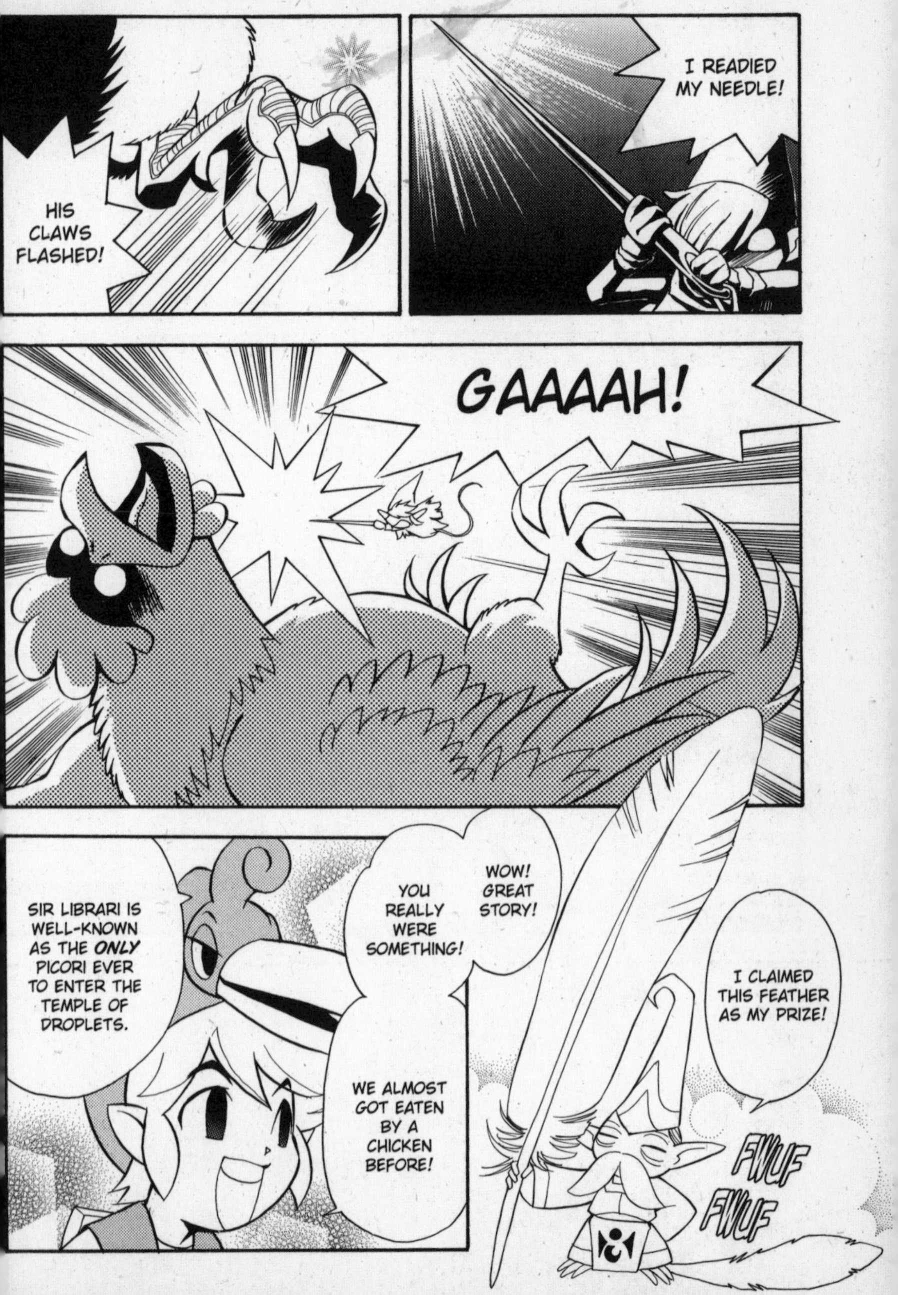
I READIED MY NEEDLE!
HIS CLAWS FLASHED!
GAAAAH!
I CLAIMED THIS FEATHER AS MY PRIZE!
FWUF FWUF
WOW! GREAT STORY!
YOU REALLY WERE SOMETHING!
SIR LIBRARI IS WELL-KNOWN AS THE *ONLY* PICORI EVER TO ENTER THE TEMPLE OF DROPLETS.
WE ALMOST GOT EATEN BY A CHICKEN BEFORE!

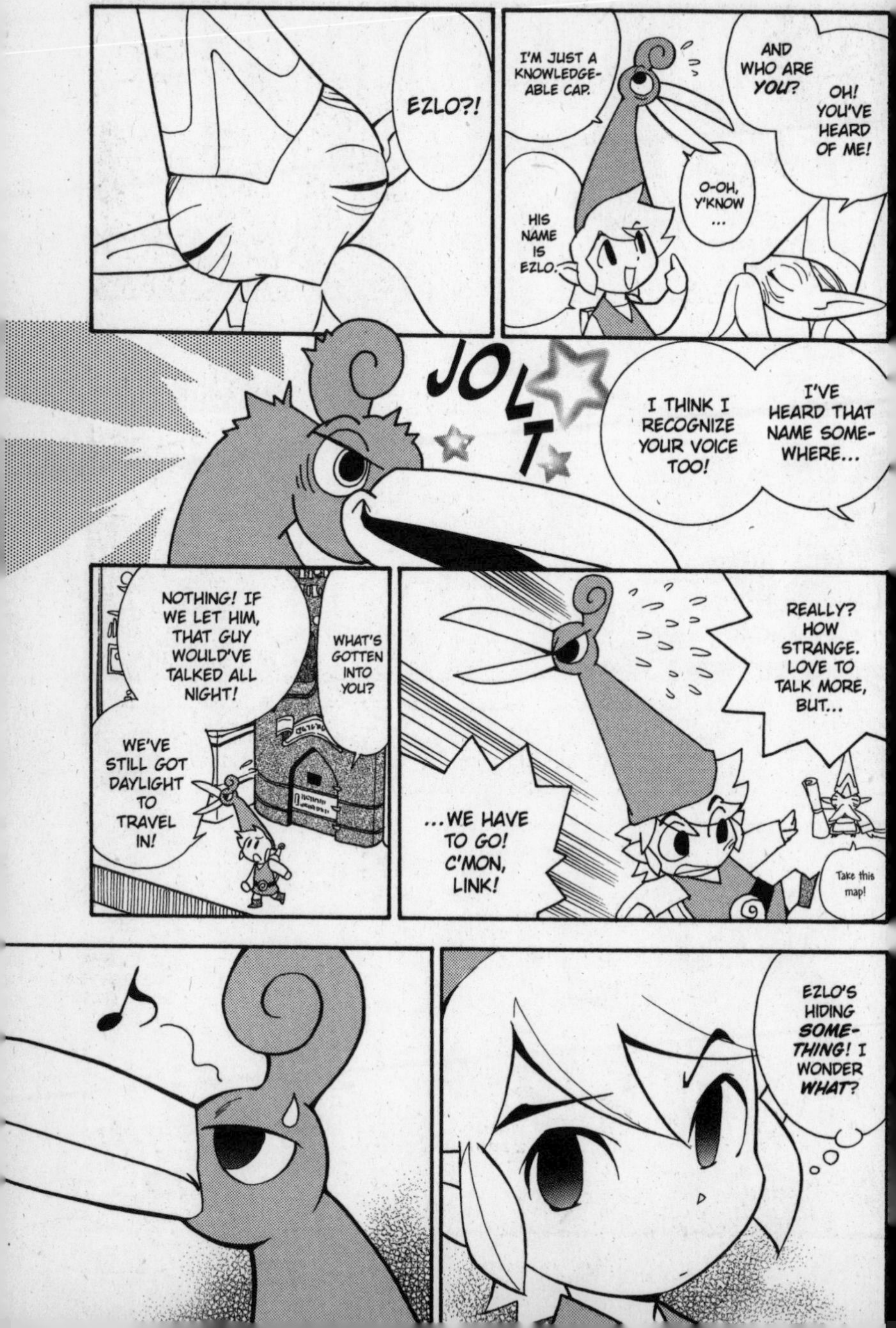
AND WHO ARE YOU?
OH! YOU'VE HEARD OF ME!
I'M JUST A KNOWLEDGE-ABLE CAP.
O-OH, Y'KNOW ...
HIS NAME IS EZLO.
EZLO?!
I'VE HEARD THAT NAME SOME-WHERE...
I THINK I RECOGNIZE YOUR VOICE TOO!
JOLT
REALLY? HOW STRANGE. LOVE TO TALK MORE, BUT...
Take this map!
...WE HAVE TO GO! C'MON, LINK!
WHAT'S GOTTEN INTO YOU?
NOTHING! IF WE LET HIM, THAT GUY WOULD'VE TALKED ALL NIGHT!
WE'VE STILL GOT DAYLIGHT TO TRAVEL IN!
EZLO'S HIDING SOME-THING! I WONDER WHAT?

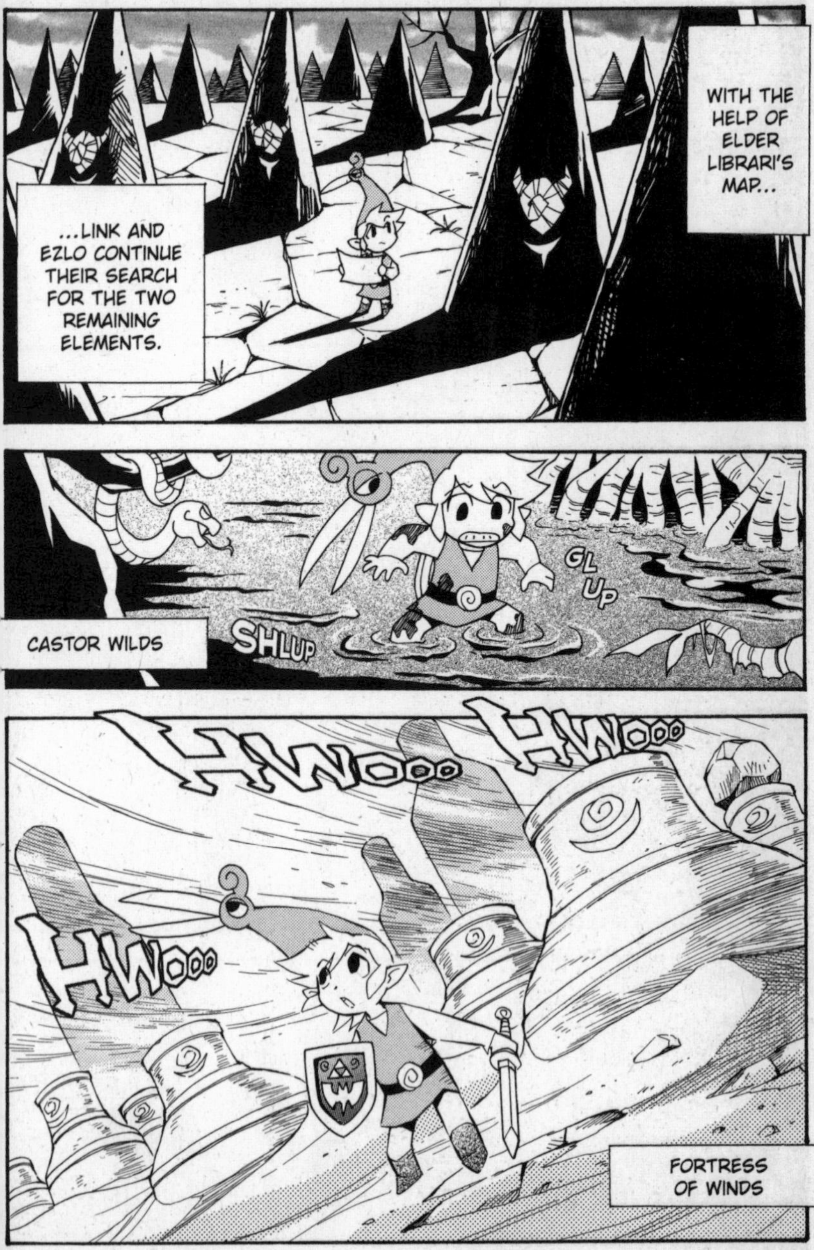
WITH THE HELP OF ELDER LIBRARI'S MAP...
...LINK AND EZLO CONTINUE THEIR SEARCH FOR THE TWO REMAINING ELEMENTS.
GLUP
SHLUP
CASTOR WILDS
HWOOO
HWOOO
HWOOO
FORTRESS OF WINDS

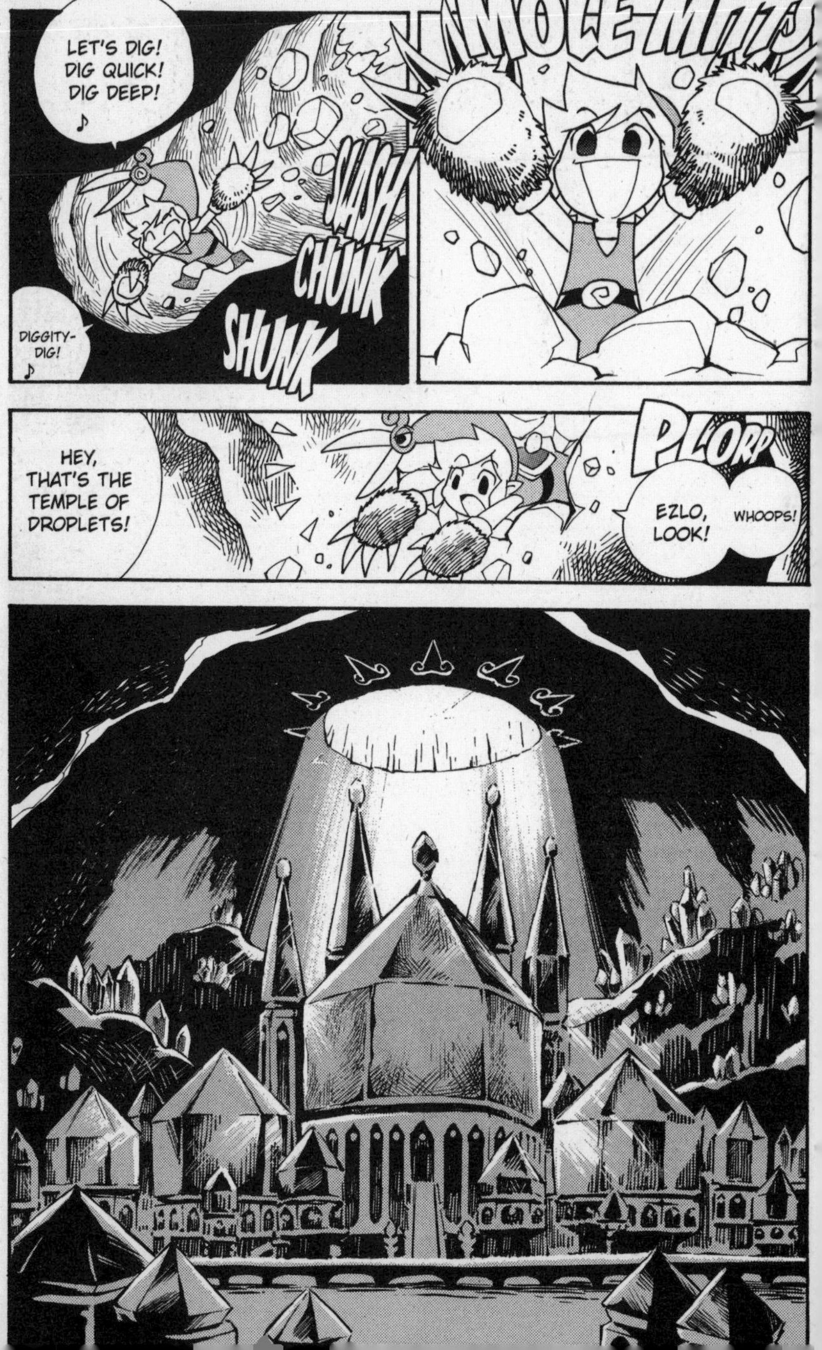
MOLE MITTS
LET'S DIG! DIG QUICK! DIG DEEP! ♪
SLASH
CHUNK
SHUNK
DIGGITY-DIG! ♪
PLORP
WHOOPS!
EZLO, LOOK!
HEY, THAT'S THE TEMPLE OF DROPLETS!

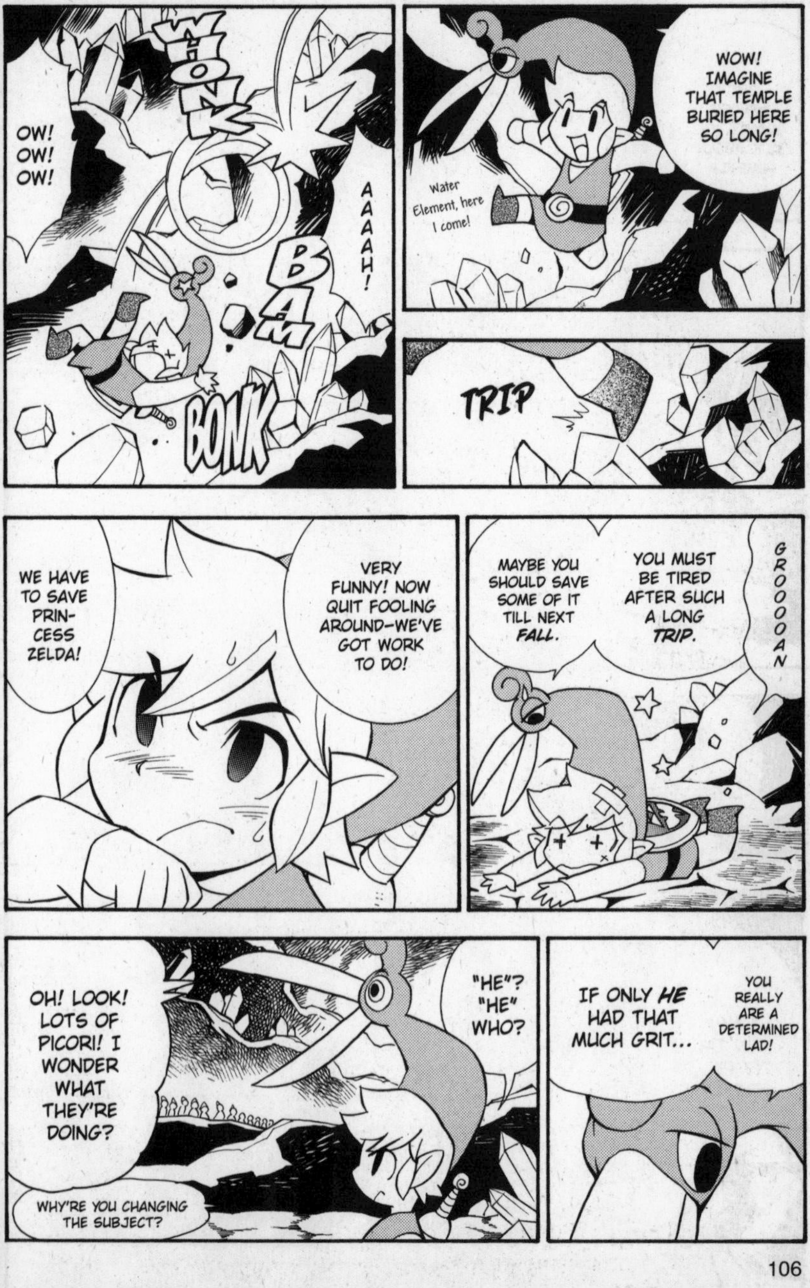
WOW! IMAGINE THAT TEMPLE BURIED HERE SO LONG!
Water Element, here I come!
TRIP
WHONK
AAAAAH!
OW! OW! OW!
BAM
BONK
GROOOOAN
YOU MUST BE TIRED AFTER SUCH A LONG ***TRIP***.
MAYBE YOU SHOULD SAVE SOME OF IT TILL NEXT ***FALL***.
VERY FUNNY! NOW QUIT FOOLING AROUND—WE'VE GOT WORK TO DO!
WE HAVE TO SAVE PRIN-CESS ZELDA!
YOU REALLY ARE A DETERMINED LAD!
IF ONLY ***HE*** HAD THAT MUCH GRIT...
"HE"? "HE" WHO?
OH! LOOK! LOTS OF PICORI! I WONDER WHAT THEY'RE DOING?
WHY'RE YOU CHANGING THE SUBJECT?

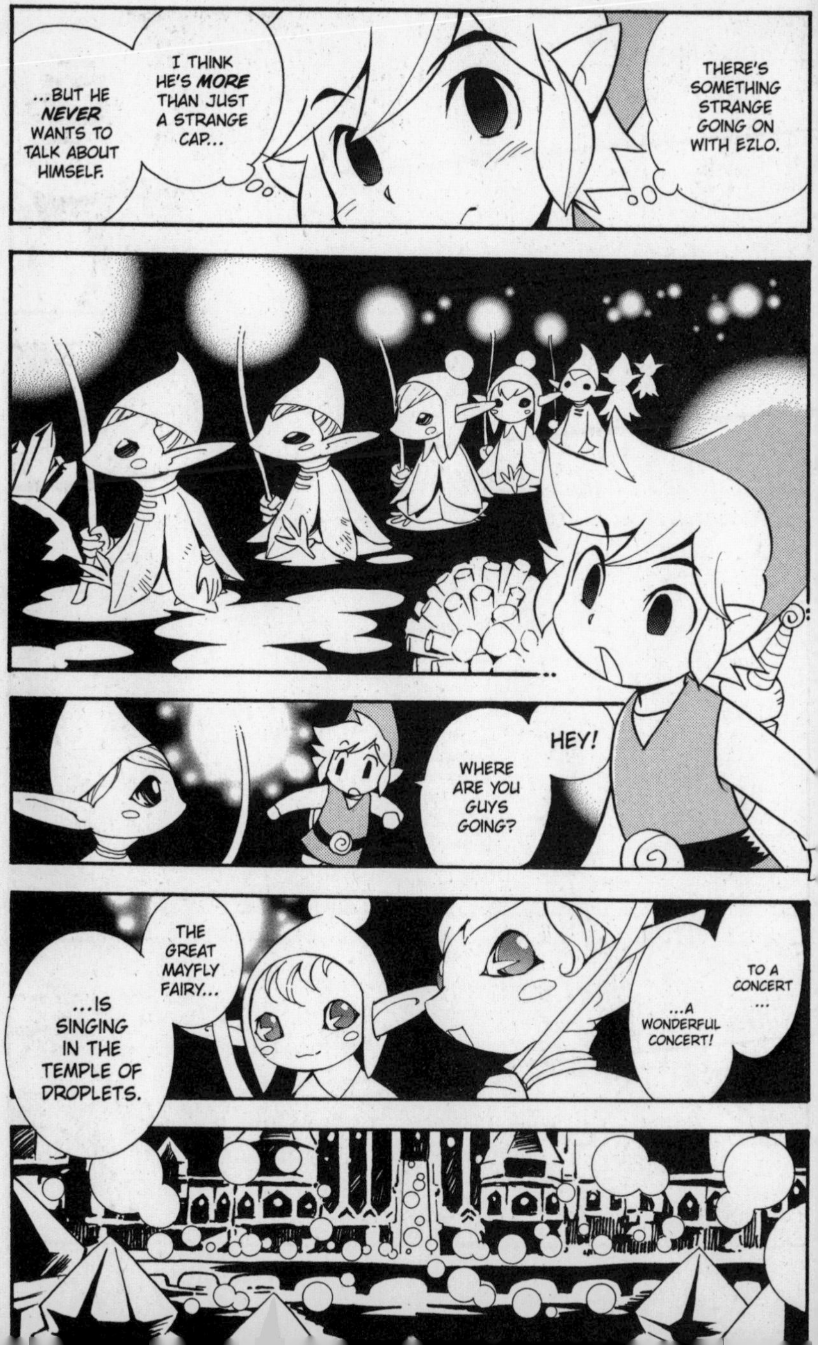
THERE'S SOMETHING STRANGE GOING ON WITH EZLO.
I THINK HE'S **MORE** THAN JUST A STRANGE CAP...
...BUT HE **NEVER** WANTS TO TALK ABOUT HIMSELF.
HEY!
WHERE ARE YOU GUYS GOING?
TO A CONCERT ...
...A WONDERFUL CONCERT!
THE GREAT MAYFLY FAIRY...
...IS SINGING IN THE TEMPLE OF DROPLETS.

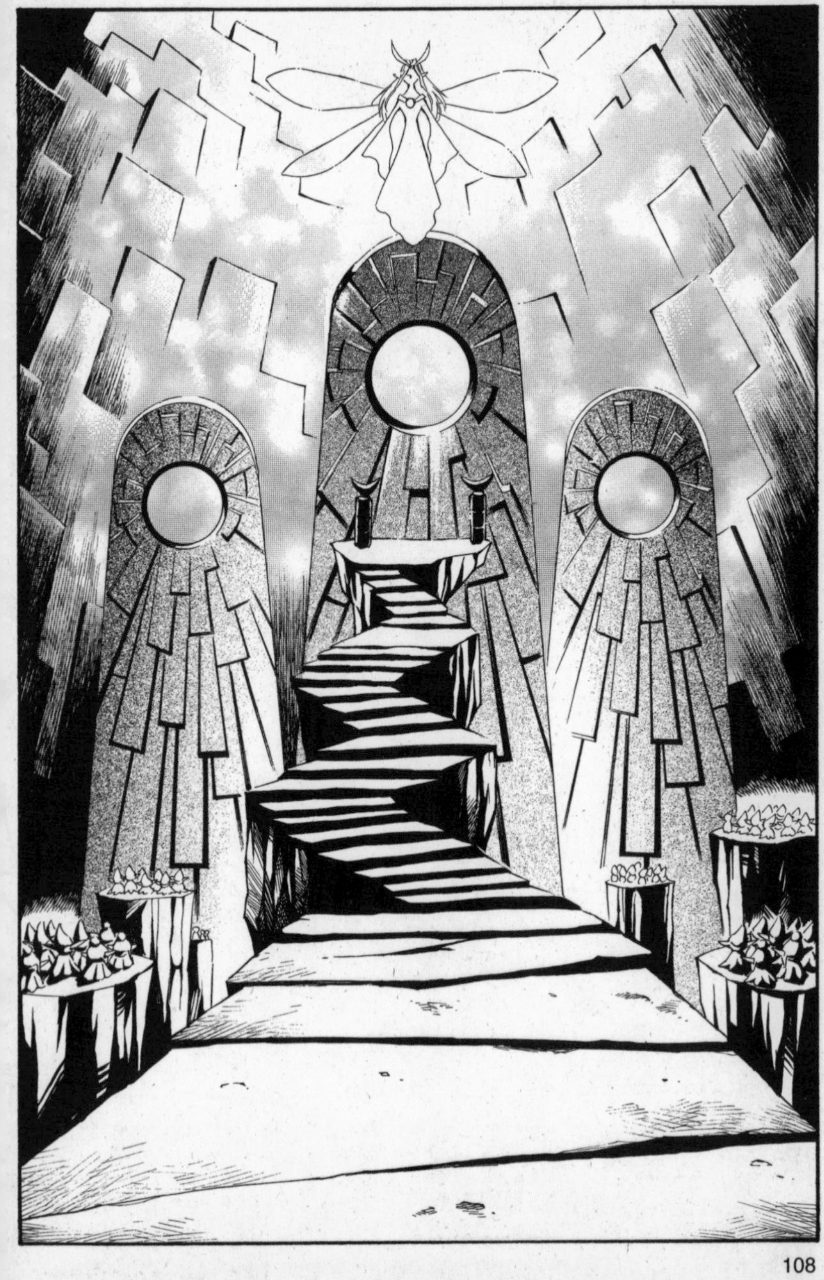

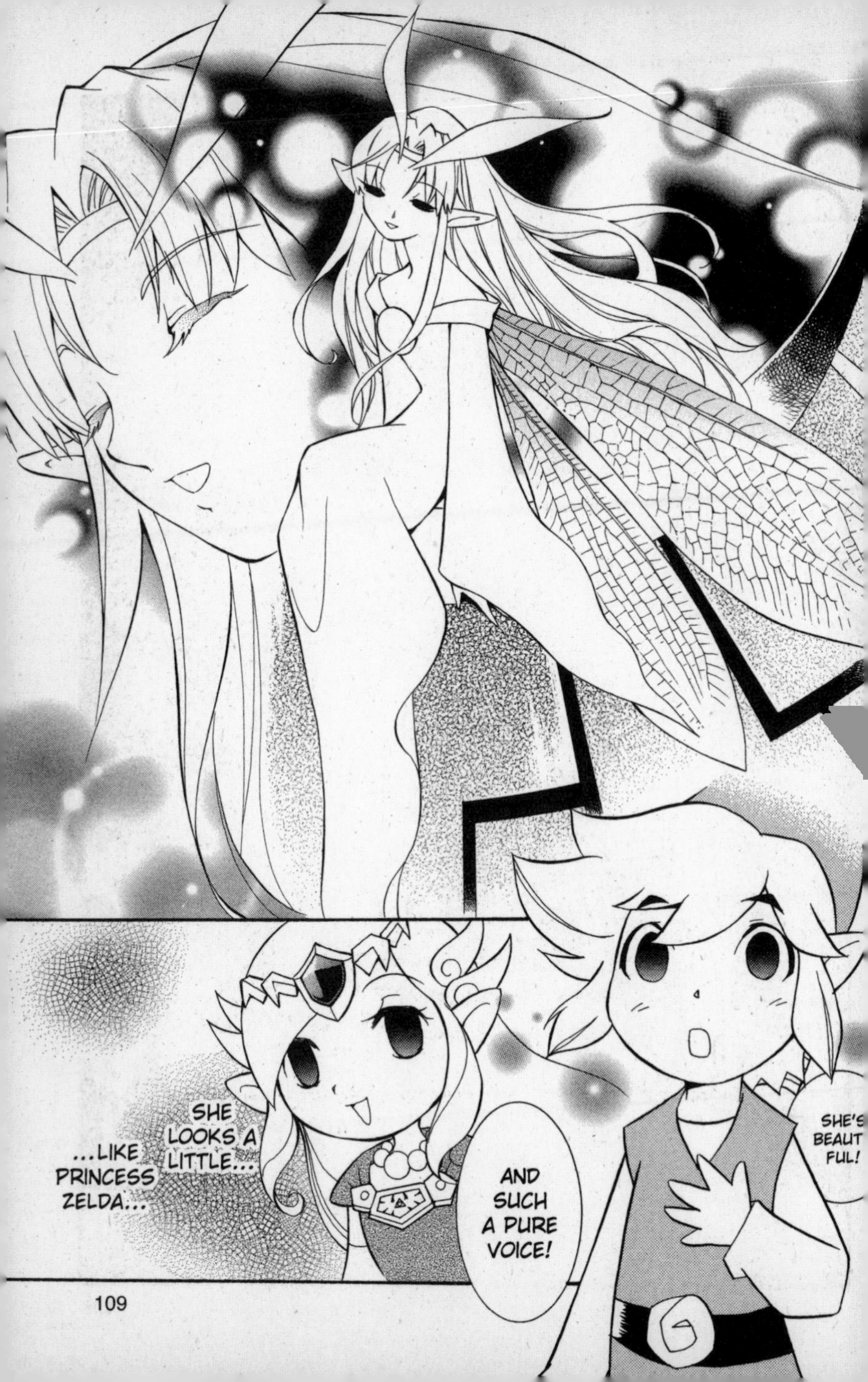
SHE'S BEAUT FUL!
AND SUCH A PURE VOICE!
SHE LOOKS A LITTLE...
...LIKE PRINCESS ZELDA...

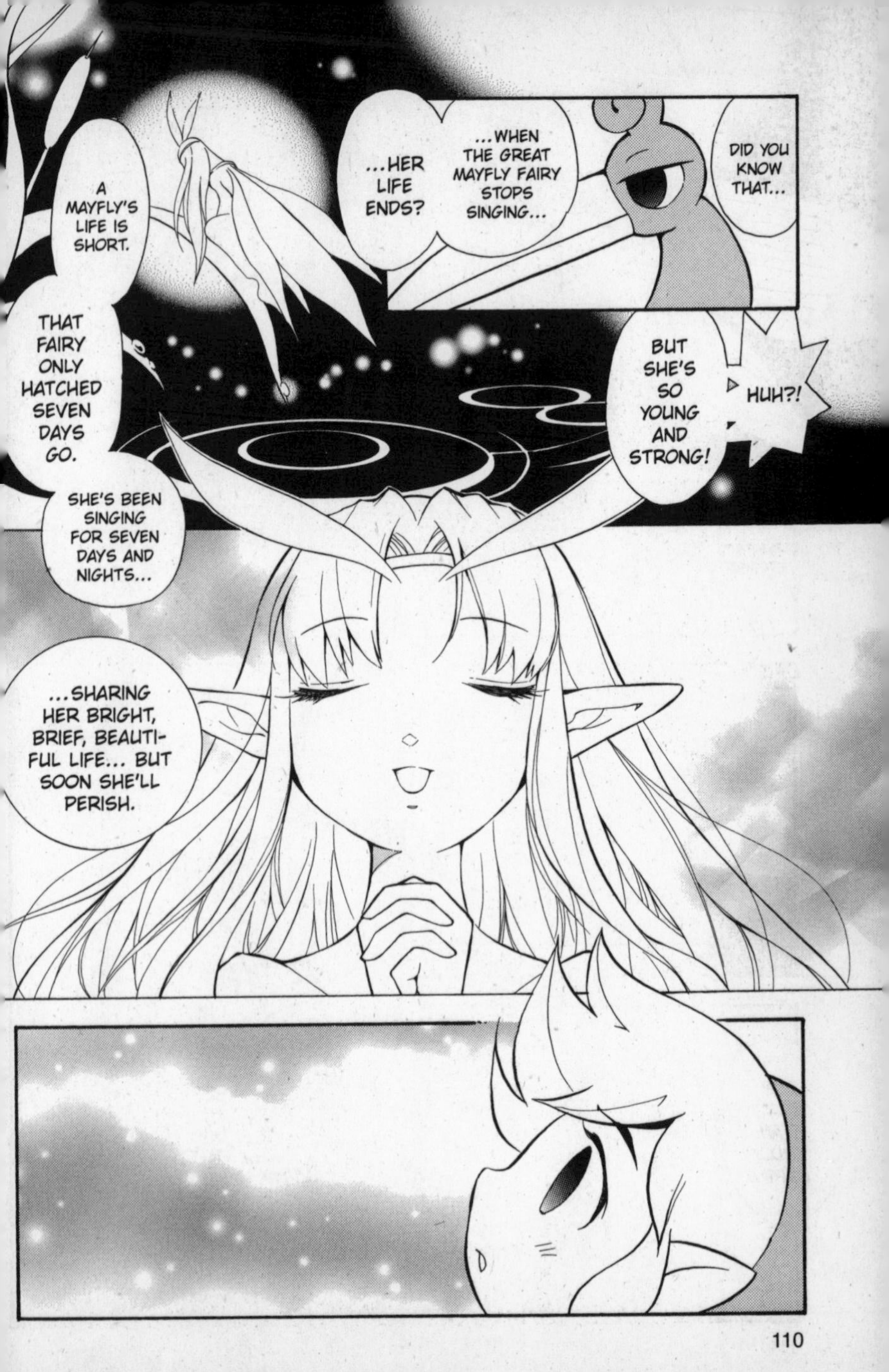
DID YOU KNOW THAT...
...WHEN THE GREAT MAYFLY FAIRY STOPS SINGING...
...HER LIFE ENDS?
A MAYFLY'S LIFE IS SHORT.
HUH?!
BUT SHE'S SO YOUNG AND STRONG!
THAT FAIRY ONLY HATCHED SEVEN DAYS GO.
SHE'S BEEN SINGING FOR SEVEN DAYS AND NIGHTS...
...SHARING HER BRIGHT, BRIEF, BEAUTIFUL LIFE... BUT SOON SHE'LL PERISH.

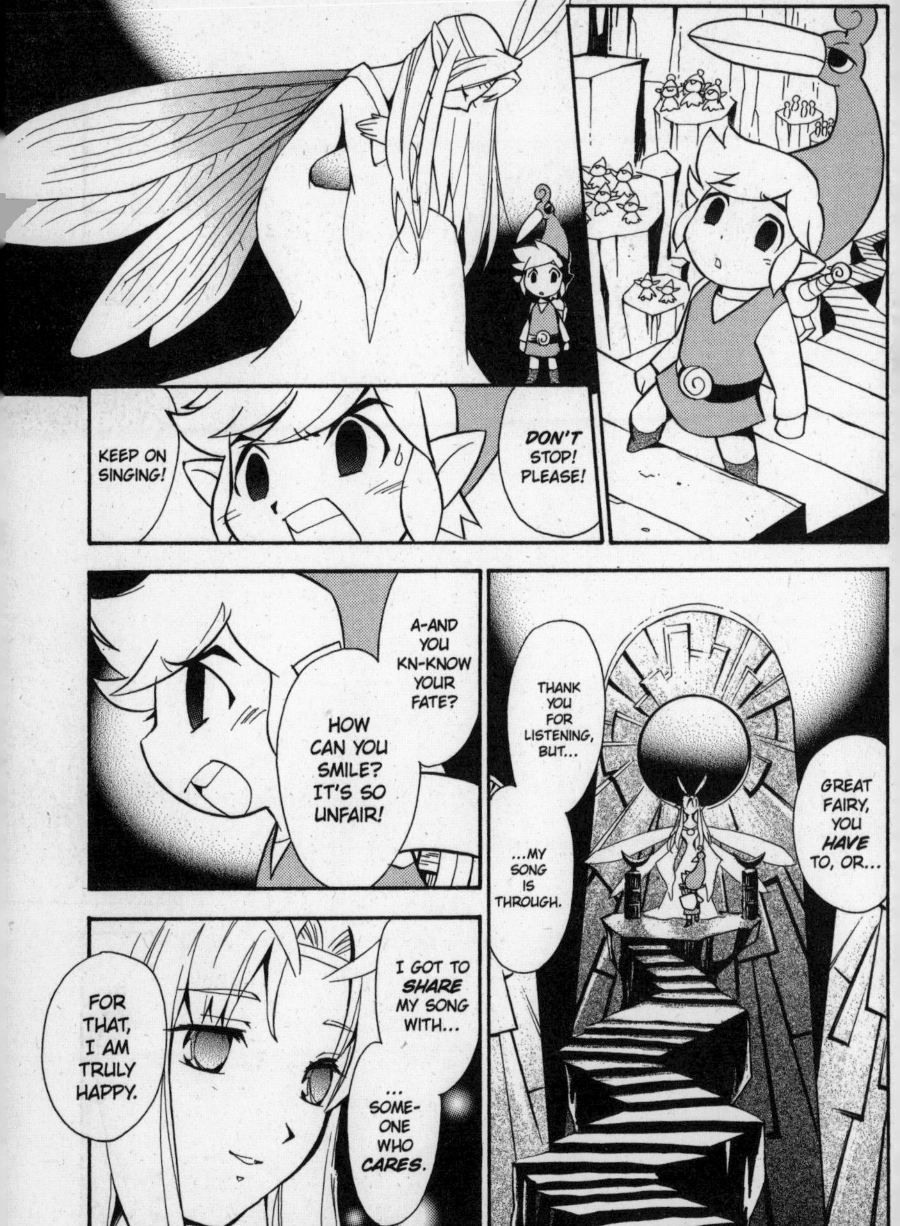
DON'T STOP! PLEASE!
KEEP ON SINGING!
GREAT FAIRY, YOU HAVE TO, OR...
THANK YOU FOR LISTENING, BUT...
...MY SONG IS THROUGH.
A-AND YOU KN-KNOW YOUR FATE?
HOW CAN YOU SMILE? IT'S SO UNFAIR!
I GOT TO SHARE MY SONG WITH...
...SOMEONE WHO CARES.
FOR THAT, I AM TRULY HAPPY.

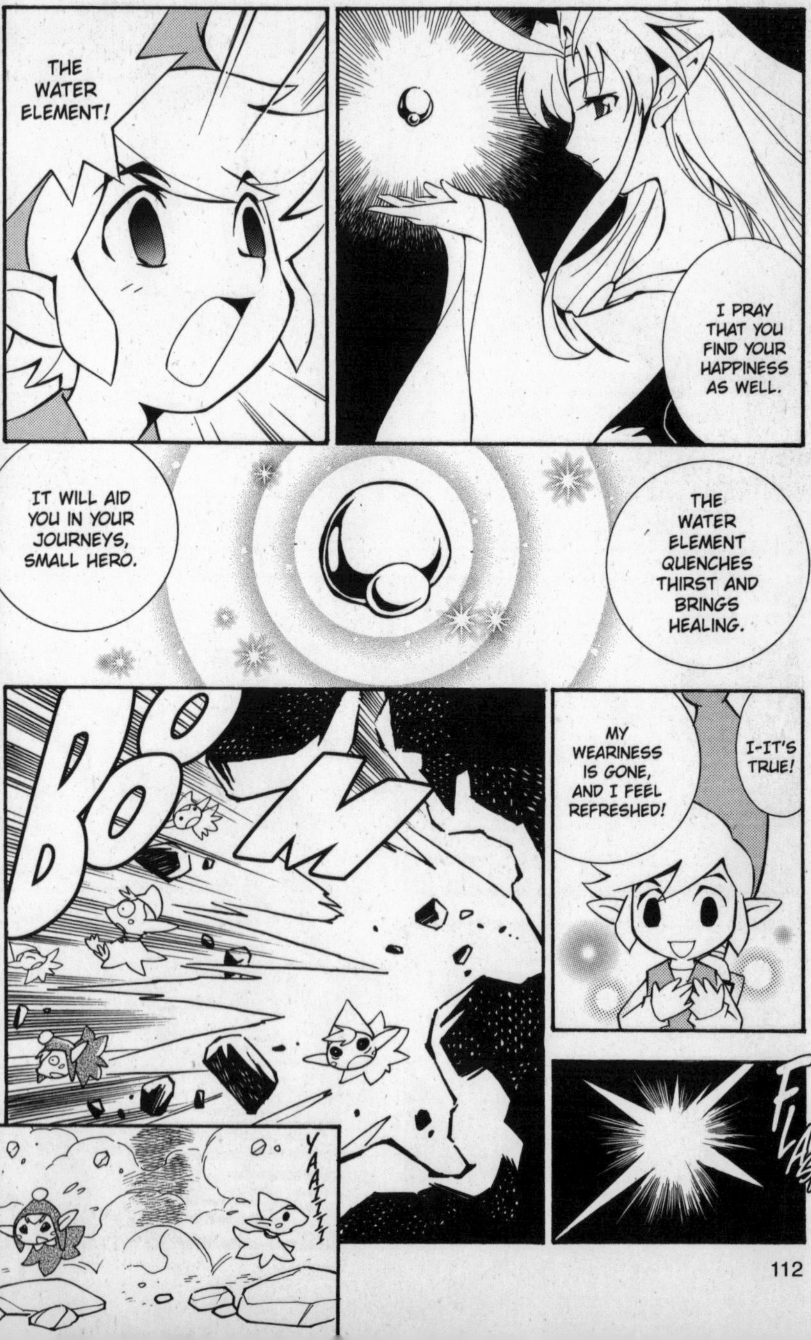
I PRAY THAT YOU FIND YOUR HAPPINESS AS WELL.
THE WATER ELEMENT!
THE WATER ELEMENT QUENCHES THIRST AND BRINGS HEALING.
IT WILL AID YOU IN YOUR JOURNEYS, SMALL HERO.
I-IT'S TRUE!
MY WEARINESS IS GONE, AND I FEEL REFRESHED!
FLASH
BOOOM
YAAIIII

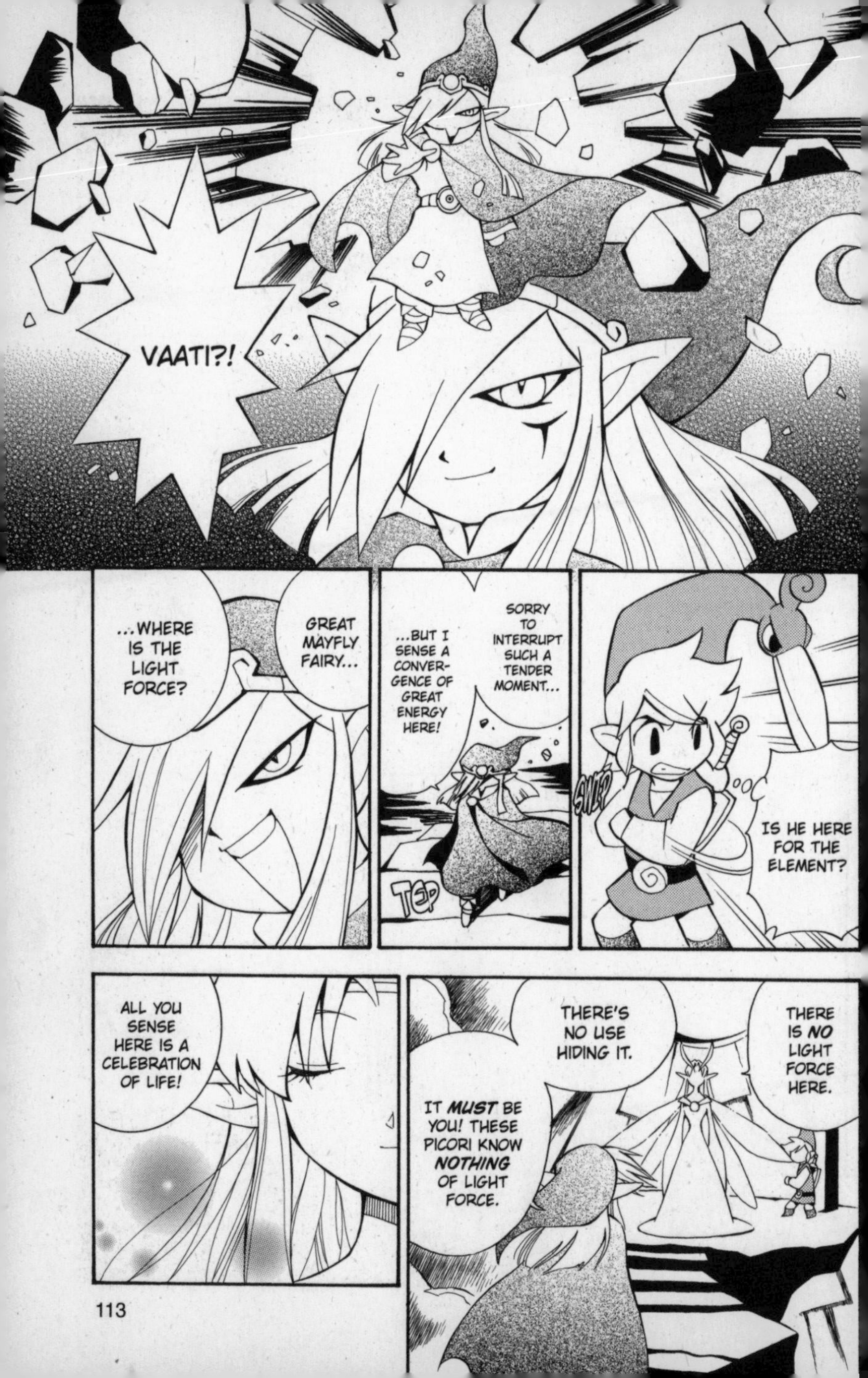
VAATI?!
IS HE HERE FOR THE ELEMENT?
SORRY TO INTERRUPT SUCH A TENDER MOMENT...
...BUT I SENSE A CONVERGENCE OF GREAT ENERGY HERE!
TEP
GREAT MAYFLY FAIRY...
...WHERE IS THE LIGHT FORCE?
THERE IS *NO* LIGHT FORCE HERE.
THERE'S NO USE HIDING IT.
IT *MUST* BE YOU! THESE PICORI KNOW *NOTHING* OF LIGHT FORCE.
ALL YOU SENSE HERE IS A CELEBRATION OF LIFE!

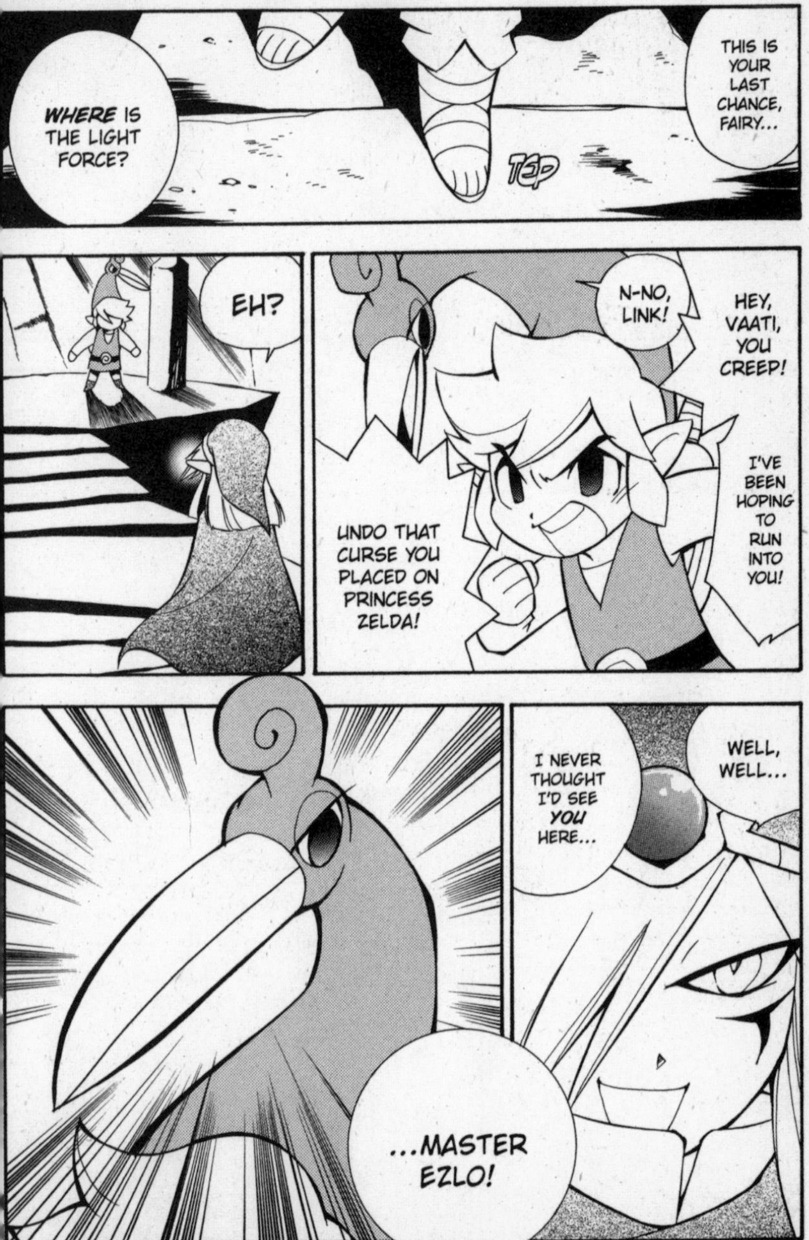
THIS IS YOUR LAST CHANCE, FAIRY...
TEP
WHERE IS THE LIGHT FORCE?
HEY, VAATI, YOU CREEP!
N-NO, LINK!
I'VE BEEN HOPING TO RUN INTO YOU!
UNDO THAT CURSE YOU PLACED ON PRINCESS ZELDA!
EH?
WELL, WELL...
I NEVER THOUGHT I'D SEE YOU HERE...
...MASTER EZLO!

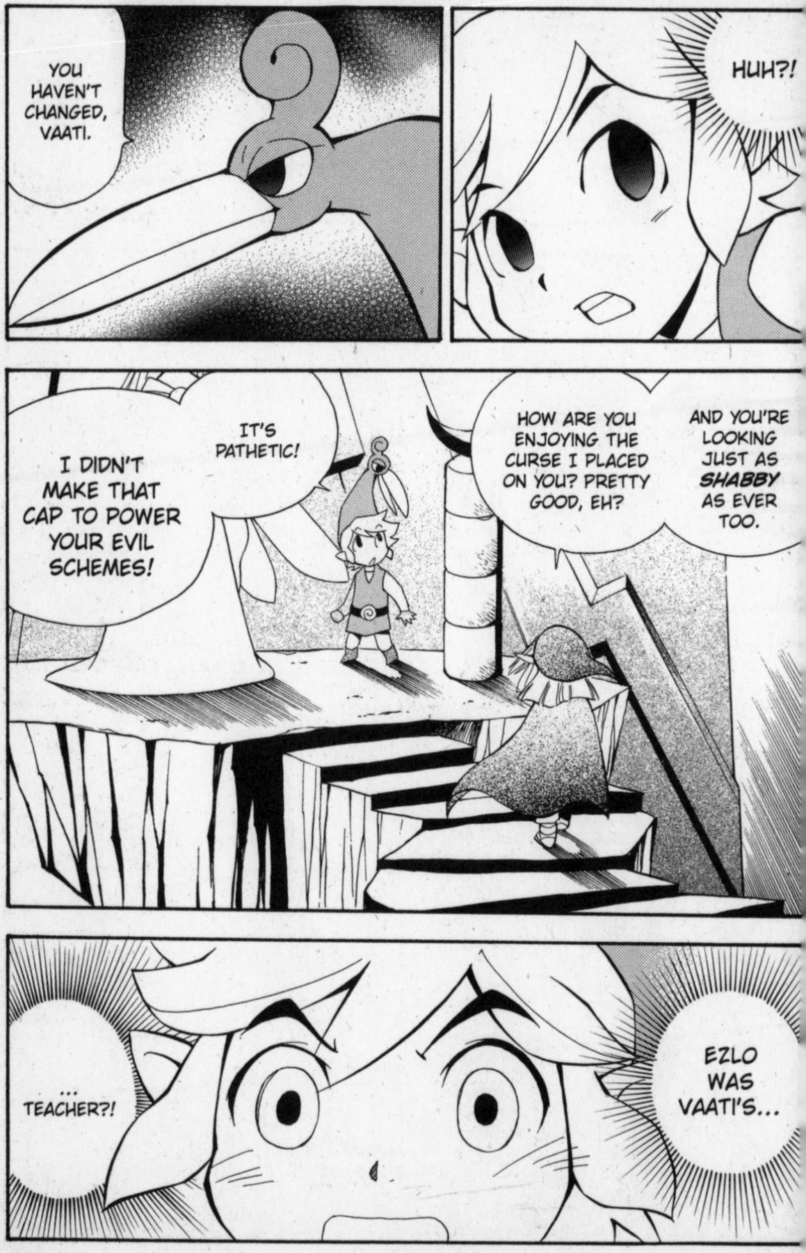
HUH?!
YOU HAVEN'T CHANGED, VAATI.
AND YOU'RE LOOKING JUST AS *SHABBY* AS EVER TOO.
HOW ARE YOU ENJOYING THE CURSE I PLACED ON YOU? PRETTY GOOD, EH?
IT'S PATHETIC!
I DIDN'T MAKE THAT CAP TO POWER YOUR EVIL SCHEMES!
EZLO WAS VAATI'S...
...TEACHER?!

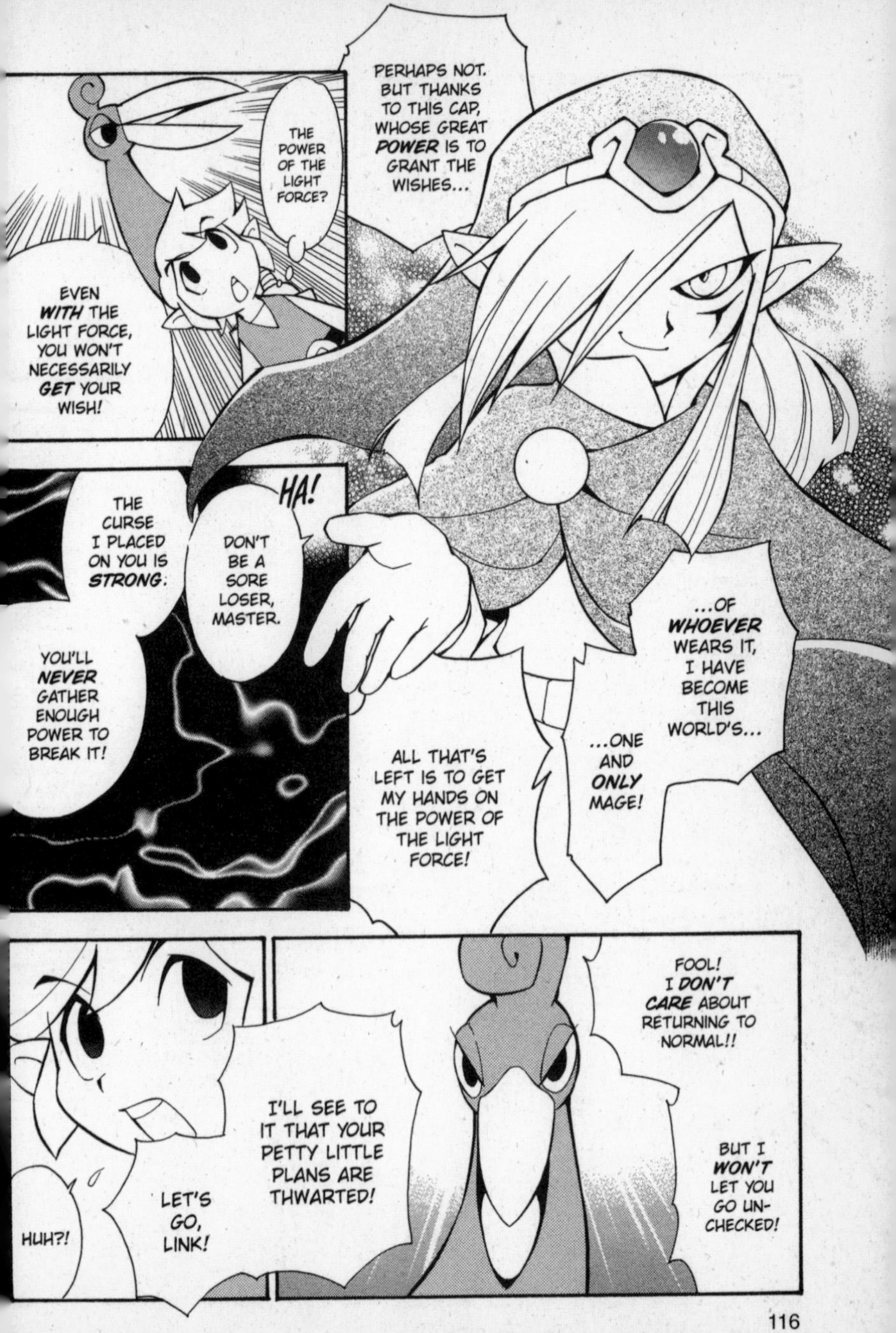
THE POWER OF THE LIGHT FORCE?
EVEN WITH THE LIGHT FORCE, YOU WON'T NECESSARILY GET YOUR WISH!
PERHAPS NOT. BUT THANKS TO THIS CAP, WHOSE GREAT POWER IS TO GRANT THE WISHES...
...OF WHOEVER WEARS IT, I HAVE BECOME THIS WORLD'S...
...ONE AND ONLY MAGE!
ALL THAT'S LEFT IS TO GET MY HANDS ON THE POWER OF THE LIGHT FORCE!
HA!
DON'T BE A SORE LOSER, MASTER.
THE CURSE I PLACED ON YOU IS STRONG.
YOU'LL NEVER GATHER ENOUGH POWER TO BREAK IT!
FOOL! I DON'T CARE ABOUT RETURNING TO NORMAL!!
BUT I WON'T LET YOU GO UN-CHECKED!
I'LL SEE TO IT THAT YOUR PETTY LITTLE PLANS ARE THWARTED!
LET'S GO, LINK!
HUH?!

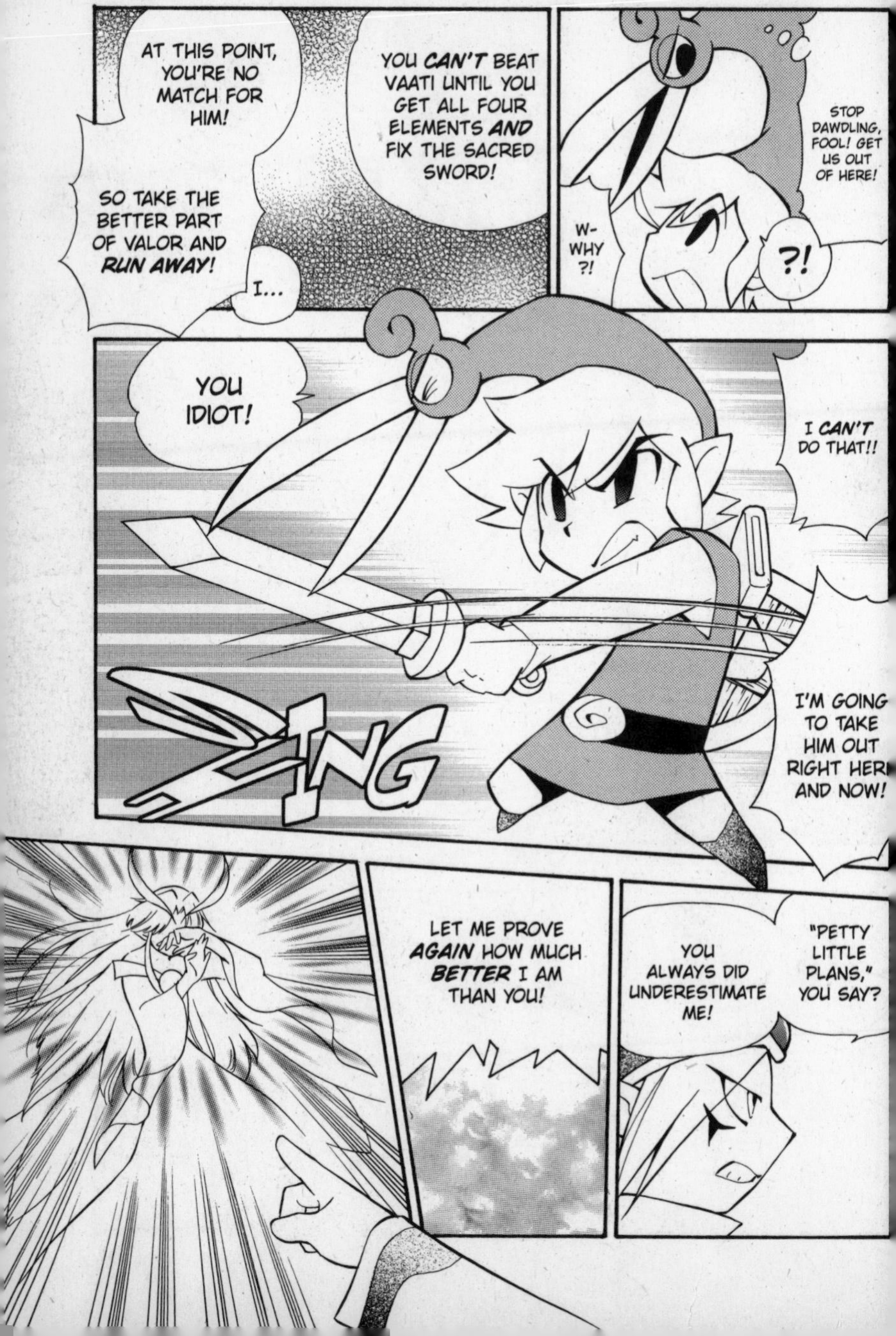
STOP DAWDLING, FOOL! GET US OUT OF HERE!
?!
W-WHY?!
YOU CAN'T BEAT VAATI UNTIL YOU GET ALL FOUR ELEMENTS AND FIX THE SACRED SWORD!
AT THIS POINT, YOU'RE NO MATCH FOR HIM!
SO TAKE THE BETTER PART OF VALOR AND RUN AWAY!
I...
I CAN'T DO THAT!!
I'M GOING TO TAKE HIM OUT RIGHT HER AND NOW!
YOU IDIOT!
ZING
"PETTY LITTLE PLANS," YOU SAY?
YOU ALWAYS DID UNDERESTIMATE ME!
LET ME PROVE AGAIN HOW MUCH BETTER I AM THAN YOU!

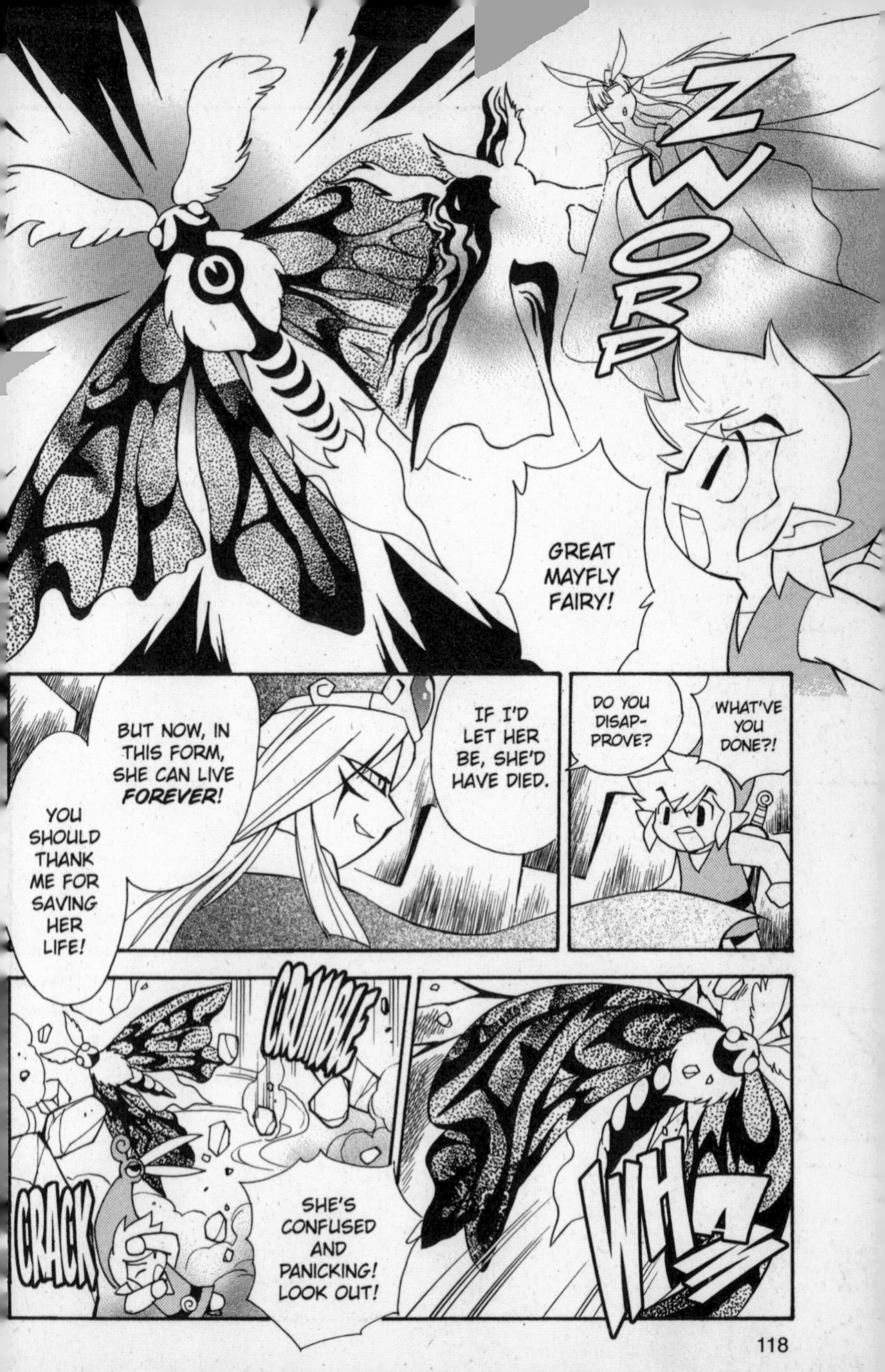
ZWORP
GREAT MAYFLY FAIRY!
WHAT'VE YOU DONE?!
DO YOU DISAP-PROVE?
IF I'D LET HER BE, SHE'D HAVE DIED.
BUT NOW, IN THIS FORM, SHE CAN LIVE ***FOREVER***!
YOU SHOULD THANK ME FOR SAVING HER LIFE!
WHA
CRUMBLE
CRACK
SHE'S CONFUSED AND PANICKING! LOOK OUT!

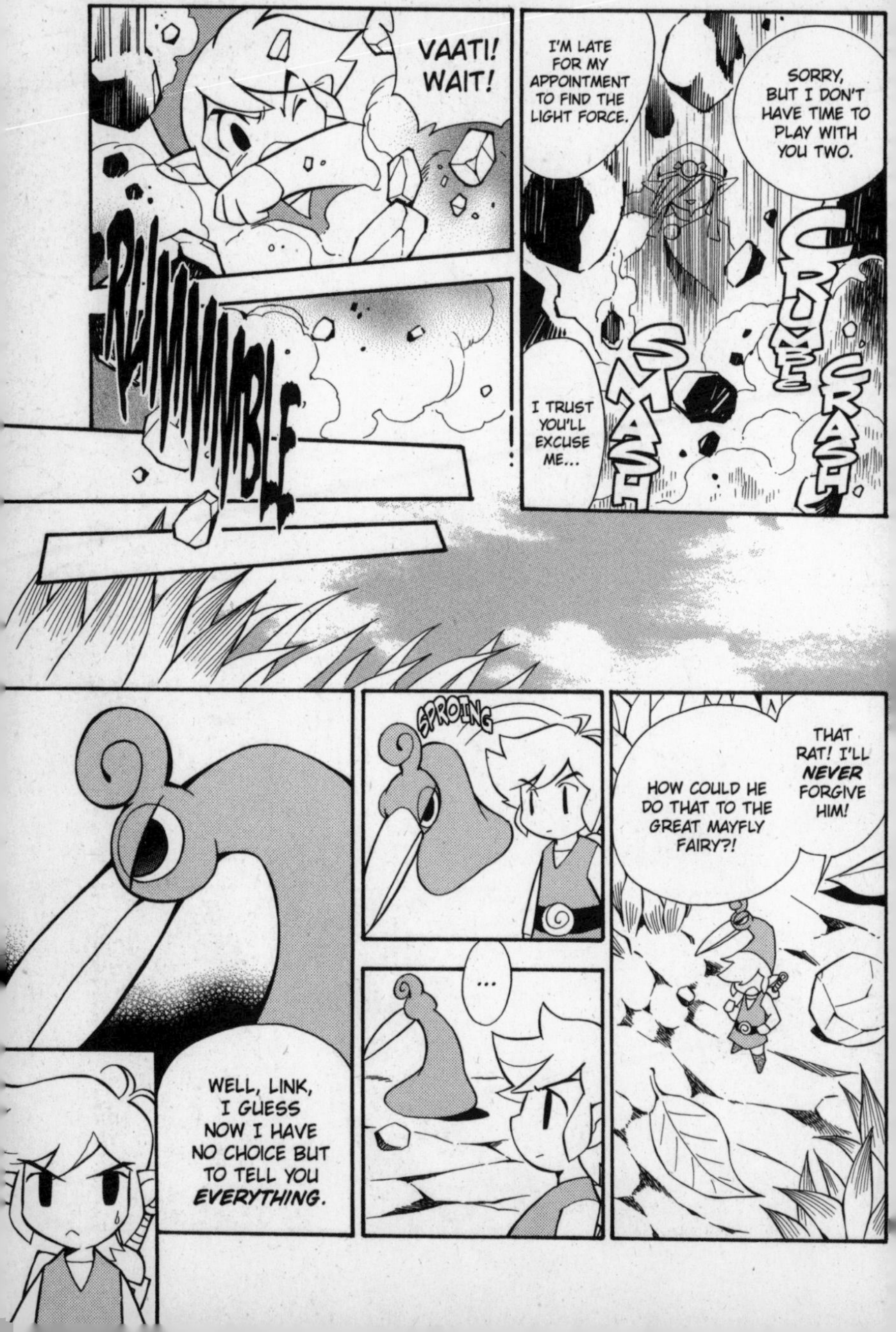
SORRY, BUT I DON'T HAVE TIME TO PLAY WITH YOU TWO.
I'M LATE FOR MY APPOINTMENT TO FIND THE LIGHT FORCE.
CRUMBLE
CRASH
SMASH
I TRUST YOU'LL EXCUSE ME...
VAATI! WAIT!
RUMMMBLE
THAT RAT! I'LL *NEVER* FORGIVE HIM!
HOW COULD HE DO THAT TO THE GREAT MAYFLY FAIRY?!
SPROING
...
WELL, LINK, I GUESS NOW I HAVE NO CHOICE BUT TO TELL YOU *EVERYTHING*.

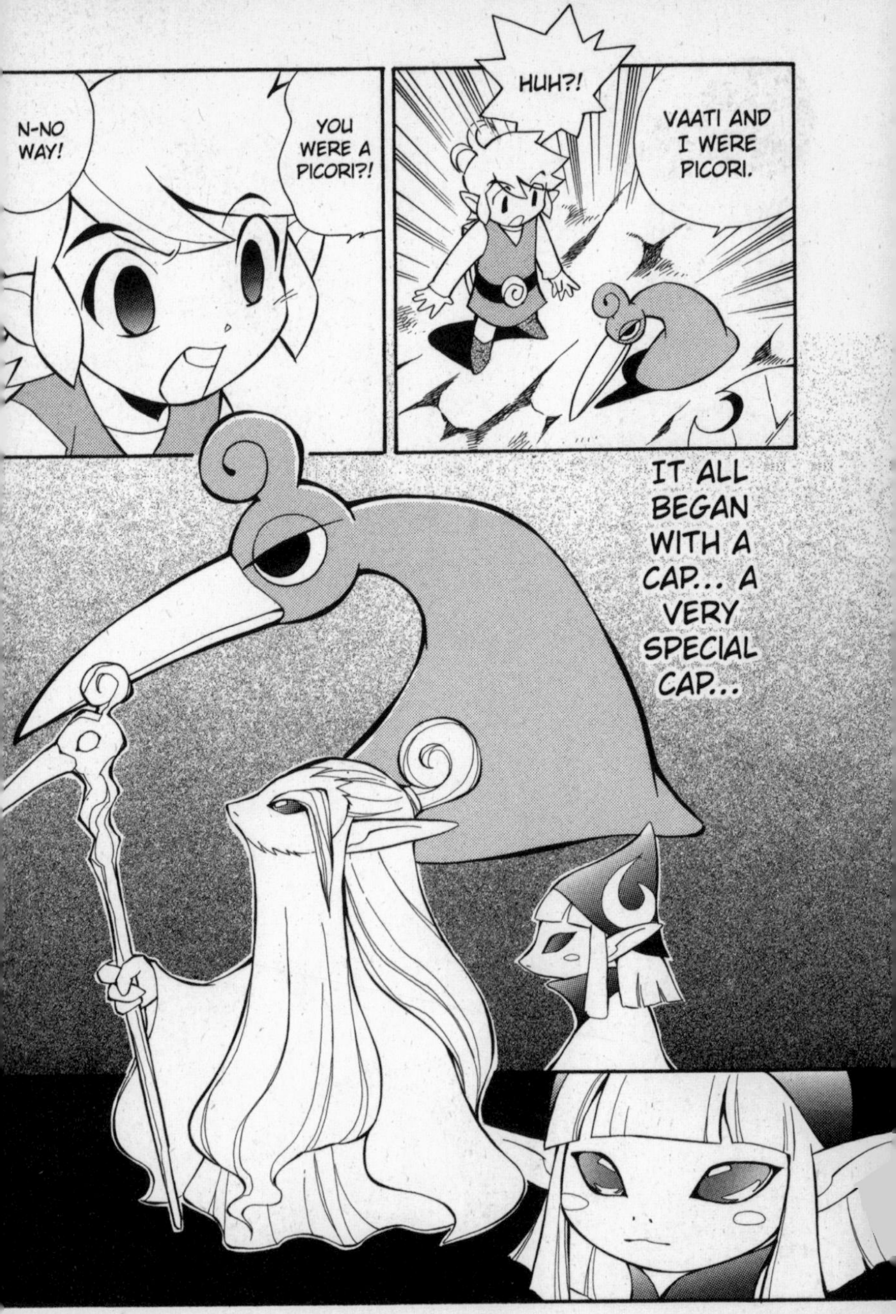
VAATI AND I WERE PICORI.
HUH?!
YOU WERE A PICORI?!
N-NO WAY!
IT ALL BEGAN WITH A CAP... A VERY SPECIAL CAP...

CHAPTER 5

THE KING AND THE WIND TRIBE

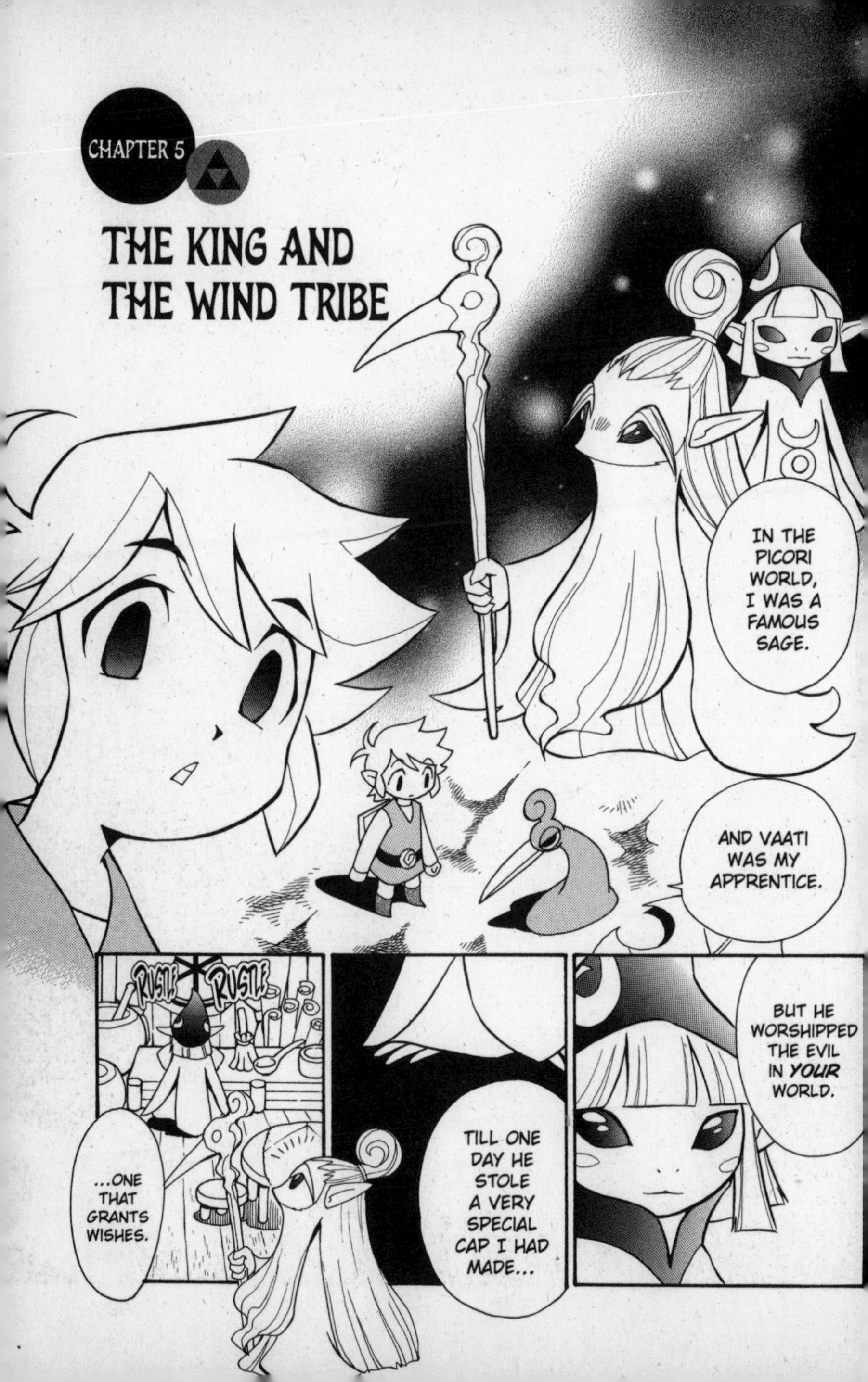
IN THE PICORI WORLD, I WAS A FAMOUS SAGE.
AND VAATI WAS MY APPRENTICE.
BUT HE WORSHIPPED THE EVIL IN *YOUR* WORLD.
TILL ONE DAY HE STOLE A VERY SPECIAL CAP I HAD MADE...
RUSTLE RUSTLE
...ONE THAT GRANTS WISHES.

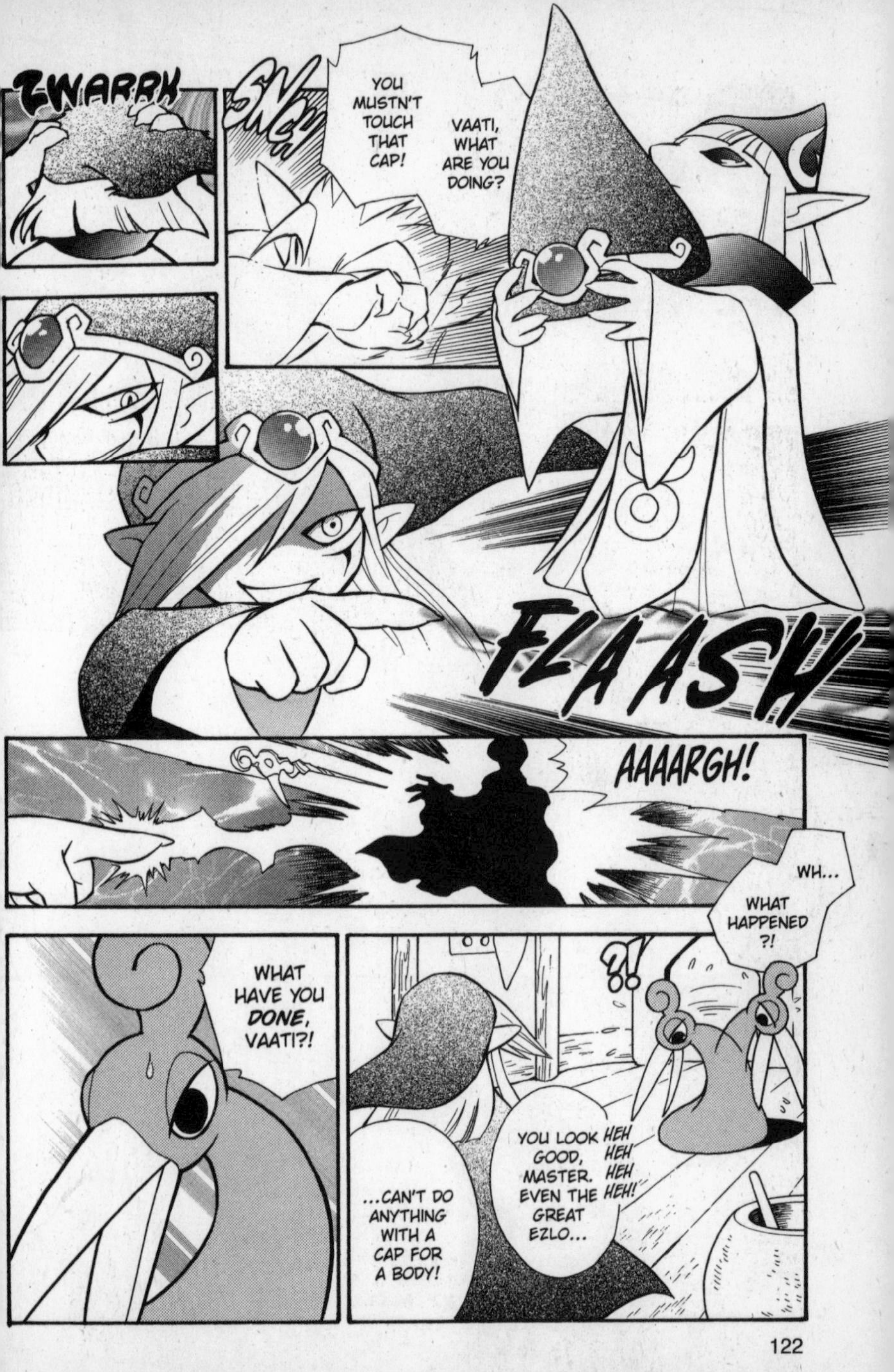
VAATI, WHAT ARE YOU DOING?
YOU MUSTN'T TOUCH THAT CAP!
SNAG
ZWARRK
FLAASH
AAAARGH!
WH...
WHAT HAPPENED?!
HEH HEH HEH HEH!
YOU LOOK GOOD, MASTER. EVEN THE GREAT EZLO...
...CAN'T DO ANYTHING WITH A CAP FOR A BODY!
WHAT HAVE YOU *DONE*, VAATI?!

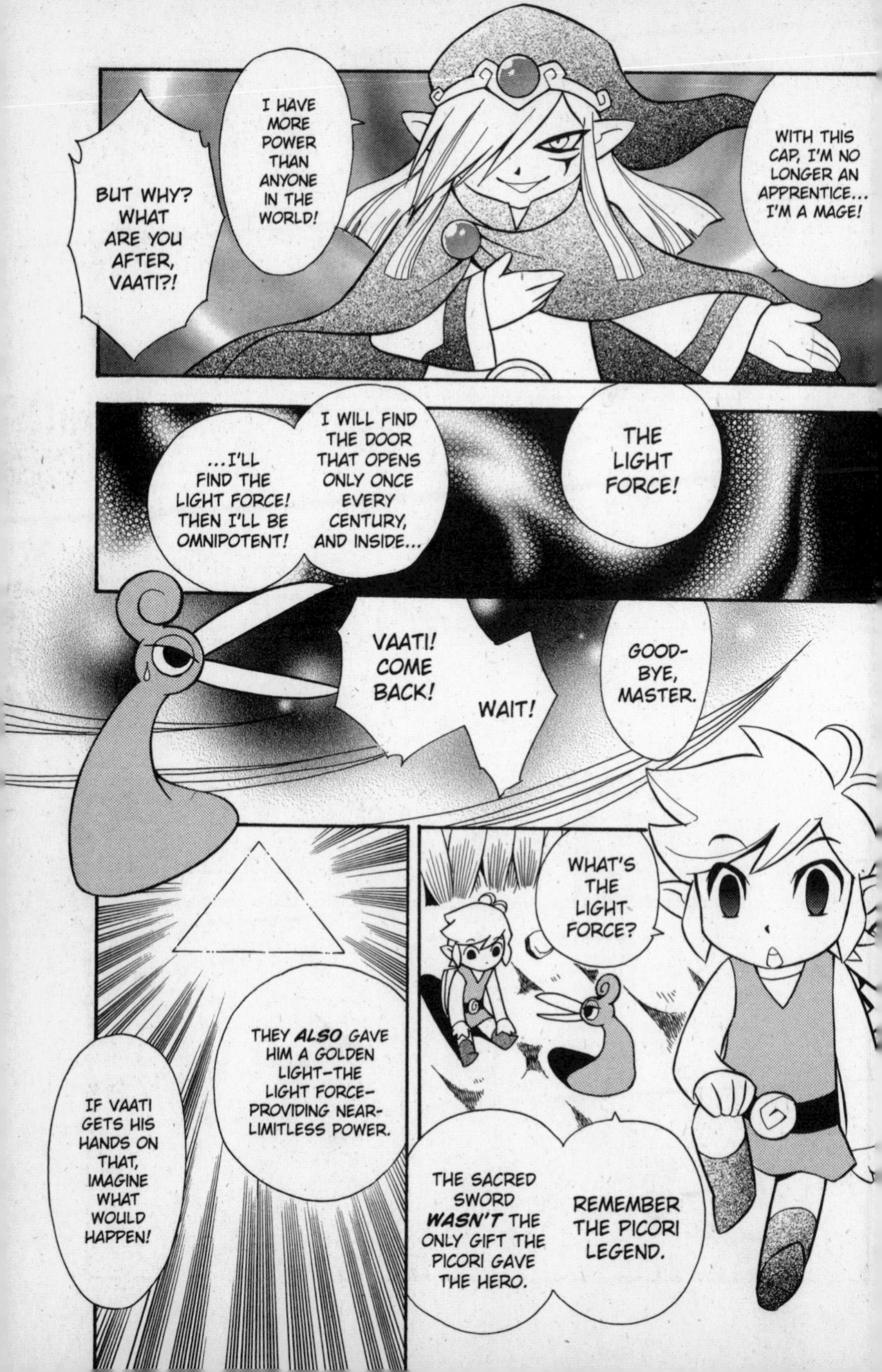
WITH THIS CAP, I'M NO LONGER AN APPRENTICE... I'M A MAGE!
I HAVE MORE POWER THAN ANYONE IN THE WORLD!
BUT WHY? WHAT ARE YOU AFTER, VAATI?!
THE LIGHT FORCE!
I WILL FIND THE DOOR THAT OPENS ONLY ONCE EVERY CENTURY, AND INSIDE...
...I'LL FIND THE LIGHT FORCE! THEN I'LL BE OMNIPOTENT!
GOOD-BYE, MASTER.
WAIT!
VAATI! COME BACK!
WHAT'S THE LIGHT FORCE?
REMEMBER THE PICORI LEGEND.
THE SACRED SWORD **WASN'T** THE ONLY GIFT THE PICORI GAVE THE HERO.
THEY **ALSO** GAVE HIM A GOLDEN LIGHT—THE LIGHT FORCE—PROVIDING NEAR-LIMITLESS POWER.
IF VAATI GETS HIS HANDS ON THAT, IMAGINE WHAT WOULD HAPPEN!

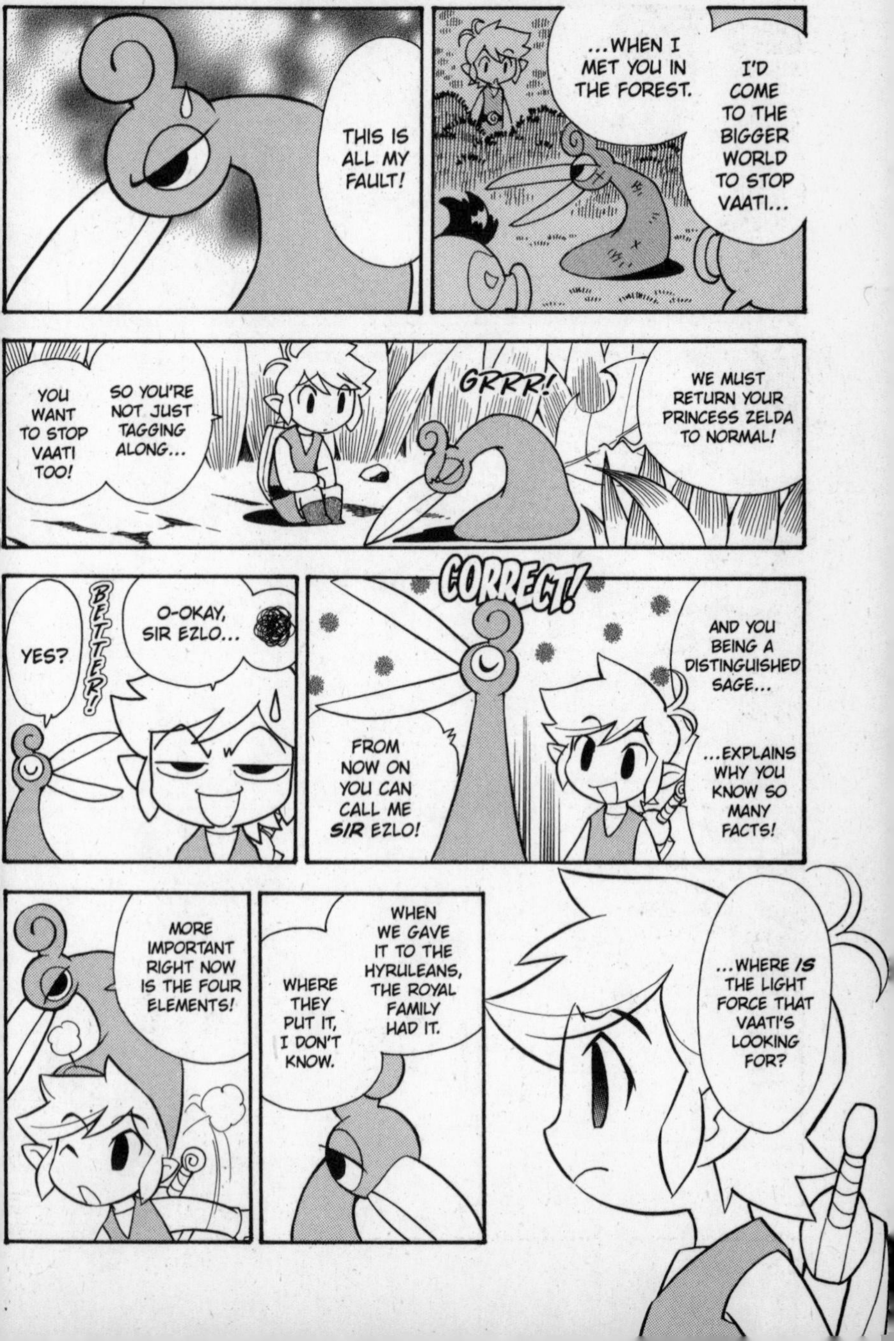
I'D COME TO THE BIGGER WORLD TO STOP VAATI...
...WHEN I MET YOU IN THE FOREST.
THIS IS ALL MY FAULT!
WE MUST RETURN YOUR PRINCESS ZELDA TO NORMAL!
GRRR!
SO YOU'RE NOT JUST TAGGING ALONG...
YOU WANT TO STOP VAATI TOO!
CORRECT!
AND YOU BEING A DISTINGUISHED SAGE...
...EXPLAINS WHY YOU KNOW SO MANY FACTS!
FROM NOW ON YOU CAN CALL ME *SIR* EZLO!
O-OKAY, SIR EZLO...
BETTER!
YES?
...WHERE *IS* THE LIGHT FORCE THAT VAATI'S LOOKING FOR?
WHEN WE GAVE IT TO THE HYRULEANS, THE ROYAL FAMILY HAD IT.
WHERE THEY PUT IT, I DON'T KNOW.
MORE IMPORTANT RIGHT NOW IS THE FOUR ELEMENTS!

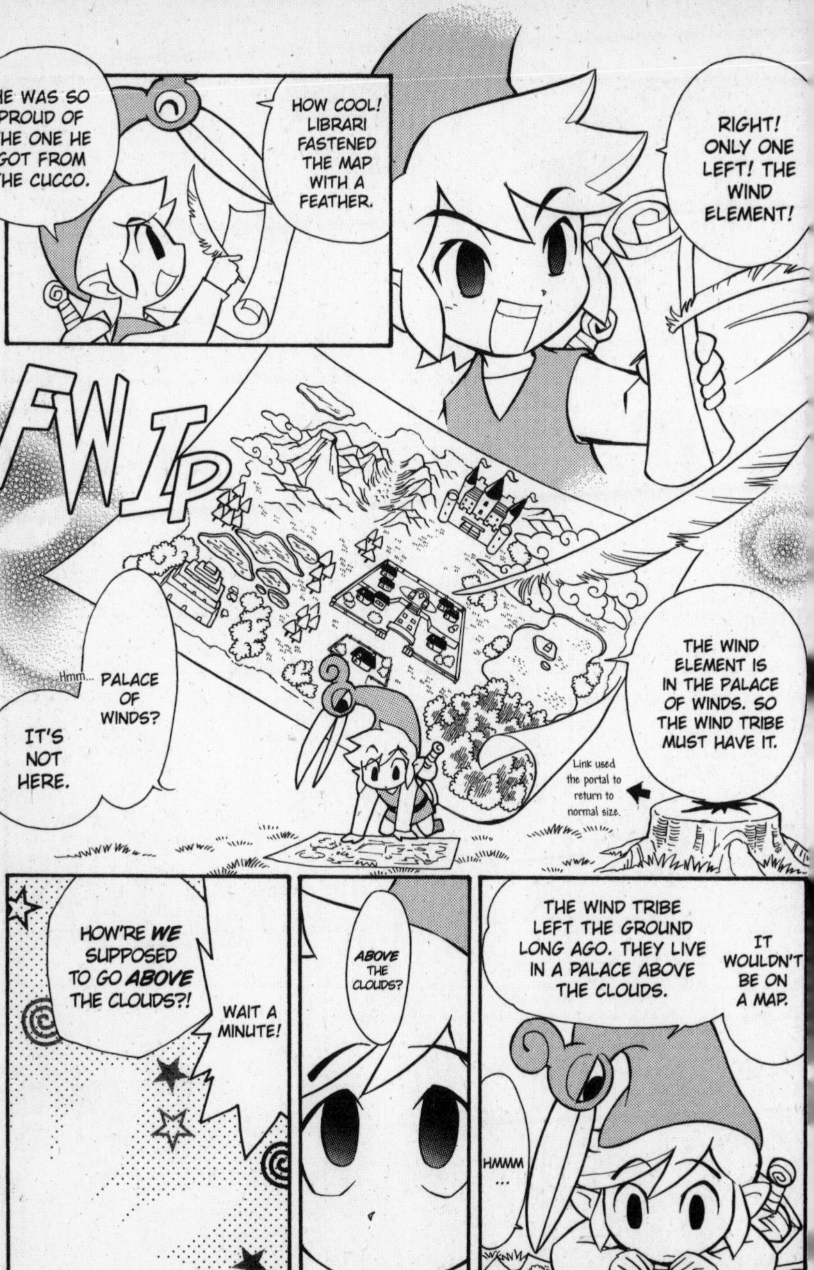
RIGHT! ONLY ONE LEFT! THE WIND ELEMENT!
HOW COOL! LIBRARI FASTENED THE MAP WITH A FEATHER.
HE WAS SO PROUD OF THE ONE HE GOT FROM THE CUCCO.
FWIP
THE WIND ELEMENT IS IN THE PALACE OF WINDS. SO THE WIND TRIBE MUST HAVE IT.
Link used the portal to return to normal size.
Hmm... PALACE OF WINDS?
IT'S NOT HERE.
THE WIND TRIBE LEFT THE GROUND LONG AGO. THEY LIVE IN A PALACE ABOVE THE CLOUDS.
IT WOULDN'T BE ON A MAP.
HMMM...
ABOVE THE CLOUDS?
WAIT A MINUTE!
HOW'RE WE SUPPOSED TO GO ABOVE THE CLOUDS?!

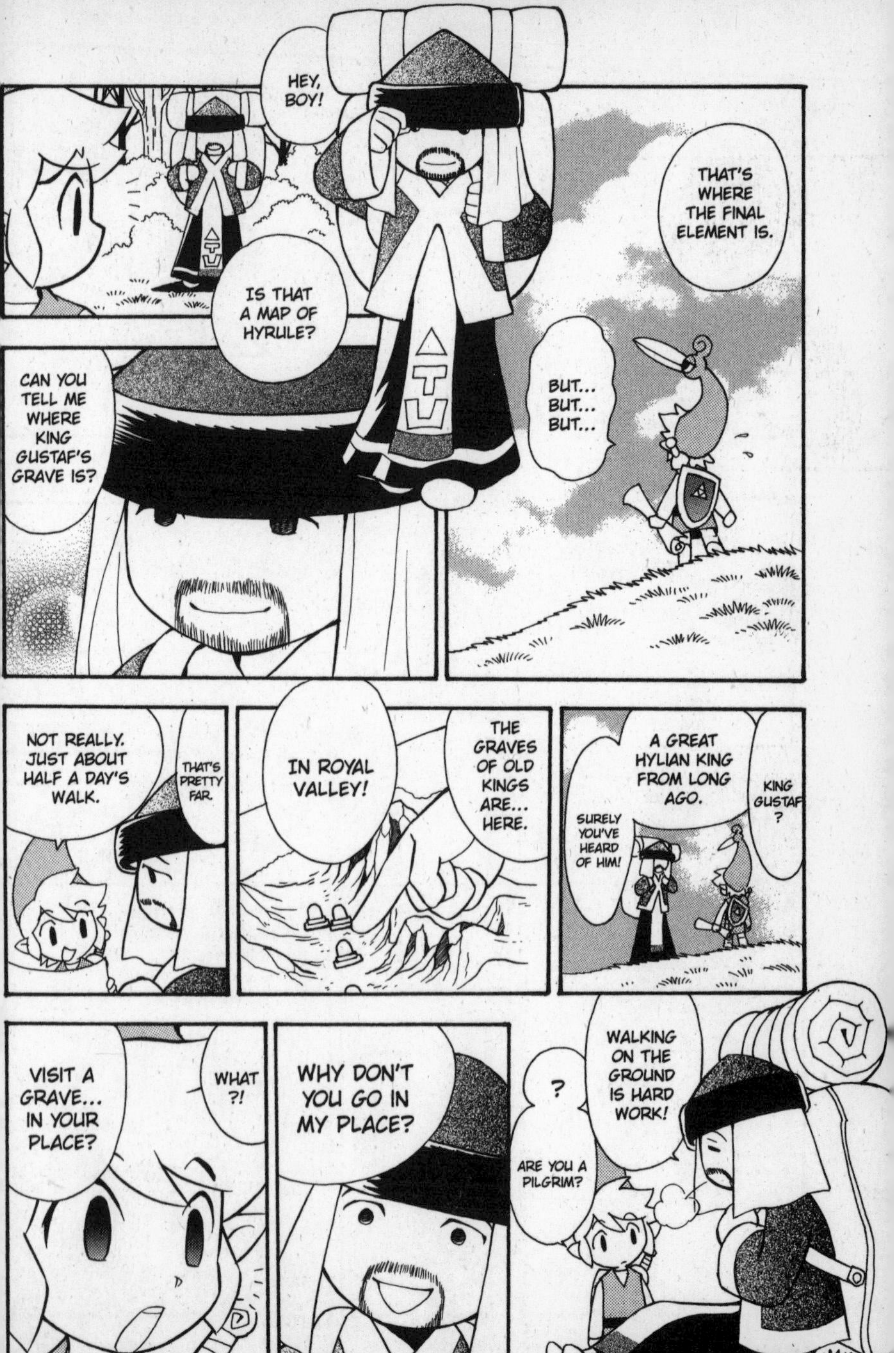
THAT'S WHERE THE FINAL ELEMENT IS.
BUT... BUT... BUT...
HEY, BOY!
IS THAT A MAP OF HYRULE?
CAN YOU TELL ME WHERE KING GUSTAF'S GRAVE IS?
KING GUSTAF?
A GREAT HYLIAN KING FROM LONG AGO.
SURELY YOU'VE HEARD OF HIM!
THE GRAVES OF OLD KINGS ARE... HERE.
IN ROYAL VALLEY!
THAT'S PRETTY FAR.
NOT REALLY. JUST ABOUT HALF A DAY'S WALK.
WALKING ON THE GROUND IS HARD WORK!
?
ARE YOU A PILGRIM?
WHY DON'T YOU GO IN MY PLACE?
WHAT?!
VISIT A GRAVE... IN YOUR PLACE?

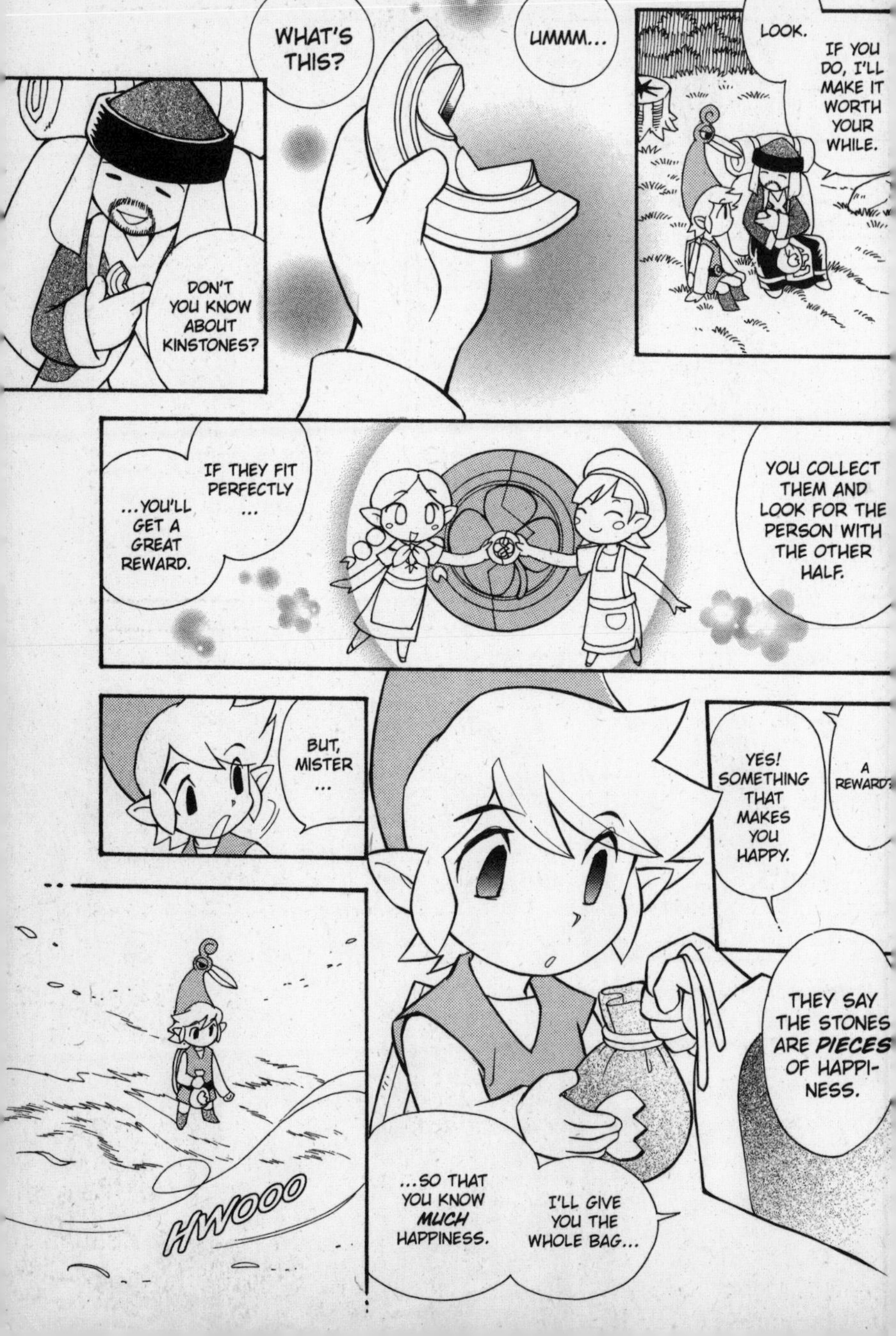
LOOK.
IF YOU DO, I'LL MAKE IT WORTH YOUR WHILE.
UMMM...
WHAT'S THIS?
DON'T YOU KNOW ABOUT KINSTONES?
YOU COLLECT THEM AND LOOK FOR THE PERSON WITH THE OTHER HALF.
IF THEY FIT PERFECTLY ...
...YOU'LL GET A GREAT REWARD.
A REWARD?
YES! SOMETHING THAT MAKES YOU HAPPY.
BUT, MISTER ...
THEY SAY THE STONES ARE *PIECES* OF HAPPI-NESS.
I'LL GIVE YOU THE WHOLE BAG...
...SO THAT YOU KNOW *MUCH* HAPPINESS.
HWOOO

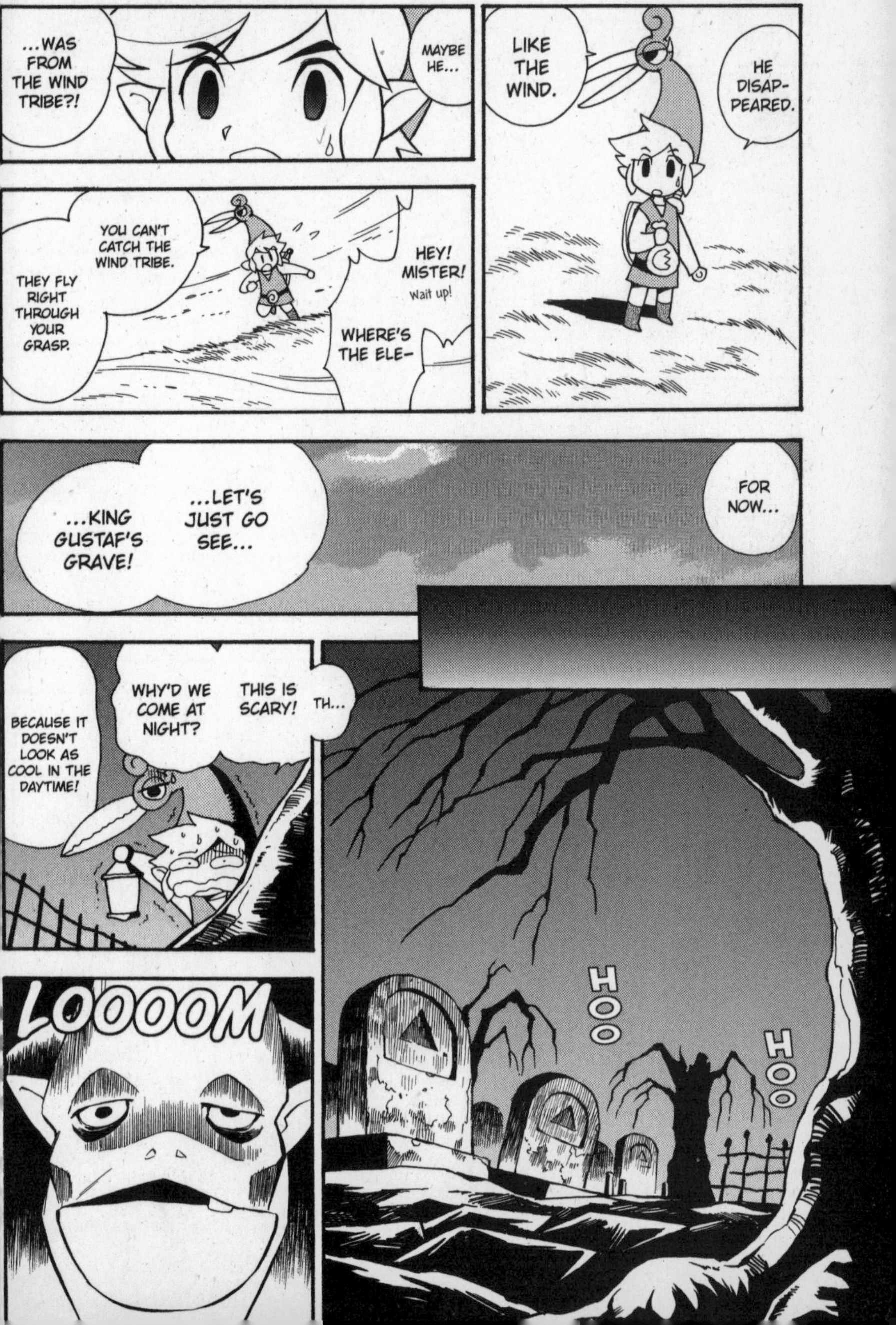
HE DISAP-PEARED.
LIKE THE WIND.
MAYBE HE...
...WAS FROM THE WIND TRIBE?!
HEY! MISTER!
Wait up!
WHERE'S THE ELE-
YOU CAN'T CATCH THE WIND TRIBE.
THEY FLY RIGHT THROUGH YOUR GRASP.
FOR NOW...
...LET'S JUST GO SEE...
...KING GUSTAF'S GRAVE!
HOO
HOO
TH...
THIS IS SCARY!
WHY'D WE COME AT NIGHT?
BECAUSE IT DOESN'T LOOK AS COOL IN THE DAYTIME!
LOOOOM

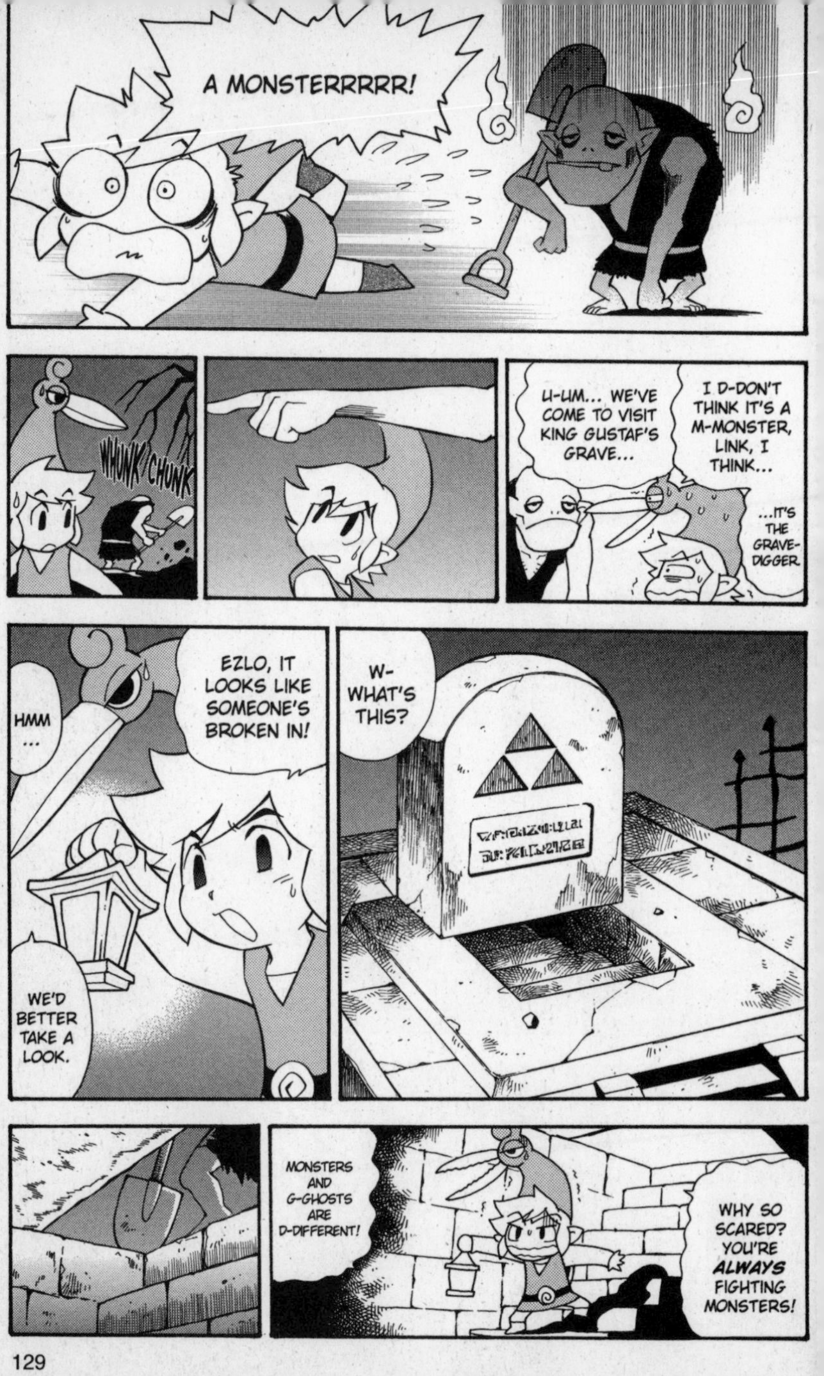
A MONSTERRRRR!
I D-DON'T THINK IT'S A M-MONSTER, LINK, I THINK...
...IT'S THE GRAVE-DIGGER.
U-UM... WE'VE COME TO VISIT KING GUSTAF'S GRAVE...
WHUNK CHUNK
W-WHAT'S THIS?
EZLO, IT LOOKS LIKE SOMEONE'S BROKEN IN!
HMM...
WE'D BETTER TAKE A LOOK.
WHY SO SCARED? YOU'RE ALWAYS FIGHTING MONSTERS!
MONSTERS AND G-GHOSTS ARE D-DIFFERENT!

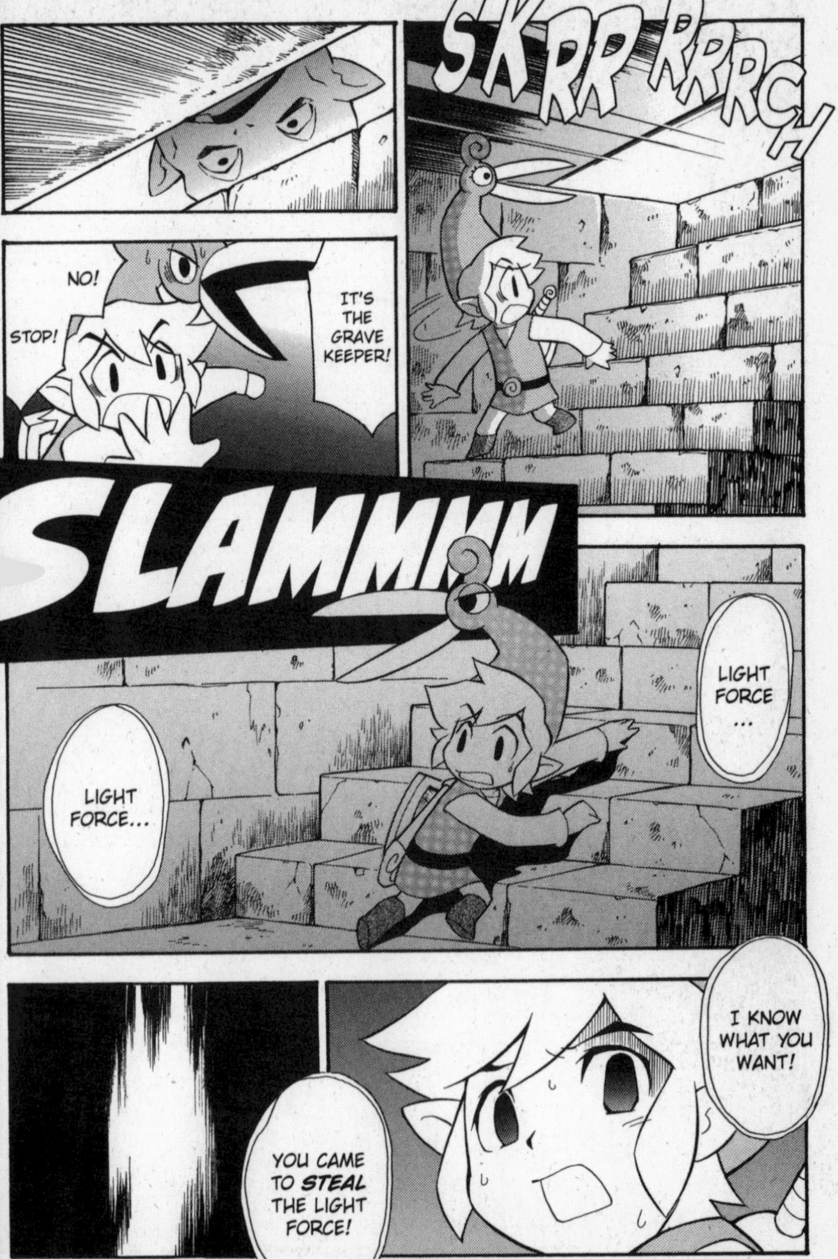
SKRRRRRCH
IT'S THE GRAVE KEEPER!
NO!
STOP!
SLAMMMM
LIGHT FORCE ...
LIGHT FORCE...
I KNOW WHAT YOU WANT!
YOU CAME TO STEAL THE LIGHT FORCE!

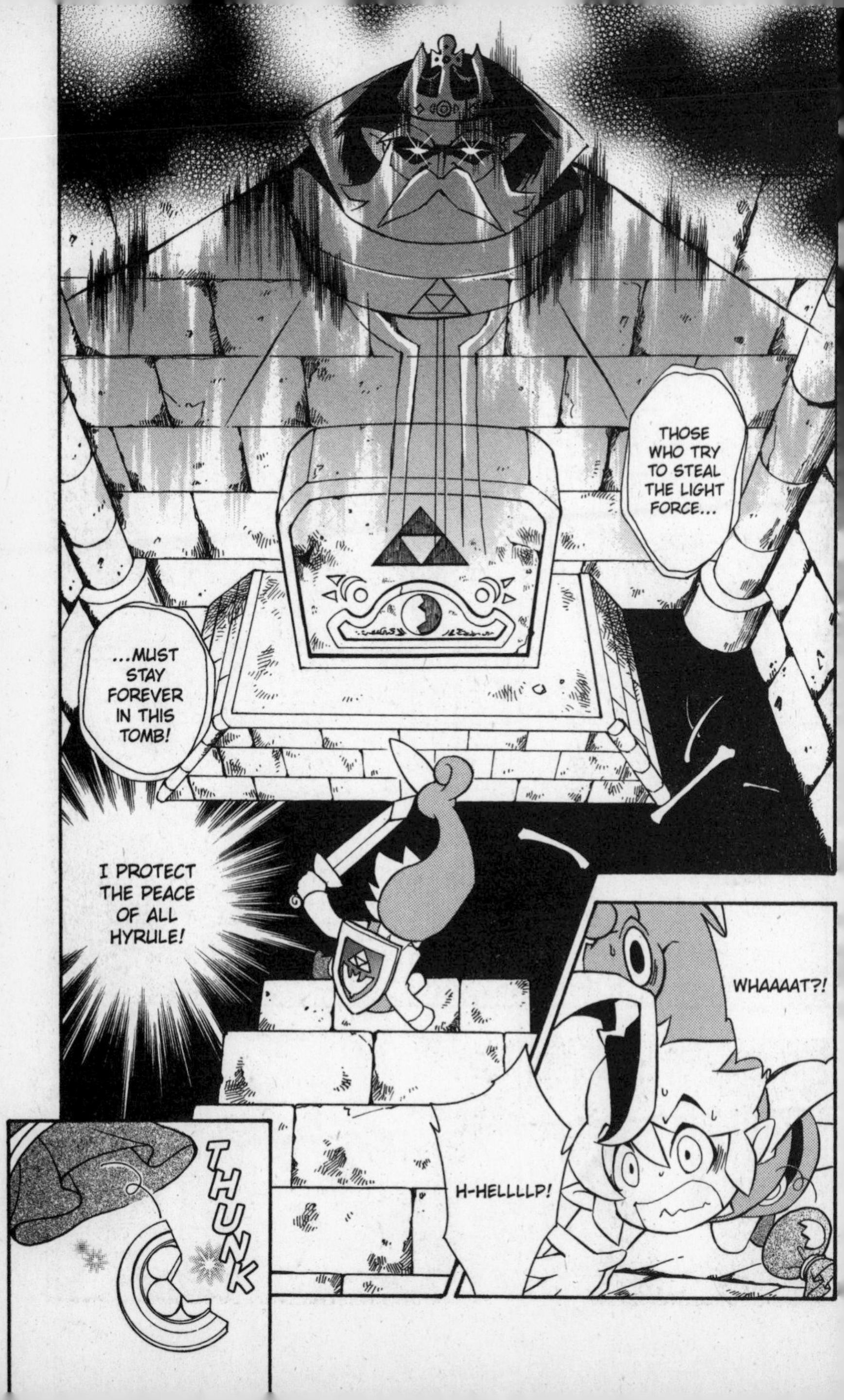
THOSE WHO TRY TO STEAL THE LIGHT FORCE...
...MUST STAY FOREVER IN THIS TOMB!
I PROTECT THE PEACE OF ALL HYRULE!
WHAAAAT?!
H-HELLLLP!
THUNK

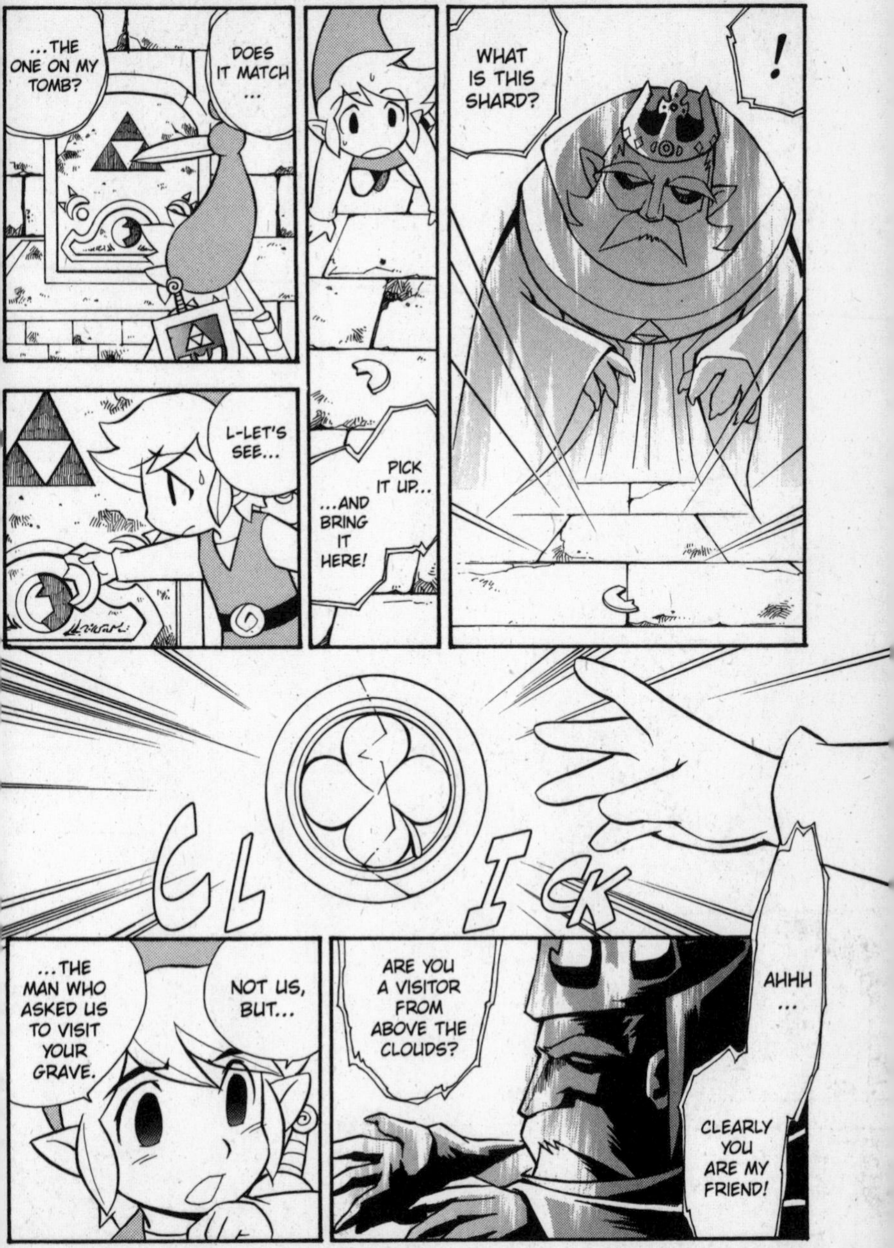
WHAT IS THIS SHARD?
!
DOES IT MATCH...
...THE ONE ON MY TOMB?
PICK IT UP...
...AND BRING IT HERE!
L-LET'S SEE...
CLICK
AHHH...
CLEARLY YOU ARE MY FRIEND!
ARE YOU A VISITOR FROM ABOVE THE CLOUDS?
NOT US, BUT...
...THE MAN WHO ASKED US TO VISIT YOUR GRAVE.

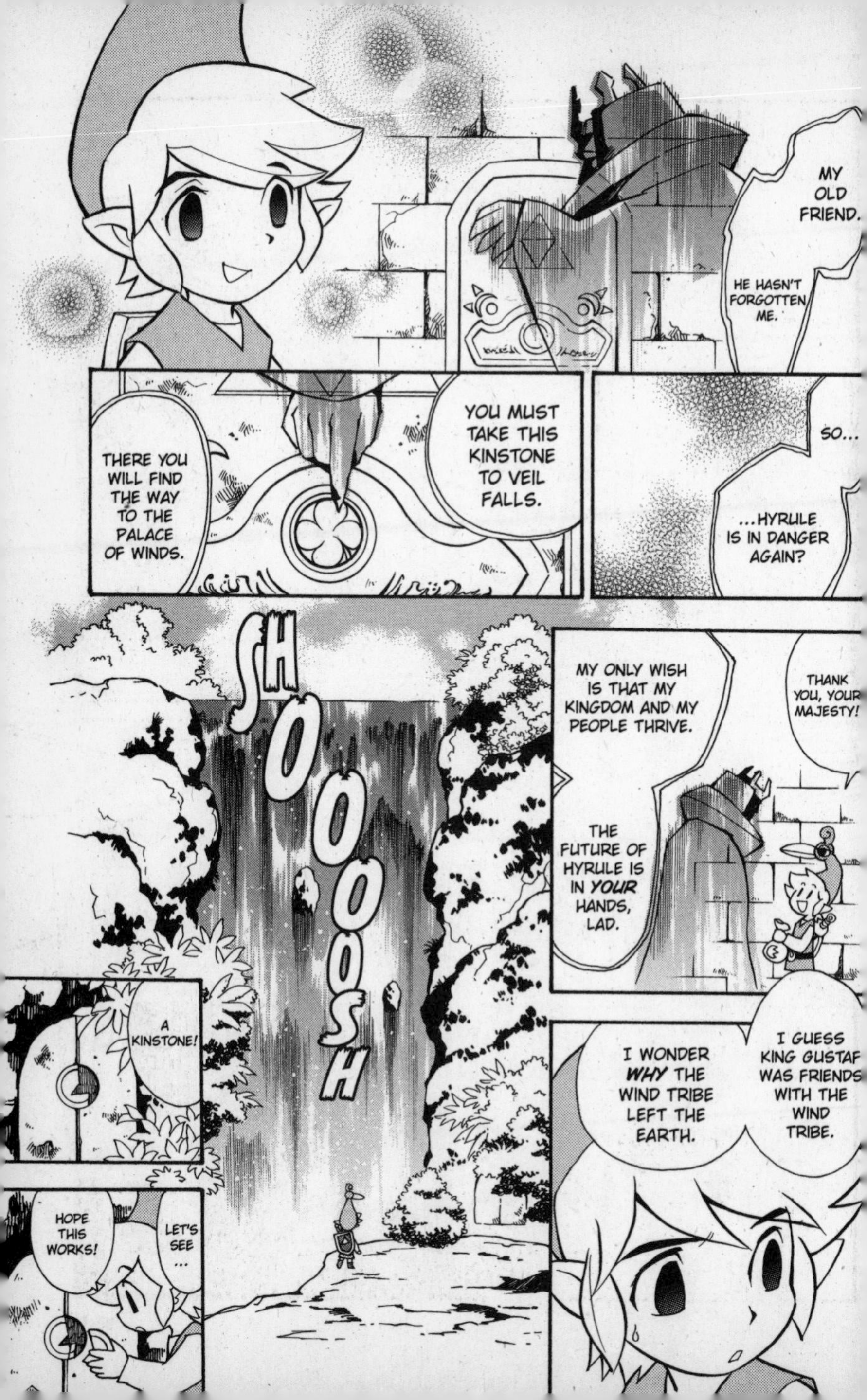
MY OLD FRIEND.
HE HASN'T FORGOTTEN ME.
SO...
...HYRULE IS IN DANGER AGAIN?
YOU MUST TAKE THIS KINSTONE TO VEIL FALLS.
THERE YOU WILL FIND THE WAY TO THE PALACE OF WINDS.
THANK YOU, YOUR MAJESTY!
MY ONLY WISH IS THAT MY KINGDOM AND MY PEOPLE THRIVE.
THE FUTURE OF HYRULE IS IN *YOUR* HANDS, LAD.
I GUESS KING GUSTAF WAS FRIENDS WITH THE WIND TRIBE.
I WONDER *WHY* THE WIND TRIBE LEFT THE EARTH.
SHOOOOOSH
A KINSTONE!
LET'S SEE...
HOPE THIS WORKS!

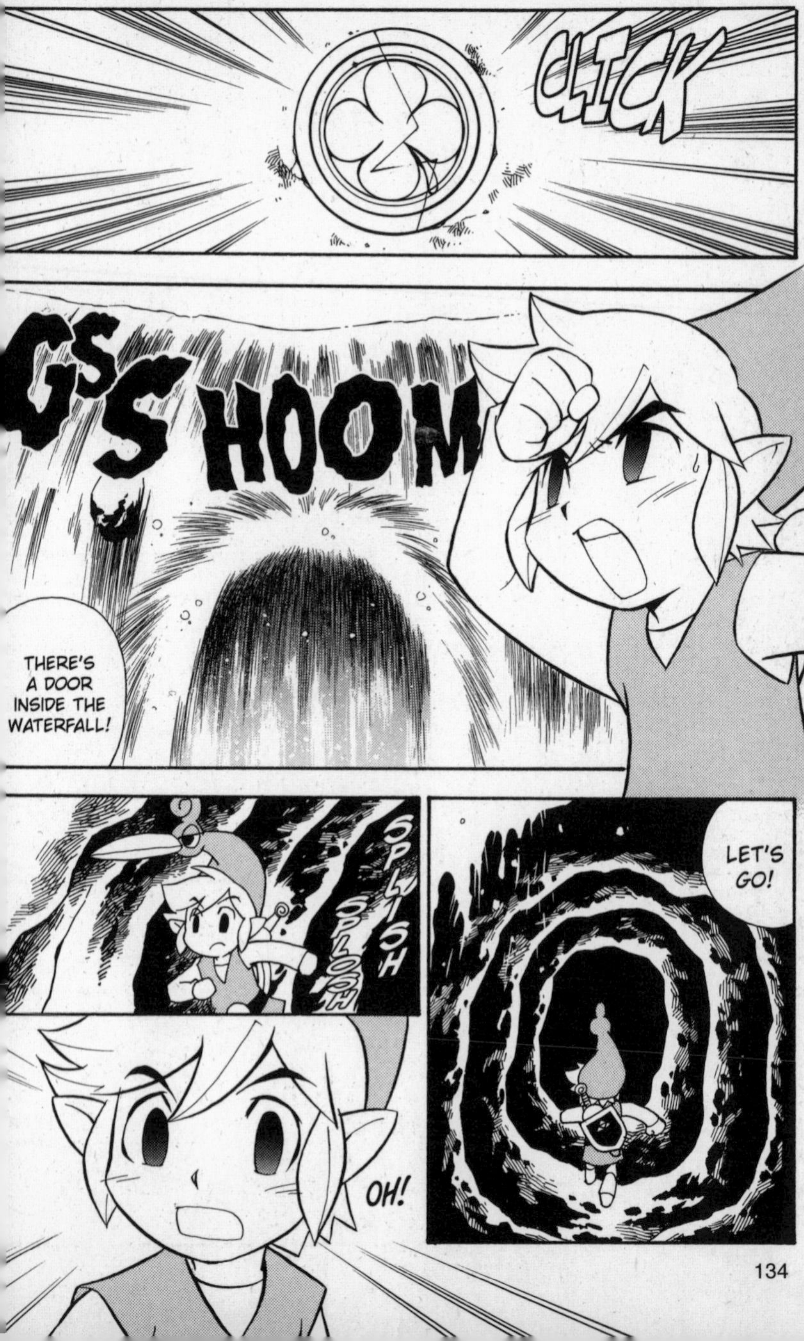
CLICK
GSSHOOM
THERE'S A DOOR INSIDE THE WATERFALL!
LET'S GO!
SPLISH
SPLOOSH
OH!

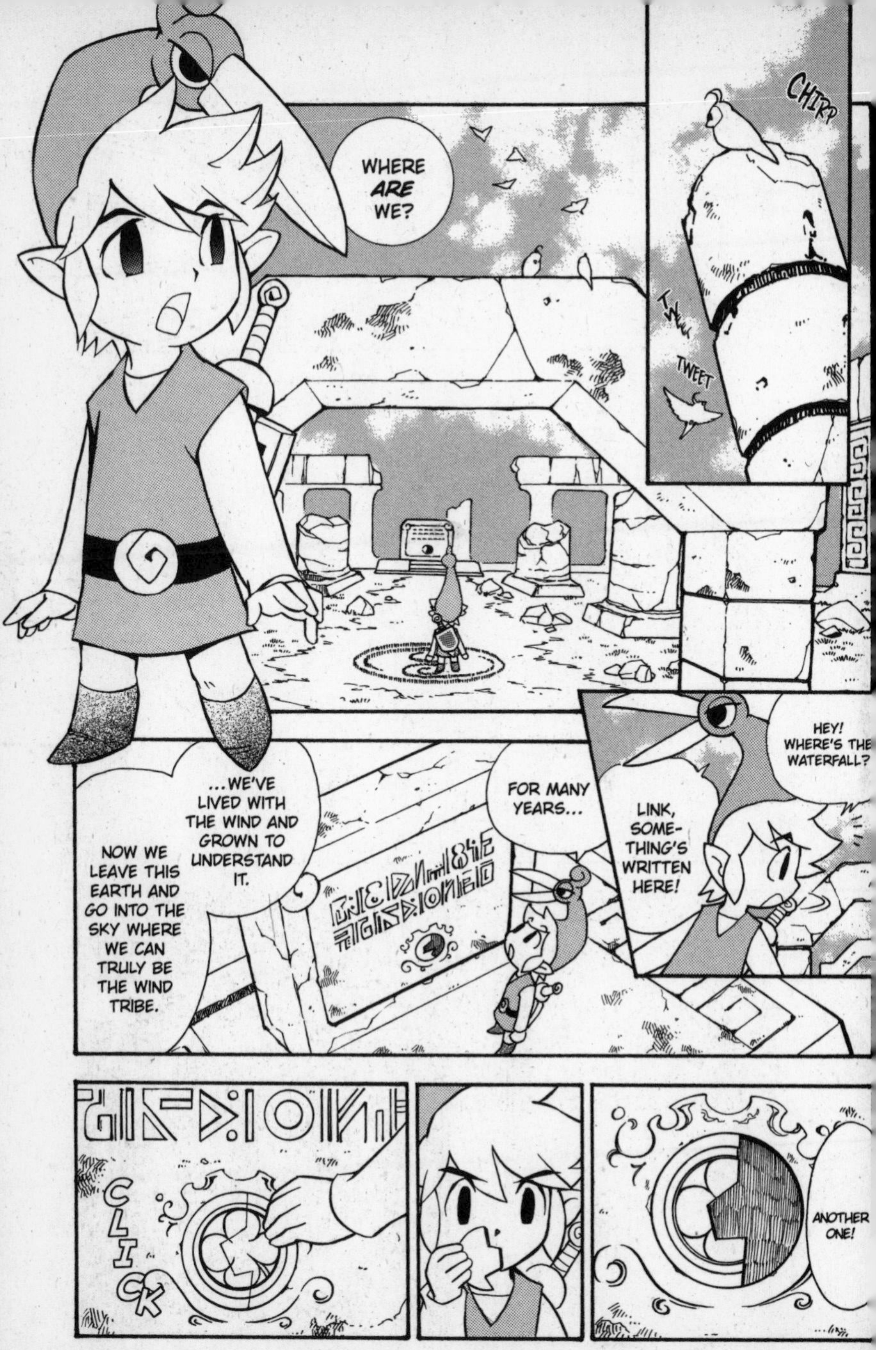
CHIRP
TWEET
WHERE *ARE* WE?
HEY! WHERE'S THE WATERFALL?
LINK, SOME-THING'S WRITTEN HERE!
FOR MANY YEARS...
...WE'VE LIVED WITH THE WIND AND GROWN TO UNDERSTAND IT.
NOW WE LEAVE THIS EARTH AND GO INTO THE SKY WHERE WE CAN TRULY BE THE WIND TRIBE.
ANOTHER ONE!
CLICK

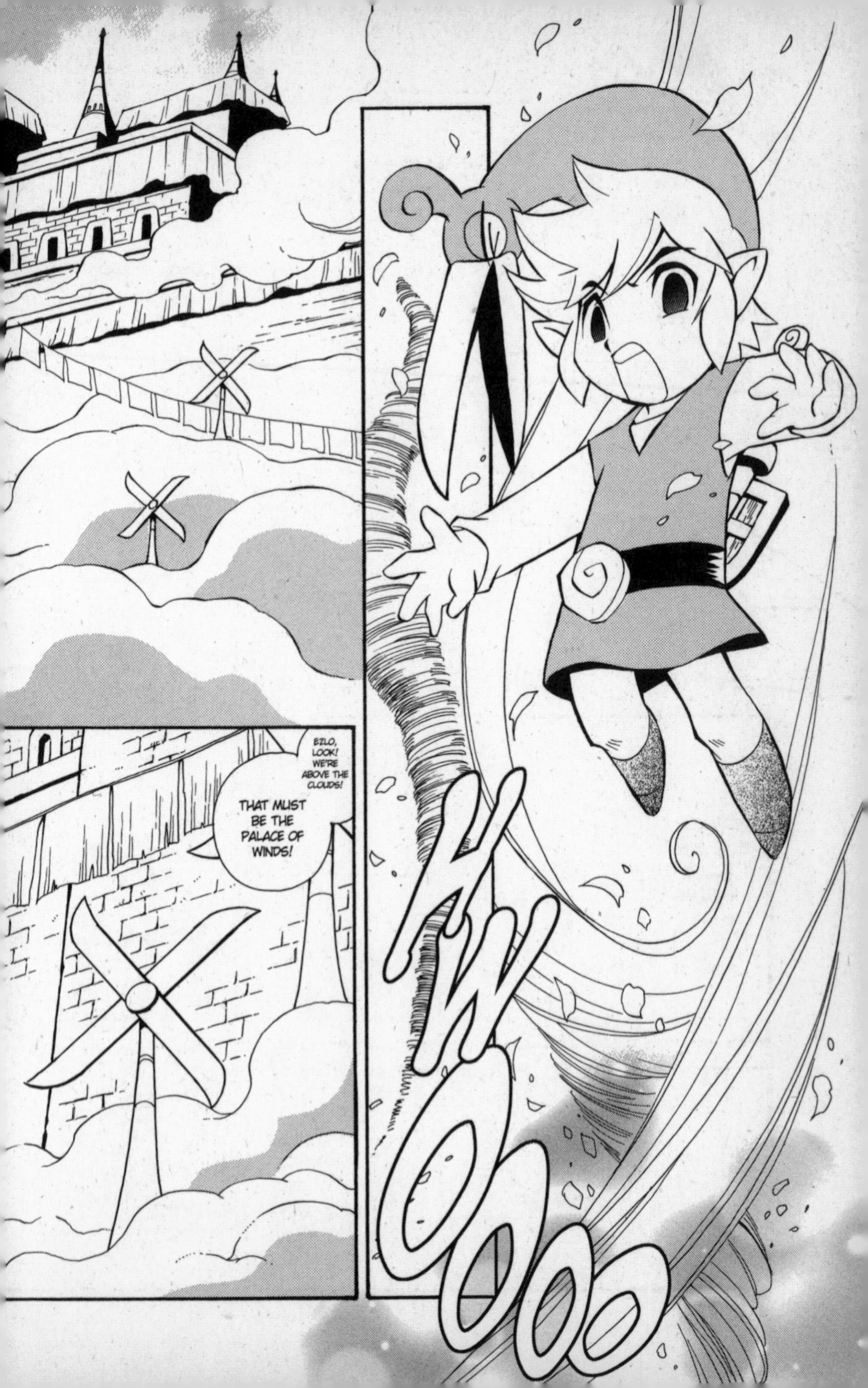
EZLO, LOOK! WE'RE ABOVE THE CLOUDS!
THAT MUST BE THE PALACE OF WINDS!

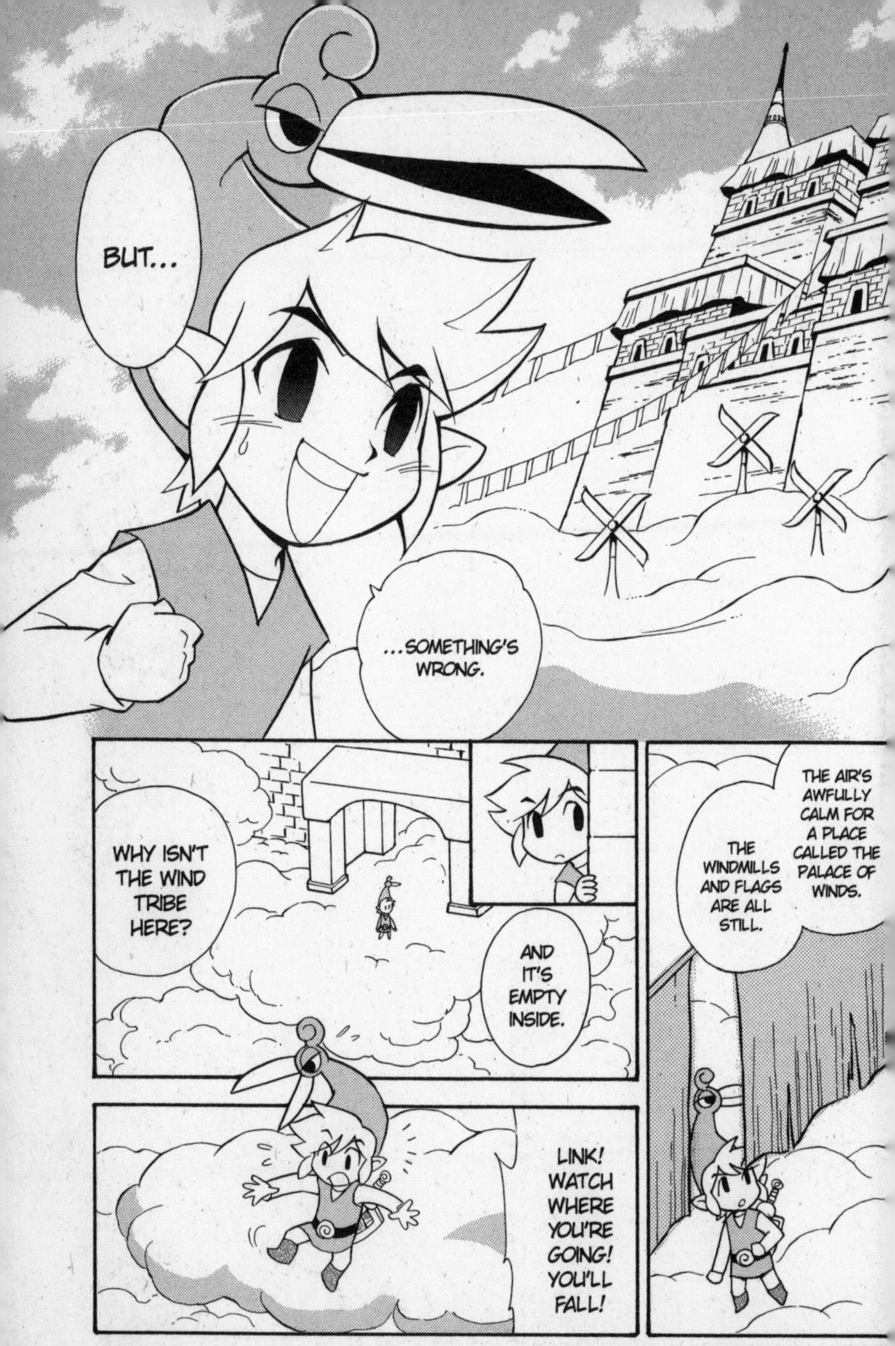
BUT...
...SOMETHING'S WRONG.
THE AIR'S AWFULLY CALM FOR A PLACE CALLED THE PALACE OF WINDS.
THE WINDMILLS AND FLAGS ARE ALL STILL.
AND IT'S EMPTY INSIDE.
WHY ISN'T THE WIND TRIBE HERE?
LINK! WATCH WHERE YOU'RE GOING! YOU'LL FALL!

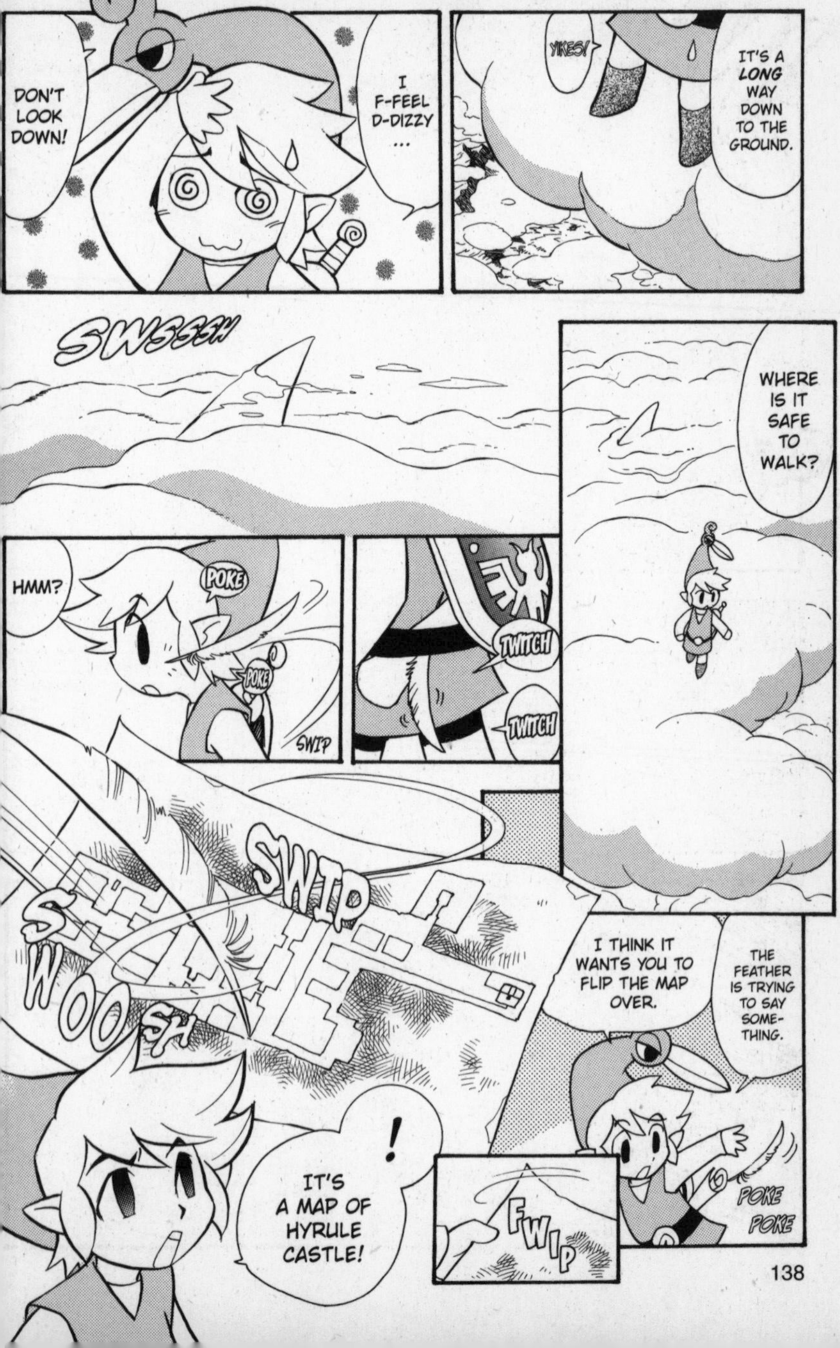

IT'S A LONG WAY DOWN TO THE GROUND.
YIKES!
I F-FEEL D-DIZZY ...
DON'T LOOK DOWN!
WHERE IS IT SAFE TO WALK?
SWSSSH
TWITCH
TWITCH
HMM?
POKE
POKE
SWIP
SWIP
SWOOSH
THE FEATHER IS TRYING TO SAY SOME-THING.
I THINK IT WANTS YOU TO FLIP THE MAP OVER.
POKE
POKE
FWIP
!
IT'S A MAP OF HYRULE CASTLE!

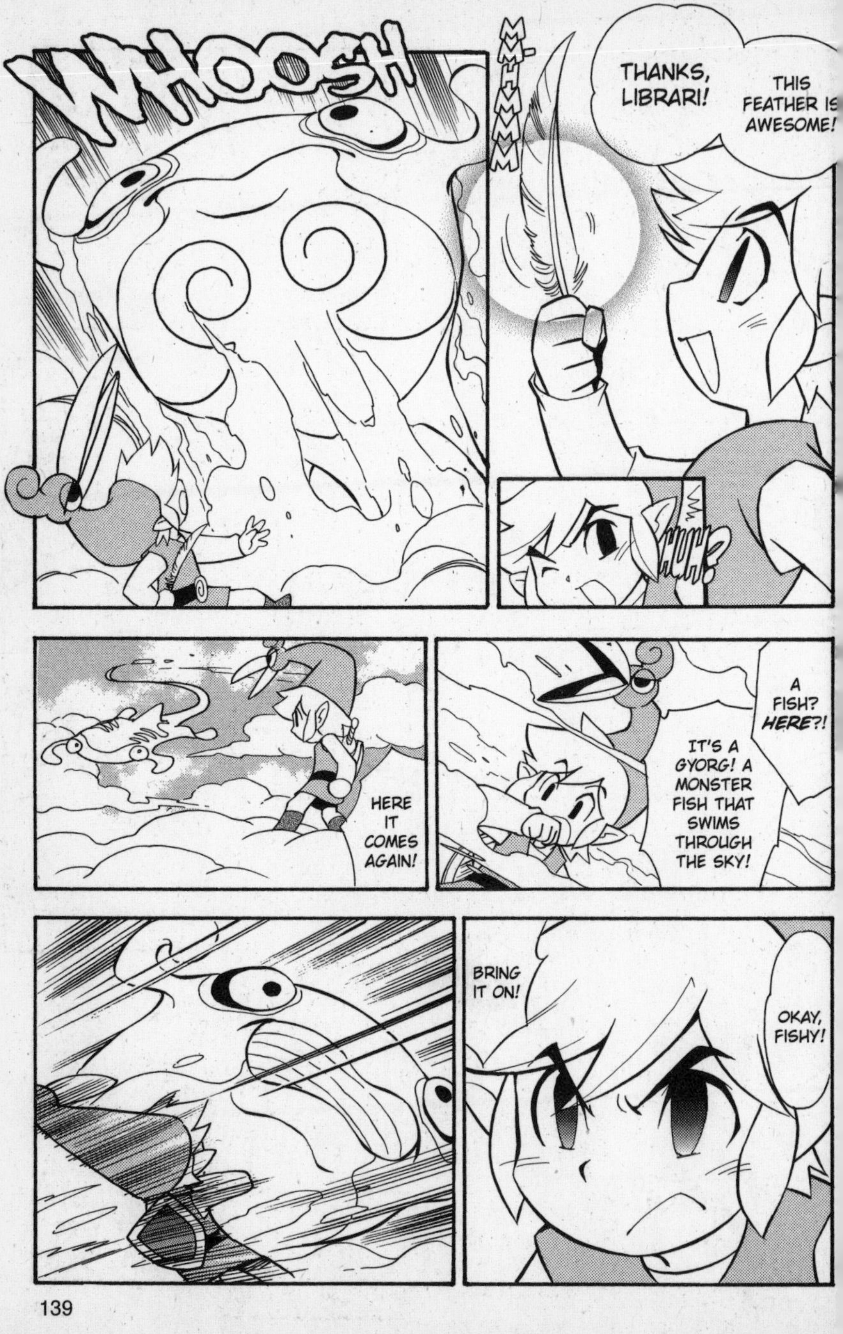
THANKS, LIBRARI! THIS FEATHER IS AWESOME!
HUH?!
WHOOSH
A FISH? HERE?!
IT'S A GYORG! A MONSTER FISH THAT SWIMS THROUGH THE SKY!
HERE IT COMES AGAIN!
OKAY, FISHY!
BRING IT ON!

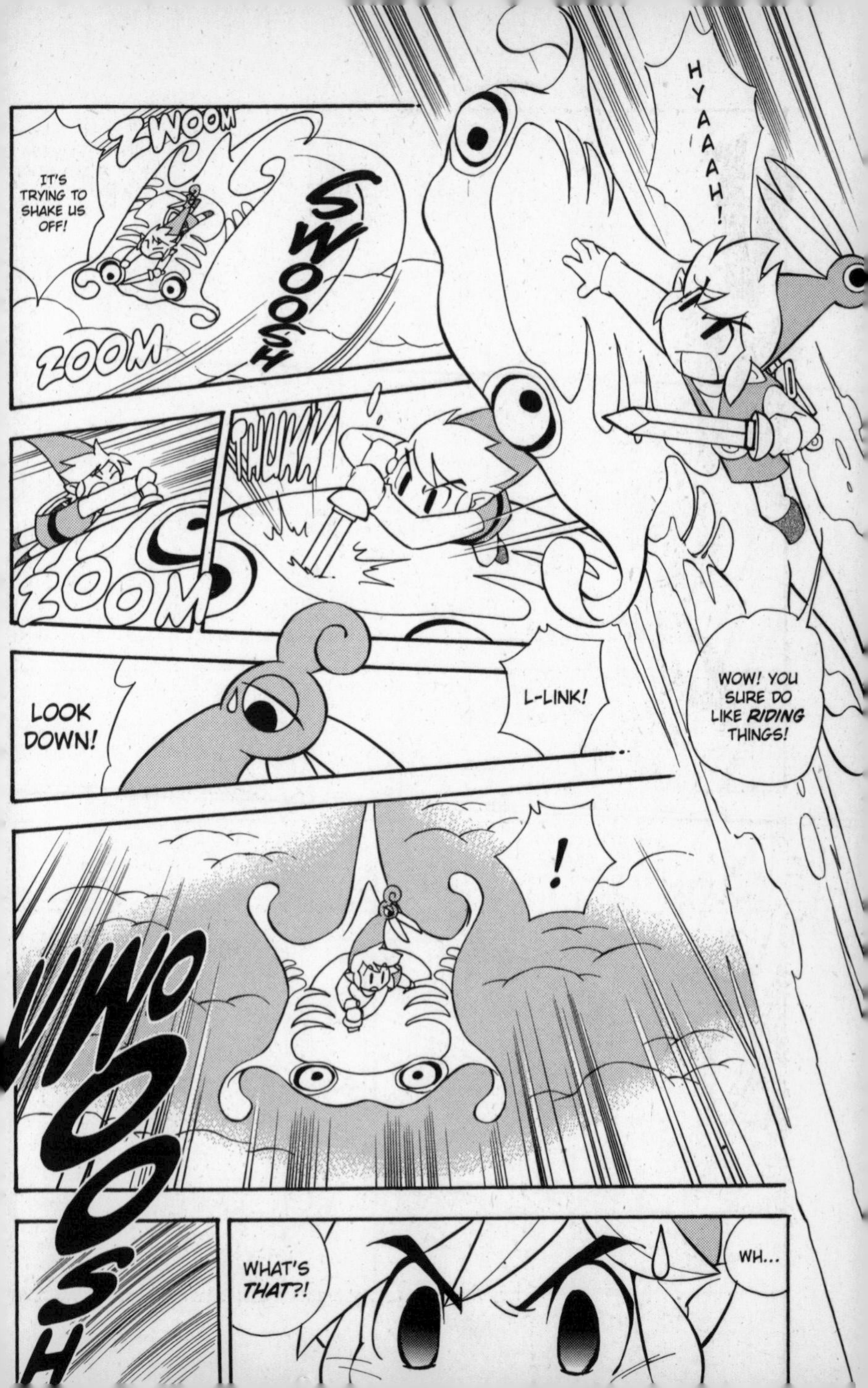
HYAAAH!
WOW! YOU SURE DO LIKE *RIDING* THINGS!
ZWOOM
IT'S TRYING TO SHAKE US OFF!
SWOOOSH
ZOOM
THUNK
ZOOM
L-LINK!
LOOK DOWN!
!
WHOOSH
WH...
WHAT'S *THAT*?!

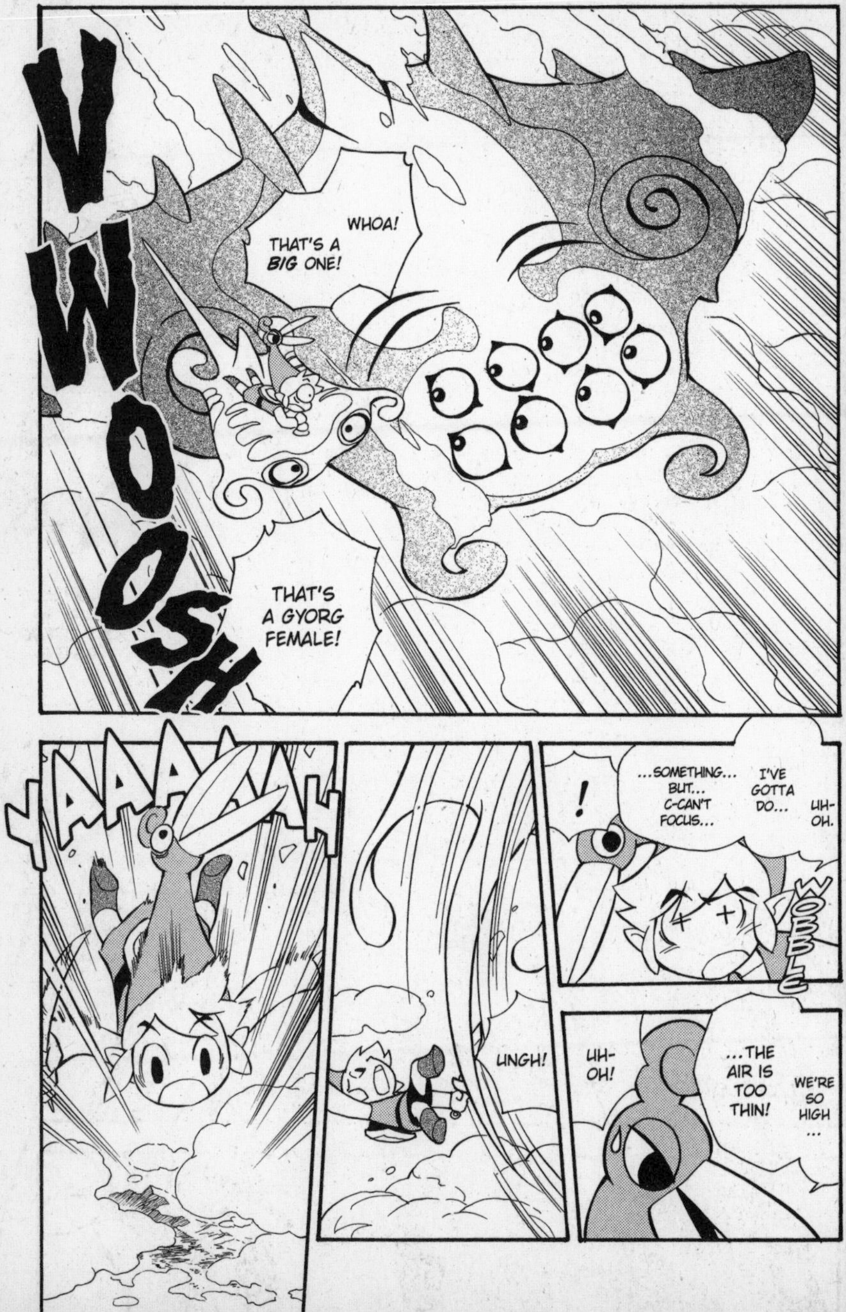
VWOOSH
WHOA!
THAT'S A *BIG* ONE!
THAT'S A GYORG FEMALE!
UH-OH.
I'VE GOTTA DO...
...SOMETHING... BUT... C-CAN'T FOCUS...
!
WOBBLE
WE'RE SO HIGH ...
...THE AIR IS TOO THIN!
UH-OH!
UNGH!
YAAAAAH

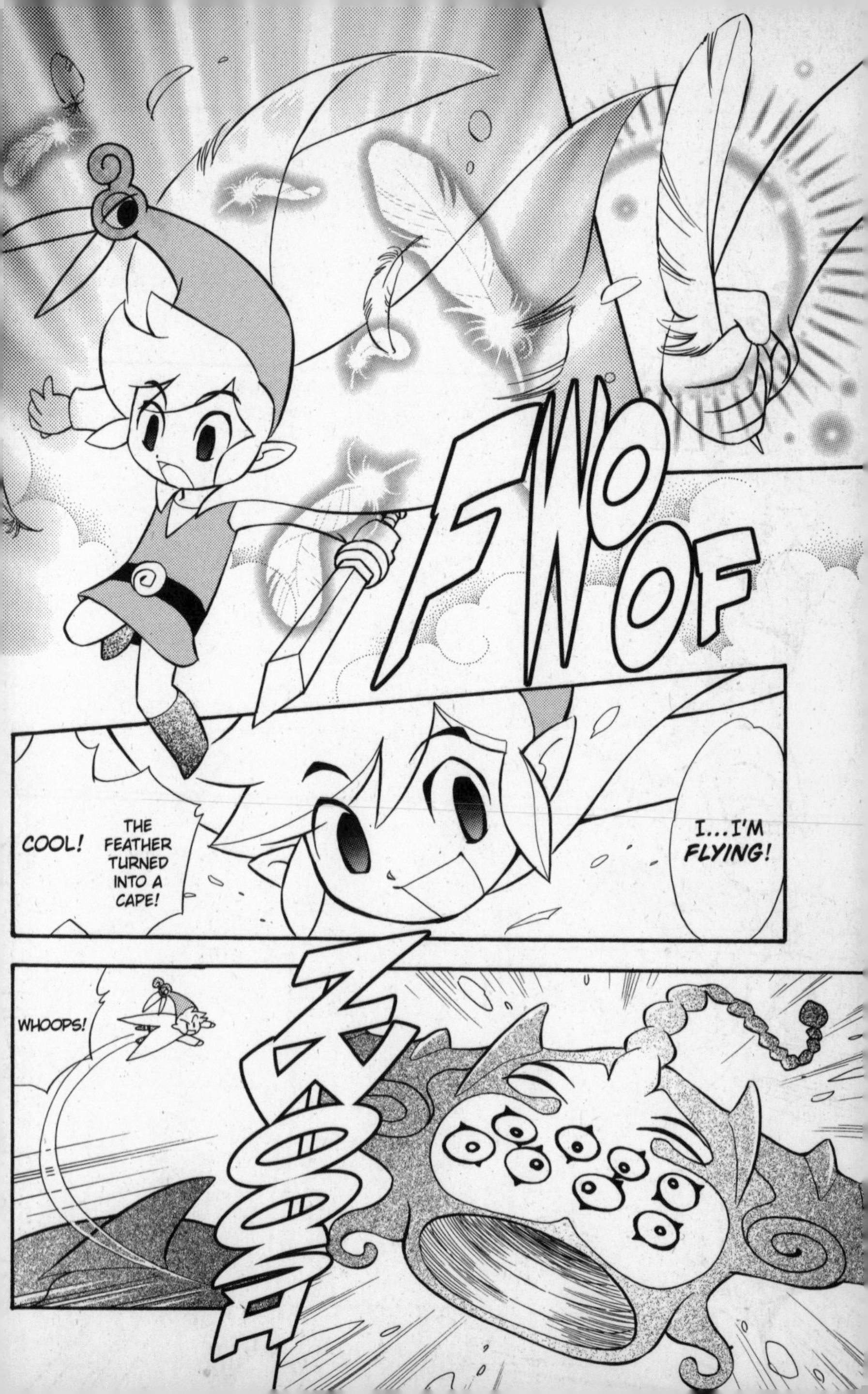
FWOOF
I...I'M FLYING!
THE FEATHER TURNED INTO A CAPE!
COOL!
WHOOSH
WHOOPS!

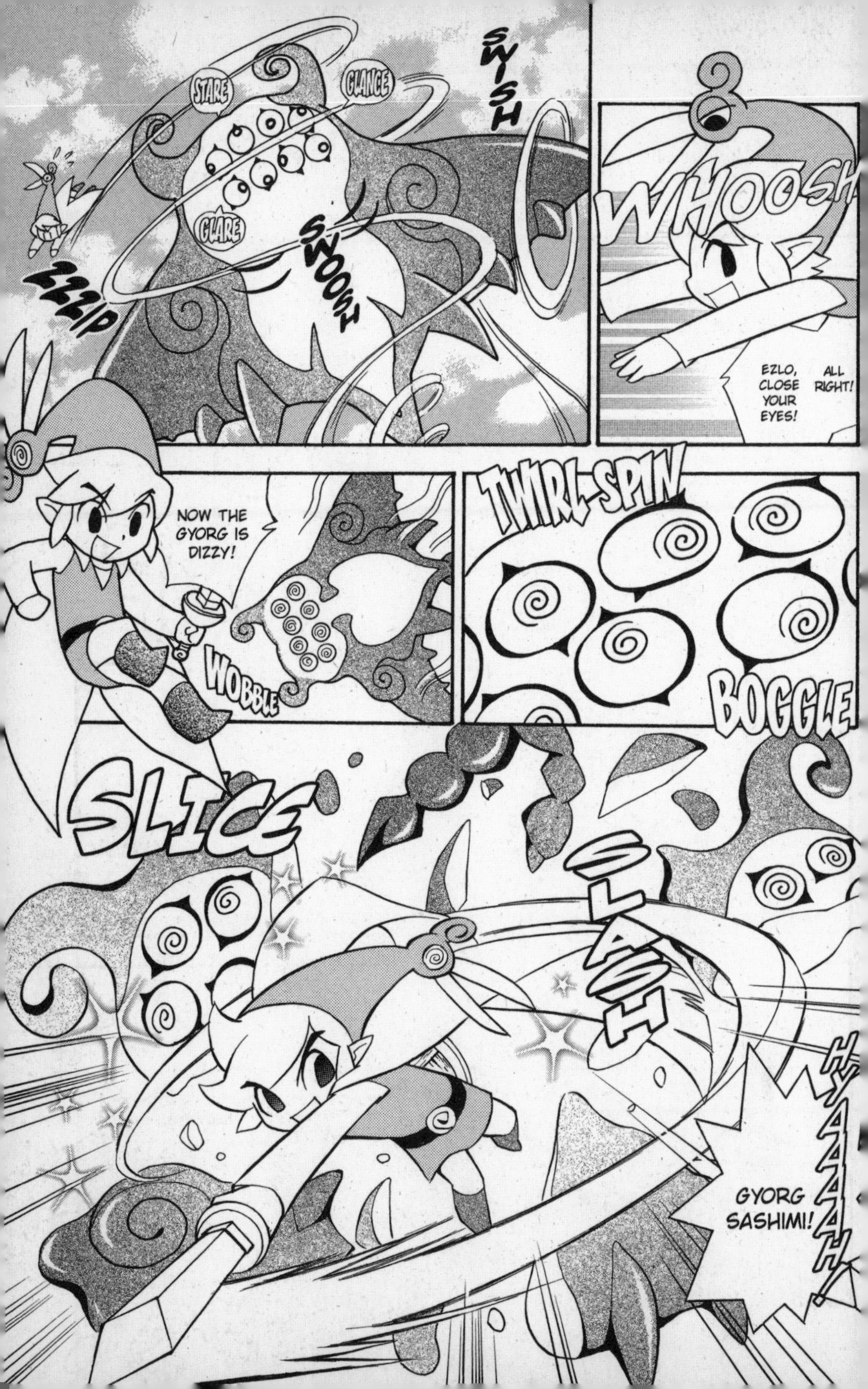
WHOOSH
EZLO, CLOSE YOUR EYES!
ALL RIGHT!
SWISH
GLANCE
STARE
GLARE
SWOOSH
ZZZIP
TWIRL-SPIN
BOGGLE
NOW THE GYORG IS DIZZY!
WOBBLE
HYAAAAAH!
GYORG SASHIMI!
SLASH
SLICE

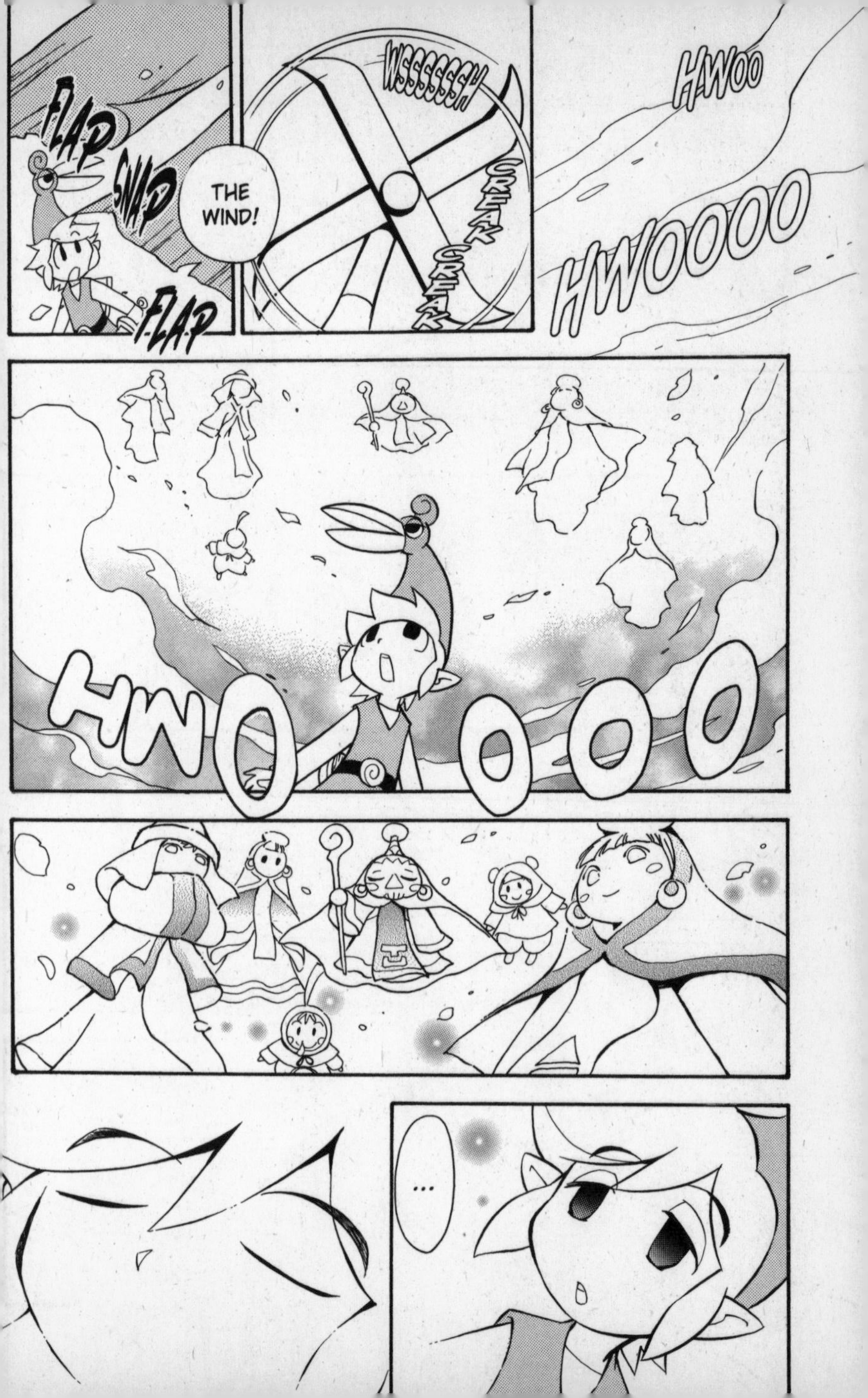
HWOO
HWOOOOO
WSSSSSSH
THE WIND!
CREAK CREAK
FLAP
SNAP
FLAP
HWOOOO
...

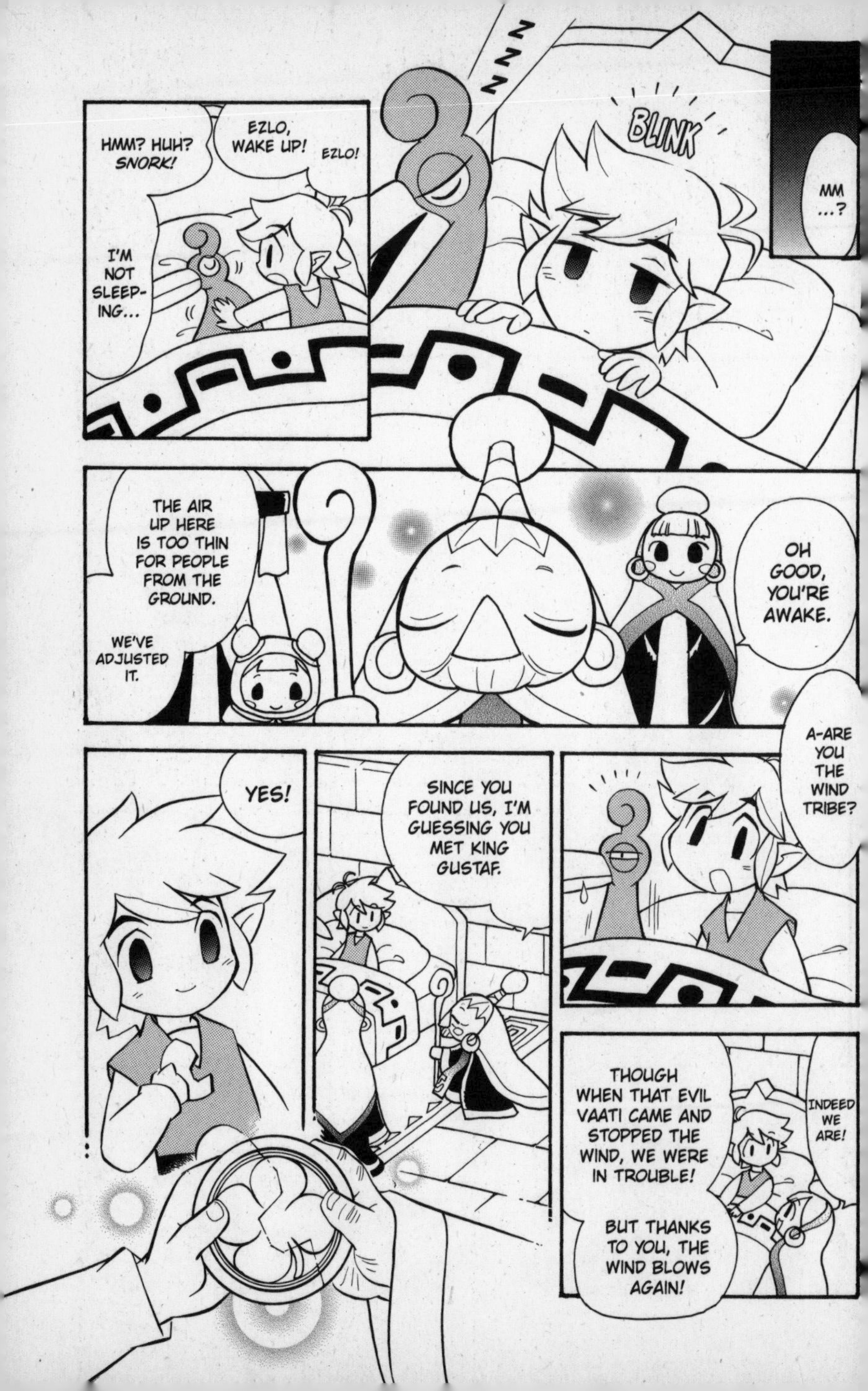
MM ...?
Z Z Z
BLINK
EZLO!
EZLO, WAKE UP!
HMM? HUH? SNORK!
I'M NOT SLEEPING...
OH GOOD, YOU'RE AWAKE.
THE AIR UP HERE IS TOO THIN FOR PEOPLE FROM THE GROUND.
WE'VE ADJUSTED IT.
A-ARE YOU THE WIND TRIBE?
INDEED WE ARE!
THOUGH WHEN THAT EVIL VAATI CAME AND STOPPED THE WIND, WE WERE IN TROUBLE!
BUT THANKS TO YOU, THE WIND BLOWS AGAIN!
SINCE YOU FOUND US, I'M GUESSING YOU MET KING GUSTAF.
YES!

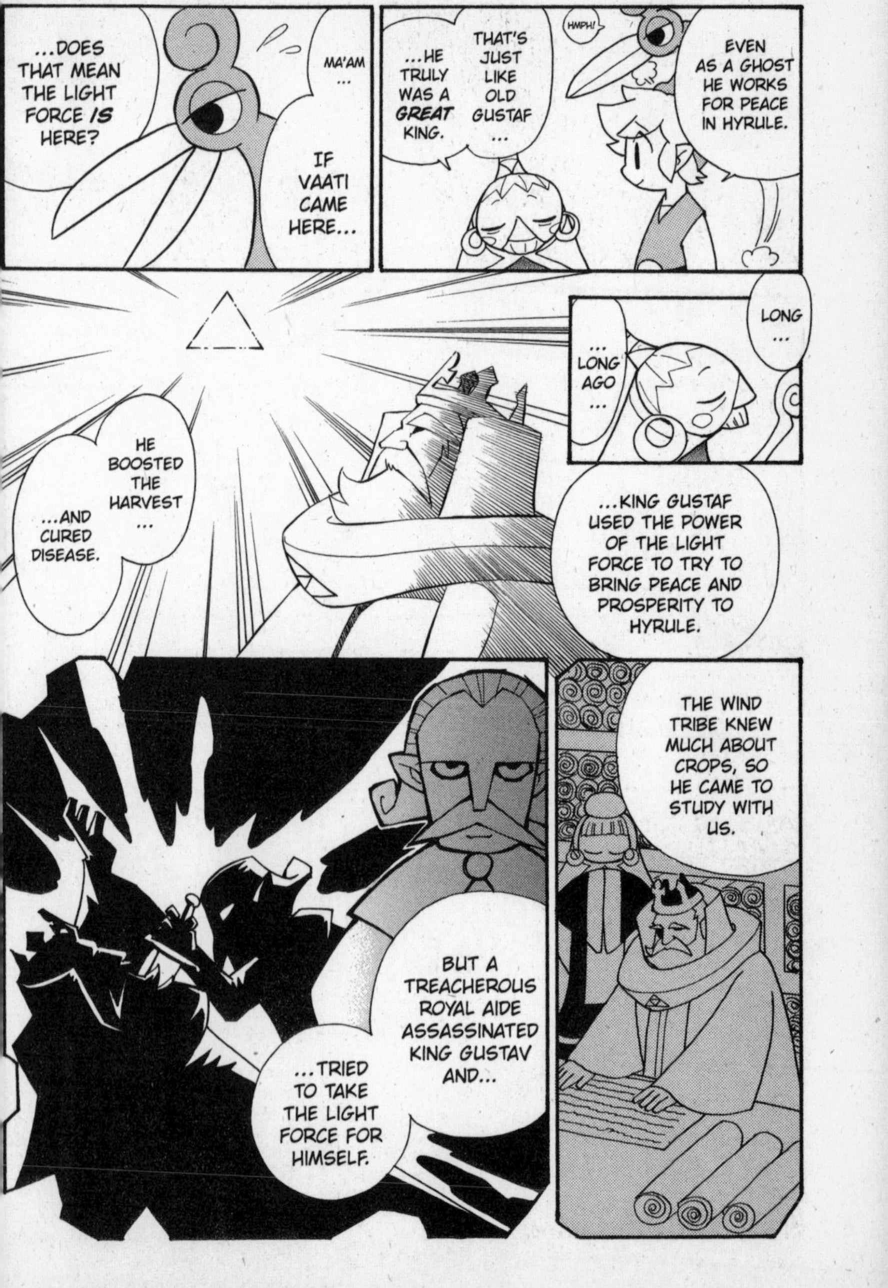
HMPH!
EVEN AS A GHOST HE WORKS FOR PEACE IN HYRULE.
THAT'S JUST LIKE OLD GUSTAF ...
...HE TRULY WAS A *GREAT* KING.
MA'AM ...
IF VAATI CAME HERE...
...DOES THAT MEAN THE LIGHT FORCE *IS* HERE?
LONG ...
... LONG AGO ...
...KING GUSTAF USED THE POWER OF THE LIGHT FORCE TO TRY TO BRING PEACE AND PROSPERITY TO HYRULE.
HE BOOSTED THE HARVEST ...
...AND CURED DISEASE.
THE WIND TRIBE KNEW MUCH ABOUT CROPS, SO HE CAME TO STUDY WITH US.
BUT A TREACHEROUS ROYAL AIDE ASSASSINATED KING GUSTAV AND...
...TRIED TO TAKE THE LIGHT FORCE FOR HIMSELF.

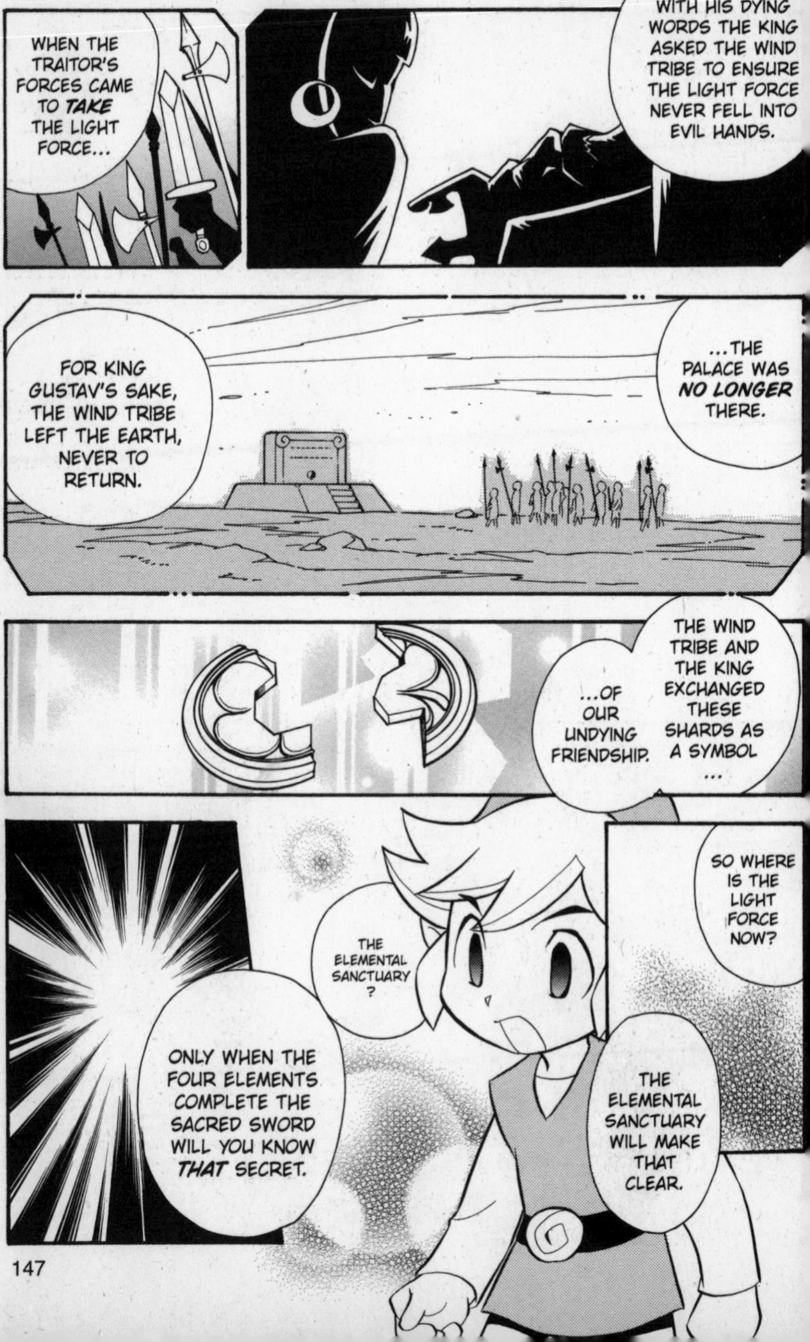
WITH HIS DYING WORDS THE KING ASKED THE WIND TRIBE TO ENSURE THE LIGHT FORCE NEVER FELL INTO EVIL HANDS.
WHEN THE TRAITOR'S FORCES CAME TO *TAKE* THE LIGHT FORCE...
...THE PALACE WAS *NO LONGER* THERE.
FOR KING GUSTAV'S SAKE, THE WIND TRIBE LEFT THE EARTH, NEVER TO RETURN.
THE WIND TRIBE AND THE KING EXCHANGED THESE SHARDS AS A SYMBOL...
...OF OUR UNDYING FRIENDSHIP.
SO WHERE IS THE LIGHT FORCE NOW?
THE ELEMENTAL SANCTUARY WILL MAKE THAT CLEAR.
THE ELEMENTAL SANCTUARY?
ONLY WHEN THE FOUR ELEMENTS COMPLETE THE SACRED SWORD WILL YOU KNOW *THAT* SECRET.

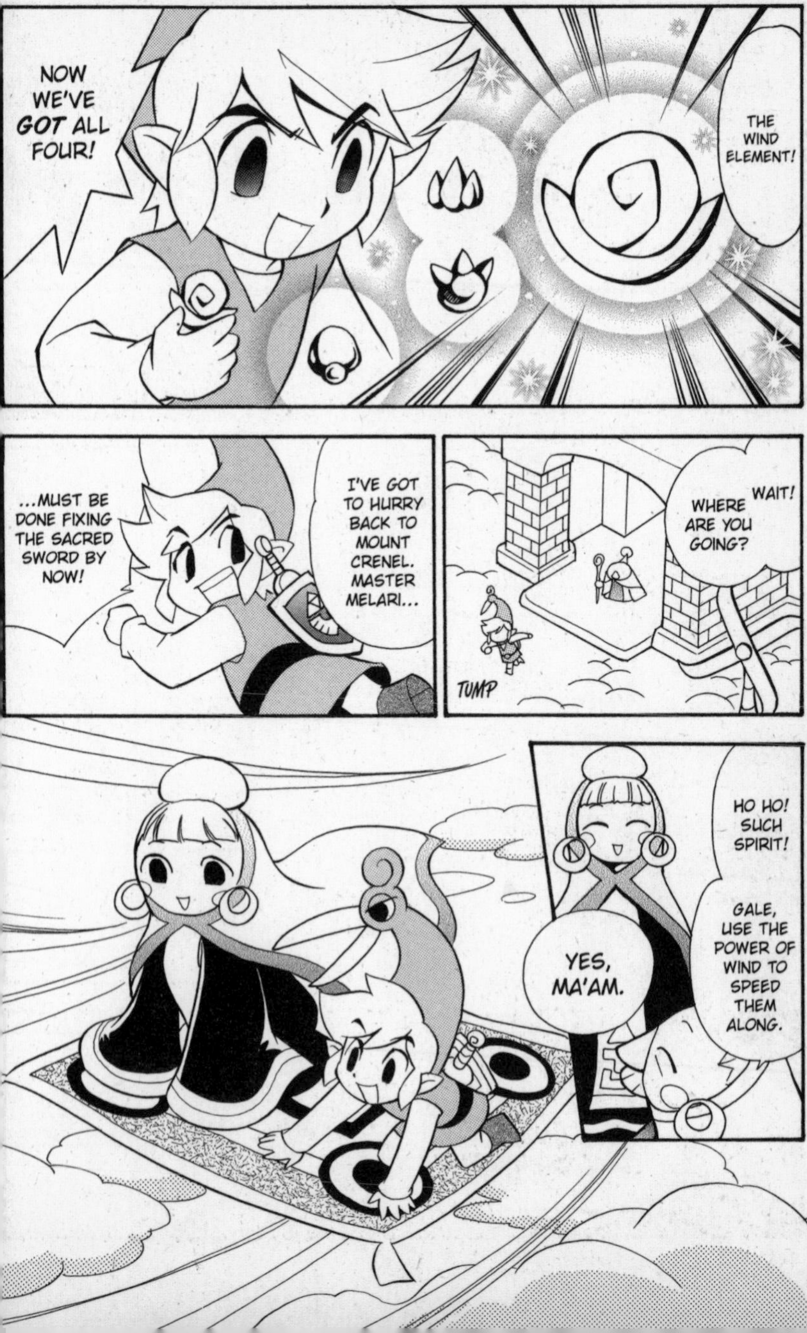
THE WIND ELEMENT!
NOW WE'VE GOT ALL FOUR!
WAIT!
WHERE ARE YOU GOING?
TUMP
I'VE GOT TO HURRY BACK TO MOUNT CRENEL. MASTER MELARI...
...MUST BE DONE FIXING THE SACRED SWORD BY NOW!
HO HO! SUCH SPIRIT!
GALE, USE THE POWER OF WIND TO SPEED THEM ALONG.
YES, MA'AM.

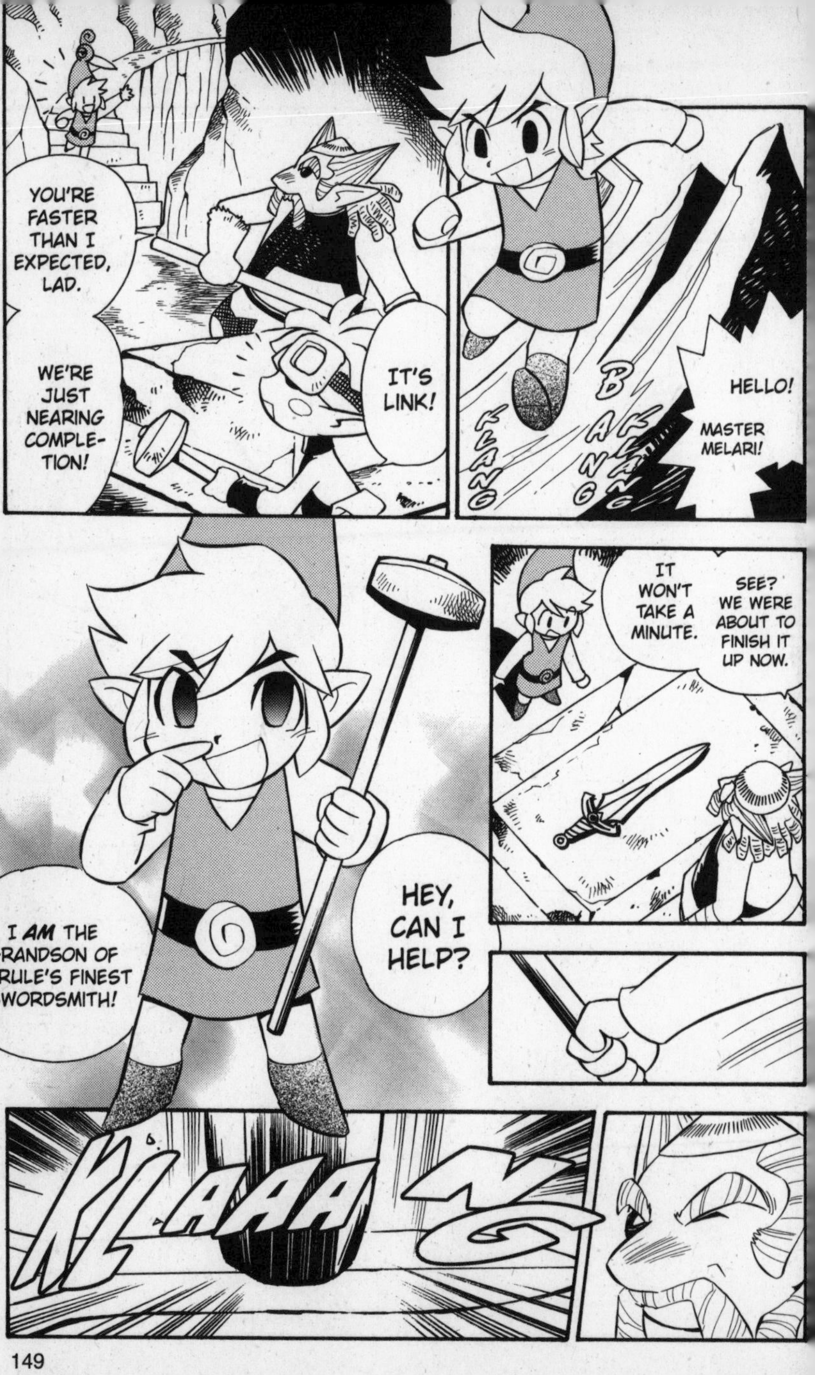
HELLO!
MASTER MELARI!
KLANG
BANG
KLANG
IT'S LINK!
YOU'RE FASTER THAN I EXPECTED, LAD.
WE'RE JUST NEARING COMPLE-TION!
SEE? WE WERE ABOUT TO FINISH IT UP NOW.
IT WON'T TAKE A MINUTE.
HEY, CAN I HELP?
I *AM* THE GRANDSON OF HYRULE'S FINEST SWORDSMITH!
KLAAANG

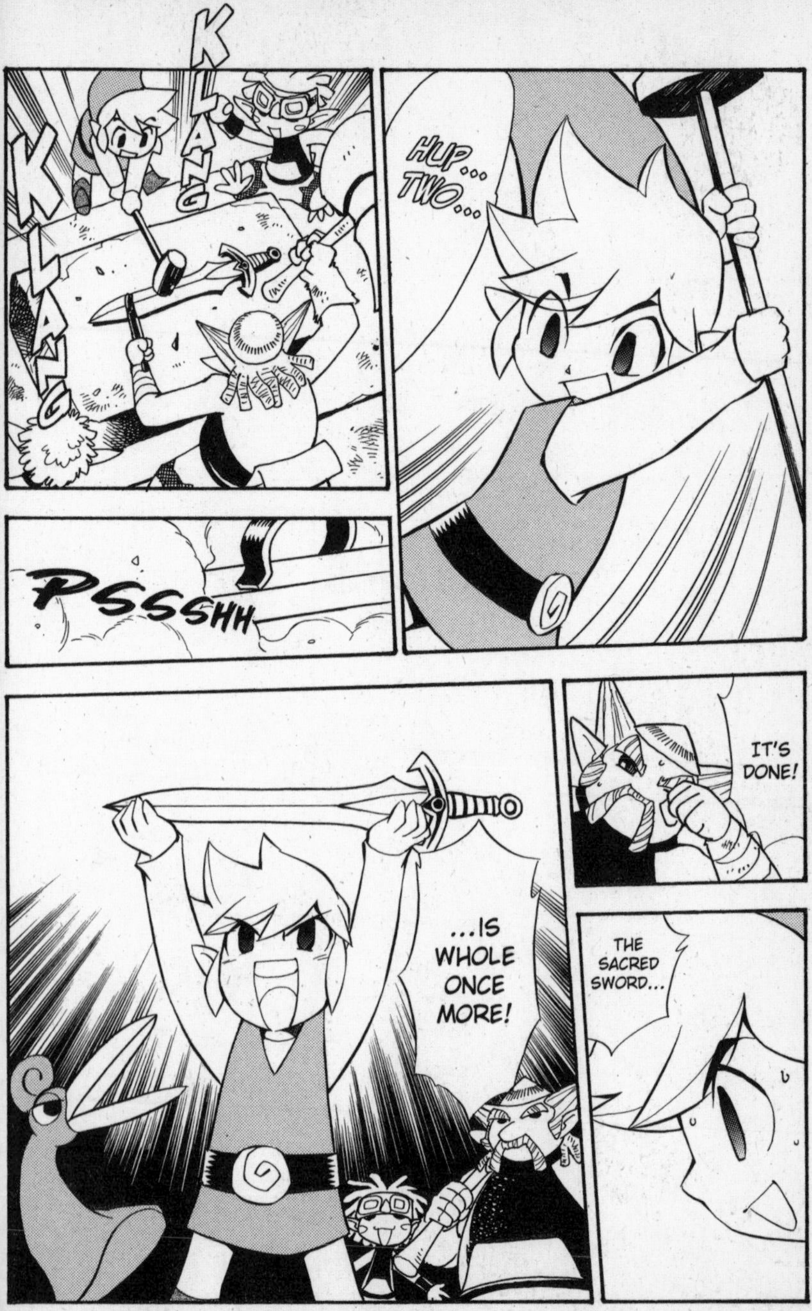
HUP...
TWO...
KLANG
KLANG
PSSSHH
IT'S DONE!
THE SACRED SWORD...
...IS WHOLE ONCE MORE!

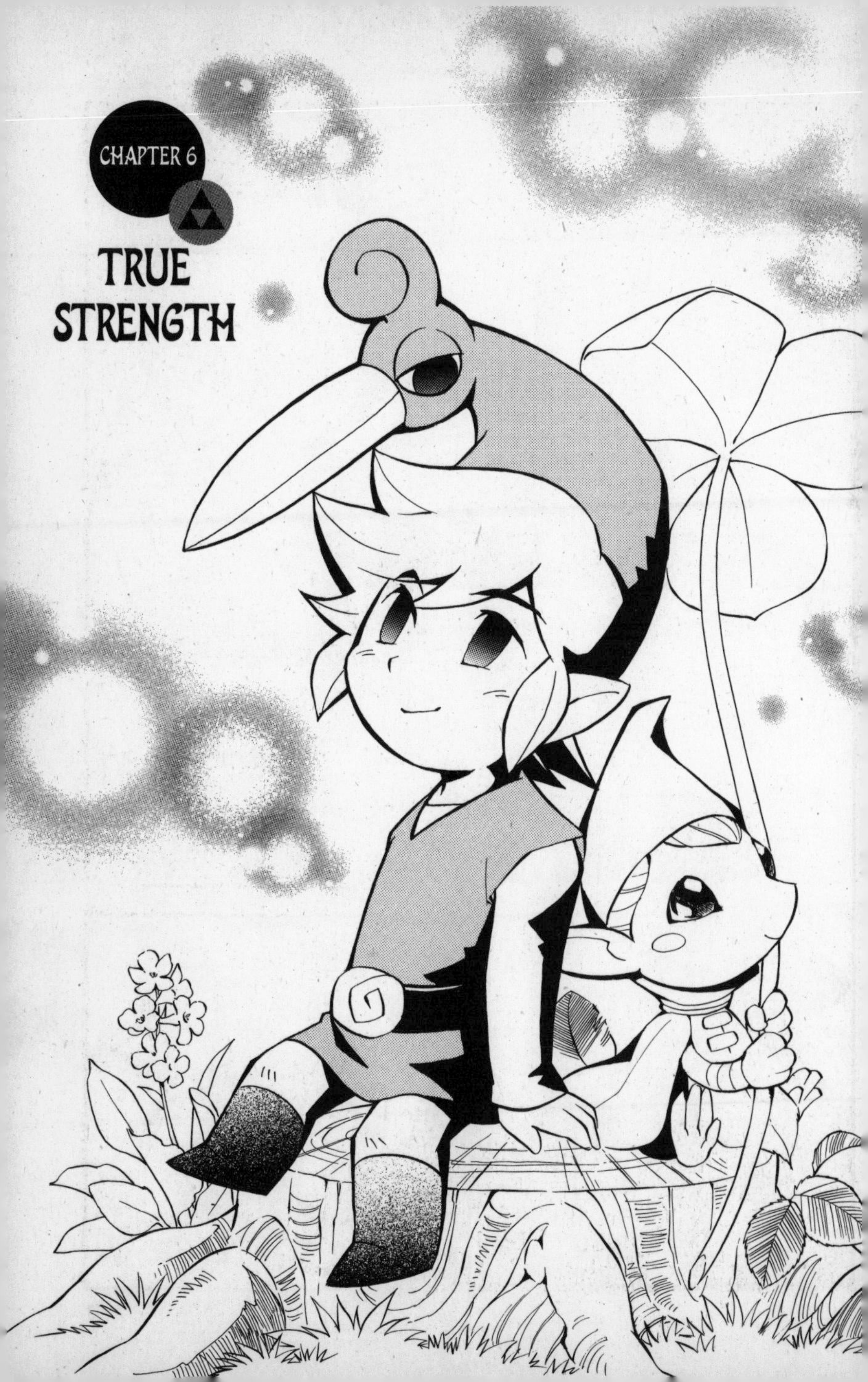
CHAPTER 6
TRUE STRENGTH

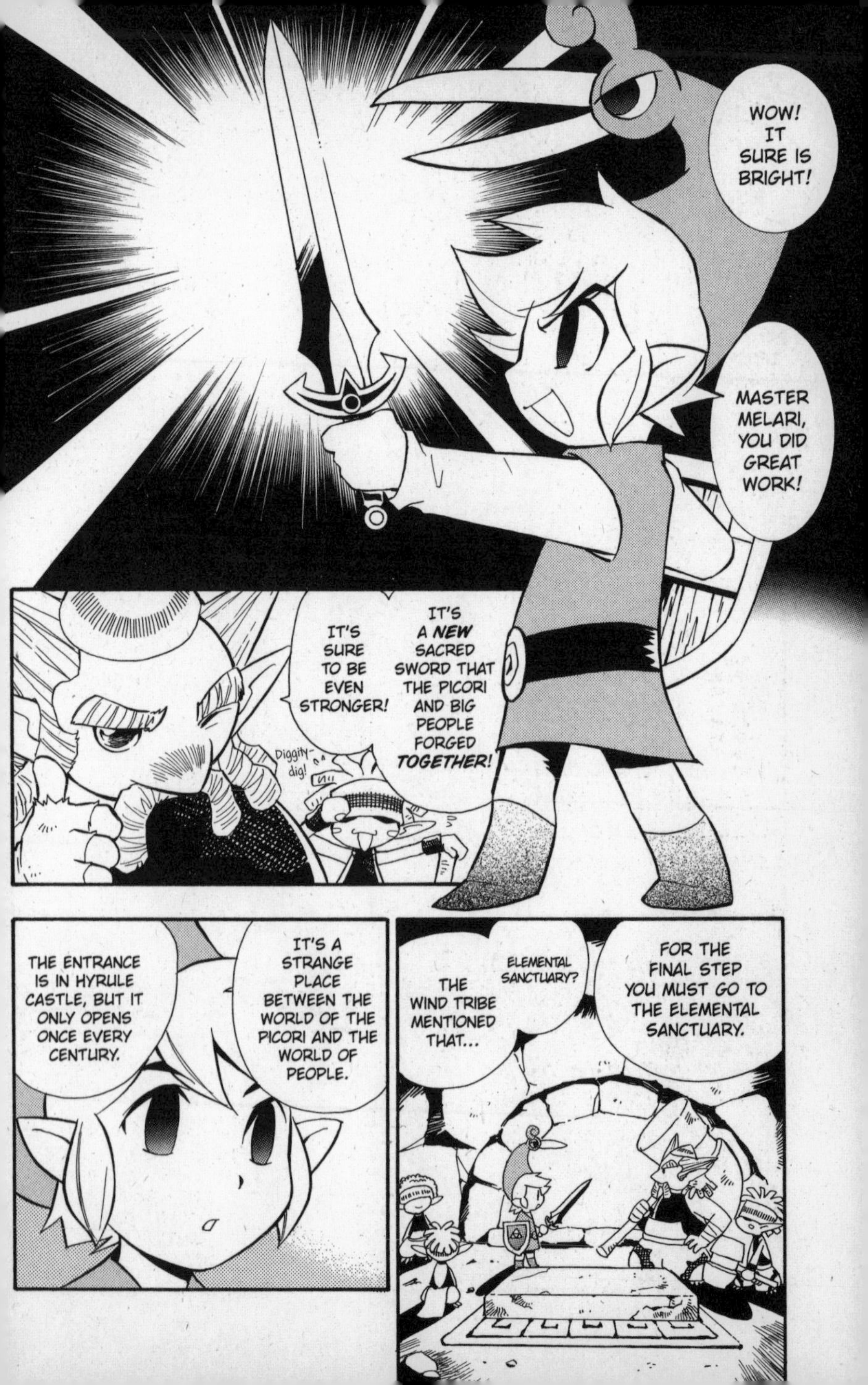
WOW! IT SURE IS BRIGHT!
MASTER MELARI, YOU DID GREAT WORK!
IT'S A *NEW* SACRED SWORD THAT THE PICORI AND BIG PEOPLE FORGED ***TOGETHER***!
IT'S SURE TO BE EVEN STRONGER!
Diggity-dig!
FOR THE FINAL STEP YOU MUST GO TO THE ELEMENTAL SANCTUARY.
ELEMENTAL SANCTUARY?
THE WIND TRIBE MENTIONED THAT...
IT'S A STRANGE PLACE BETWEEN THE WORLD OF THE PICORI AND THE WORLD OF PEOPLE.
THE ENTRANCE IS IN HYRULE CASTLE, BUT IT ONLY OPENS ONCE EVERY CENTURY.

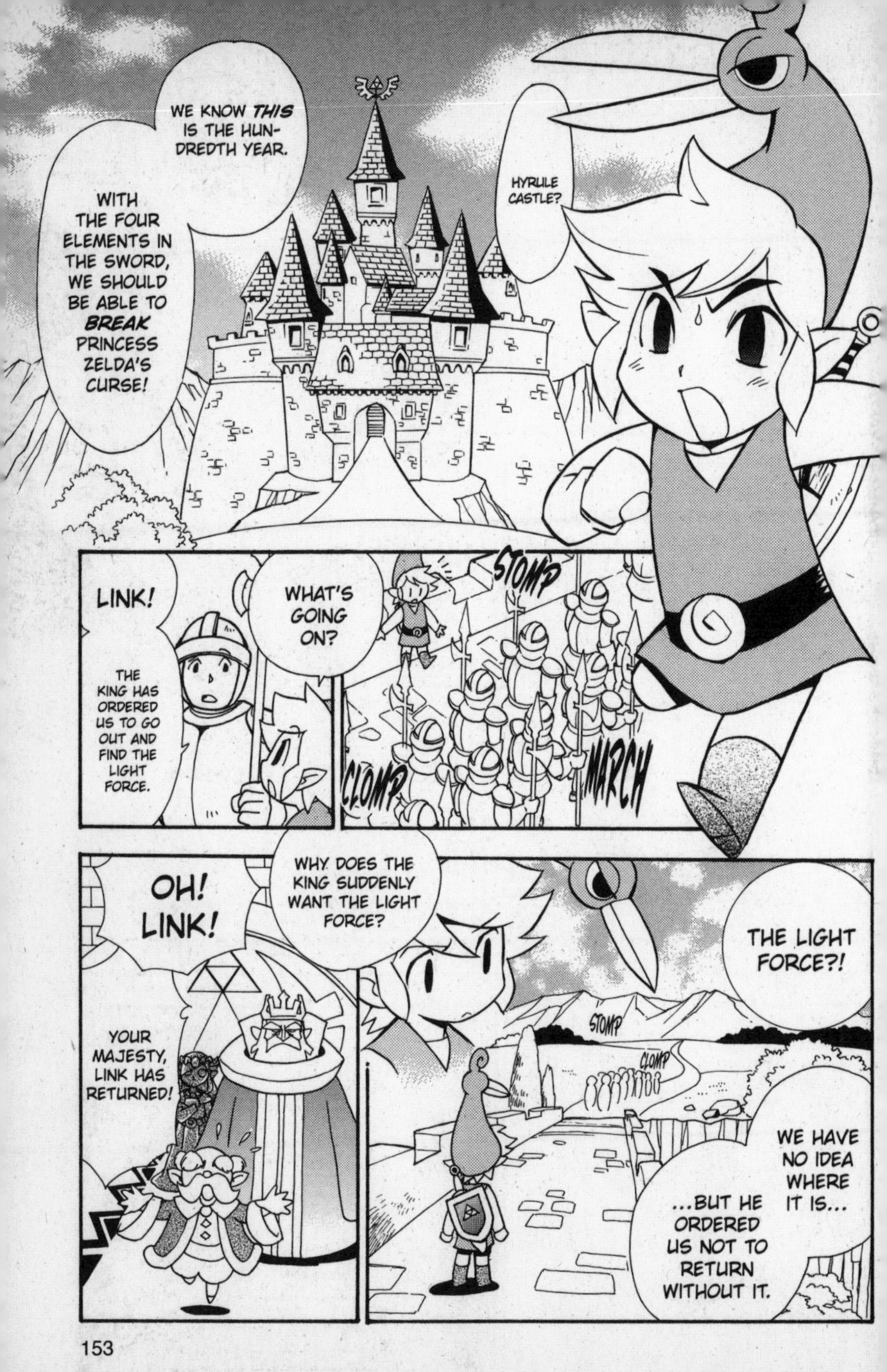
HYRULE CASTLE?
WE KNOW *THIS* IS THE HUNDREDTH YEAR.
WITH THE FOUR ELEMENTS IN THE SWORD, WE SHOULD BE ABLE TO *BREAK* PRINCESS ZELDA'S CURSE!
STOMP
MARCH
CLOMP
WHAT'S GOING ON?
LINK!
THE KING HAS ORDERED US TO GO OUT AND FIND THE LIGHT FORCE.
THE LIGHT FORCE?!
WHY DOES THE KING SUDDENLY WANT THE LIGHT FORCE?
STOMP
CLOMP
WE HAVE NO IDEA WHERE IT IS...
...BUT HE ORDERED US NOT TO RETURN WITHOUT IT.
OH! LINK!
YOUR MAJESTY, LINK HAS RETURNED!

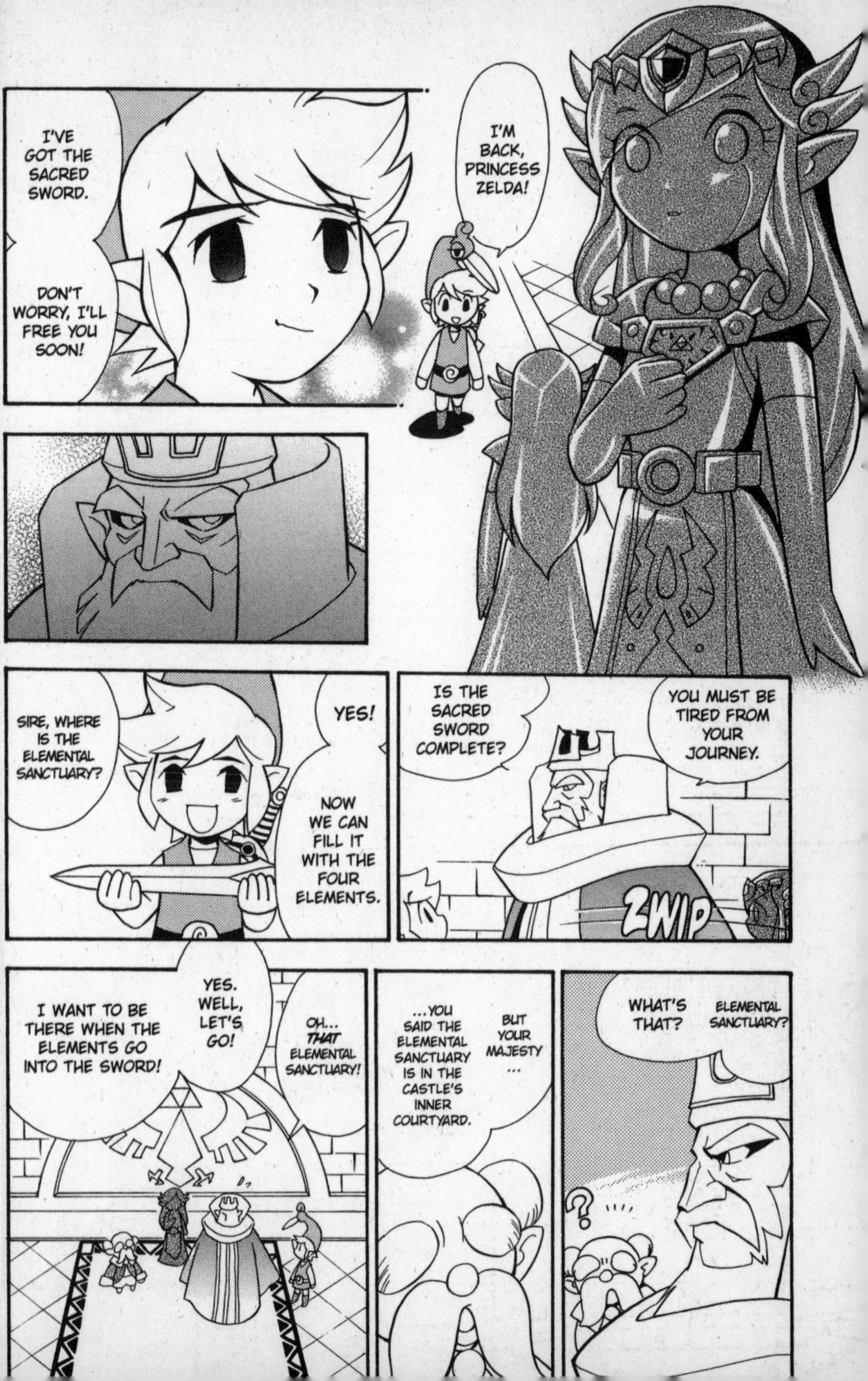
I'M BACK, PRINCESS ZELDA!
I'VE GOT THE SACRED SWORD.
DON'T WORRY, I'LL FREE YOU SOON!
YOU MUST BE TIRED FROM YOUR JOURNEY.
IS THE SACRED SWORD COMPLETE?
ZWIP
YES!
NOW WE CAN FILL IT WITH THE FOUR ELEMENTS.
SIRE, WHERE IS THE ELEMENTAL SANCTUARY?
ELEMENTAL SANCTUARY?
WHAT'S THAT?
BUT YOUR MAJESTY ...
...YOU SAID THE ELEMENTAL SANCTUARY IS IN THE CASTLE'S INNER COURTYARD.
OH... *THAT* ELEMENTAL SANCTUARY!
YES. WELL, LET'S GO!
I WANT TO BE THERE WHEN THE ELEMENTS GO INTO THE SWORD!

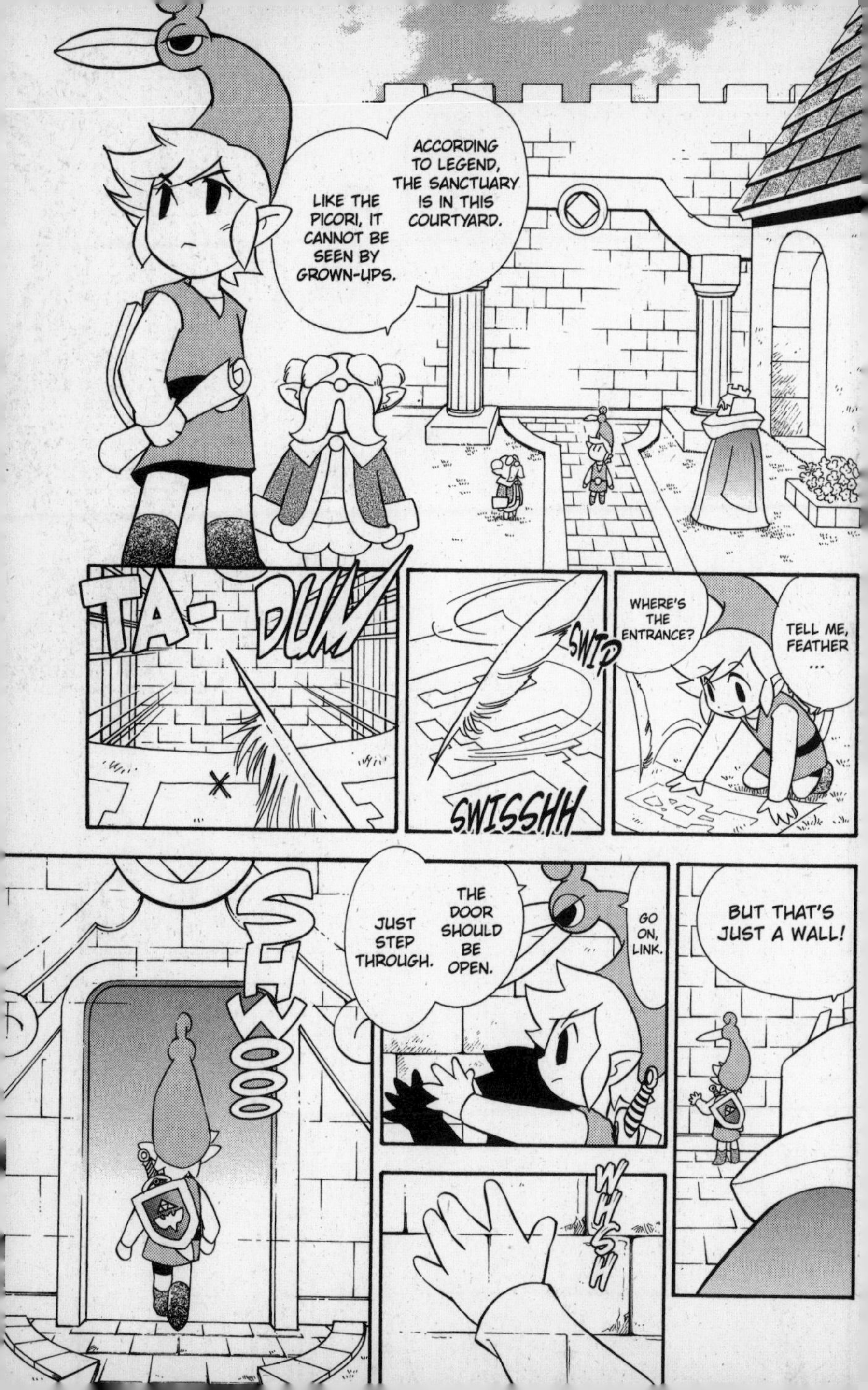
ACCORDING TO LEGEND, THE SANCTUARY IS IN THIS COURTYARD.
LIKE THE PICORI, IT CANNOT BE SEEN BY GROWN-UPS.
TELL ME, FEATHER ...
WHERE'S THE ENTRANCE?
SWIP
SWISSHH
TA-DUM
BUT THAT'S JUST A WALL!
GO ON, LINK.
THE DOOR SHOULD BE OPEN.
JUST STEP THROUGH.
WHSH
SHWOOO

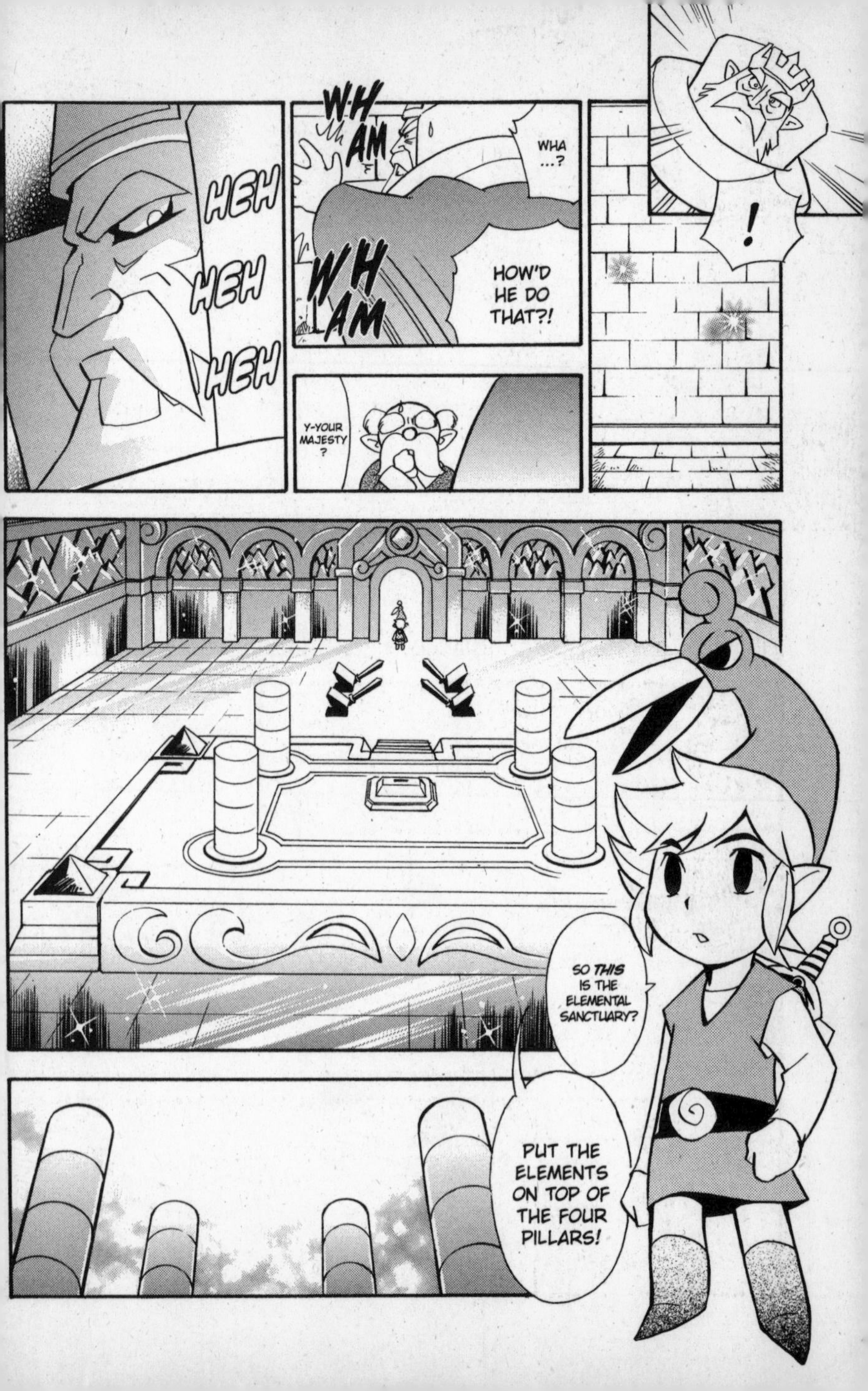
!
WHA ...?
WHAM
HOW'D HE DO THAT?!
WHAM
Y-YOUR MAJESTY ?
HEH HEH HEH
SO THIS IS THE ELEMENTAL SANCTUARY?
PUT THE ELEMENTS ON TOP OF THE FOUR PILLARS!

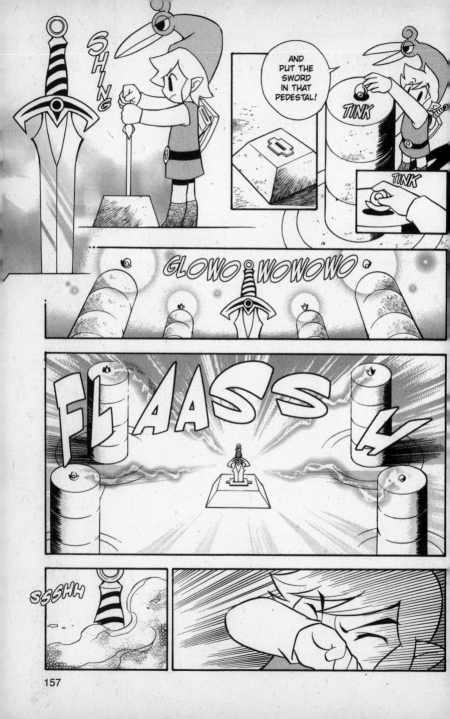

SHING

AND PUT THE SWORD IN THAT PEDESTAL!

TINK

TINK

GLOWO WOWOWO

FLAASS

SSSHH

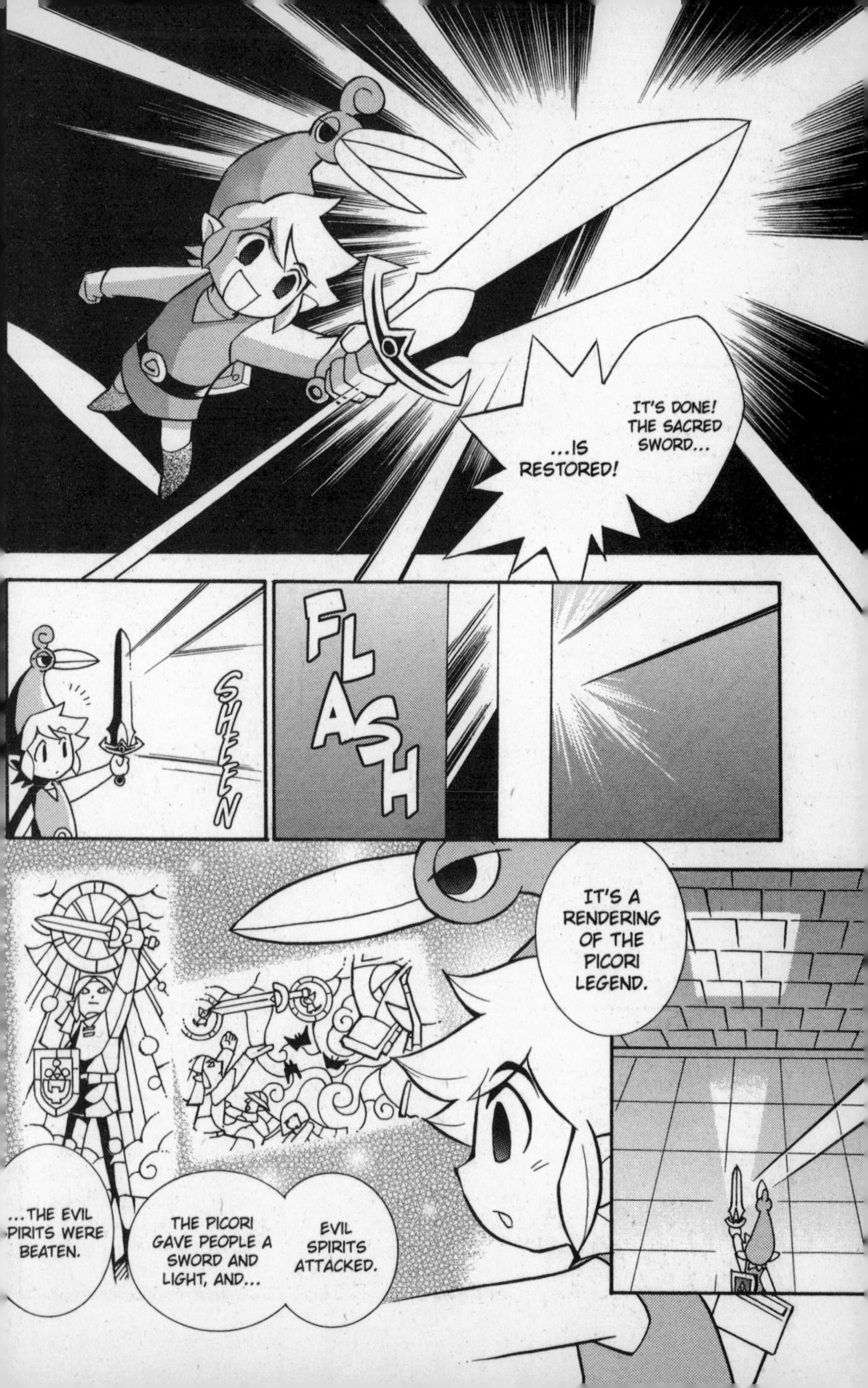
IT'S DONE! THE SACRED SWORD...
...IS RESTORED!
FLASH
SHEEN
IT'S A RENDERING OF THE PICORI LEGEND.
EVIL SPIRITS ATTACKED.
THE PICORI GAVE PEOPLE A SWORD AND LIGHT, AND...
...THE EVIL PIRITS WERE BEATEN.

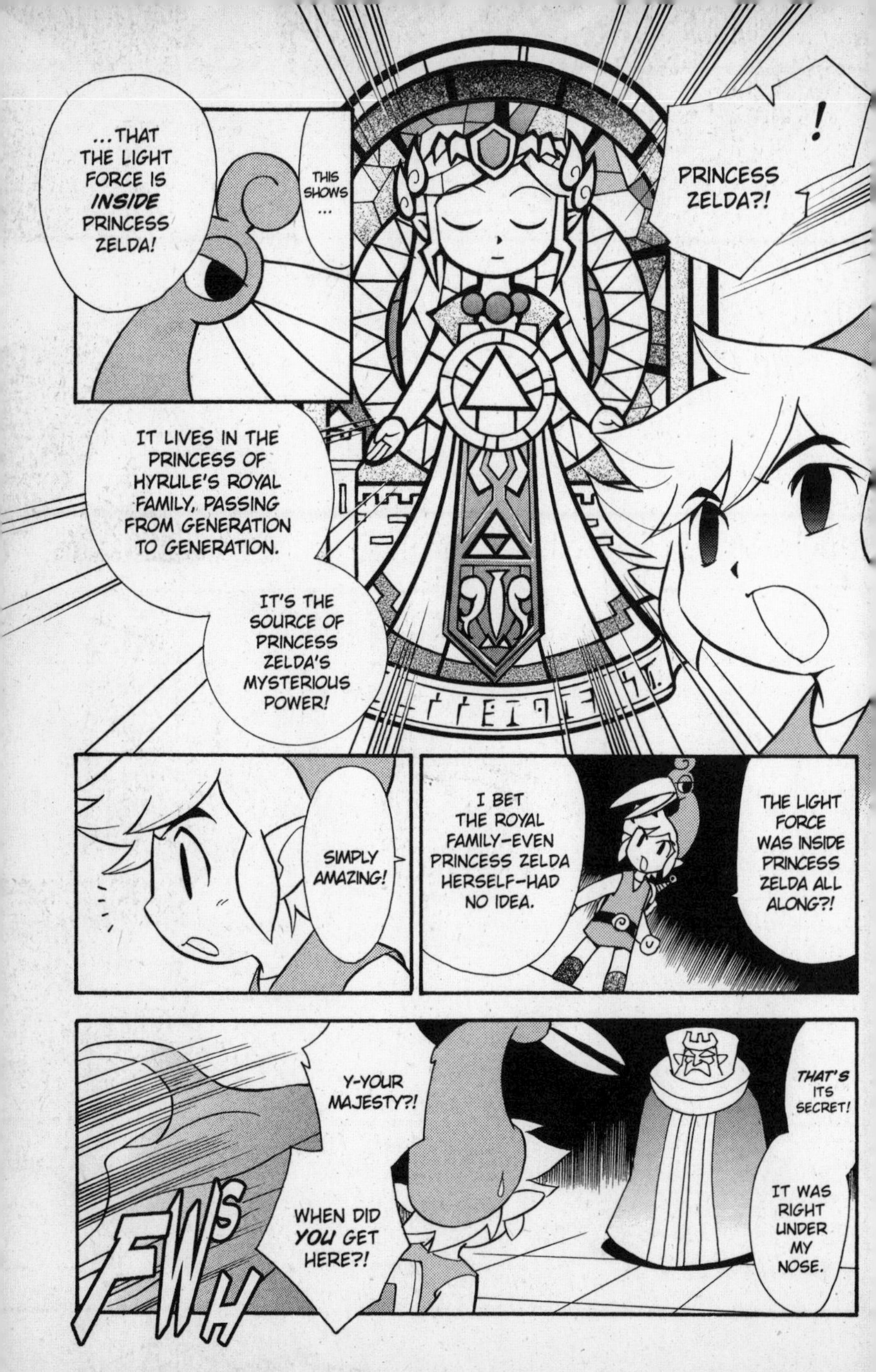
!
PRINCESS ZELDA?!
THIS SHOWS...
...THAT THE LIGHT FORCE IS *INSIDE* PRINCESS ZELDA!
IT LIVES IN THE PRINCESS OF HYRULE'S ROYAL FAMILY, PASSING FROM GENERATION TO GENERATION.
IT'S THE SOURCE OF PRINCESS ZELDA'S MYSTERIOUS POWER!
THE LIGHT FORCE WAS INSIDE PRINCESS ZELDA ALL ALONG?!
I BET THE ROYAL FAMILY—EVEN PRINCESS ZELDA HERSELF—HAD NO IDEA.
SIMPLY AMAZING!
THAT'S ITS SECRET!
IT WAS RIGHT UNDER MY NOSE.
Y-YOUR MAJESTY?!
WHEN DID *YOU* GET HERE?!
FWISH

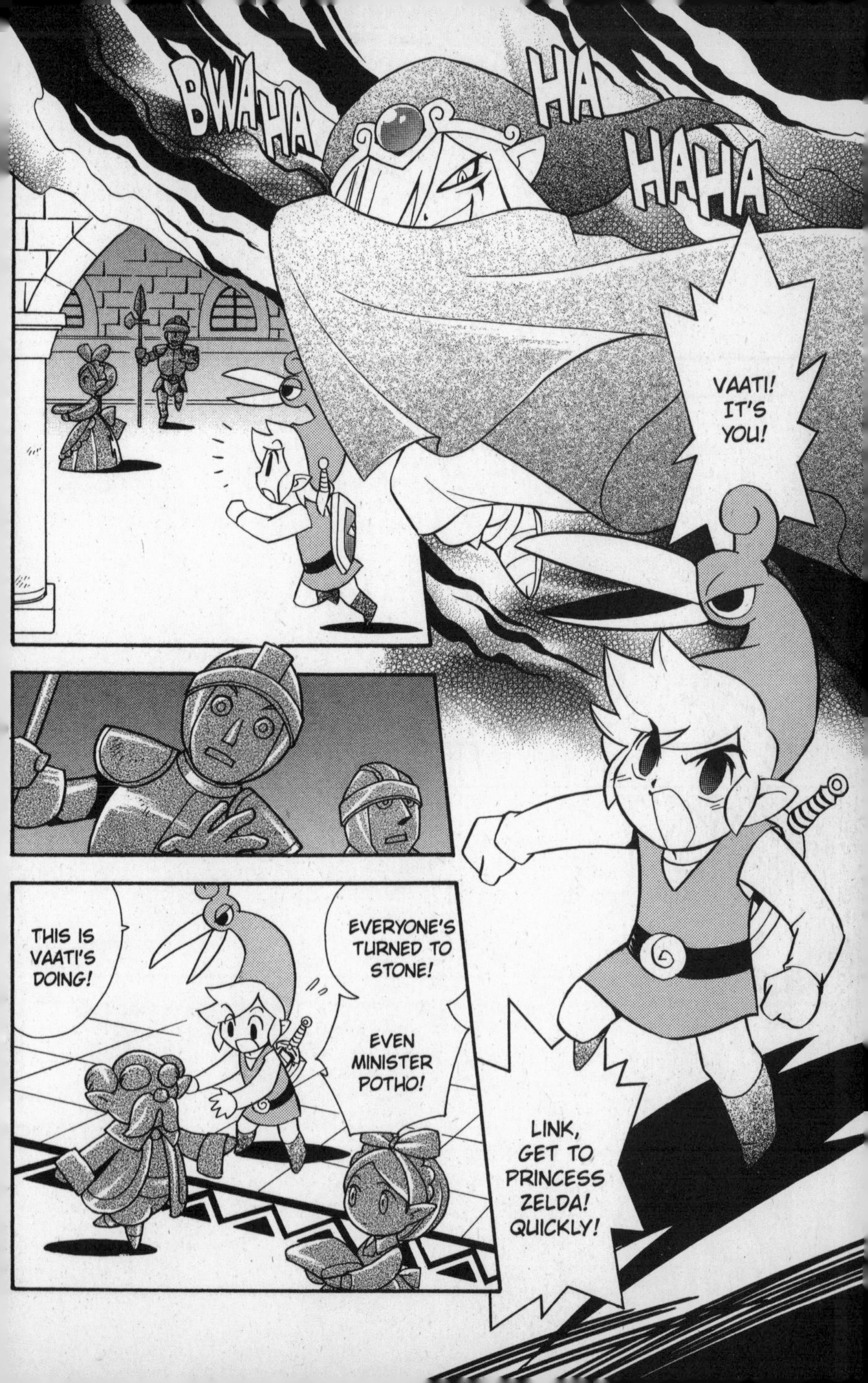
BWAHA HA HAHA
VAATI! IT'S YOU!
EVERYONE'S TURNED TO STONE!
EVEN MINISTER POTHO!
THIS IS VAATI'S DOING!
LINK, GET TO PRINCESS ZELDA! QUICKLY!

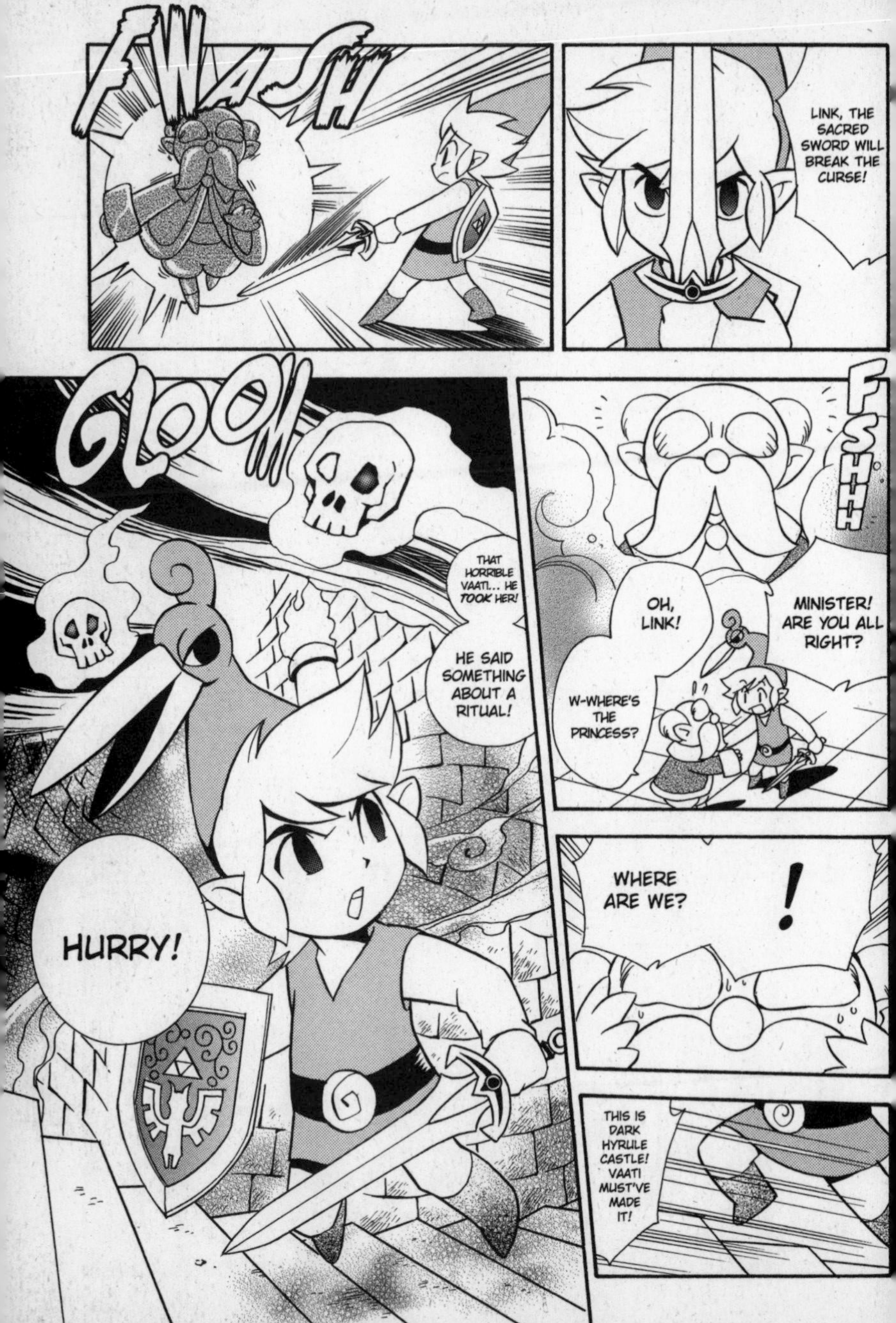
LINK, THE SACRED SWORD WILL BREAK THE CURSE!
FWASH
FSHHH
MINISTER! ARE YOU ALL RIGHT?
OH, LINK!
W-WHERE'S THE PRINCESS?
WHERE ARE WE?
!
THIS IS DARK HYRULE CASTLE! VAATI MUST'VE MADE IT!
GLOOM
THAT HORRIBLE VAATI... HE *TOOK* HER!
HE SAID SOMETHING ABOUT A RITUAL!
HURRY!

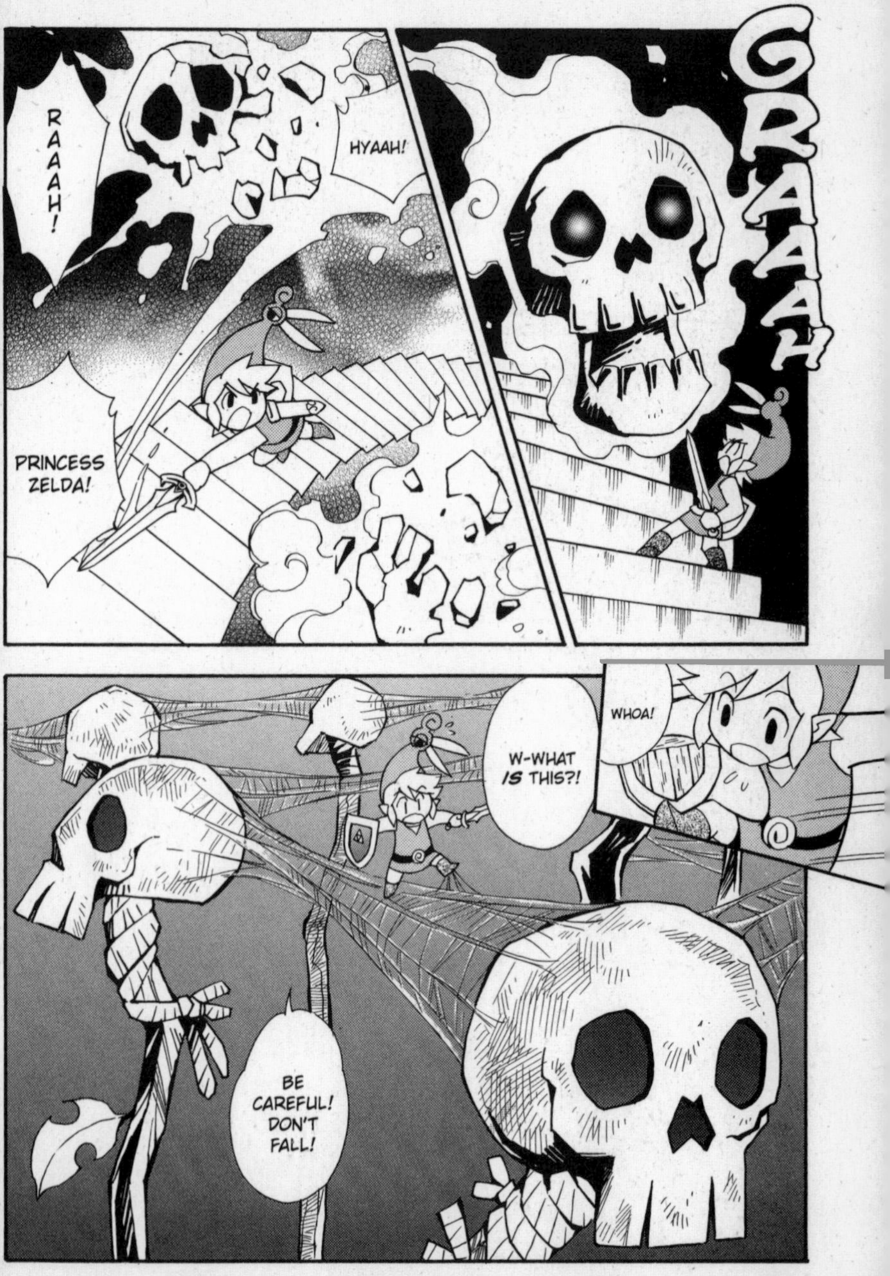
GRAAAH
HYAAH!
RAAAAH!
PRINCESS ZELDA!
WHOA!
W-WHAT *IS* THIS?!
BE CAREFUL! DON'T FALL!

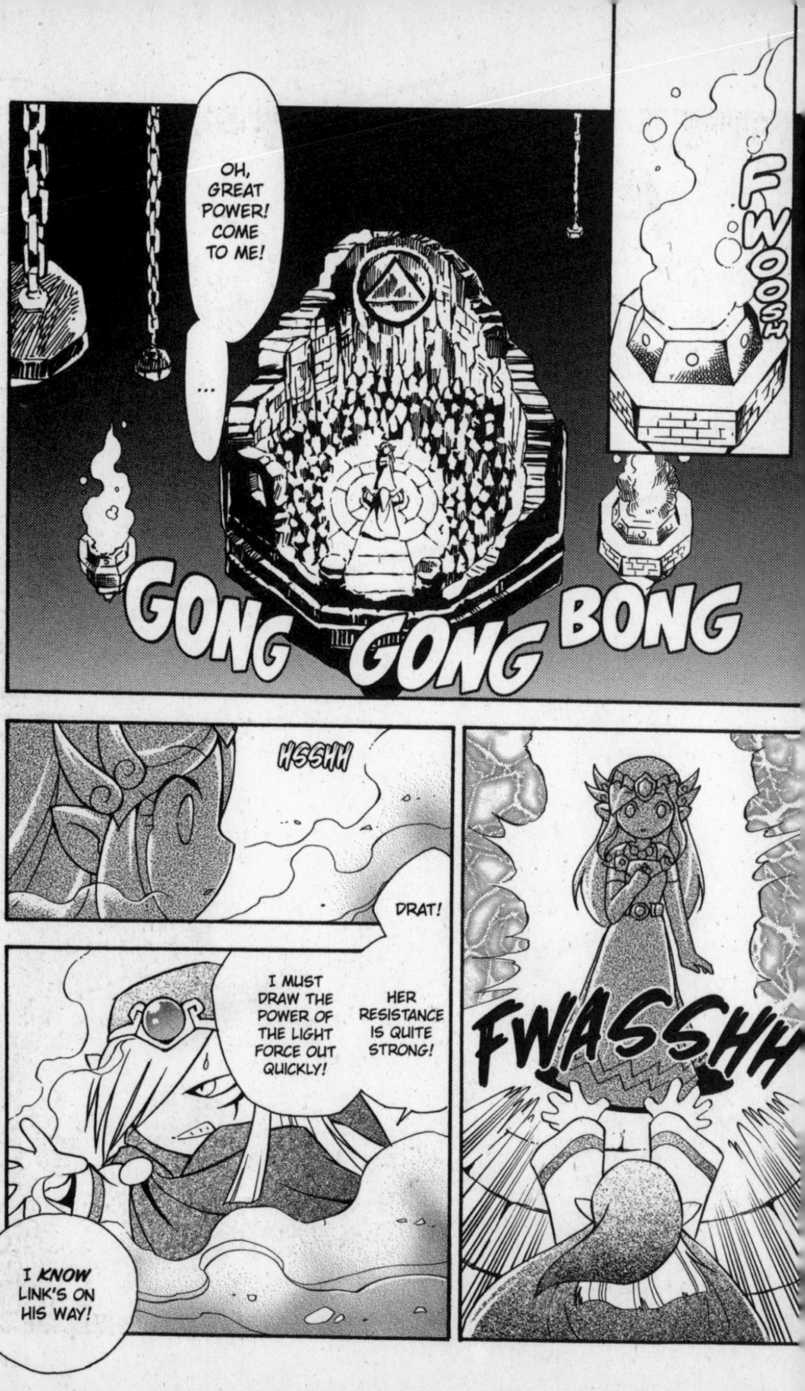
FWOOSH
OH, GREAT POWER! COME TO ME!
...
GONG GONG BONG
FWASSHH
HSSHH
...
DRAT!
HER RESISTANCE IS QUITE STRONG!
I MUST DRAW THE POWER OF THE LIGHT FORCE OUT QUICKLY!
I *KNOW* LINK'S ON HIS WAY!

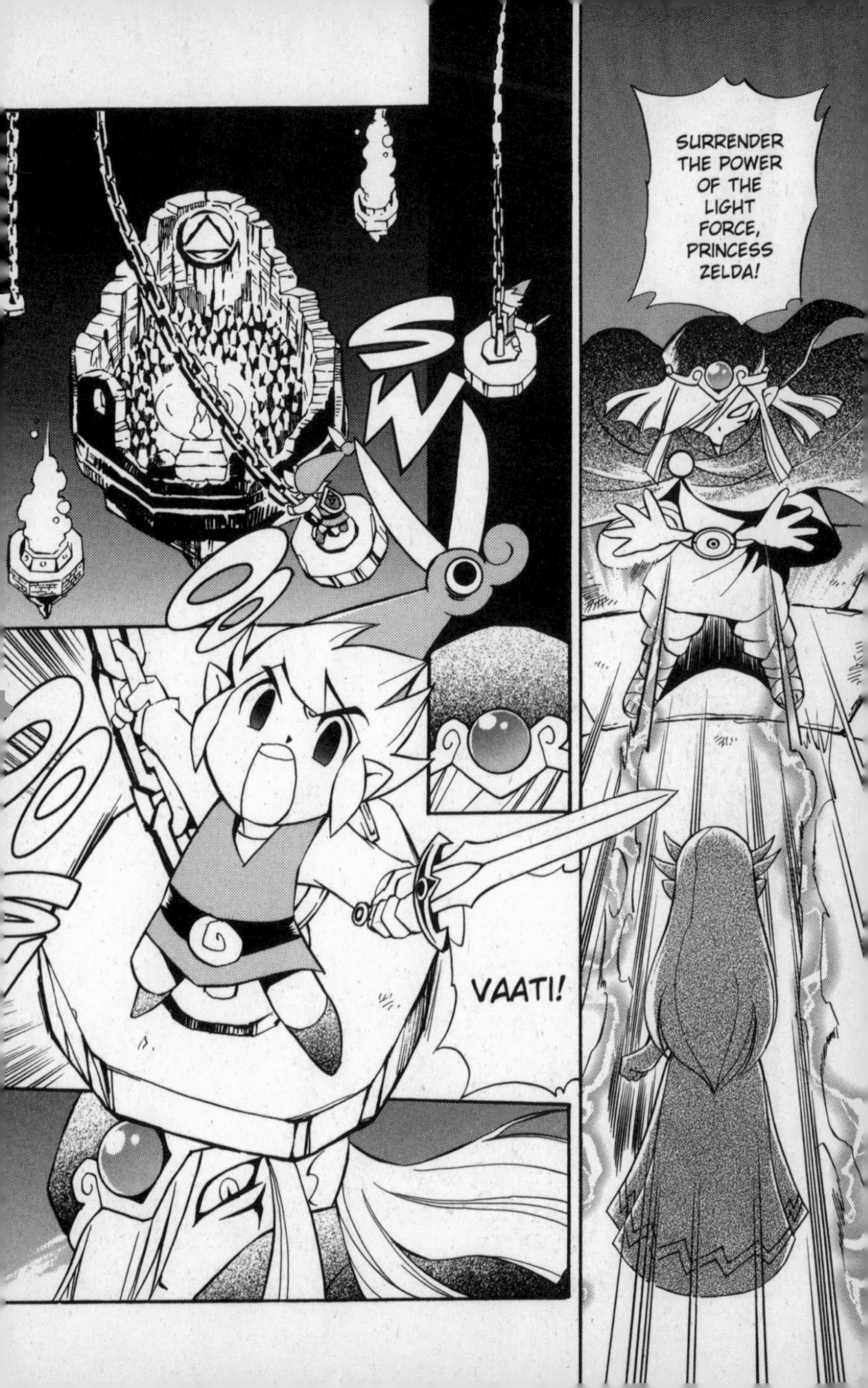
SURRENDER THE POWER OF THE LIGHT FORCE, PRINCESS ZELDA!
VAATI!

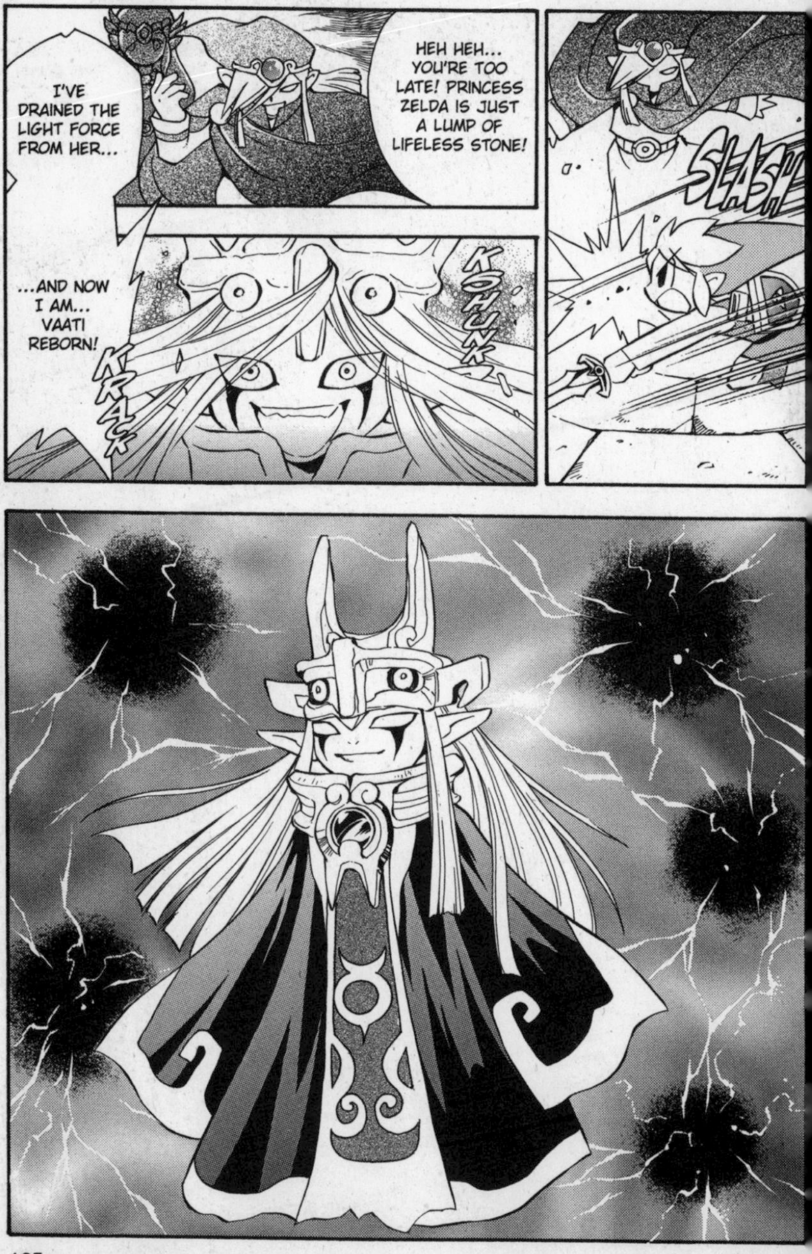
SLASH!
HEH HEH... YOU'RE TOO LATE! PRINCESS ZELDA IS JUST A LUMP OF LIFELESS STONE!
I'VE DRAINED THE LIGHT FORCE FROM HER...
KOHUNK!
...AND NOW I AM... VAATI REBORN!
KRACK

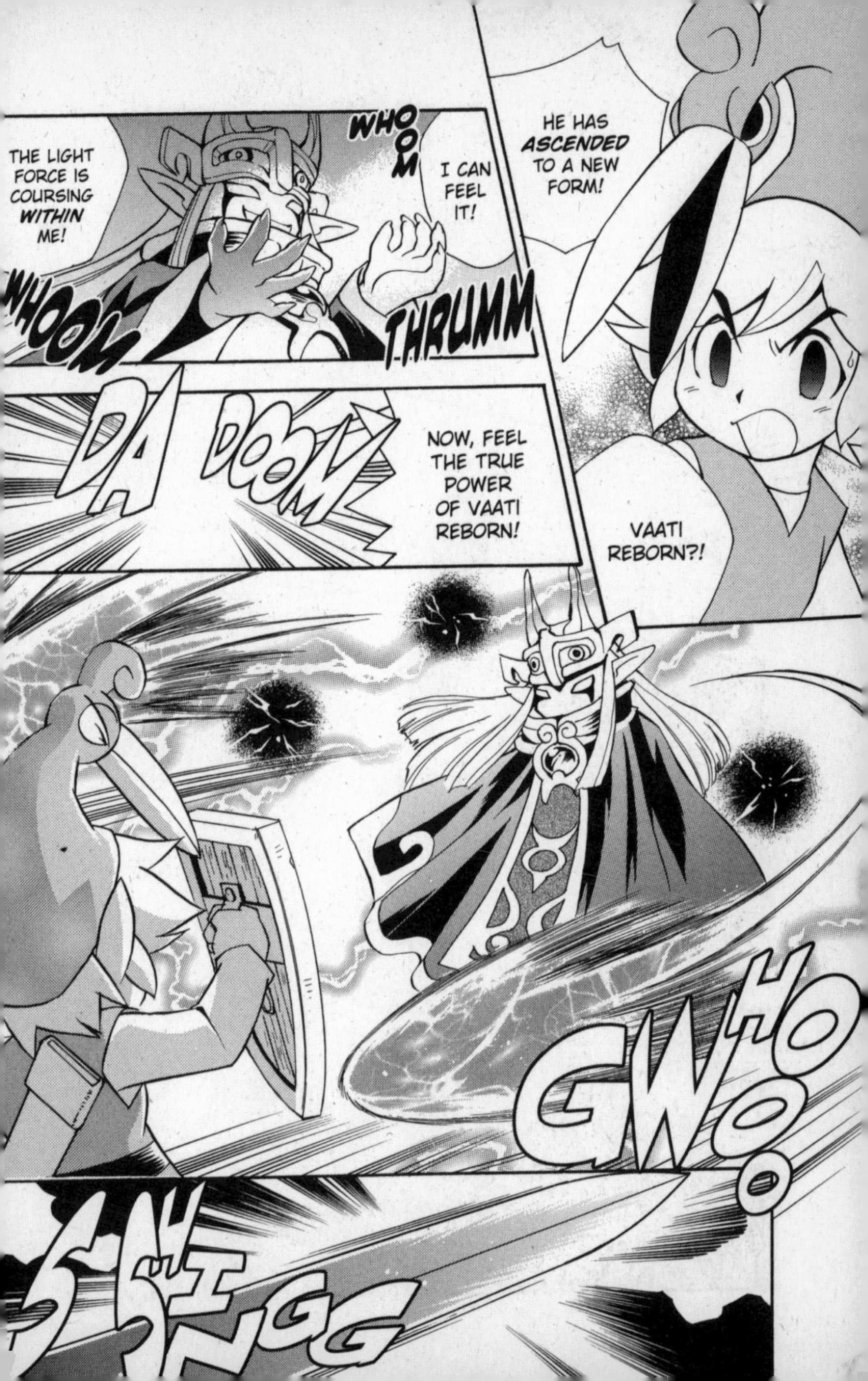
HE HAS ASCENDED TO A NEW FORM!
VAATI REBORN?!
WHOOM
I CAN FEEL IT!
THE LIGHT FORCE IS COURSING WITHIN ME!
THRUMM
WHOOM
NOW, FEEL THE TRUE POWER OF VAATI REBORN!
DA DOOM
GWHOOO
SSHINGG

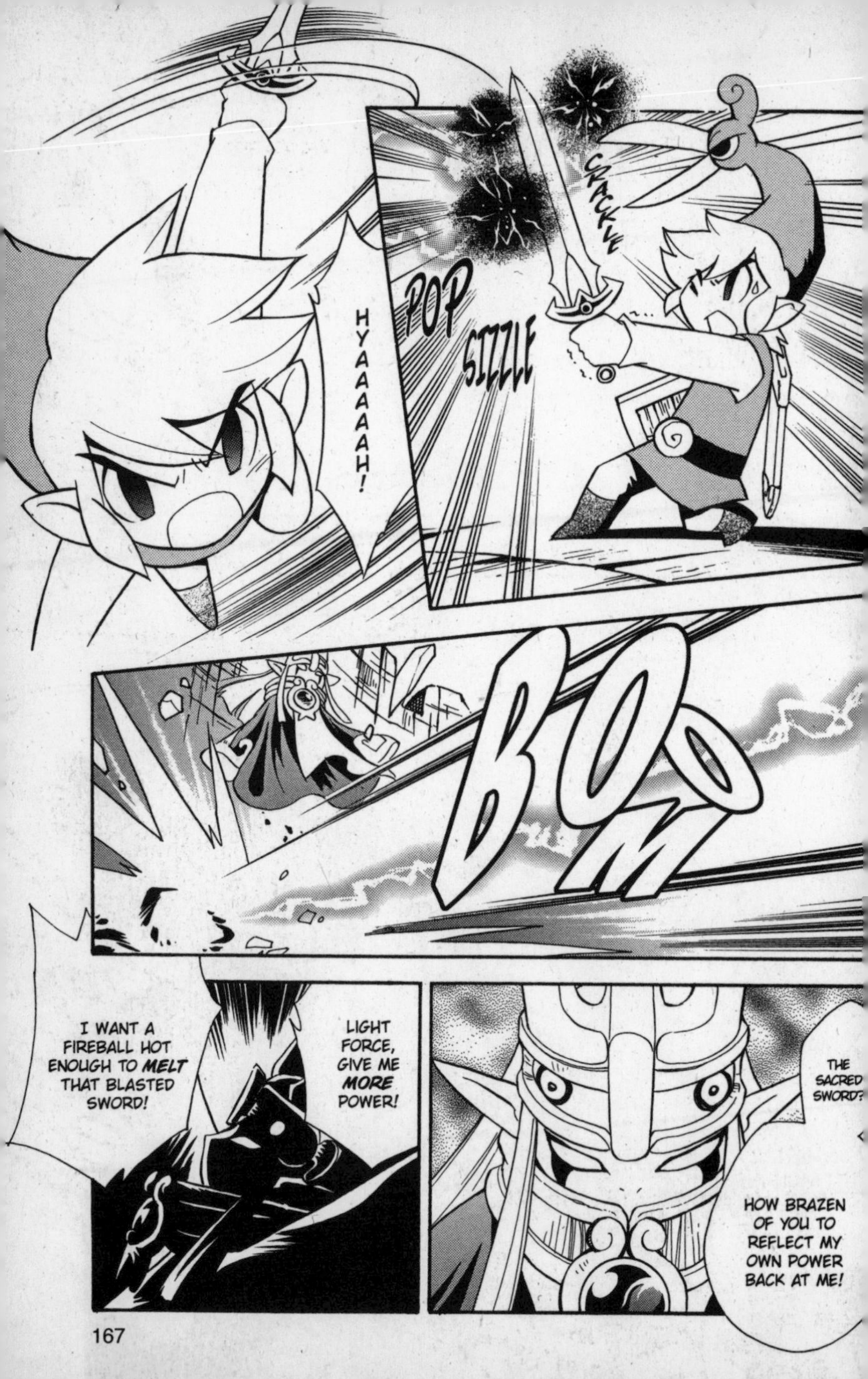
CRACKLE
POP
SIZZLE
HYAAAAAAAH!
BOOM
THE SACRED SWORD?
HOW BRAZEN OF YOU TO REFLECT MY OWN POWER BACK AT ME!
LIGHT FORCE, GIVE ME *MORE* POWER!
I WANT A FIREBALL HOT ENOUGH TO *MELT* THAT BLASTED SWORD!

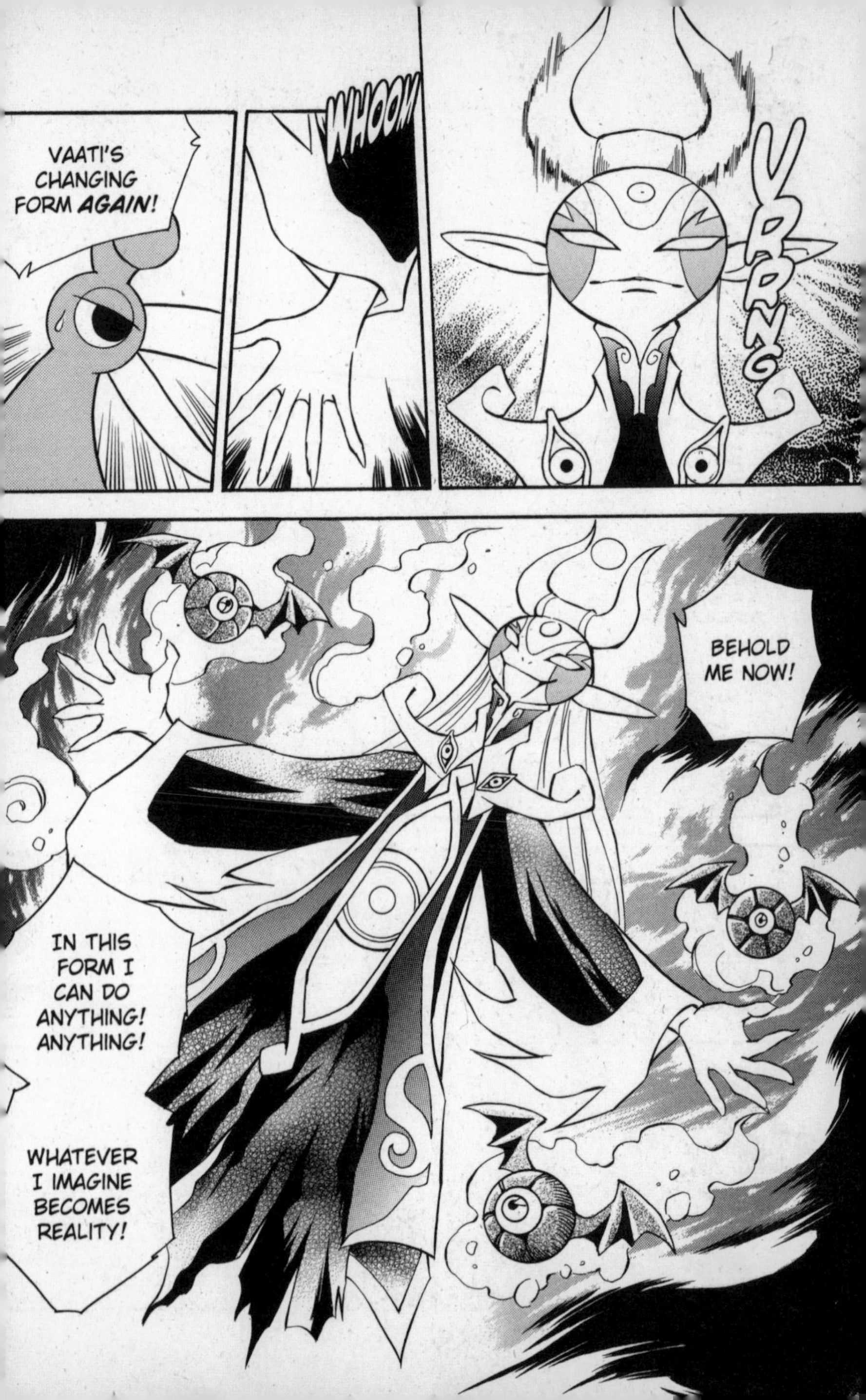
VRRNG
WHOOM
VAATI'S CHANGING FORM AGAIN!
BEHOLD ME NOW!
IN THIS FORM I CAN DO ANYTHING! ANYTHING!
WHATEVER I IMAGINE BECOMES REALITY!

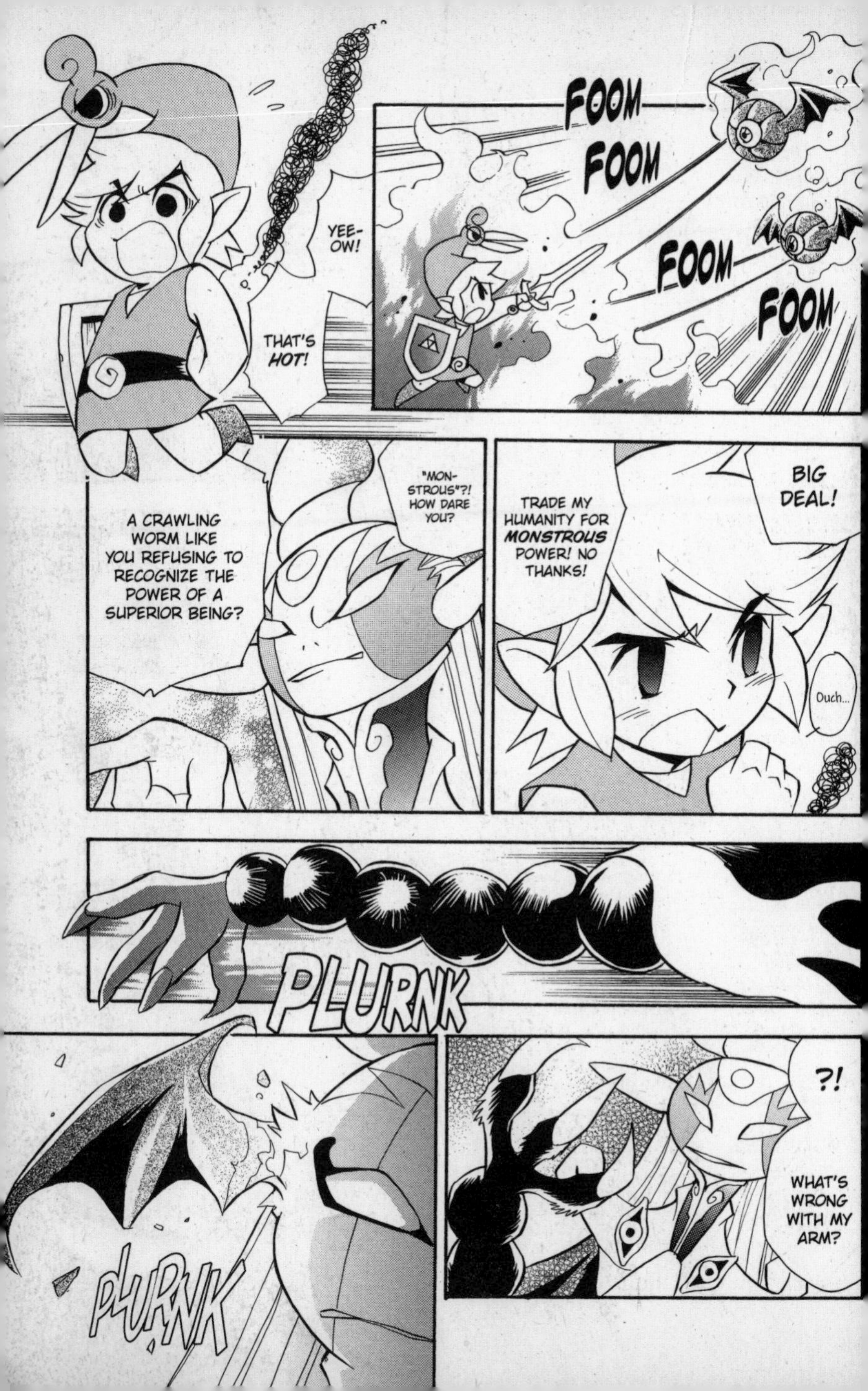
FOOM
FOOM
FOOM
FOOM
YEE-OW!
THAT'S *HOT!*
BIG DEAL!
TRADE MY HUMANITY FOR *MONSTROUS* POWER! NO THANKS!
Ouch...
"MON-STROUS"?! HOW DARE YOU?
A CRAWLING WORM LIKE YOU REFUSING TO RECOGNIZE THE POWER OF A SUPERIOR BEING?
PLURNK
?!
WHAT'S WRONG WITH MY ARM?
PLURNK

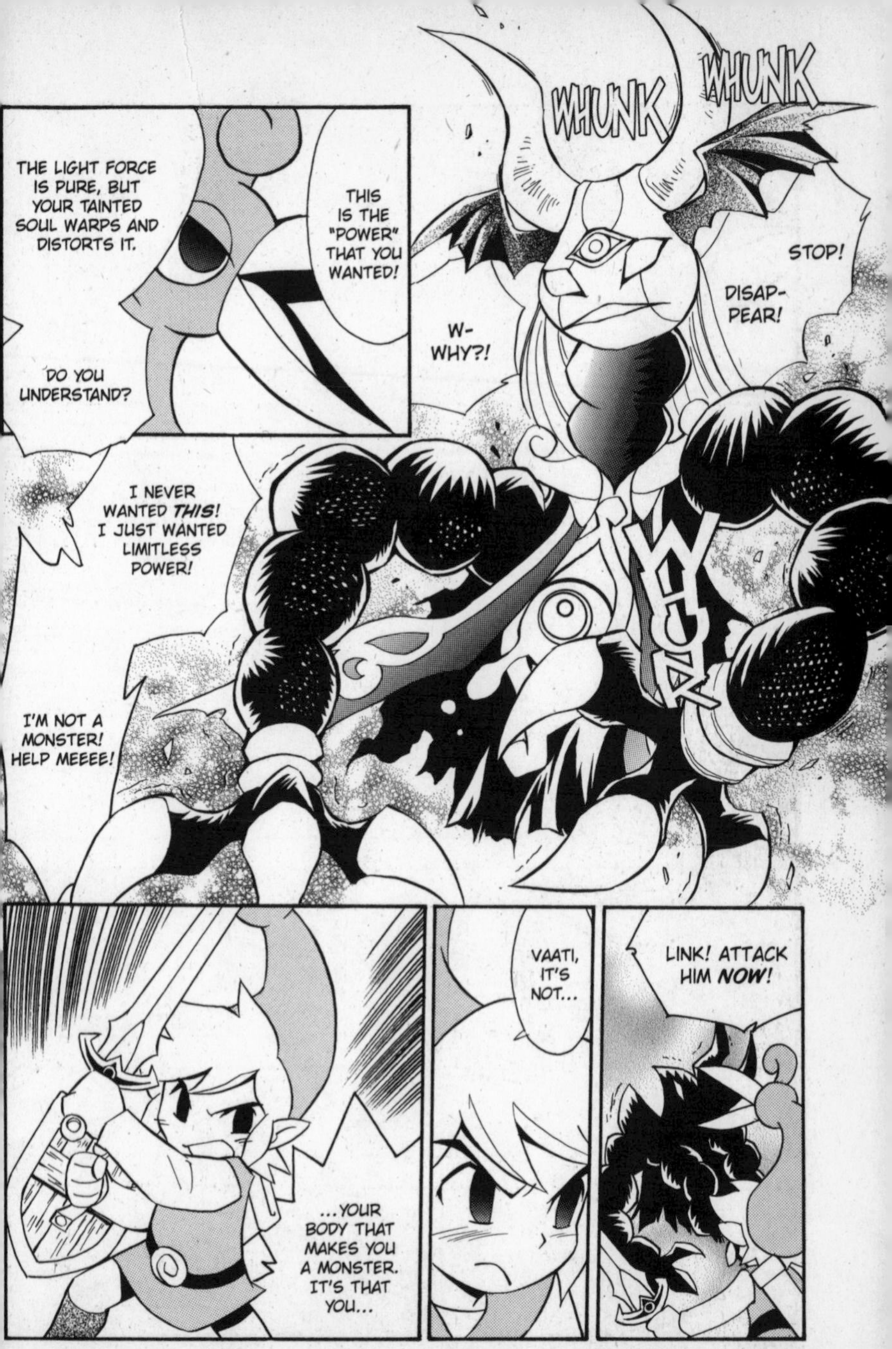
WHUNK
WHUNK
STOP!
DISAP-PEAR!
W-WHY?!
THIS IS THE "POWER" THAT YOU WANTED!
THE LIGHT FORCE IS PURE, BUT YOUR TAINTED SOUL WARPS AND DISTORTS IT.
DO YOU UNDERSTAND?
I NEVER WANTED *THIS*! I JUST WANTED LIMITLESS POWER!
I'M NOT A MONSTER! HELP MEEEE!
LINK! ATTACK HIM ***NOW***!
VAATI, IT'S NOT...
...YOUR BODY THAT MAKES YOU A MONSTER. IT'S THAT YOU...

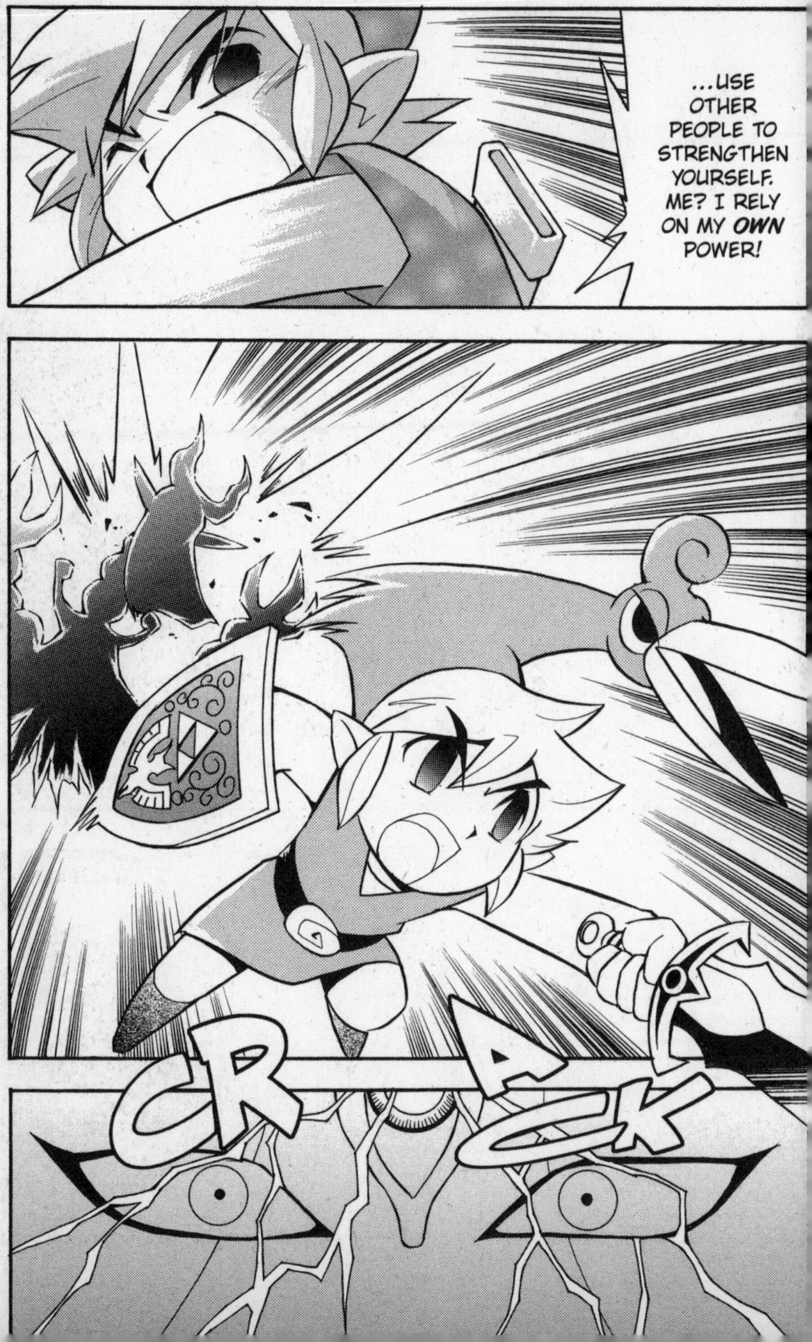
...USE OTHER PEOPLE TO STRENGTHEN YOURSELF. ME? I RELY ON MY *OWN* POWER!
CRACK

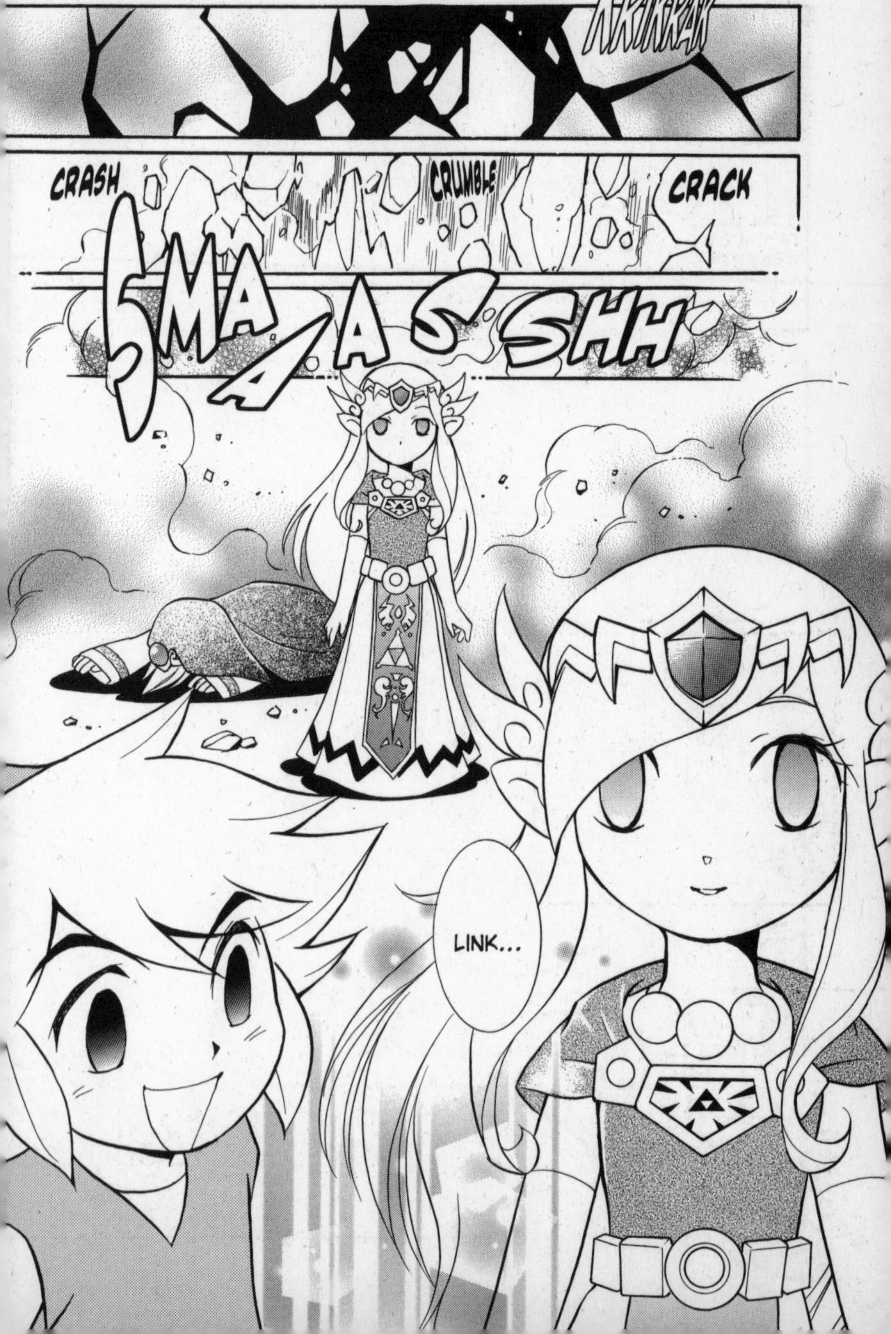
KRIKRAK
CRACK
CRUMBLE
CRASH
SMAAASHH
LINK...

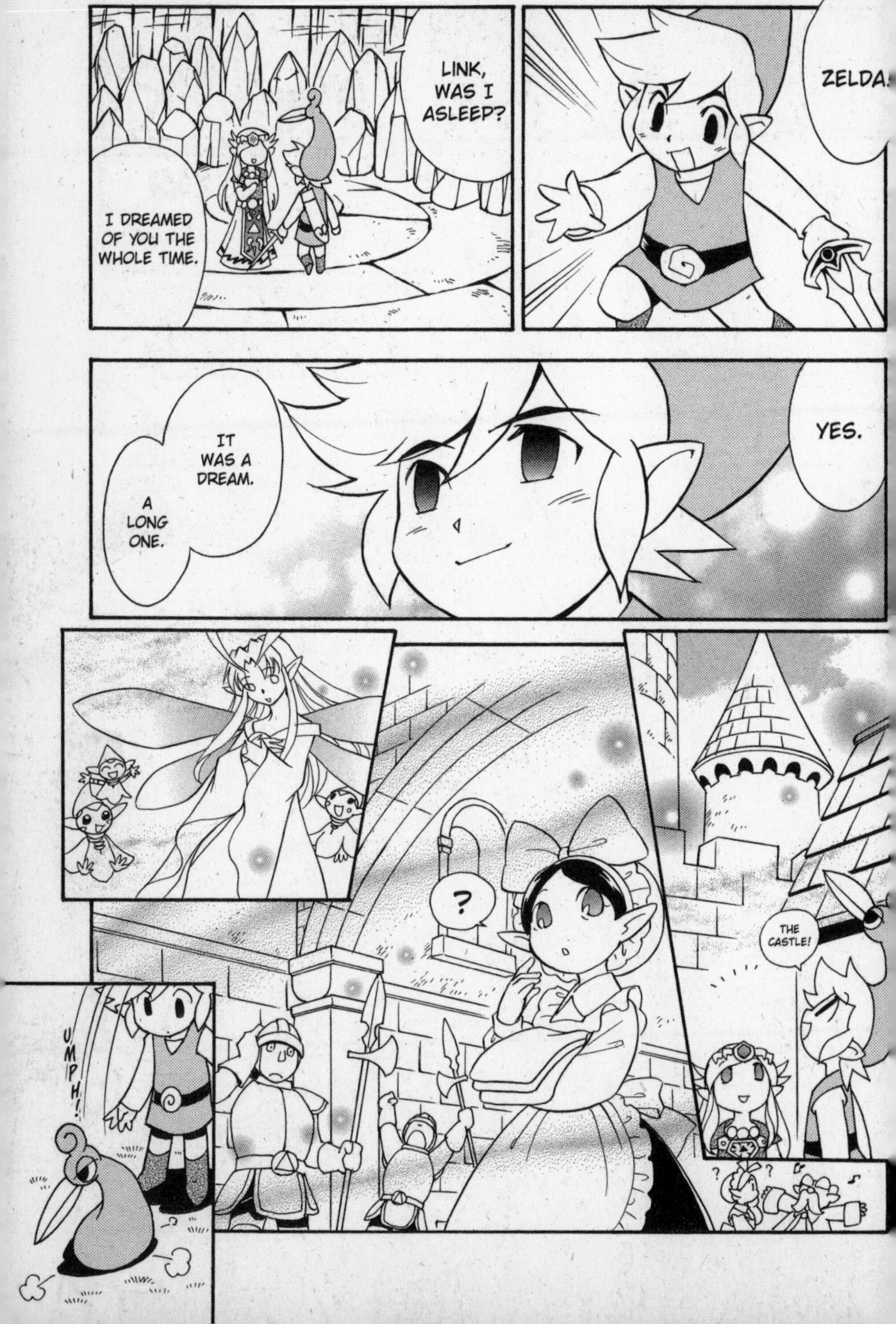
ZELDA!
LINK, WAS I ASLEEP?
I DREAMED OF YOU THE WHOLE TIME.
YES.
IT WAS A DREAM.
A LONG ONE.
THE CASTLE!
?
UMPH!

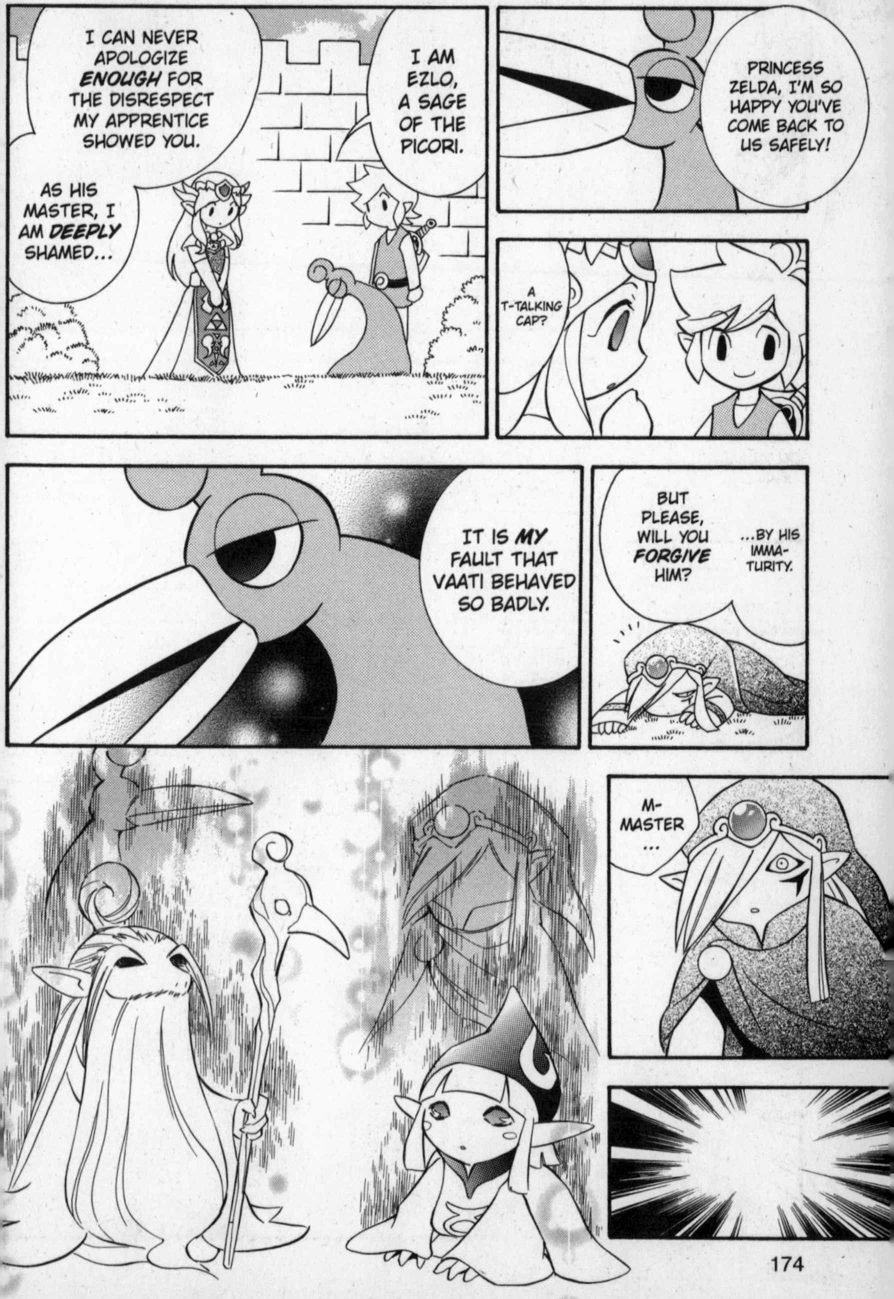
PRINCESS ZELDA, I'M SO HAPPY YOU'VE COME BACK TO US SAFELY!
A T-TALKING CAP?
I AM EZLO, A SAGE OF THE PICORI.
I CAN NEVER APOLOGIZE ENOUGH FOR THE DISRESPECT MY APPRENTICE SHOWED YOU.
AS HIS MASTER, I AM DEEPLY SHAMED...
...BY HIS IMMATURITY.
BUT PLEASE, WILL YOU FORGIVE HIM?
IT IS MY FAULT THAT VAATI BEHAVED SO BADLY.
M-MASTER...

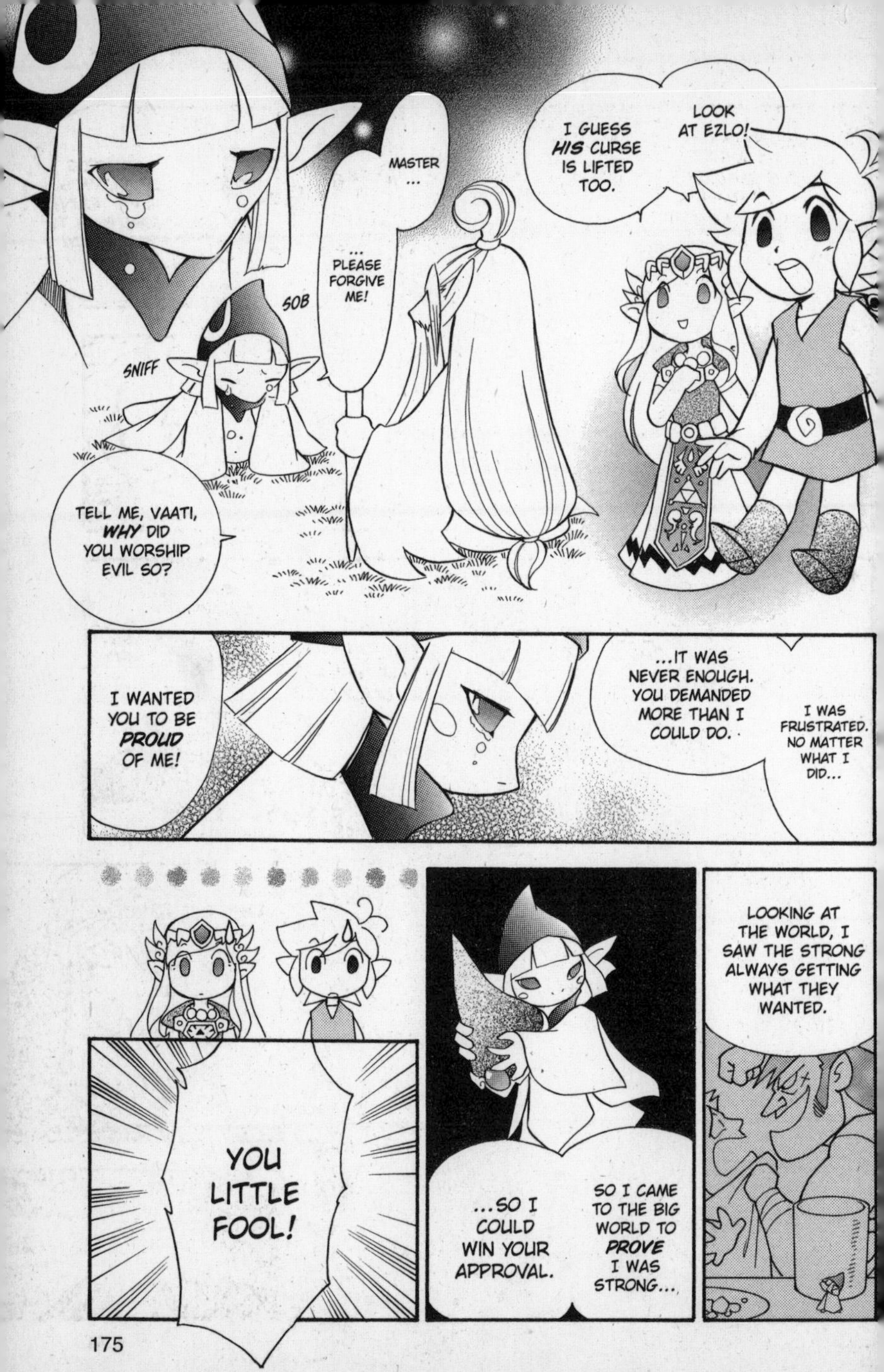
LOOK AT EZLO!
I GUESS HIS CURSE IS LIFTED TOO.
MASTER ...
... PLEASE FORGIVE ME!
SOB
SNIFF
TELL ME, VAATI, WHY DID YOU WORSHIP EVIL SO?
I WAS FRUSTRATED. NO MATTER WHAT I DID...
...IT WAS NEVER ENOUGH. YOU DEMANDED MORE THAN I COULD DO.
I WANTED YOU TO BE PROUD OF ME!
LOOKING AT THE WORLD, I SAW THE STRONG ALWAYS GETTING WHAT THEY WANTED.
SO I CAME TO THE BIG WORLD TO PROVE I WAS STRONG...
...SO I COULD WIN YOUR APPROVAL.
YOU LITTLE FOOL!

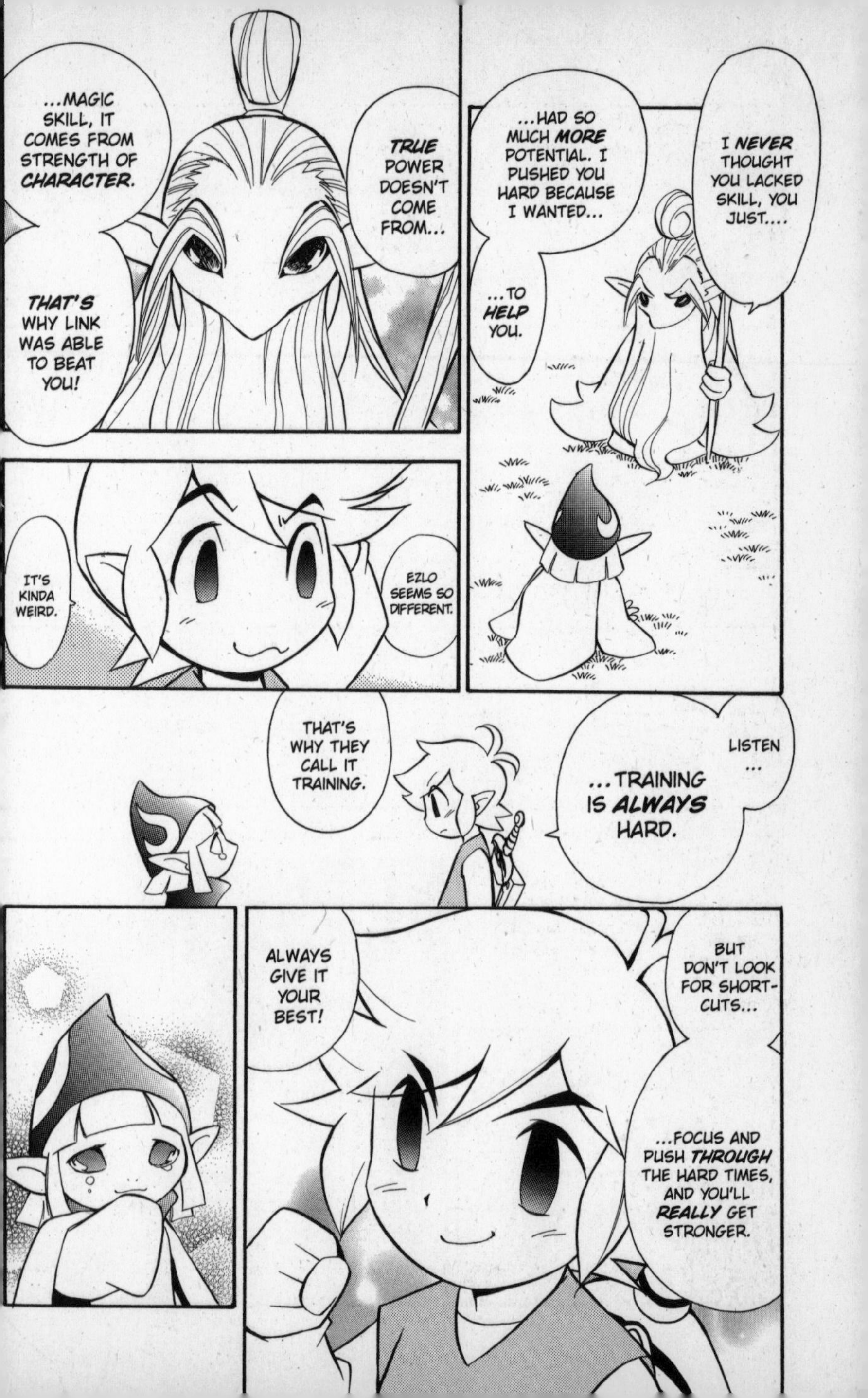
I NEVER THOUGHT YOU LACKED SKILL, YOU JUST....
...HAD SO MUCH MORE POTENTIAL. I PUSHED YOU HARD BECAUSE I WANTED...
...TO HELP YOU.
TRUE POWER DOESN'T COME FROM...
...MAGIC SKILL, IT COMES FROM STRENGTH OF CHARACTER.
THAT'S WHY LINK WAS ABLE TO BEAT YOU!
EZLO SEEMS SO DIFFERENT.
IT'S KINDA WEIRD.
LISTEN...
...TRAINING IS ALWAYS HARD.
THAT'S WHY THEY CALL IT TRAINING.
BUT DON'T LOOK FOR SHORT-CUTS...
...FOCUS AND PUSH THROUGH THE HARD TIMES, AND YOU'LL REALLY GET STRONGER.
ALWAYS GIVE IT YOUR BEST!

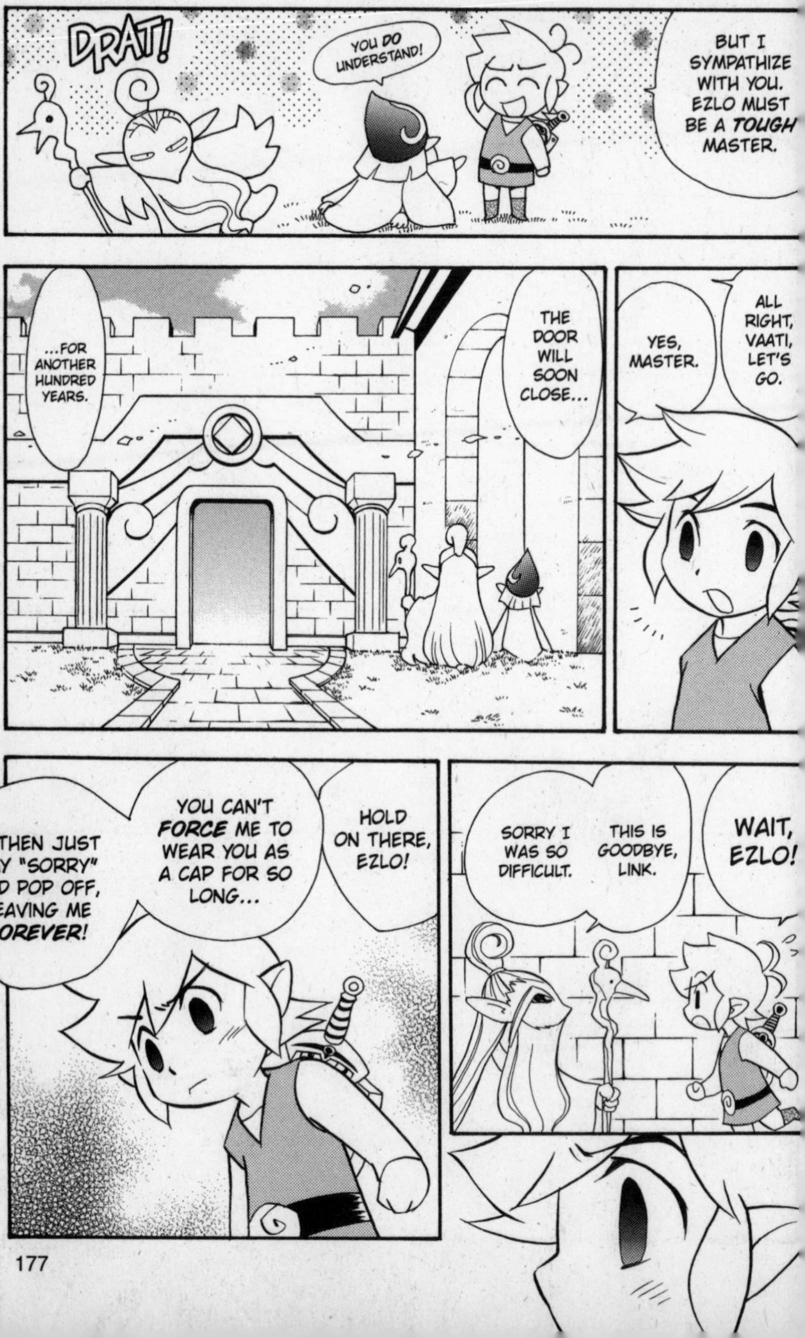
BUT I SYMPATHIZE WITH YOU. EZLO MUST BE A TOUGH MASTER.
YOU DO UNDERSTAND!
DRAT!
ALL RIGHT, VAATI, LET'S GO.
YES, MASTER.
THE DOOR WILL SOON CLOSE...
...FOR ANOTHER HUNDRED YEARS.
WAIT, EZLO!
THIS IS GOODBYE, LINK.
SORRY I WAS SO DIFFICULT.
HOLD ON THERE, EZLO!
YOU CAN'T FORCE ME TO WEAR YOU AS A CAP FOR SO LONG...
...THEN JUST SAY "SORRY" AND POP OFF, LEAVING ME FOREVER!

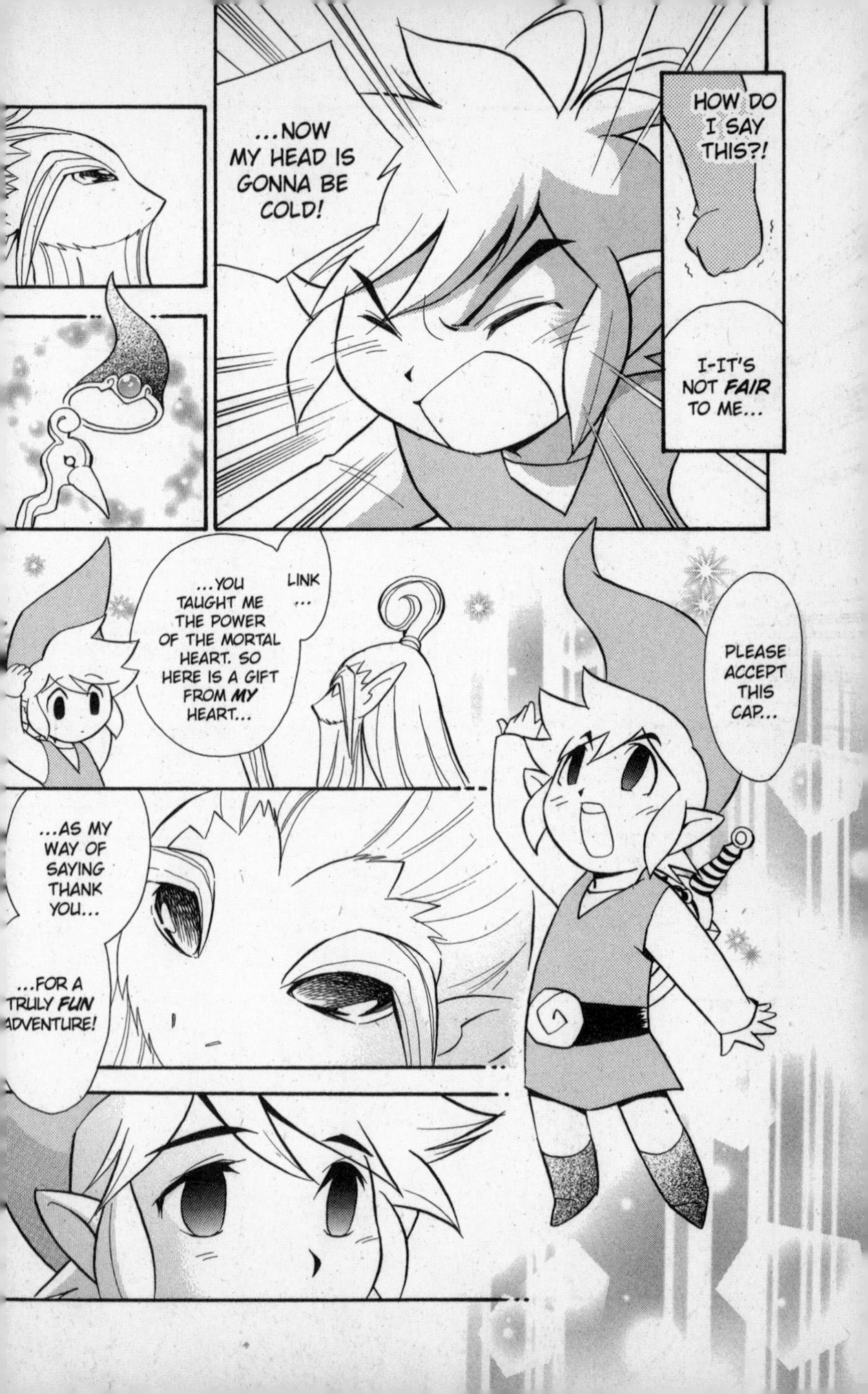
HOW DO I SAY THIS?!
I-IT'S NOT *FAIR* TO ME...
...NOW MY HEAD IS GONNA BE COLD!
PLEASE ACCEPT THIS CAP...
LINK ...
...YOU TAUGHT ME THE POWER OF THE MORTAL HEART. SO HERE IS A GIFT FROM *MY* HEART...
...AS MY WAY OF SAYING THANK YOU...
...FOR A TRULY *FUN* ADVENTURE!

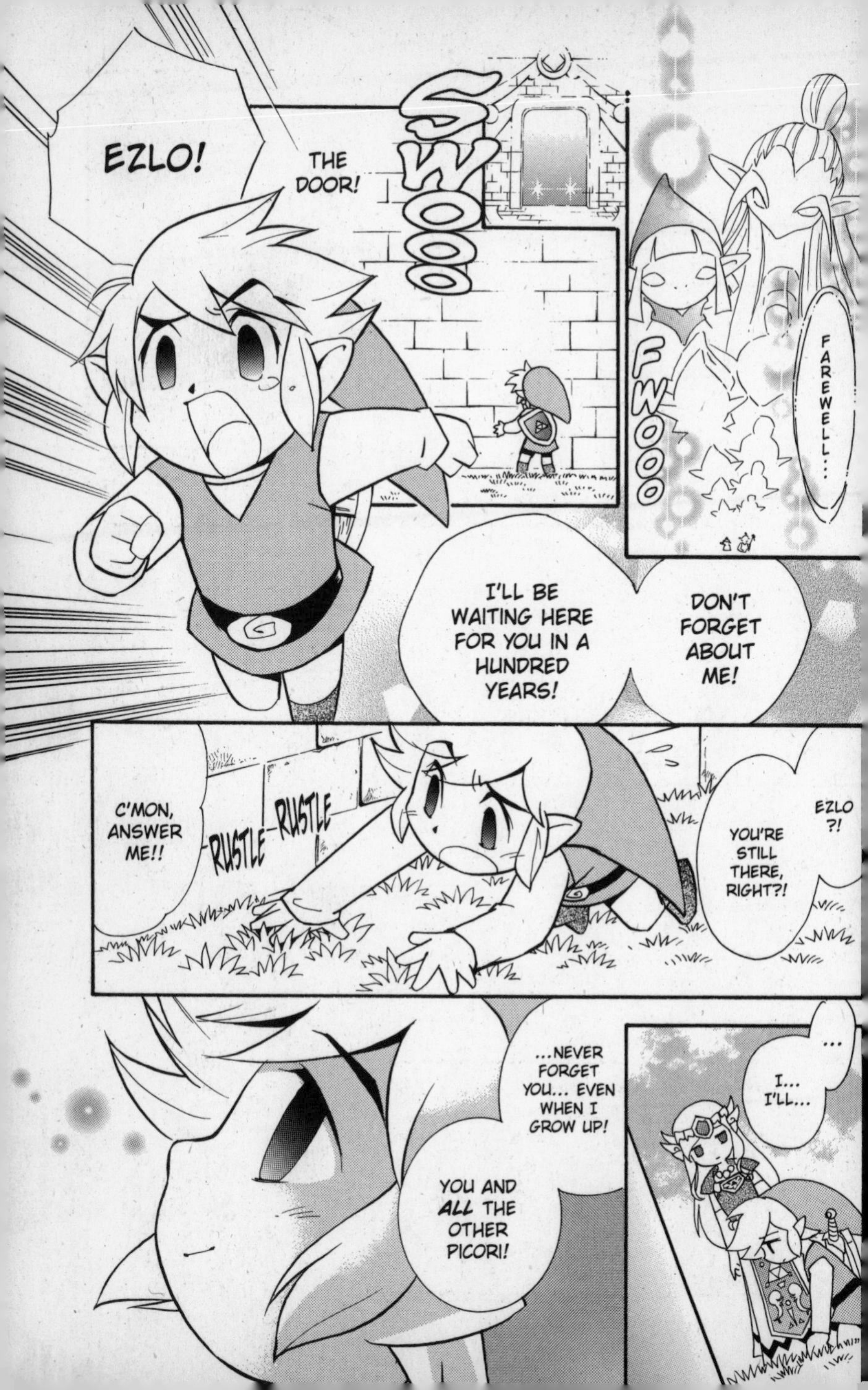
FAREWELL...
FWOOO
SWOOO
THE DOOR!
EZLO!
DON'T FORGET ABOUT ME!
I'LL BE WAITING HERE FOR YOU IN A HUNDRED YEARS!
EZLO ?!
YOU'RE STILL THERE, RIGHT?!
RUSTLE
RUSTLE
C'MON, ANSWER ME!!
...
I... I'LL...
...NEVER FORGET YOU... EVEN WHEN I GROW UP!
YOU AND ALL THE OTHER PICORI!

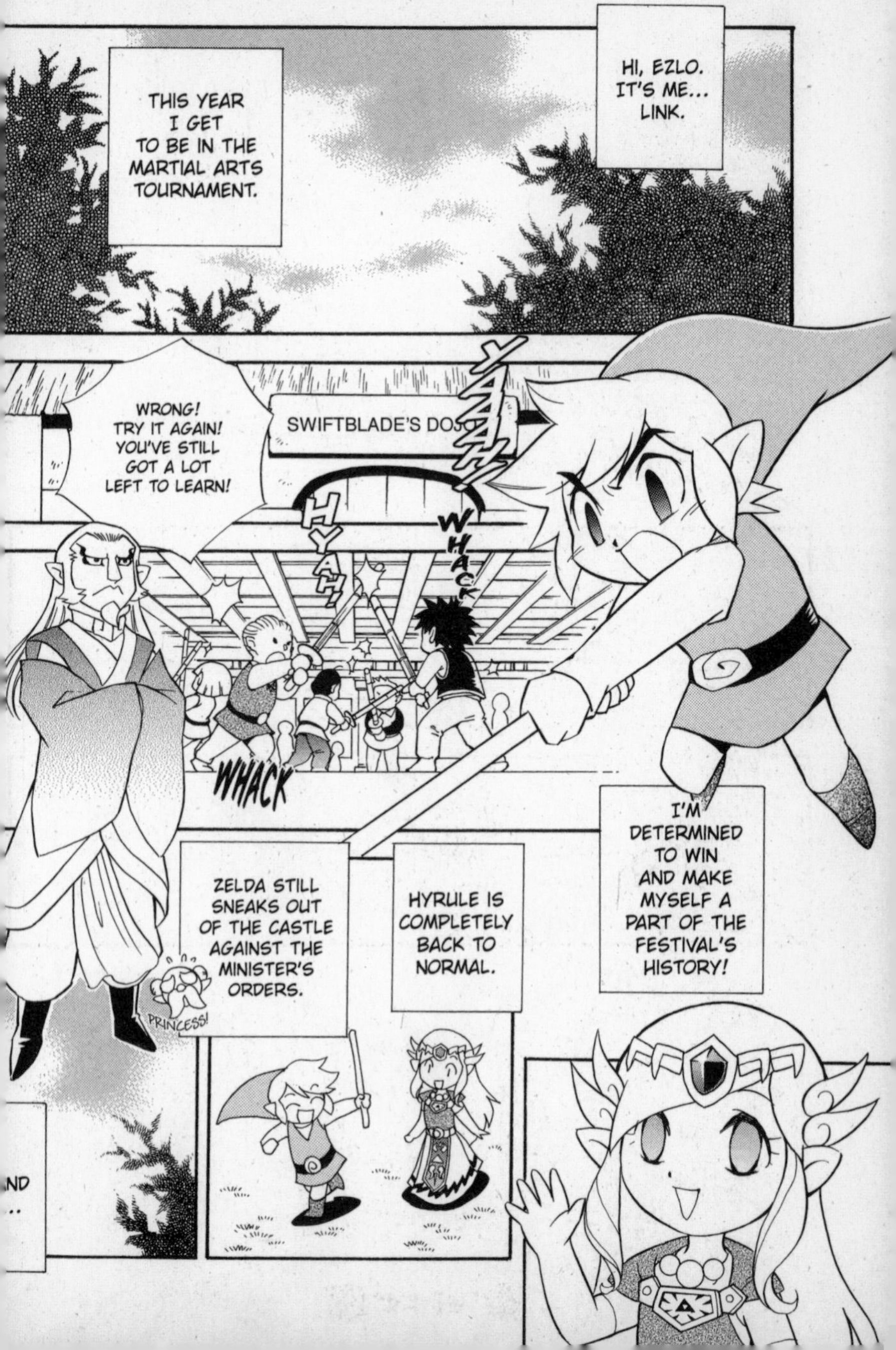

HI, EZLO. IT'S ME... LINK.
THIS YEAR I GET TO BE IN THE MARTIAL ARTS TOURNAMENT.
YAAAH!
WHACK
SWIFTBLADE'S DOJO
HYAH!
WRONG! TRY IT AGAIN! YOU'VE STILL GOT A LOT LEFT TO LEARN!
WHACK
I'M DETERMINED TO WIN AND MAKE MYSELF A PART OF THE FESTIVAL'S HISTORY!
HYRULE IS COMPLETELY BACK TO NORMAL.
ZELDA STILL SNEAKS OUT OF THE CASTLE AGAINST THE MINISTER'S ORDERS.
PRINCESS!

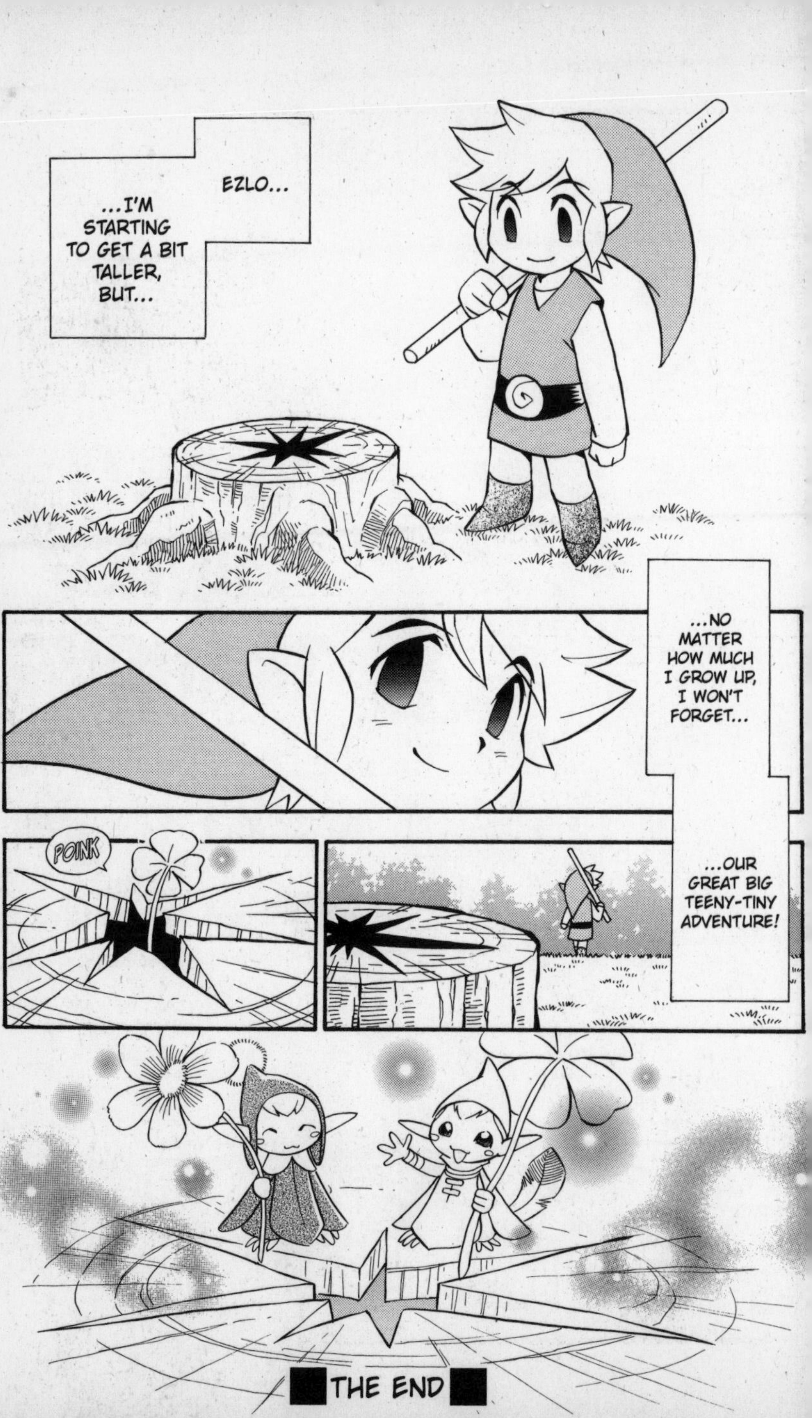
EZLO...
...I'M STARTING TO GET A BIT TALLER, BUT...
...NO MATTER HOW MUCH I GROW UP, I WON'T FORGET...
...OUR GREAT BIG TEENY-TINY ADVENTURE!
POINK
THE END

BONUS MANGA

VAATI DURING TRAINING

AKIRA HIMEKAWA

DEPARTURE

ONCE UPON A TIME...
...THERE WAS A YOUNG AND VERY SERIOUS PICORI NAMED VAATI.
RUSTLE
HE WAS QUITE TIMID...
CRINGE
ONE DAY I'M GONNA BE SUPER AWESOME!
...BUT FULL OF AMBITION.
I'M GONNA BE THE MOST FAMOUS PICORI EVER...
...AND SUPER RICH TOO!

MASTER AND PUPIL MEET

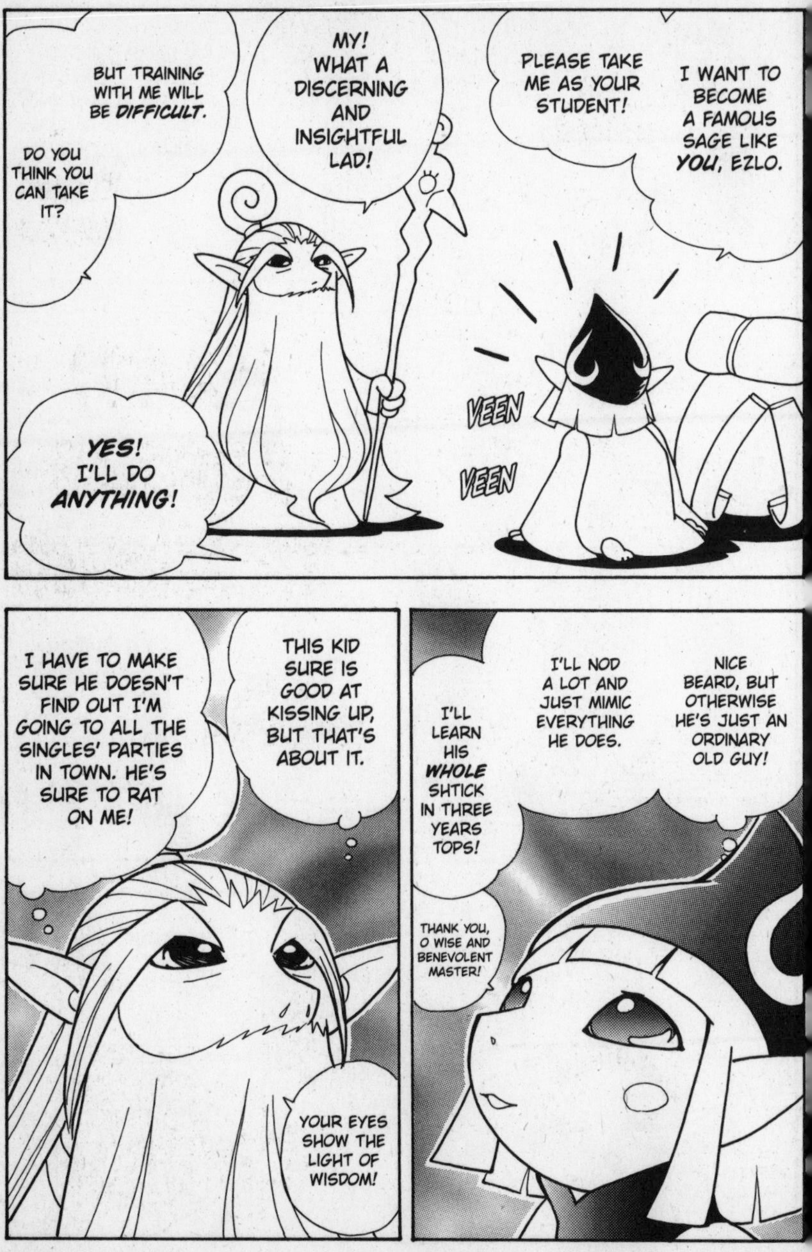
I WANT TO BECOME A FAMOUS SAGE LIKE YOU, EZLO.
PLEASE TAKE ME AS YOUR STUDENT!
MY! WHAT A DISCERNING AND INSIGHTFUL LAD!
BUT TRAINING WITH ME WILL BE DIFFICULT.
DO YOU THINK YOU CAN TAKE IT?
VEEN
VEEN
YES! I'LL DO ANYTHING!
NICE BEARD, BUT OTHERWISE HE'S JUST AN ORDINARY OLD GUY!
I'LL NOD A LOT AND JUST MIMIC EVERYTHING HE DOES.
I'LL LEARN HIS WHOLE SHTICK IN THREE YEARS TOPS!
THANK YOU, O WISE AND BENEVOLENT MASTER!
THIS KID SURE IS GOOD AT KISSING UP, BUT THAT'S ABOUT IT.
I HAVE TO MAKE SURE HE DOESN'T FIND OUT I'M GOING TO ALL THE SINGLES' PARTIES IN TOWN. HE'S SURE TO RAT ON ME!
YOUR EYES SHOW THE LIGHT OF WISDOM!

FIRST TRAINING ASSIGNMENT

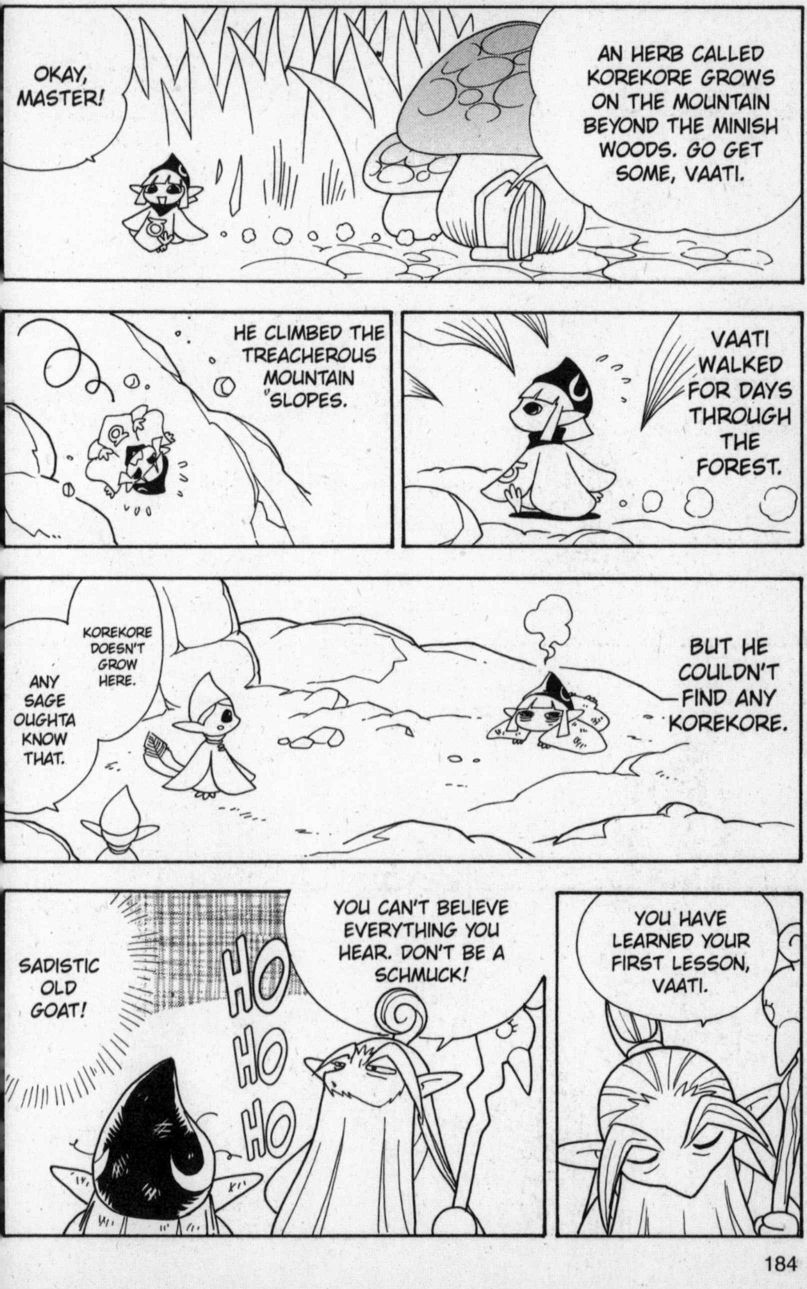
AN HERB CALLED KOREKORE GROWS ON THE MOUNTAIN BEYOND THE MINISH WOODS. GO GET SOME, VAATI.
OKAY, MASTER!
VAATI WALKED FOR DAYS THROUGH THE FOREST.
HE CLIMBED THE TREACHEROUS MOUNTAIN SLOPES.
BUT HE COULDN'T FIND ANY KOREKORE.
KOREKORE DOESN'T GROW HERE.
ANY SAGE OUGHTA KNOW THAT.
YOU HAVE LEARNED YOUR FIRST LESSON, VAATI.
YOU CAN'T BELIEVE EVERYTHING YOU HEAR. DON'T BE A SCHMUCK!
HO HO HO HO
SADISTIC OLD GOAT!

SECOND TRAINING ASSIGNMENT

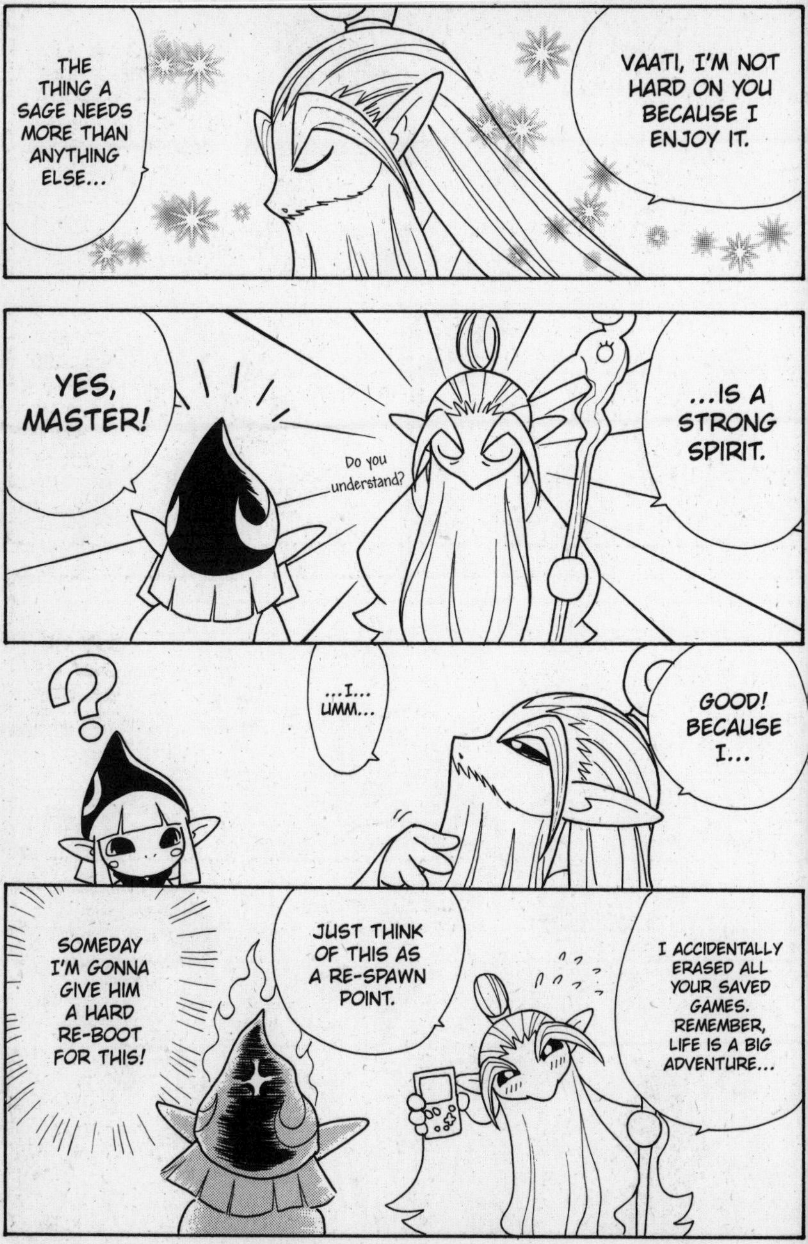
VAATI, I'M NOT HARD ON YOU BECAUSE I ENJOY IT.
THE THING A SAGE NEEDS MORE THAN ANYTHING ELSE...
...IS A STRONG SPIRIT.
Do you understand?
YES, MASTER!
GOOD! BECAUSE I...
...I... UMM...
I ACCIDENTALLY ERASED ALL YOUR SAVED GAMES. REMEMBER, LIFE IS A BIG ADVENTURE...
JUST THINK OF THIS AS A RE-SPAWN POINT.
SOMEDAY I'M GONNA GIVE HIM A HARD RE-BOOT FOR THIS!

A SURPRISE BOX

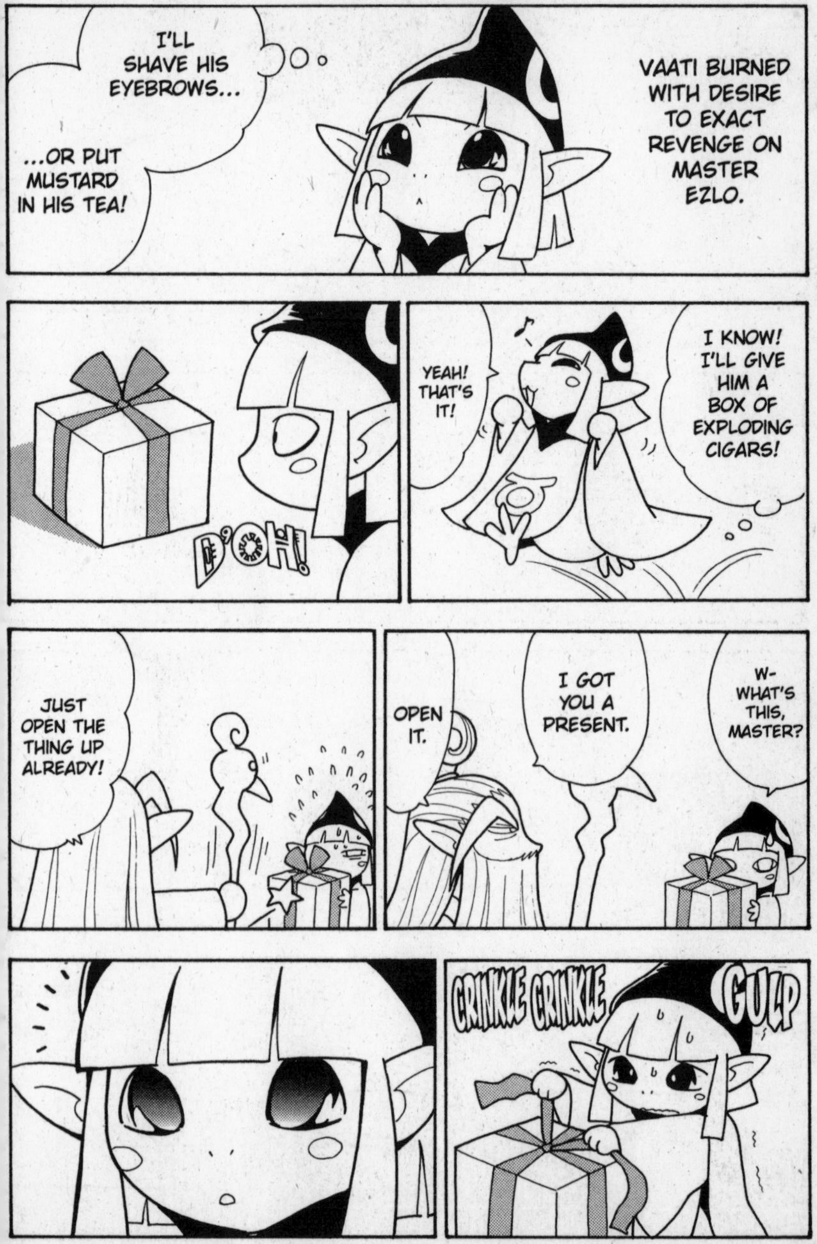
VAATI BURNED WITH DESIRE TO EXACT REVENGE ON MASTER EZLO.
I'LL SHAVE HIS EYEBROWS...
...OR PUT MUSTARD IN HIS TEA!
I KNOW! I'LL GIVE HIM A BOX OF EXPLODING CIGARS!
YEAH! THAT'S IT!
D'OH!
W-WHAT'S THIS, MASTER?
I GOT YOU A PRESENT.
OPEN IT.
JUST OPEN THE THING UP ALREADY!
GULP
CRINKLE CRINKLE